The European Model of Sport

This is the first book to present a critical analysis of the concept of the European Model of Sport (EMS). The EMS concept is widely used by policymakers at the national and EU levels, and by some sports organisations, yet it has never been comprehensively defined in official documents.

This book asks whether the EMS is real or imagined, evaluates its significance in a rapidly evolving European context and for world sport more broadly, and compares it against other models of sport in different regions of the world. The first section of this book is a multi-disciplinary analysis of the EMS, putting the EMS in historical context and examining the concept from political, economic, socio-cultural and legal perspectives. The second section of this book looks at different models of sport within Europe, including Germany, the UK, Scandinavia and South-East Europe, and how they intersect with EU policy. The final section of this book looks at models of sport in North America, Latin America, China, Africa and the Arab World, highlighting key differences and similarities in order to illuminate our understanding of sport governance, policy and management around the world. Throughout, this book includes consideration of grassroots sport, going beyond traditional analyses that have focused primarily on professional sport.

In an era in which sport represents a dynamic arena for competition between corporations, NGOs, international organisations and nation-states, this book is an essential reference for anybody with an interest in sport policy, sport governance, sport management, sport law, EU policy and law, the history of European integration or the relationship between sport and wider society.

Borja García is Reader in sport policy and governance in the School of Sport, Exercise and Health Sciences at Loughborough University, UK. He is also a founding member of the Association for the Study of Sport and the European Union (www.sportandeu.com). He has published extensively in top journals such as the *Journal of European Public Policy*, the *Journal of Common Market Studies* and *European Sport Management Quarterly*.

Vanja Smokvina is Associate Professor of sports law, labour and social security law at the Faculty of Law at the University of Rijeka, Croatia. He is the Head of the Institute of Sports Law, Sports Policies and Sports Diplomacy and holder of the Jean Monnet Chair in EU Sports Law, Policy & Diplomacy (2022–2025). Vanja is also an Arbitrator of the Court of Arbitration for Sport in Lausanne, Switzerland, and member of the Scientific Committee of the UEFA Football Law Programme.

Routledge Research in Sport Business and Management

The European Model of Sport

Myth or Reality?

Edited by Borja García
and Vanja Smokvina

Routledge
Taylor & Francis Group

LONDON AND NEW YORK

First published 2026
by Routledge
4 Park Square, Milton Park, Abingdon, Oxon OX14 4RN

and by Routledge
605 Third Avenue, New York, NY 10158

Routledge is an imprint of the Taylor & Francis Group, an informa business

British Library Cataloguing-in-Publication Data
A catalogue record for this book is available from the British Library

ISBN: 978-1-032-66513-9 (hbk)
ISBN: 978-1-032-66514-6 (pbk)
ISBN: 978-1-032-66515-3 (ebk)

DOI: 10.4324/9781032665153

Typeset in Times New Roman
by codeMantra

To David J. Allen for believing this was possible, and to my family for supporting me all the way. (Borja García)

To Maris, Gabriel and Patricia, my inspiration. (Vanja Smokvina)

Contents

Contributors

Mahfoud Amara is Associate Professor in sport social sciences and management in the Physical Education Department of the College of Education at Qatar University, Qatar. Dr Amara has a number of publications on sport, business, culture, politics and society in the Arab region.

Jaime Andreu Romeo is a retired civil servant of the European Commission. He was Head of the Sports Unit within DG Education and Culture. At the European Commission, he worked in two main areas: sports—he was responsible for the documents "The European Model of Sport" and "The Helsinki Report on Sport"—and institutional communication.

Marko Begović is Associate Professor at Molde University College in Norway, senior lecturer at the Faculty of Sport in Belgrade, Serbia, and Associate Professor at UBT in Saudi Arabia. Between 2021 and 2022, he served as Director in charge of sport and youth affairs within the Government of Montenegro. In parallel, Begović acted as Programme Director for the Master of Sport Management programme at the American University in the Emirates and Visiting Professor at the University of Montenegro. Previously, he was a member of the Governing Bureau for Sports and Task Force on Good Governance and Gender Equality Rapporteur at the Council of Europe.

Pascal Camara is a PhD student in the Institute of Sport History at the German Sport University Cologne, Germany, and Sport Science Research Manager with ICSSPE. He also worked as Programme Officer at the National Sports Council of the Gambia. He holds a BSc in sport management at Universidad Deportiva del Sur, Venezuela, and an MA in international sport development and politics at the German Sport University Cologne.

Shushu Chen is Associate Professor in sport policy and management at the University of Birmingham, UK. Her research stands out for its transdisciplinary approach, often conducted through collaborative partnerships, and for challenging the traditional boundaries of the field to develop a theory-driven understanding of sport policy and programme impacts. With a strong focus on informing and enhancing policymaking, Dr Chen brings valuable cross-cultural perspectives, offering deep insights into both Western and non-Western emerging sports landscapes.

Mathew Dowling is senior lecturer in sport management in the School of Sport, Exercise and Health Sciences at Loughborough University, UK. He has a PhD in physical education and recreation from the University of Alberta, Canada. His research interests focus on sport governance, organisational change and comparative methodology in sport.

Antonia Hannawacker is a PhD student in the Institute of Sport Science at Johannes Gutenberg University Mainz, Germany. She studied at the University of Würzburg (BA sport and sports science) and the University of Mainz (MSc international sport management).

Spencer Harris is Professor in the College of Business and Administration at the University of Colorado, Colorado Springs, USA. He has a PhD in sport policy and sport management from Loughborough University, UK. His research interests focus on sport policy, sport governance and sport development.

Mauricio Hernández Londoño is an academic and activist dedicated to advancing sports governance in Latin America and Colombia. He is the founder of the civil society organisation Transparency in Sport and holds academic roles at the University of Antioquia, the National School of Sports, Colombia, and the International University of Ecuador. In addition, he coordinates the implementation of sports policy for the Mayor's Office of Pereira, Colombia.

Mara Verena Konjer works as a postdoctoral researcher at the Institute for Sport and Exercise Science at the University of Münster, Germany. Mara conducts research in the fields of economic sociology, econometrics, communication and media as well as gender studies in sport and has published articles in *Managing Sport and Leisure*, *Soccer & Society*, the *Journal of Gender Studies* and others.

Jörg Krieger is Associate Professor in the Department of Public Health at Aarhus University, Denmark, and Professor II in the Department of Organisation, Leadership and Management at Inland Norway University, Norway. He holds a PhD in sport history and his research focuses on the history of international elite sport.

Ramón Llopis-Goig is Professor of sociology in the Faculty of Social Sciences at the University of Valencia, Spain. He has been visiting scholar at the University of Leicester, UK, at the European University Institute of Florence, Italy, and at the University of Cork, Ireland.

Henk Erik Meier is Professor for the social sciences of sport at the Institute for Sport and Exercise Science at the University of Münster, Germany. Henk Erik's research is focused on sport governance, sport media and sport policymaking. He has published articles in *Public Administration*, the *Journal of Common Market Studies*, *European Sport Management Quarterly* and others.

Louis Moustakas is Professor of sports management and sport sociology at the University of Applied Sciences Kufstein, Austria. His work focuses on the intersection between sport, social development and policy. Amongst others, his work has been featured in the *International Journal of Sport Policy and Politics*, *Sport in Society* and the *European Journal of Sport and Society*.

Sarah Muhanna Al-Naimi is a PhD candidate in "Gulf Studies" at Qatar University. Her research interests include the role of sport on enhancing small states power and status, the relationship between sport diplomacy and foreign policy and the pluralism of actors in sport diplomacy planning and delivering.

Svein Erik Nordhagen is Associate Professor of sport management in the Department of Organisation, Leadership and Management at Inland Norway University, Norway. He has a PhD in sport sociology and his research interests are sporting events, sport history and the Olympic movement.

Néstor Ordóñez Saavedra is Director of the master's programme in sports sciences at the University of Applied and Environmental Sciences (UDCA) in Colombia. He is also President of the Colombian College of Sports Training, Secretary General of the Colombian Olympic Academy and President of the Colombian Association of Faculties of Sports and Physical Education (ARCOFADER).

Milena M. Parent is Full Professor in sport (event) governance at the University of Ottawa, Canada. She is also the Director of the MEMOS (Executive Master's in Sport Organisation Management) English Programme from the International Olympic Committee/Olympic Solidarity.

Richard Parrish is Professor of sports law and Associate Head of the School of Law, Criminology and Policing at Edge Hill University, UK. He is the Director of the Centre for Sports Law Research, and between 2016 and 2019, he was awarded Jean Monnet Chair of EU Sports Law and Policy by the European Commission.

David Patterson is senior governance advisor with the United States Olympic and Paralympic Committee, USA. Previously, David has been the CEO of the Canada Games Council, Water Ski and Wakeboard Canada and Ringette Canada.

Daniel Plumley is principal lecturer in sport finance in the Department of Finance, Accounting and Business Systems in the Sheffield Business School at Sheffield Hallam University, UK. He is an active researcher, delivering funded projects for ESRC, and regularly consults with the industry on sport finance matters. He is also a Chartered Global Management Accountant (CGMA).

Holger Preuß is Professor of sports economics and sociology at the Johannes Gutenberg University Mainz, Germany, Adjunct Professor at the University of Ottawa, Canada, and international scholar at the State University of New York (Cortland), USA. His research focuses on sport's economic and socio-economic aspects, in particular, analysing the socio-economic impact of mega-events like the Olympic Games and the FIFA World Cup.

Maximilian Seltmann is research associate at the Institute of European Sport Development and Leisure Studies, German Sport University Cologne, Germany. His main areas of research are athlete rights, EU sport policy and good governance in sport. He currently coordinates the EU-funded project Assessing, Evaluating and Implementing Athletes' Social Protection in Olympic Sports (SOPROS).

Qi Wang is a PhD student at the University of Birmingham, UK, specialising in the legacies of major sporting events and their impact on sport participation. Her doctoral research focuses on two high-profile case studies: the Beijing 2022 Winter Olympics and the Birmingham 2022 Commonwealth Games, where she explores the long-term effects these events have on communities and sporting engagement.

Merle Wiehl is research student assistant in the Institute for Sport and Exercise Science at Münster University, Germany.

Rob Wilson is Professor of applied sport finance at University Campus of Football Business (UCFB), UK. He has been involved in academic and applied work in sport finance and governance since 2010 and has published extensively on topics including financial health, governance, economic decision-making and resilience, with his PhD focusing on the factors affecting financial performance in professional team sports. He presents his work all over the world, serves on several editorial boards for leading journals and has a rich network in the boardrooms of professional clubs.

Xiaoyan Xing is Professor of sport management at the Capital University of Physical Education and Sports in Beijing, China. She earned her PhD from the University of Texas at Austin, USA, and has previously served as a faculty member at Laurentian University in Canada. Her research focuses on sport participation behaviour, particularly in relation to hosting sporting events.

Foreword

I am delighted to welcome this collection of essays under the title *The European Model of Sport: Myth or Reality?* Never has a question mark been more appropriate. Is it myth or is it reality? More than that: are we addressing a model or models, a model of sport or of sports? Is it even European, or is it more narrowly EU-specific or more widely is it apt for a global role? So many question marks. And so many ambiguities. The European Model of Sport has no firmly defined character. It is a contested concept.

The thematic ambiguity which characterises the European Model of Sport may be tasted across a wide and colourful canvas of policy documents, work plans and legal texts. If I had to select one example to capture the nuances at stake, it would be the litigation generated by UEFA's attempts to block football's superleague. This is Case C-333/21. Just before Christmas in 2022 Advocate General Rantos published an explosive Opinion. Article 165 TFEU, he advised, gives expression "to the constitutional recognition of the European Sports Model". Glee for UEFA, dismay for the *superleaguers*: EU law, it seems, does not peer cautiously at the European Sports Model, instead it elevates it to the very summit of the hierarchy of legal norms, it has constitutional status. And yet, twelve months later, there was none of this in the Court's authoritative judgement, which instead took pains to insist on the limited role played by Article 165 in EU law and included not one word about any European Sports Model. Glee and dismay reversed? (That question mark once again). Yes and no (that ambiguity once again). The Court said nothing explicit about a model of sport, yet its judgement is larded with recognition of principles which are constitutive of most understandings of that concept—such as the need for homogeneous regulatory and technical conditions to underpin the holding of sporting competitions based on equal opportunities, openness and merit, supported by solidarity redistribution within football.

Be sure, the European Model of Sport is far from finished as a source of questions and ambiguities. In this vein, this book provides rich material to relish. Let the debates continue.

Stephen Weatherill
Emeritus Professor of European Law,
Oxford University, UK

Preface

Good things in life often happen on a sunny day around a cup of coffee. And this is also true of this collective book. The idea of this book was born and shaped during our many morning coffee conversations in the sunny terrace of the Faculty of Law at the University of Rijeka in Croatia overlooking the Mediterranean in the autumn of 2022. The concept of the "European Model of Sport" (or "European Sport Model", as the official Commission and Council documents like to call it nowadays) has been ever present since we both started studying and researching European sport policy and law. As academics, what caught our attention was not necessarily the concept *per se*, but the way in which it has been used by stakeholders time after time, always in an attempt to shape the policy or legal agenda. It probably is the best example of a socially constructed concept that we have ever seen, and we have been first-row spectators to how it was constructed over the years.

Very early in our conversations, we agreed that we did not want to get bogged down into the debate of whether a European Model of Sport (EMS) exists or not. We wanted to go well beyond and to interrogate the EMS from a multi-disciplinary perspective. Specially we wanted to move the debate beyond governance structures and the pyramid of sport, which seemed to be the only feature of the EMS that was constantly discussed. We did not intend this book to be a simple collection of European Union Member States' sport models either. And we quickly agreed we really wanted the book to be global. It is always easy to think global when staring into the Mediterranean. Finally, we set ourselves a small challenge, as if we were in an expedition: Could we find out who was the author of the famous European Commission 1998 document so widely cited? We had an intuition… and we were right! We managed to confirm our hypothesis, and we are pleased to have Jaime Andreu, former Head of the European Commission's Sport Unit, opening this book.

This collective book is a team effort, though. As editors, it would not have been possible without the enthusiasm and collaboration of many people. First, Simon Whitmore, who was extremely receptive and positive about our idea. Second, we cannot thank enough all the chapter authors. This has been a long process due to the complexities of the project, and all the authors have been outstanding, not just in writing their brilliant chapters but also in engaging with all our queries and emails as editors. Finally, we would like to thank the University of Rijeka, whose generous contribution made possible Borja García's research visit in autumn 2022 to start working on this project. Equally, Borja García would like to thank Loughborough University's School of Sport, Exercise and Health Sciences for awarding the School Fellowship that made possible his research visit to the Faculty of Law in Rijeka and work at the Institute of Sports Law, Sports Policies and Sports Diplomacy and its Jean Monnet Chair in EU Sports Law, Policy & Diplomacy. He would like to thank especially the generous efforts of all the colleagues that covered his duties during that time.

Borja García and Vanja Smokvina

Chapter 1

Introduction

The European Model of Sport, a Political Concept That Was Never Meant to Be

Borja García and Vanja Smokvina

Origin and Development of the European Model of Sport as an EU Policy Concept

In 1998, the European Commission's Directorate General for Education and Culture (DG EAC, with responsibility for sport, then also known as DG X) drafted an internal consultation document entitled 'The European Model of Sport[1]: Consultation Document of DG X' (European Commission, 1998). The purpose of that non-paper was to inform European Commission's thinking on the application of European Union (EU) law to sport following the well-known ruling of the Court of Justice of the European Union (CJEU) in the Bosman case. It also aimed at contributing to the Commission's dialogue with sports organisations (García, 2009).

Ten of the document's 23 pages were used by DG EAC to define the 'features of sport in Europe' (European Commission, 1998, pp. 4–5) and to identify the structures of the 'organisation of sport in Europe' (European Commission, 1998, pp. 2–4). The organisational structures of European sport identified in the document were two. On the one hand, a pyramidal structure of top-down vertical governance with one federation per sport sitting at the top. This includes a hierarchical top-down nature of sport governance and regulation emanating from the federations down to the stakeholders. On the other hand, an open system of competition that includes promotion and relegation and therefore implies interdependence between the different levels of competition.

The European Commission identified three features of sport in Europe: a grassroots approach, commitment to national identity and the existence of international competitions (European Commission, 1998, pp. 4–5). The grassroots approach is extremely important. First, it recognises the relevance of grassroots and amateur sport in social terms. But more importantly, DG EAC suggested that such a grassroots approach includes the fact that professional sport is inextricably linked to amateur sport and, therefore, it has a duty of care towards it. If this is accepted as a feature of European sport, then it has important consequences for funding and financial redistribution, as two chapters explore in the book. The commitment to national identity reflects the sociopolitical nature of sport in Europe, that goes beyond mere commercial activities. Finally, the existence of international

DOI: 10.4324/9781032665153-1

competition relates, according to DG EAC, to those competitions and tournaments where representatives of different Member States face one another, such as European football, basketball or rugby club competitions.

The author of that document, Jaime Andreu (now a retired European Commission official), explains in the book's next chapter that the paper was initially intended to inform internal reflection within the European Commission. But it went well beyond its intended purpose. It ignited a political debate that is still alive almost 30 years after. The Commission's internal document never meant to be a building block for EU sport policy development, although it informed the thinking behind the European Commission's so-called *Helsinki Report on Sport* (European Commission, 1999). A few years later, however, the European Commission's *White Paper on Sport* considered 'unrealistic to try to define a unified model of organisation of sport in Europe' (European Commission, 2007, p. 12). This was an attempt to, at least, downgrade the relevance of the European Model of Sport (EMS) as a concept in EU sport policy debates, if not to dismiss it altogether (García, 2009).

Regardless of the European Commission's intentions, the reality is that the concept of an EMS took a life of its own within the EU sport policy community. It has been used and revisited by EU institutions and sport stakeholders alike over the last three decades at different times. The latest 'resurgence' of the EMS is linked to the failed attempt to launch a European football superleague (Meier et al., 2022a), with the Council of the EU, the European Parliament and Member States strongly supporting the EMS and counter efforts of the CJEU to restrict its use in the application of EU law to sport.

Member States have been a constant support of the EMS. The Council of the EU incorporated the EMS as one of the priorities in the 2021–2024 EU Work Plan for Sport (Council of the European Union, 2020). The Work Plan explains that, under this priority, the goal is to build knowledge and to analyse the factual and legal situation on the 'impact of closed sport competitions on the system of organised sport, taking into account the specificity of sport', and the 'possible challenges faced by European sport organisations and federations' (Council of the European Union, 2020, Part Annex I).

Former European Commission Vice-President, Margaritis Schinas (2021) used social network X (formerly known as Twitter) on 19th April 2021 to post that 'we must defend a values-driven European model of sport based on diversity and inclusion'. This was done in a personal capacity, yet it was posted from Schinas' EU Commission X institutional profile during the convoluted events that surrounded the proposal and dismissal of the so-called European football superleague (Meier et al., 2022a; Meier et al., 2022b). Not long after, the European Commission published a study on the EMS authored by consultancy firm Ecorys (European Commission et al., 2022). The study, funded by the European Commission, was part of the list of activities included in the EU Work Plan for Sport 2021–2024, so it was not a direct consequence of the debates sparked by the European football superleague. Therefore, it demonstrates the salience of the EMS in the European Commission's sport policy agenda.

Political support for the EMS amongst EU institutions reached a high in the autumn of 2021. European sport ministers meeting in the Council of the EU under the Slovenian presidency adopted conclusions calling for the protection of the EMS. In that resolution, the representatives of the Member States affirmed that the EMS's 'key features include a pyramidal structure, organised sport, structured on a national basis, and by one federation per sport, solidarity with lower-tier sport levels and the promotion of open competitions' (Council of the European Union, 2021). Furthermore, and in a very similar tone, the European Parliament adopted its own resolution around the same time, in which it called to enhance and protect 'the principles of a European sport model' (European Parliament, 2021).

It is true that, even in the case of the Work Plan, none of these documents are of a regulatory nature. Nevertheless, the alignment between the European Commission, the Council of the EU and the European Parliament in 2021 clearly signals how the EMS has risen in salience within the EU sport policy agenda and, to some extent, in wider EU politics.

But even at this moment in time, with a relatively similar tone coming from Council of the EU, European Parliament and European Commission documents, consensus about the EMS is fragile. This is no better seen than in the recent rulings of the CJEU in sport-related cases, namely the cases of the International Skating Union,[2] the football superleague,[3] and Royal Antwerp's challenge to UEFA's rules on homegrown players,[4] finishing with the Diarra case on FIFA's players transfer rules.[5]

One of the most noticeable features of the CJEU rulings is that the Court does not make a single mention across the four judgements to the EMS using these precise words. However, careful reading reveals a more nuanced approach. Whereas the CJEU did not mention the EMS, it is possible to find in the rulings subtle references to elements that have been linked to the EMS. For example, in the preliminary considerations, the Court acknowledges that 'sporting activity carries considerable social and educational importance, henceforth reflected in Article 165 TFEU, for the Union and for its citizens'.[6] It then elaborates that 'a sporting activity undeniably has specific characteristics which, whilst relating especially to amateur sport, may also be found in the pursuit of sport as an economic activity',[7] in a paragraph that is repeated in all three decisions.

In doing so, the Court is recognising, explicitly, the so-called specificity of sport and, perhaps more importantly, it acknowledges that the specific features of European sport can be found both in amateur and commercial sport. This is extremely relevant, because it goes straight to the heart of the EMS as defined by the other EU institutions: its 'grassroots approach' linking together professional and amateur sport. This argument is particularly reinforced by the Court in *Superleague* when discussing collective selling of television and commercial rights.

First, the Court declares that it finds 'prima facie convincing'[8] the arguments of FIFA, UEFA, the European Commission and national governments that sport needs

to ensure some form of *"solidarity redistribution"*, to the benefit not only of professional football clubs participating in those competitions, but also *those not participating*, amateur clubs, professional players, women's football, young players and other categories of stakeholders in football.[9]

Second, the Court agrees that 'there is *a trickle-down effect* from those [UEFA international club] competitions into smaller professional football clubs and amateur football clubs which, whilst *not participating* therein, invest at local level in the recruitment and training of young, talented players'.[10] Third, the CJEU recognises 'the solidarity role of football', because it 'serves to bolster its educational and social function within the European Union'.[11] Finally, the Court enumerates a wide list of possible beneficiaries from financial solidarity and redistribution, including professional and amateur clubs and 'other stakeholders in football'.[12]

Although the ruling in the *Superleague* case only concerns football, with this discussion the Court is clearly arguing for and endorsing solidarity and redistribution in sport. It is of particular relevance for our purpose here the Court's mention of non-participant and amateur clubs (which was not necessary in the context of the case), for it concedes and even wider remit to the concepts of financial solidarity and redistribution. In doing so, the CJEU strongly suggests that there exists a link between the professional top and the grassroots bottom of the sporting pyramid. It is also relevant to the fact that the Court acknowledges football's educational and social function. All these are, at their very core, key features of the EMS as defined by the European Commission and endorsed recently by the European Parliament and the Council of the EU.

Thus, our argument is that even without directly mentioning the EMS in any of its recent judgments, the Court effectively acknowledges the existence and relevance of some of the most important characteristics defined in the EMS by the political interventions of other EU institutions. Yet, it is also clear that the CJEU approaches European sport structures in a more critical and, perhaps crucially, less political way than its counterparts in the EU institutional framework.

Therefore, we find ourselves at a juncture in which the EMS has taken again centre stage in the EU sport policy agenda after some years of being relegated in the list of priorities in favour of implementing the nascent supporting competence established in Article 165 TFEU. However, such a resurgence has been met with different levels of support from EU institutions, national governments and non-institutional stakeholders. Indeed, the heterogeneity of approaches towards the EMS is likely to be maintained because sport stakeholders, such as sport federations, International Olympic Committee, athletes, supporters, clubs or leagues, have all expressed contradicting views and different levels of support (or opposition) to the concept of the EMS. This is the starting point for this collective volume. As editors, we felt it is a good moment to pause, analyse and reflect on what the 'European Model of Sport' means not only across Europe but also beyond. We have surrounded ourselves by an excellent team of chapter authors in search of answers and reflections.

Book Objectives: What Does 'Sport' Mean for Europeans and Beyond?

With this context, the aim of this collective book is to present a critical analysis of the concept of the EMS. We start from the premise that the EMS is a ubiquitous concept that has never been officially defined, yet it is used by many institutional and non-institutional actors at national and EU level to drive their own strategies and policy agendas. The EMS is, therefore, a case of an expression widely used in debates about sport in Europe, but scarcely reflected upon. It could even be argued that the EMS is a socially constructed concept.

This book seeks to offer a much-needed calm, reflective and analytical approach. The book is not, however, an attempt to simply describe or define the EMS. And perhaps more importantly, we do not aim to debate whether an EMS does exist. Our collective objective is to go beyond that (often superficial) dichotomic discussion in search of a more critical, multidisciplinary and comparative analysis of the way in which sport is organised, financed, regulated, thought about and governed in Europe and beyond.

Interdisciplinarity is, indeed, one of our aims for this book. We depart from the traditional approaches to the EMS, mostly based just on political sciences and law to offer reflections also from a historical, sociopolitical, sociological, economic and grassroots perspective.

Book Structure

The book is divided into three parts. In the first part titled 'A multidisciplinary analysis of the European Model of Sport', there are six chapters which give an overview and critically discuss the EMS from a historical, political, legal, socio-cultural, financial and statistical point of view. The second and third parts of the book provide an overview of different models of sport throughout Europe and the rest of the world. Let us summarise briefly the contributions of each chapter.

First, **Jaime Andreu** explains in Chapter 2 how the 1998 European Commission internal document on the EMS came about. He explains that the document was intended for internal purposes, but also to inform debates with sport stakeholders and Member States. He also reflects on the way the concept has been used and the extent to which European sport has changed (or not) since 1998. This collective volume is the first academic publication in which Jaime Andreu, the author of such an influential document in the evolution of EU sport policy, explains the origin of that document and reflects on its content. As volume editors, we are incredibly grateful for his contribution.

In Chapter 3, **Richard Parrish** discusses the EMS from a legal point of view. He analyses the impact of recent CJEU rulings on the regulations and structures that sustain the EMS, especially focusing on sport federations' rules on authorisation of competitions, financial solidarity redistribution, nationality and arbitration of stakeholder disputes.

In Chapter 4, **Henk Erik Meier** and **Merle Wiehl** collect and analyse strategy and policy documents of EU Member States at national level to discuss whether there appears to be any commonly shared set of socio-cultural values around sport that underpin the way in which sport is perceived and conceptualised in European public policy and politics.

Chapter 5 moves to economic aspects of European sport. **Holger Preuß** and **Antonia Hannawacker** analyse the patters of financing sports in Europe. The chapter focuses on the overarching financing patterns which are based on common European regulations.

Following on, in Chapter 6 **Ramón Llopis Goig** uses Eurobarometer data to create a typology of sport cultures in Europe that focuses specifically on the role of grassroots sport. This is one of the most innovative contributions of this volume, because despite the constant reference to grassroots sport in EMS debates, this aspect was never analysed in depth because most academic and non-academic contributions have focused on the legal, economic or political regulation of professional sport.

The look at the financial aspects of the EMS is complemented in Chapter 7 by **Daniel Plumley** and **Rob Wilson**, who make use of an impressive data set of sport financial data to determine the extent to which there is redistribution and financial solidarity in European sport, as claimed by those most in favour of the EMS and suggested by the European Commission in 1998. This is also another of the most innovative contributions of this volume, because despite claims on the relevance of redistribution for European sport, there has been scarce attention to analysing whether EMS structures do actually ensure acceptable levels of financial solidarity or not.

The second and third parts of this book provide an overview of different models of sport throughout Europe and the rest of the world. In Europe, the focus is on the models of sport in Scandinavia, Western and Central Europe, South-Eastern Europe and, because of its specificity, the United Kingdom. Chapter authors in this second part were asked to take as a starting point for discussion the EMS definition articulated by the European Commission in 1998. Authors were also given freedom to analyse other aspects that they considered relevant to understand how sport is organised, regulated and socially understood in their respective geographical areas. It is important to point out that the book does not intend to present an exhaustive comparison of sport structures country by country. We decided against that idea from the outset of this project because there are already excellent academic contributions on comparative sport policy (Bergsgard et al., 2007; Hallman & Petry, 2013; Houlihan, 1997; Houlihan & Green, 2008; Kristiansen et al., 2017), and because the book's objective is, as pointed out above, to provide a platform for a multidisciplinary reflection on the common understandings of sport in Europe and not a microanalysis of structures at the national level. For those reasons, we opted for chapters not focused on just one country (except the UK), but that present general trends across slightly wider European regions. We accept this might make the analysis perhaps more generic and less detailed, but it has the advantage of focusing on the united diversity of sport across Europe and wider trends.

Thus, in Chapter 8, **Jörg Krieger** and **Svein Erik Nordhagen** present the historical development of sport in Scandinavia with a focus on the strong links between professional and amateur sport as one of its defining characteristics.

In Chapter 9, **Mara Verena Konjer** and **Henk Erik Meier** examine the Western and Central EMS using Germany as an example. They argue that sport in that part of Europe represents elements of the EMS in many aspects, but the public interest in amateur sport and volunteer sport clubs is giving rise to different neo-corporatist arrangements.

Marko Begovic in Chapter 10 presents the model of sport in south-eastern Europe, with a strong focus on the countries of the former Yugoslavia. He argues that sport structures in that part of Europe transitioned in accordance with the sociopolitical realm, confirming the close interplay between sport and politics.

The second part of the book is concluded with Chapter 11, where **Spencer Harris** and **Mathew Dowling** explain how the United Kingdom was an early pioneer of many of the structures identified in the EMS, but it has to be seen now as a contemporary revisionist, for many of the neo-liberal and commercial dynamics that are often identified as endangering the EMS structures have been pioneered in the UK with the commercialisation of professional sport.

Finally, the book introduces a third and final part in which we seek to discuss the global impact of the EMS. The aim is to understand the extent to which we encounter (or not) any similarities or differences with the EMS in sport systems well beyond the European continent. For this purpose, again, we asked authors to have as a starting point of reflection the features identified in the 1998 European Commission document, but we allowed them the necessary freedom to reflect on the structures and dynamics of their sport models. Like in the second part, these chapters do not intend to present a systematic and very wide geographical comparison. Our intention was to present contributions that, like small pills, contribute to our reflection and debate on how sport is understood, conceptualised and structured. Something that we wanted to address, though, was the inclusion of parts of the world that are often overlooked in existing academic literature on comparative sport policy, which could be found in the chapters on Africa, the Arab World and Colombia (as a Latin American example).

Thus, in Chapter 12, **Milena Parent** and **David Patterson** discuss the US and Canadian models of sport. They argue that there is a tendency in Europe to homogenise both systems under the common label of 'American model of sport'. However, they argue that there are clear differences whereby sport in Canada is more closely aligned with the features identified in the EMS.

In Chapter 13, **Shushu Chen**, **Xiaoyan Xing** and **Qi Wang** present the Chinese model of sport explaining that it is a clear outlier in respect to the EMS. They argue that the Chinese model of sport system is heavily influenced by Confucianism and by the strong role of the state and government in China.

Chapter 14 presents another of the original contributions of the volume. **Sarah Muhanna Al-Naimi** and **Mahfoud Amara** discuss the model of sport in the Arab World, an area that is often overlooked except, perhaps, in geopolitical debates. They analyse the strong similarities to the EMS that can be found in the models of sport in the Arab World, which are attributed to the colonial past and to the close geographical and cultural proximity to Europe, especially in the case of northern African countries.

In Chapter 15, **Mauricio Hernández Londoño** and **Nestor Ordóñez Saavedra** present the Colombian model of sport, which we have included as an example of sport structures in Latin America, another geographical area traditionally neglected in the academic literature on sport policy and governance. This chapter emphasises the mixed institutional design of Colombian sport, where public and private entities collaborate under the oversight of the State. The chapter discusses the strong role of public authorities in the regulation and funding of sport, a feature that is common across Latin America.

The final contribution in the third part of the book is Chapter 16, where **Pascal Camara, Louis Moustakas**, and **Maximilian Seltmann** use archival material and an analysis of national and organisational documents to examine the historical emergence of parallel pillars of sport structures in the continent and many African countries. They argue that decolonisation and the emergence of independent states led to the formation and consolidation of sport organisations at national and continental level deeply rooted in Pan-Africanist principles and anchored on the nation-state. Their contribution rounds up the book's third part.

This collective endeavour culminates with a concluding chapter in which we take stock of the many conceptual reflections and the geographical spread of sport structures. It is difficult to make justice in a concluding chapter to the excellent contributions that our chapter authors have made. We are forever grateful for their enthusiasm, support and patience through the long process of this collective volume. We feel, however, that together we have created an outstanding contribution to academic and political debates on sport policy, governance, regulation and law in Europe.

In the end, one may conclude that there is no unique '[the] European Model of Sport' present on the European soul or worldwide, but different varieties which could be defined as models coming under the same umbrella as 'a European Model of Sport' since they do have (to certain and varying extents) some of the core elements initially defined by the European Commission in 1998 (and discussed by Jaime Andreu in this book), but not others. Furthermore, European sport governing bodies and EU institutions could perhaps be proud that those core elements are strongly present also worldwide, with the notable exception of the USA and, to a lesser extent, Canada.

Notes

1 The editors will use the term European Model of Sport (EMS) although the EU institutions, academics and others on different occasions use also the term 'European Sport Model'.
2 Case C-124/21 P –*International Skating Union* v *Commission*.
3 Case C-333/21, *European Superleague Company SL* v *Unión de Federaciones Europeas de Fútbol (UEFA)*, *Fédération internationale de football association (FIFA)*.

4 Case C-680/21, *SA Royal Antwerp Football Club* v *Union royale belge des sociétés de football association ASBL, Union des associations européennes de football (UEFA).*
5 Case C-650/22, *Fédération internationale de football association (FIFA)* v *BZ.*
6 *Superleague*, par. 102, *Royal Antwerp*, par. 70.
7 *Superleague*, par. 103, *Royal Antwerp*, par. 71, *ISU*, par. 95.
8 *Superleague*, par. 235.
9 *Superleague*, par. 234.
10 *Superleague*, par. 235.
11 *Superleague*, par. 235.
12 *Superleague*, par. 236.

References

Bergsgard, N. A., Houlihan, B., Mangset, P., Nodland, S. I., & Rommetvedt, H. (Eds.). (2007). *Sport Policy: A Comparative Analysis of Stability and Change.* Butterworth-Heinemann.
Council of the European Union. (2020, December 4). *Resolution of the Council and of the Representatives of the Governments of the Member States Meeting Within the Council on the European Union Work Plan for Sport (1 January 2021–30 June 2024) (2020/C 419/01).* Art. 2020/C 419/01. https://eur-lex.europa.eu/legal-content/EN/TXT/?uri=CELEX%3A42020Y1204%2801%29
Council of the European Union. (2021, November 30). Sport: Council resolution stresses key features of values-based sport model. *Press Release.* https://www.consilium.europa.eu/en/press/press-releases/2021/11/30/sport-council-resolution-stresses-key-features-of-values-based-sport-model/
European Commission. (1998). *The European Model of Sport: Consultation Document of DG X.* European Commission.
European Commission. (1999). The Helsinki Report on Sport. In *Report from the European Commission to the European Council with a View to Safeguarding Current Sports Structures and Maintaining the Social Function of Sport within the Community Framework* (Issue COM (1999) 644 final).
European Commission. (2007). *White Paper on Sport* (Issue COM (2007) 391 final). https://ec.europa.eu/assets/eac/sport/library/documents/whitepaper-full_en.pdf
European Commission, Directorate-General for Education Sport and Culture, Y., Sennett, J., Le Gall, A., Kelly, G., Cottrill, R., Goffredo, S., & Spyridopoulos, K. (2022). *Study on the European Sport Model: A Report to the European Commission.* Publications Office of the European Union. https://data.europa.eu/doi/10.2766/28433
European Parliament. (2021, November 23). *European Parliament Resolution of 23 November 2021 on EU Sports Policy: Assessment and Possible Ways Forward 2021/2058(INI).* https://www.europarl.europa.eu/doceo/document/TA-9-2021-0463_EN.html
García, B. (2009). Sport governance after the White Paper: The demise of the European model? *International Journal of Sport Policy and Politics, 1*(3), 267–284. https://doi.org/https://doi.org/10.1080/19406940903265541
Hallman, K., & Petry, K. (Eds.). (2013). *Comparative Sport Development : Systems, Participation and Public Policy.* Springer.
Houlihan, B. (1997). *Sport, Policy and Politics: A Comparative Analysis.* Routledge.
Houlihan, B., & Green, M. (Eds.). (2008). *Comparative Elite Sport Development: Systems, Structures and Public Policy.* Butterworth Heinemann.

Kristiansen, E., Parent, M. M., & Houlihan, B. (Eds.). (2017). *Elite Youth Sport Policy and Management : A Comparative Analysis*. Routledge is an imprint of the Taylor & Francis Group, an Informa Business.

Meier, H. E., García, B., Konjer, M., & Jetzke, M. (2022a). The short life of the European Super League: A case study on institutional tensions in sport industries. *Managing Sport and Leisure, 29*(3), 1–22. https://doi.org/10.1080/23750472.2022.2058071

Meier, H. E., García, B., Yilmaz, S., & Chakawata, W. (2022b). The capture of EU football regulation by the football governing bodies. *Journal of Common Market Studies, 61*(3), 692–711. https://doi.org/10.1111/jcms.13405

Schinas, M. (2021, April 19). We must defend a values-driven European Model of Sport based on diversity and inclusion. *Twitter*. https://twitter.com/MargSchinas/status/138390 8874101530625?s=20

Part I

A Multidisciplinary Analysis of the European Model of Sport

Chapter 2

How the Concept of the "European Model of Sport" Was Coined

Jaime Andreu Romeo

Introduction

The European Union legal system emerged during the 1990s as the primary authority to address the novel categories of conflicts resulting from sports activities, instilling confidence in its efficacy and reassuring all stakeholders. The 1990s were a time of profound change for sport in Europe, mostly due to the surge in private television, leading to a TV sports' rights boom. That increase in TV rights for sport sparked tensions between sports organisations and broadcasters since they highlighted the inadequacy of the existing legal framework. However, as important as it was, the fights around TV and commercial rights were not the only significant changes that European sport underwent in that seismic period of the late 1990s.

At that time, a complaint for a possible breach of the free movement of workers was lodged at the Court of Justice of the European Union (CJEU) by a Belgian football player: the now well-known Bosman case.[1] This case would significantly alter the landscape of the sports industry, marking a monumental shift. The arrival of TV rights' cash also caused problems between sports regulations and the sports industry. Ticketing was no longer the primary source of revenue; TV rights and sponsorship contracts replaced it.

Amidst all those very profound changes in the context of sport, FIFA and UEFA (the major players in European sports), approached the European Commission for negotiations in the aftermath of the Bosman ruling. They proposed to remove national barriers for players, thereby avoiding the ruling of the CJEU in the Bosman case. In return, they sought complete control over the management of television broadcasting, including establishing blackout periods to prevent oversaturation of football on the screen. Notably, football federations negotiated without consulting other international sports federations.

Another critical event happened at that exact moment. Professional clubs challenged international sports federations' monopolistic power for the first time. Indeed, negotiations between the International Basketball Federation (FIBA) and European professional basketball clubs broke down, resulting in a split between both parties and the creation of the Basketball Euroleague.

DOI: 10.4324/9781032665153-3

At the time, Competition Commissioners Karel van Miert and Mario Monti, along with the Commissioner for Education and Sport, Viviane Reding, played a very active role in all these questions. Their proactive approach was evident in the creation of the European Commission's Sports Unit within the Directorate General on Education and Culture, a recognition of the need for a global political view on sports matters, as was the case for Culture. Thus, it is in that context that the European Commission had the need to reflect on how to approach sport and its interplay with the common market.

The European Model of Sport Working Paper: Where Did It Come From?

The combination of all those events led the federations to increase their pressure and lobbying on the governments of the Member States. This pressure resulted in the Declaration on sport attached to the Treaty of Amsterdam, known as the Amsterdam Declaration on Sport (European Council, 1997). The Declaration is a vague and short text, mostly because of the division among Member States. It underlines the social significance of sport and calls to the bodies of the European Union to listen to sports organisations when important questions affecting sport are at issue, mainly concerning amateur sports. The Member States have maintained a neutral distance between sport and other economic sectors, namely the media and sports industry.

As the Commission was mandated to analyse the follow-up of the Amsterdam Declaration on Sport, the Sports Unit embarked on a reflective process to understand the reasons behind the significant flow of litigation on sport-related issues. This introspection led to the (now) well-known working paper on the European Model of Sport (European Commission, 1998), a key document in understanding the evolution of sport in Europe.

Because of the impact of American sports in Europe, the Commission approached the subject by analysing the differences between the American and European models of sport. After the Second World War, two prominent sports models dominated the international scene: the American, based on the principles of free economy, and the Soviet, anchored on state interventionism. Between the two superpowers, Western Europe developed a third way of organising sport – a mixed model combining the autonomy of sports organisations and the intervention of the state. Within the European territory, it was possible to identify two differentiated approaches: on the one hand, a French and Mediterranean framework, with a high degree of interventionism and a heavy legislative corpus; on the other hand, a Nordic/Anglo-Saxon model based on the autonomy of sport organisations and a light legal/regulatory system.

The Commission analysed the current system to identify what were, until that moment, the characteristics of the European model: the monopolistic situation of the federations, the promotion/relegation system, the pyramidal structure of European sports, and solidarity between professional and amateur sports.

It is also essential to refer to the audiovisual industry. Indeed, sport, very much similar to the case of music, can be considered as both practice and an entertainment show for large publics. Sport as entertainment is associated with the development of the media industry. As some authors have indicated, it is a symbiotic relationship. We know that symbiotics can have two meanings: one is positive when the two parts benefit from the interaction; the other is negative, the idea of parasitism when one part takes dominance over the other, harming it.

While the audiovisual industry operated under the free market principle in the USA, the hegemonic model in Western Europe was the public audiovisual service, organised at national and European levels. This structure of the television market under the control of public television channels helps to explain the arrival of continental sporting competitions, a natural characteristic of Europe. However, the state monopoly on the television industry was broken during the 1980s with private television operators' arrival and new technological developments, such as satellite television.

This change in the audiovisual model resulted in a massive flow of money into sports organisations, with ticket sales ceasing to be the primary source of income for clubs and federations. The selling of audiovisual rights was to become now the first source of income for professional sport. However, the owners of television stations demanded an improvement in the quality of the sporting spectacle. This request explains, for example, the opening of the Olympic Games to professionalism or the creation of the UEFA Champions League. The aim was to ensure uncertainty in the outcome and that the participants would attract the spectators.

The European Commission's conclusion was obvious: the legal framework regulating this relationship needed to be revised because it was outdated.

The Commission was also of the view that the evolution of audiovisual systems challenged the model – we were still far from the new interactive media – and that a set of reforms were necessary if the political wish of the Member States was to maintain such structures. Furthermore, the collapse of the Eastern bloc implied substantial political reforms of the sports organisations in those countries. After 40 years of state interventionism, most of them moved to the Nordic model, giving autonomy to the sports organisations and ensuring only the necessary financing of their activities so they can fulfil their social role. Nevertheless, the arrival of autocratic governments and ramping Nationalism have modified the initial approach to national sports organisations. In some states, the framework has returned to more interventionist positions. But this is a different debate outside the scope of this chapter.

In this wider political, economic, legal, and sporting context, the European Commission organised the so-called *General States of European Sport*, held in Olympia (Greece) on 20–23 May 1999. It was at that meeting of the *General States of European Sport* where the European Commission's sports unit presented its document/reflection on the European Model of Sport. Interestingly, the first conclusion of the participants was that the European Model of Sport does not exist. For the Commission, it was not a real surprise. Politically speaking, it was clear that the gap between the highly interventionist French model and the British liberal model could never merge.

The fear of European harmonisation pushed both governmental and non-governmental organisations to refuse the term the European model and to circumscribe it only to a standard model of organising competitions. The Commission was also persuaded of the impossibility of imposing a unilateral legal solution to regulate a common model of sport across the European Union.

The Helsinki Report on Sport (1999) clearly expressed that a large consensus would be necessary to fill the gap (European Commission, 1999). Commissioner Mario Monti also warned that other forms of sports organisations could arrive on the scene. This announcement was made in 2001 and ratified by the Court of Justice in the Superleague case ruling of December 2023.[2]

Conclusion: A Debate That Has Never Been Closed

This book's interest lies in reviewing whether Governments and sports organisations have analysed their working methods to consider the evolution of sporting activities, and the already influential CJEU jurisprudence generated since the 1990s. Sports organisations should admit that they are not operating alone on the market but that their decisions can seriously concern other vital economic sectors, mainly the audiovisual and goods sports industry.

Twenty-five years after its publication, the working paper "The European Model of Sport" has proved its significance since it triggered a debate that has not yet been closed. National governments and sport organisations should also admit that their current operating models must adjust to the present social and economic situation to preserve their identity. Lobbying for legal exemptions is not the only way to do this necessary *aggiornamento*; the problem requires a deep review of the different models. Seventy years ago Di Lampedusa warned about immobilism tactics: "If we want things to stay as they are, things will have to change".

Notes

1 Case C-415/93, Union royale belge des sociétés de football association ASBL v Jean-Marc Bosman, Royal club liégeois SA v Jean-Marc Bosman and others and Union des associations européennes de football (UEFA) v Jean-Marc Bosman, ECLI:EU:C:1995:463.
2 Case C-333/21 *European Superleague Company SL v FIFA and UEFA* [2023] ECLI:EU:C:2023:1011.

References

European Commission. (1998). *The European Model of Sport: Consultation Document of DG X*. European Commission.

European Commission. (1999). The Helsinki Report on Sport. In *Report from the European Commission to the European Council with a View to Safeguarding Current Sports Structures and Maintaining the Social Function of Sport within the Community Framework* (Issue COM (1999) 644 final).

European Council. (1997). Declaration No. 29, on Sport. In *Attached to the Treaty of Amsterdam Amending the Treaty on European Union, the Treaties Establishing the European Communities and Certain Related Acts*.

Chapter 3

A Legal Assessment of the Status of the European Model of Sport Following the Judgements of the Court of Justice on 21 December 2023

Richard Parrish

Introduction

On 21 December 2023, the Court of Justice of the European Union reignited the debate on the merits of the so-called "European Model of Sport", despite not even referring to it in the judgements. In *ISU*, *Superleague*, and *Royal Antwerp*, the Court considered the legality of several sporting rules considered fundamental to the structural integrity of the pyramidic sports model.[1] This contribution examines four such rules on: prior authorisation, solidarity, nationality, and arbitration. It argues that the Court has not deconstructed the European model by calling into question the ability of sports governing bodies to continue to act as regulators of their respective sports, but that this regulatory autonomy is conditioned on governing bodies drafting, implementing, and enforcing sporting rules within a framework of good governance. Scholars of this field will recognise this message and might assume that it is judicial endorsement the EU's sport policy developed by the European Commission, the European Parliament, and the Member States. In fact, the Court declined to make reference to the policy messaging, instead side-lining those contributions through dismissive treatment of Article 165 TFEU and a refusal to even recognise that a sports "policy" exists at all. Does this matter given that there has been a convergence of messaging between the policy and legal streams, or will politics want to reassert itself and wrestle oversight of international sports governance away from judicial adjudication?

The European Model of Sport

In organisational terms, the European model is frequently depicted as resembling a pyramid in which international sports federations reside at the pinnacle exercising monopolistic regulatory powers over their respective sports. This power is then partly devolved to continental and national regulatory bodies that similarly act as monopolists within their respective jurisdictions. In competitive terms, the structure implies a strong connection between the top of the pyramid (the elite level) and its base (the grassroots). This connection is supported by an open system of promotion and relegation which allows for sporting merit to determine sporting

DOI: 10.4324/9781032665153-4

outcomes, redistributive solidarity payments, investments into the development of young athletes, and the nurturing of volunteering and the socio-cultural dimensions of sport. The model has a distinct national character with national leagues and national competitions being prominent. Conflict is regulated internally with mandatory arbitration clauses seeking to keep sports disputes out of the court room.

Whether these features amount to a model is contested. Nafziger (2008, 100) reminds us that models are general representations of reality rather than precise descriptions of organisational structures. A cursory glance across the European sporting landscape reveals a bewildering diversity of sporting structures and methods of private and state regulation (Chaker, 1999). At best, one might be able to identify *a* European model, such as *a* football model, or recognise some characteristics common across some sports, but to claim the existence of *the* European model is a stretch in so far as it implies a degree of universality. With this caveat, this chapter proceeds to use the phrase "the European model".

It is not surprising that the sports movement claims the existence of such a model, for those who define the structure are more able to control what goes on within it. However, given the diversity of approaches observable across sports and the increasing commercial nature of the sector that has attracted new and litigious stakeholders, it is somewhat surprising that the term has embedded itself in the European political discourse on sport, although not within judicial discourse, as will be discussed later.

In 1998 the European Commission confidently declared that "[T]here is a European model of sport with its own characteristics" and "[T]his model has been exported to almost all other continents and countries, with the exception of North America" (European Commission, 1998, 5). The Commission subsequently spent several years rowing back on that position, no doubt mindful of the need to avoid the perception that it had fallen victim to regulatory capture. Only a year later in its Helsinki Report on Sport, reference to the European model was dropped in favour of reference to "common features" and a "European approach to sport" (European Commission, 1999).

By the time of its 2007 White Paper on Sport, the Commission had all but abandoned the use of the term by acknowledging that "[I]n view of the diversity and complexities of European sport structures… it is unrealistic to try to define a unified model of organisation of sport in Europe" (European Commission, 2007, 12). This view was repeated in the Commission's 2011 Communication on Sport, in which it reiterated that "it is not possible to define a single model of governance in European sport across different disciplines and in view of various national differences" (European Commission, 2011, 10).

Rather than focussing on the entire structure, EU sport policy concentrated on the values of the model. It articulated a line conditioning the conversion of these values into concrete sporting rules only if governing bodies adhered to principles of good governance. In the White Paper, the European Commission concluded that continued self-regulation of sport rests on adherence to "a common set of principles for good governance in sport, such as transparency, democracy, accountability and representation of stakeholders" (European Commission 2007, 13). In the Communication on Sport good governance was highlighted as being "a condition for addressing challenges regarding sport and the EU legal framework" (European Commission, 2011, 10). Successive EU Work Plans on Sport have also highlighted the importance of good governance in sport (Council of the European Union 2017, 2020). Several expert groups on good governance have been established[2] and multiple projects focussed on good governance in the sports sector have been funded under the Erasmus+ Sport programme.[3] The EU institutions have also attempted to foster debate on good governance through structured and social dialogue.[4] Although constitutionally hamstrung due to the location of sport at the base of the EU's competence pecking order, EU sport policy has been far from inactive in advancing the importance of good governance.

A glance at how another international organisation handled the question of the existence of the European model highlights the linguistic sensitivity surrounding the issue. By 2018, the Council of Europe decided to commence a process to revise its "European Sports Charter", a process completed in 2021 (Council of Europe, 2021). On its website, it acknowledged that the "Charter does not make reference to it [the European model of sport] as there is no intergovernmental consensus regarding its definition or even its existence".[5] Instead, the Charter refers to "common features of a framework for European sport and its organisation, *understood* by the sports movement as the European sport model" (Article 2(2)).

Just because some understand certain common features as corresponding to a European model does not make it a reality – a view expressed by EU Athletes, a multi-sport federation of athlete and player trade unions. In its contribution to the revision of the Sports Charter, EU Athletes stated that it

> is strongly opposed to any attempts to recognise codify or protect the European sport model as proposed by the Olympic movement. In our opinion, it is little more than a continuation of the long running and unsuccessful campaign for sport to be exempt from European laws.
>
> (EU Athletes, 2021)

The proposal, announced in April 2021, to establish a breakaway European Super League rehabilitated the use of the term "European Model of Sport" within EU political circles. The Vice-President of the European Commission highlighted the need to "protect the European sport model, which is based on a balance between clubs and national competitions, in order to ensure the development of the discipline in an open and non-discriminatory area" (Brocard & Anglade, 2021, 3). The EU's Work Plan for Sport 2021–2024 established the "European Model of Sport" as a priority theme committing it to investigate the impact of closed sport competitions on the system of organised sport (Council of the European Union, 2020). The Commission subsequently funded a study on the European sport model, published in April 2022 (European Commission, 2022) and in December 2021 the Sports Ministers adopted a Resolution on the key features of a European Sport Model

(Council of the European Union, 2021). The slight nuance, for those who noticed, was that the resolution made reference to *a* (and not *the*) European model. The sentiments expressed in the resolution were reaffirmed in a 2024 Declaration by European Sports Ministers on the European Sport Model (Ministère des Sports et des Jeux Olympiques et Paralympiques, 2024).

The Super League proposal has therefore allowed the notion of a European Model of Sport to regain political traction. But whilst the model has been reacquainted with an old friend, it is far from certain that politics can deliver what the sports movement wants. The weaponry of politics is light. The embodiment of EU sports policy, Article 165 TFEU, lacks bite as a supporting competence. Its voice struggles to be heard in Luxembourg where the Court of Justice is often asked to assess the validity of certain sporting rules considered to be the cement holding the European sports pyramid together. For the sports movement, the fear is that the Court is, or will in future, dismantle the pyramid one stone at a time.

EU Law and Sport

As established in *Walrave*, sport falls under the orbit of EU law "only in so far as it constitutes an economic activity".[6] Across its judgements of 21 December 2023, the Court added that "only certain specific rules which were adopted solely on non-economic grounds and which relate to questions of interest solely to sport per se must be regarded as being extraneous to any economic activity".[7] As examples, the Court offered rules excluding foreign players from the composition of national teams or the determination of ranking criteria used to select the athletes participating individually in competitions. Beyond those limited exceptions, most sporting rules must be drafted, implemented and enforced in compliance with EU law, most notably with regard to the requirements of Article 45 TFEU (free movement of workers), Article 56 (freedom to provide services), Article 101 TFEU (prevention, restriction or distortion of competition) and Article 102 TFEU (abuse of a dominant position).[8]

Even though many sporting rules will require an assessment of compatibility with EU law, it is now well established that not all of these rules will give rise to restrictions of free movement or competition. In *Deliège*, the Court rejected a claim that selection rules could restrict a judoka's freedom to provide services by finding that "such a limitation is inherent in the conduct of an international high-level sports event, which necessarily involves certain selection rules or criteria being adopted".[9] In *Meca-Medina*, this logic was extended to competition law as the Court found that anti-doping rules do not necessarily constitute a restriction of competition since any limitation "is inherent in the organisation and proper conduct of competitive sport and its very purpose is to ensure healthy rivalry between athletes".[10]

Even if it is determined that the inherent rules doctrine does not apply, EU free movement and competition law permit arguments to be presented justifying restrictions. Measures that impede free movement can be justified with reference to the pursuit of legitimate objectives in the public interest. Measures that prevent, restrict, or distort competition can be exempt under Article 101(3) TFEU if a number of cumulative conditions are met including whether the contested measure improves the functioning of the market whilst allowing the benefits of this to be shared amongst those operating within it. Although the exemption criteria are crafted in the language of markets, the Court has acknowledged that account can be taken of "the particularities and specific characteristics of the sector(s) or market(s) concerned" if these considerations are decisive for the outcome of that examination.[11] A justificatory regime also operates in Article 102 TFEU where conduct likely to fall under the 102 prohibitions can be justified if the body holding the position of dominance can demonstrate that its conduct is objectively necessary, or that the exclusionary effect produced may be counterbalanced or even outweighed by advantages in terms of efficiency which also benefit the consumer.[12]

The Court has given practical articulation to the above justificatory regimes. For example, in *Bosman*, the Court acknowledged that "…the aims of maintaining a balance between clubs by preserving a certain degree of equality and uncertainty as to results and of encouraging the recruitment and training of young players must be accepted as legitimate".[13] In *Superleague* and *Royal Antwerp* the Court accepted the pursuit of "sporting merit" as a potential source of justification.[14]

Whether or not the inherent rules doctrine or more traditional justifications are invoked, the Court requires proportionality control to take place. Measures must be suitable to achieve the stated legitimate objectives and not go beyond what is necessary to achieve them. In its judgements of 21 December 2023, the Court wanted to see governing bodies bring forward "convincing arguments and evidence" to satisfy proportionality control and where the case was referred via the Article 267 TFEU root, it required the referring court to robustly interrogate these arguments.[15]

The above assessment advances the argument that the specific nature of sport *can* be taken into account at all stages of the process of applying EU law to contested sporting rules. Since the adoption of Article 165 TFEU, the question has been asked whether it *must* be taken into account. Article 165 TFEU requires the EU to "contribute to the promotion of European sporting issues, while taking account of the specific nature of sport". In his Opinion in *Superleague*, Advocate General Rantos claimed that Article 165 TFEU "is, by its very nature, a 'horizontal' provision, inasmuch as it must be taken into consideration when implementing other EU policies".[16] With regard to the challenges faced by the European Model of Sport from proposals such as that presented by the Superleague company, Rantos claimed that

> it is precisely in response to the other models which exist that the EU legislature decided to incorporate the concept of the 'European Sports Model' into the Treaty in order to draw a clear distinction between it and those other models and to guarantee its protection through the adoption of Article 165 TFEU.[17]

The Opinion of AG Rantos raises political and legal questions. Politically, is there any evidence that Member States supported the adoption of Article 165 TFEU as a means of offering constitutional protection to an edifice many disputed the existence of? Whilst the protection of the European model was a concern of the sporting establishment, there is scant evidence that this lay behind the Member States motivations.[18] Legally, given that Article 165 TFEU is a supporting competence, can his horizontal provision claim be supported?

In *Superleague* and *Royal Antwerp*, the Court rejected the horizontal claim by stating that Article 165 "is not a cross-cutting provision having general application" and that it "need not be integrated or taken into account in a binding manner" in the application of other Treaty provisions, notably Articles 45 and 101 TFEU. As such, Article 165 TFEU cannot be regarded as a "special rule exempting sport from all or some of the other provisions of primary EU law".[19] The Court even cast doubt on the very existence of an EU policy on sport by stating that Article 165 TFEU is a provision intended to confer only a supporting competence on the Union as per Article 6(e) TFEU and this only permits it to pursue "actions" in the area of sport rather than a "policy".[20]

Prior Authorisation Rules

For the European model to operate effectively requires participants to commit to it. A governing body possesses no divine right to organise and regulate a sport to the exclusion of others. It derives its regulatory powers through the adoption of a set of contractual prior authorisation rules that establish terms under which a third-party event organiser can establish a competition, and the consequences for participants should they participate in an event that has not be authorised by the governing body. The commercial opportunities offered by elite sport have attracted a growing number of private entities wishing to enter the market for the organisation and commercial exploitation of sport. It is their presence that is leaving the European Model of Sport "potentially endangered" (Agafonova, 2024).

The use of prior authorisation rules is defended on the grounds that they pursue several legitimate sporting objectives.[21] They allow a governing body to ensure the uniform application of sporting rules, including both "field-of-play" rules and off-field ethical and integrity rules which are designed to ensure sporting merit prevails over commercial considerations. In the absence of such rules, commercially minded third-party event organisers could "cherry-pick" the commercially profitable elements of a sport, leaving the volunteering and solidarity functions of the governing body compromised. The commercial motivations of third-party organisers could also damage athlete and spectator health and safety should profit be prioritised over welfare, and the scheduling of events could become problematic if competition between event organisers became the norm.

Underpinning the above justifications is the assumption that traditional governing bodies operate a socio-cultural operations model whereas new market entrants are simply motivated by profit. The interrogation of motive is secondary to the question of the position the governing body holds within the sports market. Governing bodies wear two hats.[22] They are regulatory bodies and simultaneously event organisers and commercial operators. The potential for conflicts of interest to infect the European model is therefore high, even "inevitable" (Weatherill, 2017, 253). The operation of a prior authorisation system therefore has the potential to attract the interest of EU competition law.

In *MOTOE* the Court of Justice identified one such conflict concerning the system of prior authorisation in Greek motorcycling.[23] A third-party event organiser (MOTOE) complained that it was being excluded from the market due to the dual regulatory and event organising functions exercised by the body entrusted by Greek law with the task of approving motorcycling events. The Court held that the power of the body empowered to give consent to a third-party event must be exercised in such a way that is subject to restrictions, obligations, and review.[24] In coming to that conclusion, the Court declined more far-reaching solutions to mitigating conflicts of interest, such as that arrived at by the European Commission in *Fédération Internationale de l'Automobile*.[25] Here, the FIA offered a complete separation of its commercial and regulatory functions in relation to the FIA Formula One World Championship and the FIA World Rally Championship.

The question of the legality of prior authorisation rules reached its denouement on 21 December 2023. On that day in concurrent judgements, the Court of Justice established the criteria that must be applied for the adoption, implementation, and enforcement of such rules to be compatible with Articles 101 and 102 TFEU. In doing so, the Court identified deficiencies with the operation of the prior authorisation systems in speed skating and football.

The dispute in *ISU* arose following a complaint lodged to the European Commission by two speed skaters claiming that the International Skating Union's prior authorisation rules restricted competition. A third-party event organiser, Icederby International, requested permission from the ISU to stage a speed skating event. The ISU's refusal and threat of the imposition of sanctions on those who did participate left the speed skaters without the possibility to participate in a financially lucrative event and it left Icederby locked out of the market for the organisation of speed skating events. Following two appeals,[26] the case reached the Court of Justice.[27]

The *Superleague* litigation raised similar issues. The organisation of international football is the closest real-world exemplification of the European Model of Sport. The April 2021 announcement that a number of elite European football clubs intended to establish a "Super League" to rival UEFA's Champions League represented the greatest test to the structural integrity of the established pyramid. The proposal was for 12 to 15 founder clubs to be permanent members with an unspecified number of clubs joining through a qualification process. The Super League was therefore a partial closed league, a feature running contrary to the open-league model evident with the European model. The announcement was met with hostility from fan groups and the initiative was soon halted following the withdrawal of the English clubs. However, litigation was commenced in Spain by some of the remaining clubs and a referral was made to the Court of Justice. Part of the claim was that the system of prior authorisation operated by FIFA and UEFA, along with the associated threat of sanctions for those who participate in it, was in breach of EU competition law.

In both judgements, the Court explained that governing bodies are able to adopt, apply and ensure compliance with prior authorisation rules, but the power to do so is not unfettered, particularly in circumstances where the regulatory power of the governing body enables it to prevent third parties' access to the market the governing body is itself active in. In *Superleague*, the Court accepted that sporting merit "can be guaranteed only if all the participating teams face each other in homogeneous regulatory and technical conditions, thereby ensuring a certain level of equal opportunity".[28] However, whereas prior authorisation rules can be legitimately deployed to ensure equality of sporting opportunity is maintained, they cannot be used to undermine equality of opportunity for undertakings seeking access to the sports market.

In *ISU* the Court stated that the prior authorisation powers of a governing body must be "circumscribed by substantive criteria which are transparent, clear and precise... preventing it from being used arbitrarily" whilst also being "clearly set out in an accessible form, prior to any implementation of the powers that they are intended to circumscribe".[29] Such substantive criteria could include sporting considerations such as "the holding of sporting competitions based on equality of opportunity and merit".[30] The rules must be "exercised without discrimination" and the sanctions capable of being imposed must be "objective and proportionate"[31] and be "subject to suitable restrictions, obligations and review".[32] Further, the powers must be subject to "transparent and non-discriminatory detailed procedural rules", including time limits for submitting authorisation requests and for taking decisions.[33]

The judgements of 21 December 2023 have implications for the European Model of Sport. At one level, the legitimacy of the governing body to adopt, apply and enforce prior authorisation rules is preserved, but at a cost. The Court conditions this regulatory autonomy on adherence to high standards of internal governance. Consequently, prior authorisation rules must be product of a framework of substantive criteria and detailed procedural rules suitable for ensuring that they are transparent, objective, non-discriminatory, and proportionate.[34] The instinctive reaction of governing bodies is to revisit and revise prior authorisation rules to ensure adherence to this framework.[35] But is that sufficient?

Revised prior authorisation rules might be able to repel some authorisation requests, but not all (Weatherill, 2024). For example, a governing body could refuse a prior authorisation request from a third-party event organiser if the proposed event was unsafe or its rules contradicted the principle of sporting merit, such as it being a closed league. However, refusal of a request to stage a third-party event that mirrors that of the governing body could be in breach of the non-discrimination principle.

Furthermore, at paragraph 176 of *Superleague*, the Court suggests that adherence to the non-discrimination principle may be insufficient to shield the governing body from attack under EU law. Prior authorisation rules, even those adopted within the framework of good governance described above, still make it possible to deny football clubs and players the opportunity to participate in potentially innovative new competitions that may be substantially different from those being run by the incumbent governing body. This might also have the effect of completely depriving spectators and television viewers of the opportunity to attend and view these events.[36] According to Weatherill (2024), "it is here that the Court's ruling could be revolutionary". What it suggests is that in addition to requiring prior authorisation rules to be the product of a good governance framework, they must also not frustrate innovation in the market. A governing body seeking to defend its prior authorisation rules is therefore led down a further "efficiency-orientated, economic approach" in addition to the "traditional" approach based on the articulation of sporting justifications (Agafonova, 2024).

It is not new that governing bodies seek to defend contested sporting rules with reference to both sporting and economic justifications, but since the judgements of 21 December 2023, the Court of Justice is now requiring a stricter evidential burden of proof. Following *Superleague* and *Royal Antwerp* the Court is demanding "convincing arguments and evidence" to be brought forward to justify contested sporting rules under Articles 101 and 102 TFEU.[37] Furthermore, the Court is outsourcing the detailed assessment of these arguments and evidence to national courts. Consequently, whilst prior authorisation rules might pursue legitimate objectives and might be the product of a sound governance framework, they do not release the governing bodies

> from their obligation to establish, before the national court, that the pursuit of those objectives translates into genuine, quantifiable efficiency gains, on the one hand, and that they compensate for the disadvantages caused in competition terms by the rules at issue in the main proceedings, on the other.[38]

The ability of a governing body to give legal articulation to this has been made more challenging as a consequence of the Court's treatment of the inherent rules doctrine and the reach of Article 165 TFEU expressed on 21 December 2023.

Solidarity Rules

As "the guarantors of cohesion", sports bodies play an important role in ensuring effective solidarity mechanisms operate between the various levels of the sport (European Commission, 2022, 31). Specifically, resource generated at the pinnacle of the pyramid is redistributed either horizontally, for example between clubs participating in the same competition, or vertically meaning redistribution to lower levels of the pyramid including to grassroots sport. This redistribution of wealth seeks to ensure the sport remains competitive and therefore attractive to spectators, broadcasters, and sponsors, but it also supports the development and sustainability of the sport through grassroots funding.[39] The impulse for solidarity therefore reflects the pursuit of both economic and sporting objectives.

The EU has long recognised the importance of solidarity in sport. In the 2000 Nice Declaration on Sport, the Member States claimed that solidarity was "essential" to the preservation of sport's social role.[40] Successive Commission papers on sport have reiterated this point.[41] Without specifically mentioning solidarity, Article 165 TFEU implies its importance by focussing on "the specific nature of sport, its structures based on voluntary activity and its social and educational function". By their very nature, the voluntary model and the social and educational functions of sport are not profitable and therefore require support.

As discussed above, governing bodies use prior authorisation rules as a means of safeguarding their solidarity function as without them, commercially minded third-party event organisers could engage in free-riding by establishing rival events absent of a solidarity commitment. In the first instance *ISU* Decision, the Commission recognised that some form of solidarity may justify limited restrictions being placed on the economic freedoms of undertakings involved in sport but that the prevention of free-riding cannot be considered a legitimate objective in itself, but rather a claim relating to the economic efficiencies within the sector.[42]

The Commission noted some inconsistencies with the ISU's claims on the importance of prior authorisation rules for the preservation of its solidarity function including a failure to substantiate its solidarity claims and the fact that the prior authorisation rules allowed for the ISU to demand a solidarity contribution from third-party event organisers.[43] The Commission observed that the ISU considered it permissible to use this contribution to support competitive events organised by its members whereas no such funds are made available for the organisation of third-party events, thereby placing such operators at a competitive disadvantage.[44] This further supported the Commission's view that the ISU's prior authorisation rules had as their object the protection of the ISU's economic interests which cannot be considered a legitimate interest.

As explained above, solidarity functions pursue both economic and sporting objectives and disentangling those objectives is problematic given their interdependent nature. A more logical approach would be to consider the protection of the economic interests of a governing body anti-competitive only if that body unjustifiably denies a competitor market access.[45] On appeal, and contrary to the Commission's finding, the General Court found favour with that logic by stating that the ISU's conduct in seeking to protect its own economic interests was not in itself an anti-competitive objective.

Nevertheless, despite making that error, the General Court considered sound the Commission's overall assessment that the prior authorisation rules amounted to an object restriction. Furthermore, given its conflicted role in both regulating and commercially exploiting the sport, the General Court agreed with the Commission that it should not use solidarity contributions to finance its own competitive events.[46] On final appeal to the Court of Justice, the speed skaters argued that the General Court erred in its assessment of the question of the pursuit of economic interests. That ground of appeal was rejected by the Court as the skaters could derive no further advantage given that the ISU's prior authorisation rules had already been condemned.[47]

The judgement in *ISU* cannot therefore be interpreted as a rejection of the importance of the solidarity function in sport and neither does it question the use of solidarity contributions payable by would-be third-party event organisers. Rather, it requires solidarity schemes to pursue legitimate objectives, be they economic or sporting, in a manner that does not seek to unduly deprive rivals access to the market.

On the same day as *ISU*, the Court delivered *Superleague*, a case with further implications regarding the ability of a governing body to fulfil its solidarity function. For many sports, the sale of media rights represents a significant source of revenue that can then be used to support a governing body's solidarity function. A common business model employed by governing bodies is for media rights to be sold collectively on behalf of participants, such as clubs, even though the participants might, depending on national law, be the original owner of the intellectual property. The assignment of these rights by the original owner is normally a condition of participation in the events organised by the body collectively exploiting the rights. In *Superleague*, the referring Spanish court sought guidance from the Court of Justice on whether FIFA's and UEFA's use of this model conflicts with EU competition law.

The Court of Justice combined its analysis of Articles 101 and 102. It found that the collective selling arrangements were the principal source of revenue for FIFA and UEFA, but these arrangements amount to an object restriction under Article 101 and an abuse of a dominant market position under Article 102 TFEU. This is because the arrangements grant exclusive power to FIFA and UEFA to exploit the rights thereby restricting competition between the clubs that are denied the opportunity to exploit the rights on an individual basis. Collective selling also affects the functioning of competition within the market to acquire such rights (between broadcasters) as abusive prices can be demanded by the monopolist seller which has consequential impacts on consumers and television viewers.[48]

Given that the Court classified the conduct as an object restriction and one giving rise to an abuse of a dominant position, the ability to rely on the inherent rules doctrine to save this practice was removed.[49] The Court therefore turned to consider claims that the collective selling model could be justified. In previous Decisions, the Commission applied the exemption criteria contained within Article 101(3) to permit the collective sale model operated by UEFA, the English Premier League, and the German Bundesliga.[50] Amongst other benefits, collective selling gave rise to efficiencies by providing a single point of sale whilst offering attractive rights to broadcasters who benefit from the consistent branding offered by a single supplier of rights.

In *Superleague*, the Court noted these arguments but left it to the national court to interrogate them further. Nevertheless, the Court entered into a discussion on whether any efficiency gains claimed benefitted participants other than just FIFA and UEFA. In doing so, the Court claimed that a large share of the profit derived from the sale of rights on a collective basis is spent on fulfilling FIFA's and UEFA's solidarity function and this benefits not only participating clubs in those competitions "but also those not participating, amateur clubs, professional players, women's football, young players and other categories of stakeholders in football".[51] The benefit is further extended to supporters and consumers (television viewers) and to "all EU citizens involved in amateur sport".[52] The Court claimed that "[t]hose arguments appear prima facie to be convincing" and that the proper functioning, sustainability, and success of the competitions in question rests on them being competitively balanced, an objective served via the redistribution of wealth collective selling facilitates.[53] Without equivocation or further analysis, the Court announced that

> there is a trickle-down effect from those competitions into smaller professional football clubs and amateur football clubs which, whilst not participating therein, invest at local level in the recruitment and training of young, talented players, some of whom will turn professional and aspire to join a participating club.

Further, solidarity in football "serves to bolster its educational and social function within the European Union".[54]

Although the Court then repeated that it is for the referring court to test the veracity of such claims, its forthright stance on the wide benefits of solidarity and its connection with the pursuit of competitive balance is ground-breaking and likely to be influential.

Nationality-Based Rules

The European Model of Sport possesses a distinctly national character. National competitions, national championships, and competitions between national teams are a long-standing and entrenched feature of the European sporting landscape. To preserve this national character, eligibility to participate is often structured around nationality, and this can give rise to claims of nationality discrimination which is a protected characteristic under EU law.

In *Walrave*, the Advocate-General opined that it was "common sense" for national teams to consist only of nationals of that country.[55] The legal reasoning to support that proposition was arrived at by the Court of Justice at paragraph eight where it stated that the prohibition on nationality discrimination "does not affect the composition of sport teams, in particular national teams, the formation of which is a matter of purely sporting interest and as such has nothing to do with economic activity".[56]

In *Walrave* the Court mentioned the composition of national teams as an example of a rule potentially excluded from the scope of the Treaty. This raised expectations that other nationality-based rules, for example those used to structure eligibility in club sport, could be treated likewise. However, *Donà* and then, most notably,

Bosman dashed those expectations.[57] In *Bosman*, the so-called 3+2 nationality quota operated by UEFA and implemented by some national associations was condemned by the Court as amounting to an obstacle to a worker's freedom of movement. In coming to that conclusion the Court rejected submissions that the rule served to maintain the traditional link between each club and its country, that this was necessary to ensure a pool of players eligible to play for the national team, and that nationality restrictions are required to maintain competitive balance between clubs.[58] At paragraph 106, the Court did however accept as legitimate the aims of maintaining a balance between clubs by preserving a certain degree of equality and uncertainty as to results and of encouraging the recruitment and training of young players.

Bosman made the national boundaries of the European model more porous. When on Boxing Day in 1999, Chelsea Football Club fielded 11 non-nationals in its starting XI, the labour market implications of the judgement became clear. In particular, UEFA expressed concern that *Bosman* had contributed to diminished incentives for clubs to train players, a lack of identity in local and regional teams, the hoarding of players by clubs, problems for national teams, a diminution of competitive balance in UEFA and national competitions, and an increased link between money and sporting success (Dalziel et al., 2013, 9). The result was the introduction of its home-grown player rule.

Introduced for the 2006/07 season, the rule requires every football team entering European club competitions to name eight "home grown" players in their 25-player squad. A minimum of four of these players must be "club-trained", meaning a player who, irrespective of nationality and age, has been trained with the current club for a period of three entire seasons or of 36 months whilst between the age of 15 and 21. The remaining players must be "association-trained" meaning a player, irrespective of nationality and age, has been trained by another club in the same national association.

Despite a study funded by the European Commission finding that the rule gave rise to indirect nationality discrimination, no party complained, and the rule became an established part of football's regulatory landscape.[59] In 2014, the European Commission indirectly endorsed the rule by referring to it in a complaint raised in Spanish basketball. Here the Commission argued that whereas 32% of squad places under UEFA's rule were reserved for home-grown players, in Spanish basketball the quota ranged from 40% to 88% rendering the measure disproportionate (European Commission, 2014).

In 2020, an arbitral tribunal in Belgium rejected a complaint from a professional player and Royal Antwerp Football Club that UEFA's rule, and the corresponding rule implemented in Belgium, infringed Articles 45 and 101 TFEU, but it made a preliminary ruling request to the Court of Justice. The Belgian rule was similar in construction to that of UEFA but differed insofar as the eight home-grown players on the 25-player squad list could be sourced from clubs in the same national association and there was an obligation for clubs to field at least six players who have been trained by a Belgian club.

In *Royal Antwerp*, the third of its judgements of 21 December, the Court of Justice directed the referring Belgian Court to undertake the detailed assessment of whether the contested rules breached EU free movement and competition laws. However, the Court provided guidance on the interpretation of such provisions.

On the allegation that the contested rules infringe Article 101 TFEU, the Court accepted that sports governing bodies are able to adopt rules relating to the organisation and functioning of the sport in question and that "sporting merit… can be guaranteed only if all the participating teams face each other in homogenous regulatory and technical conditions, thereby ensuring a certain level of equal opportunity".[60] The Court even recognised that this might require the market to possess a "national requirement or criterion".[61] The home-grown player rules possess such a national character as it partially partitions the market along national lines given that the recruitment choices of clubs is partially skewed towards recruiting and training players from within the national association within which they operate.

The Court did not enter further analysis of whether, in light of those statements, the contested rules give rise to a "sufficient degree of harm to competition to be able to be regarded as having as their 'object' the restriction of competition", although it did consider the proportion of players falling within the rule as a particularly relevant factor.[62] In its assessment of the potential application of the exemption criteria contained in Article 101(3) TFEU, the Court wanted to see convincing arguments and evidence that the rules encourage professional clubs to recruit and train young players thereby intensifying competition through training.

Part of the answer to this question was implied in the Court's Article 45 TFEU assessment. Here, the Court first found that the home-grown player rules amount to indirect discrimination on the grounds of nationality but that the objective of encouraging the recruitment and training of young players is legitimate. However, the Court then appeared to cast doubt on the suitability of the rules to achieve an intensification of training. It supported the view that the club-trained element of the rule is most suited to achieve the stated objective, leaving the association-trained element potentially vulnerable as that element "might not constitute real and significant incentives for some of those clubs".[63] In that regard, the Court appears to be agreeing with the Opinion of Advocate General Szpunar who expressed doubts regarding the "general coherence" of the association-trained element.[64] The argument is that clubs with significant financial means have little incentive to develop young players if they can fill the quota by recruiting players already trained in the same national association (Parrish & Živić, 2024). As pointed out by Powell and Couse (2024), Belgium, whose rule has an association-trained focus, has one of the highest figures for the total minutes played by expatriate players.

Royal Antwerp does not prevent governing bodies from establishing rules that endow the market with a national character, but it prescribes the conditions under which it can do so. Specifically, the Court wants to see convincing arguments and evidence that such rules are suitable and necessary for the fulfilment of the stated legitimate objectives. *Royal Antwerp* indirectly concerned nationality-based eligibility rules in teams sport, but what of the picture for individual sports? A study funded by the European Commission highlighted the extent to which nationality-based rules were being routinely deployed by governing bodies (T.M.C. Asser Instituut et al., 2010). These practices included denying non-nationals access to national competitions, limiting their participation, and imposing residency and club membership requirements as a condition of participation. Amongst the many stated justifications for such rules was the desire to preserve the national character of national championships.

In *TopFit*, the Court was asked to assess the case of an Italian national, living in Germany, who was excluded from full participation in the amateur senior German athletics championships on account of his nationality.[65] The Court determined that the TFEU's non-discrimination and citizenship provisions, when read alongside Article 165 TFEU, enable an EU citizen, whether economically active or not, who is residing in another Member State to "create bonds with the society of the State to which he has moved and in which he is residing or to consolidate them".[66] The complainant's treatment therefore constituted a restriction of freedom movement.[67]

On first appearance, *TopFit* could be interpreted as a significant threat to the ability of governing bodies to continue to endow the sports market with a national character. However, the Court did not in fact unleash the "open-access" principle into sport. The full or partial exclusion of non-nationals will continue to be legitimate where the presence of non-nationals is capable of preventing a national from winning the championship and hindering the designation of the best nationals.[68] This scenario can be envisaged where the sport operates eliminatory heats or rounds such as in athletics or tennis. It is less tolerable where the presence of a non-national has no bearing on the identification of the best national, such as in a marathon where time and not placings are used to establish this.

Arbitration Clauses

The structural integrity of the European Model of Sport could undermined if sports disputes are not settled "in-house" but are subject to litigation. To mitigate this risk, sports governing bodies have deployed the "contractual solution" requiring participants operating within the European model to resolve disputes by way of arbitration (Weatherill, 2017). The Swiss-based Court of Arbitration for Sport (CAS), established in 1983, sits at the pinnacle of this system of international sports justice.

The system of mandatory arbitration in sport claims to deliver time, cost and expertise benefits, but not all have total faith in the system of sporting justice being dispensed.[69] Nevertheless, CAS has been resilient in defending claims that it lacks independence from the sports movement[70] and that arbitration is unjustifiably forced upon participants.[71] However, a different line of attack was pursued by the speed skaters in *ISU*. Here it was claimed that the arbitration rules in force in international speed skating reinforced the restrictive nature of the prior authorisation rules being challenged. The European Commission agreed[72] but the General Court found that the arbitration rules could be justified by a legitimate interest relating to the specific nature of sport such as the need to adjudicate disputes "quickly and economically" by a specialist body thereby promoting "a certain procedural uniformity" which "strengthens legal certainty".[73] On appeal, the Court of Justice restored the reasoning of the Commission.[74]

The restoration of that reasoning reflects the Court's concern, expressed across its judgements of 21 December 2023, that sporting autonomy must be conditioned on sports governing bodies demonstrating a commitment to good governance. For those subject to the monopoly power of a governing body and to a system of mandatory arbitration, the availability of effective review as a means of mitigating conflicts of interest is an irreducible minimum standard of good governance. First expressed in *MOTOE*, this logic has now been forcefully confirmed in *ISU*.

The problem identified by the Court is not that the mandatory submission of disputes to arbitration is anti-competitive per se, but that arbitral decisions of international federations such as the ISU are reviewable exclusively by CAS, which is located in Switzerland outside the EU territory. Furthermore, its decisions are reviewable exclusively by the Swiss Federal Tribunal. That court does not apply EU law and has no mechanism to refer questions to the Court of Justice in Luxembourg under the Article 267 TFEU procedure.[75] Articles 101 and 102 TFEU are provisions having direct effect, but mandatory arbitration clauses could deny individuals located within the EU the ability of seeking to ensure before a Member State court that the arbitral award to which they are subject complies with this fundamental provision of EU public policy. In arriving at that position, the Court rejected the General Court's reasoning that the effectiveness of EU law was ensured on account of the ability of an individual subject to an arbitral award to seek damages before a national court or to lodge a complaint with the Commission or a national competition authority.[76] According to the Court, the prospect of receiving damages could not compensate for the absence of effective remedy.[77]

Just as *ISU* preserved the ability of governing bodies to adopt, apply, and enforce prior authorisation rules, subject to those rules being produced with a framework of substantive criteria and detailed procedural rules, so the judgement also permitted the continued use of arbitration clauses. However, the requirement for effective judicial review located in EU law represents a challenge for CAS and the sports movement. One potential solution, but not one mandated by the Court, is for CAS to allow some arbitration panels to be seated within the territory of the EU. This would allow Member State courts to patrol the legality of awards under EU law, but it would require burdensome adjustments and disturb considerable case law based on Swiss law. Alternatively, and more realistically, the mandatory nature of arbitration could be relaxed so that participants have a choice to arbitrate or litigate, or mandatory arbitration could be preserved only for sports-related as opposed to commercial disputes. For example, with regards the FIFA Regulations on the Status and Transfer of Players (RSTP), FIFA, and by extension CAS on appeal, are competent to exclusively hear all disputes arising out of the regulations except for employment-related disputes with an international dimension where participants are able to seek redress before a national court.[78] This provision was included at the insistence of the European Commission during the framing of the original RSTP in 2001 and had input from FIFPro, the international trade union for players. As Duval argues, the judgement should encourage better governance along these lines as governing bodies should more readily engage with athletes prior to adopting rules so that they have their "buy-in" (Duval, 2024b).

Conclusion

Within the EU, the debate surrounding the existence, merits, and preservation of the European Model of Sport is framed in both political and legal terms. The political debate has oscillated between those comfortable using the term and those who are linguistically more cautious but still espouse the key values and principles on which it is founded. EU sport policy has navigated this nuance and articulated a position advancing claims that sport has a special character and that the regulatory autonomy of governing bodies should be conditioned within a framework of adherence to good governance.

The legal debate has centred on whether rules drafted, applied, and enforced that are designed to preserve the structural integrity of the European model are compatible with EU law and the extent to which an orthodox application of EU law should prevail over an approach in which specificity of sport arguments gain traction. The initial reaction to the European Court's judgements on 21 December 2023, in which the term European model was not even uttered and Article 165 TFEU side-lined, suggests that orthodox law has triumphed over politics (García, 2024).

The judgements of 21 December 2023 will no doubt give rise to claims that a political counter offensive is required. Article 165 could be strengthened or even usurped by constitutionally more robust Treaty provisions with a view to moving the EU's approach beyond ad hoc judicial adjudication of sports governance to one in which legislation and/or the establishment of an EU sports agency could protect the European model (Zglinski, 2024).

Attractive as this may appear, the proposed EU legislative solution is not remedying a mischief of the Court's making, beyond signalling political annoyance that the Court appeared to devalue the political efforts of those seeking improvements in international sports governance. There is in fact broad convergence of thinking between the political and legal streams. The judgements of 21 December 2023 give judicial endorsement to the main strand of EU sport policy, albeit without referencing it, through an insistence loaded into all three judgements that good governance lies at the heart of continued regulatory autonomy.

Consequently, the judgements do not represent an existential threat to the values and principles on which the European model is based. With regard to prior authorisation rules, the Court preserved the regulatory autonomy of governing bodies but placed good governance conditions on its exercise. Likewise, with regard to solidarity, the Court argued that this function cannot be used to unjustifiably foreclose markets, but it reinforced the importance of solidarity mechanisms in sport and even broke new ground by highlighting connections between redistribution and the pursuit of competitively balanced competitions. Regarding nationality-based rules, the Court accepted that governing bodies are able to endow the European sports market with a national character should that be suitable, necessary and evidenced, in the pursuit of legitimate sporting objectives. Finally, the Court accepted the legitimacy of arbitration clauses, even those mandatory in nature, but that good governance dictates that awards are reviewable to ensure that EU law-derived rights are protected.

None of the above is said to dismiss the scale of the governance challenges facing governing bodies, but equally the extent of the damage done to the European model by the Court should not be exaggerated.

Notes

1 Case-124/21 P *International Skating Union v Commission* [2023], ECLI:EU:C:2023:1012 (herein *ISU*); Case C-333/21 *European Superleague Company SL v FIFA and UEFA* [2023] ECLI:EU:C:2023:1011 (herein *Superleague*); & Case C-680/21 *SA Royal Antwerp Football Club v URBSFA* [2023] ECLI:EU:C:2023:1010 (herein *Royal Antwerp*).
2 See for example, European Commission (2016). Expert Group on Good Governance: Promotion of Existing Good Governance Principles, July.
3 As of March 2024, a search on the Erasmus+ Project results portal returns over 100 funded good governance projects.
4 Structured dialogue involves bi-lateral and multi-lateral discussions between the EU institutions and the sports movement, for example with the context of the annual EU Sport Forum. Social dialogue refers to discussions and potentially joint actions facilitated by the Commission but involving organisations representing the two sides of industry, namely employers and workers. It is located in Article 151–156 TFEU.
5 "Revision of the European Sports Charter", accessed at: https://www.coe.int/en/web/sport/revision-esc
6 Case 36/74 *Walrave and Koch v Association Union Cycliste Internationale* [1974] ECR 1405 (herein *Walrave*) paragraph 4.
7 Case-124/21 P *ISU* paragraph 92; Case C-333/21 *Superleague* paragraph 84 & Case C-680/21 *Royal Antwerp Football Club* paragraph 54.
8 As there is a rich literature on the application of these and other provisions of EU law to sport, only brief mention of them is made here. A notable contribution is Weatherill, S. (2017). *Principles and Practice in EU Sports Law*, Oxford University Press. See also Cattaneo, A. & Parrish, R. (2020). *Sports Law in the European Union*, Alphen aan den Rijn: Wolters Kluwer.
9 Case C-51/96 and C-191/97 *Deliège* v *Ligue Francophone de Judo et Disciplines Associées Asb* [2000] ECLI:EU:C:2000:199 paragraph 64.
10 Case C-519/04 *P David Meca-Medina and Igor Majcen* v *Commission* [2006] ECLI:EU:C:2006:492 paragraph 45. It should be noted that since the judgements of 21 December 2023, the inherent rules doctrine does not apply to object restrictions under Article 101 TFEU nor to conduct which by its very nature infringes Article 102 TFEU.
11 Case C-680/21 *Royal Antwerp* paragraph 126.
12 Case C-333/21 *Superleague* paragraph 202.
13 Case C-415/93 *Union Royale Belge Sociétés de Football Association and others* v *Bosman and others* [1995] ECR I-4921 paragraph 106 (herein *Bosman*).
14 Case C-333/21 *Superleague* paragraph 144 & Case C-680/21 *Royal Antwerp* paragraph 105.
15 See for instance Case C-680/21 *Royal Antwerp* paragraph 120.

16 Opinion of Advocate General Rantos delivered on 15 December 2022 in Case C-333/21 *Superleague*, paragraph 35.

17 Opinion of Advocate General Rantos, paragraph 33.

18 One of the few accounts of the negotiating history of Article 165 TFEU is García, B. & Weatherill, S. (2012). Engaging with the EU in Order to Minimise Its Impact: Sport and the Negotiation of the Treaty of Lisbon, *Journal of European Public Policy*, 19(2), 238–256.

19 Case C-333/21 *Superleague* paragraphs 100–101 & Case C-680/21 *Royal Antwerp* paragraph 68–69.

20 *Royal Antwerp* paragraph 67. For critical comment see See Parrish, R. & Živić, L. (2024). Royal Antwerp and Home-Grown Players: Re-shaping Sports Governance and EU Sports Law and Policy, *The International Sports Law Journal*, 23, 453–459, https://doi.org/10.1007/s40318-024-00263-y

21 In Case AT.40208 – International Skating Union's Eligibility Rules, at s.8.5.1, para's 211–224 (Do the Eligibility Rules Pursue Legitimate Objectives?) the European Commission discusses objectives.

22 Robby Houben refers to the dual function of a governing body as "double hatting". See Houben, R. (2023). Sports Governance (in football) Under Attack, *The International Sports Law Journal*, 23, 271–292.

23 Case C-49/07 *Motosykletistiki Omospondia Ellados NPID (MOTOE) v Elliniko Dimosio* [2008] ECLI:EU:C:2008:376.

24 For further discussion, see Weatherill, S. (2009). Article 82 and Sporting 'Conflicts of Interest': The Judgment in MOTOE, *The International Sports Law Journal*, 1/2, 3–7 and Miettinen, S. (2008). Policing the Boundaries Between Regulation and Commercial Exploitation: Lessons from the MOTOE Case, *The International Sports law Journal*, 3/4, 13–18.

25 COMP 35.163, Notification of FIA Regulations, COMP 36.638, Notification by FIA/FOA of agreements relating to the FIA Formula One World Championships, COMP 36.776, GTR/FIA, Notice published 13/06/2001 OJ C 169, paragraph 5.

26 Case AT.40208 – International Skating Union's Eligibility Rules was appealed to the General Court and Case T-93/18 *International Skating Union v Commission* ECLI:EU:T:2020:610 was appealed to the Court of Justice. For discussion of the General Court's approach see Cattaneo, A. (2021). International Skating Union v Commission: Pre-authorisation Rules and Competition Law, *Journal of European Competition Law and Practice*, 12(4), 318–320.

27 Case-124/21 P *ISU.*

28 Case C-333/21 *Superleague* paragraph 143.

29 Case-124/21 P *ISU*, paragraph 131.

30 Case-124/21 P *ISU* paragraph 132.

31 Case-124/21 P *ISU* paragraph 133.

32 Case-124/21 P *ISU* paragraph 144.

33 Case-124/21 P *ISU* paragraph 135.

34 Case C-333/21 *Superleague* paragraphs 120–138.

35 See for example UEFA Authorisation Rules governing International Club Competitions, Edition 2022. For a discussion of possible responses see van der Burg, T. (2024). How UEFA Can React to the Super League Ruling, *The International Sports Law Journal*, 23, 447–452, https://doi.org/10.1007/s40318-024-00260-1

36 A sentiment repeated at paragraph 146 of Case-124/21 P *ISU.*

37 Case C-333/21 *Superleague* paragraph 205 & Case C-680/21 *Royal Antwerp*, paragraph 120.

38 Case C-333/21 *Superleague* paragraph 196.

39 Examples of redistributive schemes in sport are detailed in European Commission (2022). Study on the European Sport Model, written by Sennett, J., Le Gall, A., Kelly, G., Cottrill, R., Goffredo, S., and Spyridopoulos, K., García, B. & Weatherill, S. (2012).

Engaging with the EU in Order to Minimize Its Impact: Sport and the Negotiation of the Treaty of Lisbon, Journal of European Public Policy, 19(2), 32–36.

40 Conclusions on the Presidency, European Council, Nice 7–10 December 2000, Annex IV, *Declaration on the Specific Characteristics of Sport and its Social Function in Europe, of which Account Should be Taken in Implementing Common Policies*, paragraphs 1 & 8.

41 See for example, European Commission (2007). *White Paper on Sport*, COM(2007) 391 final, Brussels, 11/07/2007.

42 Case AT.40208 – International Skating Union's Eligibility Rules, paragraphs 221 & 224.

43 Case AT.40208 – International Skating Union's Eligibility Rules, paragraphs 246–249.

44 Case AT.40208 – International Skating Union's Eligibility Rules, paragraphs 187 & 220.

45 A point made by Advocate General Rantos in Case C-124/21 P *ISU* paragraph 104.

46 Case T-93/18 *International Skating Union v Commission* paragraphs 111–114.

47 Case-124/21 P *ISU* paragraphs 205–211.

48 Case C-333/21 *Superleague* paragraphs 217–230.

49 See footnote 10.

50 Decision COMP/C.2–37.398 – Joint selling of the commercial rights of the UEFA Champions League; Case COMP/38.173, Collective selling of FA Premier League's broadcasting rights; Case COMP/C-2/37.214, Joint selling of the media rights to the German Bundesliga.

51 Case C-333/21 *Superleague* paragraph 234.

52 Case C-333/21 *Superleague* paragraph 234.

53 Case C-333/21 *Superleague* paragraph 235.

54 Case C-333/21 *Superleague* paragraph 235.

55 Opinion of Advocate-General Warner in Case 36/74 *Walrave* at 1426, first column.

56 Case 36/74 *Walrave* paragraph 8.

57 Case 13/76 *Donà v Mantero* [1976] ECR 1333 and Case C-415/93 *Bosman*.

58 Case C-415/93 *Bosman* paragraphs 121–137.

59 The study was authored by Dalziel, M., Downward, P., Parrish, R., Pearson G. & Semens, A. (2013). An Assessment of the Compatibility of UEFA's Home Grown Player Rule with Article 45 TFEU, *European Law Review*, 39(4), 493–510.

60 Case C-680/21 *Royal Antwerp* paragraph 105.

61 Case C-680/21 *Royal Antwerp* paragraph 106.

62 Case C-680/21 *Royal Antwerp* paragraphs 108–109.

63 Case C-680/21 *Royal Antwerp* paragraph 147.

64 Case C-680/21 Opinion of AG Szpunar in *Royal Antwerp* paragraph 67.

65 Case C-22/18 *TopFit e.V. and Daniele Biffi v Deutscher Leichtathletikverband e.V.* [2019], EU:C:2019:497 (herein *TopFit*). For further discussion see Lindholm, J. & Parrish, R. (2020). Horizontal Direct Effect of Union Citizenship and the Evolving Sporting Exception: TopFit, *Common Market Law Review*, 57(4), 1283–1304.

66 Case C-22/18 *TopFit* paragraph 34.

67 Case C-22/18 *TopFit* paragraph 47.

68 Case C-22/18 *TopFit* paragraph 61.

69 For one such critique see Duval, A. (2024). Embedded Lex Sportiva: The Swiss Roots of Transnational Sports Law and Governance, in Duval, A., Krüger, A. & Lindholm, J. (Eds.), *The European Roots of the Lex Sportiva: How Europe Rules Global Sport*, Oxford: Hart, pp. 17–40.

70 See *Lazutina v IOC and FIS*, Swiss Federal Tribunal, 27/05/200, 129 III 445.

71 *Mutu and Pechstein v Switzerland*, ECtHR, 02/10/2018, 40575/10 and 67474/10.

72 Case AT.40208 – International Skating Union's Eligibility Rules.

73 Case T-93/18 *International Skating Union v European Commission*, ECLI:EU:T:2020:610 paragraph 156.

74 Case-124/21 P *ISU*.

75 Case-124/21 P *ISU* paragraph 198.
76 Case-124/21 P *ISU* paragraph 200.
77 Case-124/21 P *ISU* paragraph 201.
78 Article 22, FIFA Regulations on the Status and Transfer of Players, 2023 Edition.

References

Agafonova, R. (2024). *ISU* and *Superleague* Judgments: Sports Governance in the Market-driven Era, *International Sports Law Journal*, 23, 441–446, https://doi.org/10.1007/s40318-024-00261-0

Brocard, J.M. & Anglade, M. (2021). *The European Model of Sport, Evaluation and Perspectives*, CDES: Limoges.

Cattaneo, A. (2021). International Skating Union v Commission: Pre-authorisation Rules and Competition Law, *Journal of European Competition Law and Practice*, 12(4), 318–320.

Cattaneo, A. & Parrish, R. (2020). *Sports Law in the European Union*, Alphen aan den Rijn: Wolters Kluwer.

Chaker, A.N. (1999). *Study of National Sports Legislations in Europe*, Strasbourg: Council of Europe.

Council of Europe (2021). Recommendation CM/Rec(2021)5 of the Committee of Ministers to Member States on the Revised European Sports Charter, adopted by the Committee of Ministers on 13 October 2021.

Council of the European Union (2017). European Union Work Plan for Sport (1 July 2017 – 31 December 2020) - Council Resolution, 24/05/2017, 9639/17.

Council of the European Union (2020). European Union Work Plan for Sport (1 January 2021 – 30 June 2024), Council Resolution, 04/12/2020, 2020/C 419/01.

Council of the European Union (2021). The Features of a European Sport Model, Council Resolution, 13/12/2021, 2021/C 501/01.

Dalziel, M., Downward, P., Parrish, R., Pearson, G. & Semens, A. (2013). Study on the Assessment of UEFA's Home Grown Player Rule, Study funded by the European Commission.

Duval, A. (2024a). Embedded Lex Sportiva: The Swiss Roots of Transnational Sports Law and Governance, in Duval, A., Krüger, A., & Lindholm, J. (Eds.), *The European Roots of the Lex Sportiva: How Europe Rules Global Sport*, Oxford: Hart.

Duval, A. (2024b). The *International Skating Union* Ruling of the CJEU and the Future of CAS Arbitration in Transnational Sports Governance, *International Sports Law Journal*, 23, 467–474, https://doi.org/10.1007/s40318-024-00270-z

EU Athletes (2021). EU Athletes Response to the Lobby for a 'European sports model', Brussels, 20/01/21, accessed at: https://rm.coe.int/eu-athletes-response-to-the-lobby-for-a-european-sports-model/1680a2430e

European Commission (1998). The European Model of Sport, Consultation Document of DGX.

European Commission (1999). Report from the Commission to the European Council with a View to Safeguarding Sports Structures and Maintaining the Social Function of Sport within the Community Framework – The Helsinki Report on Sport, COM/99/0644 final.

European Commission (2007). Commission Staff Working Document. Impact Assessment Accompanying the White Paper on Sport, SEC 932, 11/07/2007.

European Commission (2011). Developing the European Dimension in Sport (the Communication on Sport), final, COM(2011), Brussels, 18/01/11.

European Commission (2014). Basketball: Commission Asks Spain to End Indirect Discrimination Towards Players from Other Member States, accessed at: https://ec.europa.eu/commission/presscorner/detail/en/MEMO_14_293

European Commission (2016). Expert Group on Good Governance: Promotion of Existing Good Governance Principles, July.

European Commission (2022). Study on the European Sport Model, written by Sennett, J., Le Gall, A., Kelly, G., Cottrill, R., Goffredo, S., Spyridopoulos, K., García, B. & Weatherill, S. (2012). Engaging with the EU in Order to Minimize its Impact: Sport and the Negotiation of the Treaty of Lisbon, *Journal of European Public Policy*, 19(2), 238–256.

García, B. (2024). Down with the Politics, Up with the Law! Reinforcing EU Law's Supervision of Sport Autonomy in Europe, *International Sports Law Journal*, 23, 416–421, https://doi.org/10.1007/s40318-024-00264-x

Houben, R. (2023). Sports Governance (in football) Under Attack, *International Sports Law Journal*, 23, 271–292.

Lindholm, J. & Parrish, R. (2020). Horizontal Direct Effect of Union Citizenship and the Evolving Sporting Exception: TopFit, *Common Market Law Review*, 57(4), 1283–1304.

Miettinen, S. (2008). Policing the Boundaries Between Regulation and Commercial Exploitation: Lessons from the MOTOE Case, *The International Sports Law Journal*, 3/4, 13–18.

Ministère des Sports et des Jeux Olympiques et Paralympiques (2024). Déclaration des ministres des sports européens pour un modèle sportif basé sur la solidarité, le mérite sportif et l'impact sociétal du sport, accessed at: https://www.sports.gouv.fr/declaration-des-ministres-des-sports-europeens-pour-un-modele-sportif-base-sur-la-solidarite-le

Nafziger, J. (2008). A Comparison of the European and North American Models of Sports Organisation, *International Sports Law Journal*, 3–4.

O'Leary, L. (2024). *ISU, Royal Antwerp, European Superleague* & Employment Relations in Sport, *International Sports Law Journal*, 23, 431–435, https://doi.org/10.1007/s40318-024-00266-9

Parrish, R. & Živić, L. (2024). *Royal Antwerp* and Home-Grown Players: Re-shaping Sports Governance and EU Sports Law and Policy, *International Sports Law Journal*, 23, 453–459, https://doi.org/10.1007/s40318-024-00263-y

Powell, A. & Couse, C. (2024). Justifying Indirectly Discriminatory Restrictions: Can European Football's Home-Grown Players Rules Withstand the Proportionality Test? *International Sports Law Journal*, 23, 436–440, https://doi.org/10.1007/s40318-024-00262-z

T.M.C. Asser Instituut, Edge Hill University & Leiden University (2010). Study on the Equal Treatment of Non-Nationals in Individual Sports Competitions, Study for the European Commission.

van der Burg, T. (2024). How UEFA Can React to the Super League Ruling, *International Sports Law Journal*, 23, 447–452, https://doi.org/10.1007/s40318-024-00260-1

Weatherill, S. (2009). Article 82 and Sporting 'Conflicts of Interest': The Judgment in MOTOE, *International Sports Law Journal*, 1/2, 3–7.

Weatherill, S. (2017). *Principles and Practice in EU Sports Law*, Oxford: Oxford University Press.

Weatherill, S. (2024). Football Revolution: How Do the Court's Rulings of 21 December 2023 Affect UEFA's Role as a 'Gatekeeper'?, *EU Law Analysis*, accessed at: https://eulawanalysis.blogspot.com/2024/01/football-revolution-how-do-courts.html

Zglinski, J. (2024). Can EU Competition Law Save Sports Governance? *International Sports Law Journal*, 23, 475–481, https://doi.org/10.1007/s40318-024-00258-9

Chapter 4

Socio-Cultural Values in European Sport

A Selective Survey of Strategy and Policy Papers in EU Member States

Henk Erik Meier and Merle Wiehl

Introduction

Any account of socio-cultural values in sport runs the risk of getting lost in intricate discussions between various sub-disciplines of sport science. Scholars of sport philosophy and ethics have emphasized that sports are neither inherently good nor bad, but rather have the potential to be both (McFee, 2004; DeSensi, 2014). A sociological perspective suggests adopting an even more skeptical stance for several reasons:

First, the values of sport are often expressed in a rather lofty manner raising the question whether these values are merely 'empty signifiers' (Laclau, 1996), which have become hegemonic but nevertheless do not have any substantial and stable meaning. Hence, besides being ambiguous and vague, the values of sport as stated in the official rhetoric of the sport governing bodies have been subject to substantial changes (Chatziefstathiou, 2005).

Second, empirical research has nurtured skepticism about the validity of a key claim in the debate about values in sports. Sport and physical education have been traditionally legitimated by claiming that they serve to socialize certain values. Accordingly, sport is supposed to contribute to the internalization of values essential for industrial societies, such as teamwork, rule conformity, obeyance to authority, a competitive or work ethos, discipline, and ambition (Coakley, 2007). Although these claims have been widespread, empirical evidence for such a socializing impact of sport has remained rather rare (Roberts, 2016).

Third, empirical research has further demonstrated that values in relation to sport might be perceived quite differently by different audiences (Koenigstorfer & Preuss, 2018; Rocha et al., 2023).

Fourth, values might influence the ways of engagement in sport, but, depending on participants' attitudes, the same form of activity can be experienced in many ways and with a focus on different values (Aggerholm & Breivik, 2020).

Finally, scholars have emphasized that many sport organizations practice a 'decoupling' between official rhetoric and actual practice (Anastasiadis & Spence, 2020). For sociologists, such a decoupling is not surprising and might reflect the simple fact that 'institutional isomorphism' is a ubiquitarian phenomenon in

DOI: 10.4324/9781032665153-5

social life (Meyer & Rowan, 1977; DiMaggio & Powell, 1983). Accordingly, organizations are shaped by external cultural expectations concerning appropriate structures, practices, and behaviors rather than by functional requirements. Therefore, the rhetorical commitment to certain values by sports organizations might not reflect much more than a symbolic concession to hegemonic ideologies or coercive pressures. A decupling of talk from action becomes likely when the very actors who are responsible for implementation enjoy some agency (Bromley & Powell, 2012). Hence, the official rhetoric of international sports, which emphasizes respect, equality, international understanding, peace, and excellence, has often been contradicted by the actual practices, which involve winning at any price, commercial exploitation, intense national rivalry, cheating, and corruption (Milton-Smith, 2002). Moreover, the commitments of sports organizations and public authorities to the values of sport might not always be supported by corresponding resource endowments necessary to implement these values.

Notwithstanding these qualifications, institutional isomorphism is a socially and politically relevant phenomenon as it indicates that certain political and societal expectations have acquired hegemonic status. These considerations are particularly relevant with regard to the debate about a distinct European Model of Sports and its specific socio-cultural values. After the rapid commercialization of European sport had gathered pace since the 1990s, sport policy-makers, officials and grassroots stakeholders have debated whether such a distinct European Model of Sport exists and what its defining features could be (García, 2009). In order to determine whether a hegemonic European Model of Sport dedicated to a specific set of socio-cultural values exists, this chapter adopts an inductive perspective focusing on the member states of the European Union (EU). Although it proved impossible to include all member states, our sample shows substantial diversity. Yet, the heterogenous character of the documents is a strong caveat against too bold interpretations of the findings (Table 4.1).

In order to identify socio-cultural values, a thematic coding of these policy documents and strategy papers was performed following the steps outlined by Braun and Clarke (2006). This chapter follows previous research on values in sport (Rocha et al., 2023), which relied on Rokeach (1968) and Schwartz (1994) for operationalizing the concept of values. Accordingly, statements referring to values in sports should transcend specific situations and objects and represent higher-order contexts. More specifically, the account presented here follows Schwartz (1994) who defined human values as 'desirable trans-situational goals, varying in importance that serve as guiding principles in the life of a person or other social entity'. Based on these broad conceptual guidelines, initial codes were identified, discussed, refined, and finally defined into more abstract themes. Nevertheless, it is important to note that the rhetoric of the policy papers is characterized by vagueness and ambiguity, which makes it sometime difficult to define clearly delineated categories.

Table 4.1 Overview of analyzed policy documents

Member state	Code	Year of publication	Title of document
Bulgaria	BG	2011	National strategy for development of physical education and sport in the Republic of Bulgaria 2012–2022
Czechia	CZ	2014	Sport concept 2016–2025: Sport 2025
Denmark	DK	2016	Idrætspolitiske sigtelinjer
Estonia	EE	2014	Explanatory Memorandum to the Draft Resolution of the Riigikogu 'Fundamentals of Estonian Sports Policy until 2030'
Finland	FI	2018	Valtioneuvoston selonteko liikuntapolitiikasta
Germany	DE	2023	Sportbericht der Bundesregierung
Ireland	IE	2023	Sport Ireland: Statement of Strategy 2023–2027
Luxembourg	LU	2020	LTAD – Lëtzebuerg lieft Sport
Malta	MT	2019	Aiming higher: An overview over the national strategy for sport and physical activity in Malta
Netherlands	NL	2022	The world's sportiest nation: Dutch Sport's Strategic Plan 2032
Slovenia	SI	2014	National program of sport of the Republic of Slovenia 2014–2023
Sweden	SE	2023	Strategisk plan för idrottsrörelsen

Socio-Cultural Values as Invoked in the EU Member States

Sport and Physical Activity as Policy Vehicles

All of the papers analyzed share an instrumental perspective on sport and physical activity, which are perceived as a vehicle to achieve certain social and political goals. Intrinsic value is rarely mentioned and does not represent the primary motivation for the policies promoted by public authorities:

> The intrinsic value of physical activity in this report refers to the importance of physical activity for the individual citizen, based on the individual's own preferences and choices. The instrumental value of sport, on the other hand, refers to its role in promoting the goals desired by society, such as public health, education, training, national defense, social cohesion, etc.
>
> (Finnish Parliament, 2018, p. 3)

The finding that policy-makers pursue an instrumental perspective might not appear particular surprising, yet, it is nevertheless relevant. An instrumental perspective indicates a rejection of those traditions of European amateur sport, which emphasized the autotelic character of sport as an activity for the 'sake of it' (Gammelsæter, 2010, 2021). An instrumental perspective also implies that the liberal doctrine of the autonomy of sport, according to which sport represented a sphere of private life offering a break and retreat from politics (Allison, 2001), no longer figures in the EU member states in a strict sense. Sport is now perceived as socially and politically relevant, which comes with ambivalent implications for sports organizations. On the one hand, the emphasis of the social and political functions of sport serves to legitimize claims for public support. On the other hand, stressing sport's social and political responsibility serves to justify state interventions. These implications are very precisely expressed in the Czech strategy paper.

> Sport is a service to the public. The development of sport must be a joint effort of associations, non-profit organizations, and commercial entities, as well as state authorities and local self-government bodies.
> (The Ministry of Education, Youth and Sport, 2014, p. 4)

Therefore, sport policy initiatives supported by public authorities have to be beneficial for the sporting world and the entire society (Ministère des Sports, 2020, p. 36).

Socio-Cultural Values and Goals in Sport and Physical Activity

Contribution to Public Health

Table 4.2 indicates that all policy and strategy papers emphasize the role of sport and physical activity for public health.

In many policy papers, the emphasis on public health is explicitly motivated by concerns about declining health and fitness among citizens, which is linked to a sedentary lifestyle and obesity (e.g., Bulgaria, Czech Republic, Netherlands). Ultimately, the public health rationale is an economic one, which is driven by concerns about the negative economic impact of physical inactivity:

> Increasing physical activity also has great national economic significance. A recent report funded by the Prime Minister's Office and coordinated by UKK Institute [...] showed the large social costs in Finland caused by low physical activity, excessive sitting, and poor physical condition, which were estimated at 3.2-7.5 billion euros annually. Immobility causes additional costs in the form of direct health care costs, lost work inputs, care costs for the elderly, marginalization, and an increase in social benefits.
> (Finnish Parliament, 2018)

Table 4.2 Socio-cultural values as expressed in key policy papers

	BG	CZ	DK	EE	FI	DE	IE	LU	MT	NL	SI	SE
Socio-cultural values												
Public health												
Socialization												
Social cohesion												
National pride												
Nation branding												
Economic growth												
Political advocacy												
Defensive capability												
Turning socio-cultural values into social practice												
Broad and life-long participation												
Good governance and high-quality services												

Note: Own depiction, results of qualitative analyses of strategy and policy papers listed in Table 4.1.

The emphasis on sport's role for public health has substantial implications:

The policy focus is shifted from the traditional sport model toward a broader and more inclusive concept of (preferably) life-long physical activity (see below). Traditional sports organizations might therefore face demands to diversify their supply to meet the political demand for more inclusive and life-long participation. Traditional sports organizations might also no longer be framed as exclusive providers of physical activity. Alternative providers and forms of physical activity are likely to gain in importance. The diversification of physical activity and its relevance for public policies is well-expressed in the Dutch paper:

Dutch people like to pursue a wide range of sporting activities, which are increasingly organized and practiced in hybrid formats, both formally and informally. This might include anything from individuals playing sports in public spaces, group physical activities classes at gyms, WhatsApp groups set up by professional or amateur athletes, neighborhood 3x3 basketball teams, groups of old-age pensioners who meet regularly to play snooker at their local pub, large-scale running and cycling events with thousands of participants, national and international elite sports, professional football teams, Olympic, Paralympic and non-Olympic sports, Formula 1 and last but not least, traditional amateur sports clubs, which have always played an important role in Dutch community life. In other words, the country has a rich and thriving culture of physical activity of all kinds.

(Nocnsf, 2022, p. 4: 357)

The emphasis on diverse forms of physical activity for public health might also motivate a reallocation of public subsidies from traditional sports organizations and infrastructures to informal settings and public open spaces encouraging informal physical activity (Koohsari et al., 2015).

Sport as Socializing Agency

Notwithstanding dominant public health considerations, sport's contribution to socialization figures still strongly in the policy papers. The Czech paper provides an excellent summary of the traditional perception of sport as a socializing agency:

The social aspect of sport is becoming increasingly important due to the issues of individualization of interests and social atomization, social stratification, the passivity of civic society and social exclusion often leading to socially pathological behavior. Sport is based on cooperation and teamwork, on responsibility towards the whole. Friendships made in sport, shared memories, patriotism, positive attitude to a location and its identity, pride and patriotism are lifelong values that sport has to offer and it is hard to replace this with other activities. Sport is about promoting fair play, equality, and fairness. It combats xenophobia and actively enhances a multicultural society. The activities of sports associations represent the basis of sports activities in the Czech Republic and are at the core of social cohesion and active civil society.

(The Ministry of Education, Youth
and Sport, 2014, p. 9)

Some countries emphasize sport's role for learning democratic participation and the integration of immigrants (Denmark, Germany). Some policy papers link also elite sport to socialization:

Elite sport also makes an important overall contribution to the societal debate on values. Successful athletes often act as role models, especially for children and young people, and stand for motivation, perseverance, fairness, and team spirit.

(Deutscher Bundestag, 2023, p. 18)

Social Cohesion

Although the concept of social cohesion shows some overlap with socialization, it is here listed as a distinct category because social cohesion is insofar less ambitious as it simply emphasizes that sport and physical activity provide opportunities for social interactions.

Owing to the widening social divide, there is a strong need for the various segments of society to find common ground. Social isolation, job insecurity and inequality are all pressing social issues that play into this. But remote work as the 'new normal' has also increased people's need for community. We believe sport can play a strong role in promoting social cohesion.

(Nocnsf, 2022, p. 5: 1055)

National Pride, Patriotism, and Nation Branding

Distinguishing the emphasis on sport's role for national pride from its role for nation branding is also particularly difficult, because some papers mention both socio-cultural values in a single breath:

The achievements of our national teams promote our national identity and patriotism and our athletes, and their results have a great impact on the positive perception of the Czech Republic. Important national and international events continue to enhance the Czech Republic as a choice of tourist destinations and active leisure activities.

(The Ministry of Education, Youth
and Sport, 2014, p. 4)

Other papers simply state: 'Top sport also strengthens national identity' (Finnish Parliament, 2018). Yet, several policy papers focus not on the domestic role of elite sports for national pride and identification but primarily on external image effects for which the term of 'nation branding' has been recently coined. The Estonian policy paper defines the aim of

achieving a positive image and representativeness of Estonia through the results of competitive sports, successfully organised sports competitions and events, as well as competent and distinguished representatives – Estonia is represented in an effective and dignified way at international level.

(Riigikogu & Government of the Republic, 2014,
p. 10: 2990, emphasis in original)

Similar rationales are expressed in other policy paper:

> Sporting success at major international sporting events and a positive image of top athletes promote Germany's reputation.

(Deutscher Bundestag, 2023, p. 18)

> We believe that our sports ambassadors who proudly display the red shirts with the Maltese cross should be instantly recognized around the world.

(Parliamentary Secretary for Youth, Sport and
Voluntary Organisations, 2019, p. 2: 376)

Economic Activity

Despite the rapid and persistent commercialization of sport, the value of sport as economic activity is only explicitly mentioned by a minority of policy papers:

> When major sporting events take place on Danish soil, it attracts tourists, generates publicity and markets Denmark. Locally, cities and rural communities also use sport to brand themselves as attractive places to attractive places to live and visit – both through sporting events and through an active and attractive sports and leisure life. Sport can also contribute to creating growth and employment – locally and nationally.

(Kultur Ministeriet, 2016, p. 5)

> Sports and exercise contribute to economic growth and employment through an extensive and growing market of goods and products.

(Riigikogu & Government of
the Republic, 2014, p. 1)

> After all, sport has grown into a significant economic factor that generates turnover and added value and creates jobs.

(Deutscher Bundestag, 2023, p. 18)

Defensive Capacity

Some socio-cultural values only appear explicitly in a few policy papers. Thus, only Czech Republic, Estonia, and Finland mention sport's role for national defense or more precisely for the population's defensive capacity (The Ministry of Education,

Youth and Sport, 2014; Riigikogu & Government of the Republic, 2014, p. 1; Finnish Parliament, 2018)

Political Advocacy

Finally, some policy papers state the aim to employ sports as a vehicle for political advocacy, which is here understood as the expectation that sport takes an active stance within political or societal debates. The Dutch policy paper states:

> There are higher standards for public conduct, and the fact that politics and sports are increasingly intertwined has put sporting organisations under pressure.
>
> (Nocnsf, 2022, p. 5: 2314)

In the Dutch paper, demand for political advocacy is framed as an increase in 'the public value of elite sports' and remains rather vague.

> This includes leveraging the power of elite sports to help address various social issues.
>
> (Nocnsf, 2022, p. 16: 129)

The German policy papers is much more specific with respect to political advocacy. Sport and sports organizations are framed as being potentially threatened by right-wing extremists, which inspires calls for visible political advocacy:

> Sports clubs also have to contend with undemocratic actors who use sports structures as a platform to spread misanthropic ideas, contrary to their own understanding of values. Although exclusion, right-wing extremism, racism and anti-Semitism are not dominant in sport, they pose major challenges for clubs and associations.
>
> (Deutscher Bundestag, 2023, p. 167)

Turning Socio-Cultural Values into Practice

Broad and Lifelong Physical Activity as Means and Ultimate Value

It should be self-evident that the emphasis on sport's role for public health implies that broad and life-long participation in physical activity has to be encouraged and represents an aim in itself. Moreover, broad participation of the population is a prerequisite for all other social and political purposes associated with sport (Denmark). Hence, although the distinct EU member states are characterized by substantial differences in the level of physical activity, the policy papers analyzed define broad, inclusive, and life-long participation as key strategic aim, which is reflected in the mission statements:

"The world's sportiest nation." – Netherlands

(Nocnsf, 2022)

Ireland is an active nation where people are encouraged to start, continue to participate, progress and achieve in sport.

(Sport Ireland, 2023, p. 15)

Danes are one of the world's most sports-active populations, and their participation in exercise and sports is increasing.

(Kultur Ministeriet, 2016)

Driving forward a nation towards a new culture of physical activity and sport by promoting an inclusive framework for participants at all levels. Instilling a new generation of successful athletes with the self-belief of achieving their full potential at the highest level, whilst recognising the benefits of physical activity in creating a healthier nation.

(Parliamentary Secretary for Youth, Sport and Voluntary Organisations, 2019, p. 3: 666)

The Swedish sports movement's vision continues to be the best in the world, for everyone at all levels.

(Riksidrottsförbundet & SISU Idrottsutbildarna, 2023)

Even though these ideas seem to resemble the 'sports for all' concepts, which have been popularized since the 1970s, the focus of the more recent policy papers is on the promotion of life-long participation. Strategic guidance is often provided by the concept of 'physical literacy' (e.g., Czech Republic, Estonia, Ireland, Luxembourg, Netherlands), which is defined as 'the skills, knowledge and behaviours that give us the confidence and motivation to move throughout our lives' (Ministère des Sports et al., 2020, p. 24). The concept implies, among others, that traditional competitive sport represents just one option and one (temporary) episode in the lifetime of physically active people.

Due to the inadequate level of physical activity and stimuli in instructing children in sports, there is a decrease in physical literacy in children and youth, which makes sport an activity which is too demanding and less sought after. The development of physical literacy is one of the fundamental tasks of all sports areas, regardless of their specific objectives. The common goal is to achieve a considerable increase in the level of physical activity among the population and to help children develop as many athletic skills as possible, which is an essential condition for one's future choice of sport and for the diversity of leisure or physical activities.

(The Ministry of Education, Youth and Sport, 2014, p. 10)

We have agreed on the goals for 2025 together: that Swedish sports must work for lifelong sports in association for everyone, regardless of background, age, gender, level of ambition or other conditions. Everyone must have a place. Everyone should be able to see the sports association as a good alternative for training and competition, while Swedish sports develop a successful elite. This strategic plan is a guidepost for the entire sports movement towards 2025.

(Riksidrottsförbundet & SISU
Idrottsutbildarna, 2023, p. 3)

In terms of policy implications, physical literacy focuses on 'helping children develop their fundamental movement skills' in order to be able to engage in life-long physical activity (Nocnsf, 2022, p. 11), for later life stages high-quality offers for the entire population are needed (Ministère des Sports, 2020, p. 4). Ultimately, the emphasis on broad and life-long participation implies a shift in sport models, which the Swedish policy visualizes with a simple image (Figure 4.1).

Competitive and elite sport nevertheless still figure in the policy papers. In some cases, it seems to be simply taken for granted that nation-states have to have elite sport systems. Other policy papers depict elite sports as providing opportunities for the most talented:

Once engaged in sport, participants will have every incentive to stay involved whether as players or in one or more of the many highly valued coaching, offici-ating and voluntary support roles that are available, invested in and appreciated. They will also, where they wish to and have the requisite talent, be afforded the opportunity to progress to high levels of performance.

(Sport Ireland, 2023, p. 48)

In other policy papers, elite sports are characterized as a means, that is,

Invaluable in achieving our targets. Accomplishments of elite athletes and their overall excellence in sport are fundamental, as well as being a goal in itself. We seek to be among the most successful ten countries in the world in elite sports achievement.

(Nocnsf, 2022, p. 10)

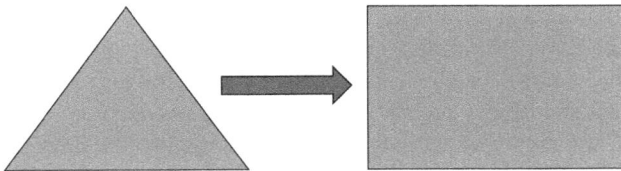

Figure 4.1 The implied shift from the traditional model of sport.

Source: Riksidrottsförbundet & SISU Idrottsutbildarna (2023, p. 15). Reproduced with per-mission from the publishers, the Swedish Sport Confederation (Riksidrottsförbundet).

Since competitive and elite sports are defined as being fundamental to achieve the targets of an activating policy, the Dutch policy paper also frames 'exciting and appealing matches, games and races, competitions' as key policy aims (Nocnsf, 2022, p. 22: 0)

Regarding participation, it should be mentioned that a number of policy papers also stresses the importance of winning and maintaining volunteers (Estonia) and educating and supporting them:

> Voluntary work is a very important source of the Slovenian and European sport outside of the education system. Despite the fact that volunteers work for free their work must be as professional as possible.
> [...] Accordingly, we will ensure systemic conditions for the social recognition of voluntary work and raise the level of competence of volunteers.
>
> (Slovenia, 2014, p. 42)

> Volunteers and professionals are a driving force in organised sport, and they are expected to perform at an even higher level as a result of the growing complexity and the importance of sport as a public good. Both the number of volunteers and professionals and the quality of the human capital merit attention. We will explore these issues in this line of action and will prioritise training and supporting volunteers, creating more competitive and appealing paid jobs in the sporting world, and improving the skills of professionals in the operating organisations.
>
> (Nocnsf, 2022, p. 21: 0)

Good Governance and High-Quality Service Provision

All policy papers explicitly name expectations in sport governance and service provisions. The minimum requirements raised are that sport represents an environment

> safeguarding and encouraging the enforcement of moral and ethical values in sport, and by respecting human dignity and security of all connected with sport.
>
> (Slovenia, 2014, p. 5)

Yet, the policy papers formulate often more ambitious and specific expectations associated with the 'good governance' (e.g., Germany). The focus is on more effective control mechanisms and activities (Bulgaria), greater transparency, integrity and active prevention of negative phenomena, such as doping, cheating, betting and throwing matches, corruption, outcome fixing, sexual abuse (e.g., Czech Republic, Denmark, Estonia, Germany), democratic governance, non-discrimination, inclusion and respect (e.g., Estonia, Finland, Germany, Ireland, Sweden), and increasingly environmental sustainability (e.g., Finland, Germany, Ireland, Sweden).

The German policy paper announces that these expectations will be enforced by conditionalizing the provision of public subsidies:

> It is important to the Federal Government that the relevant good governance principles are applied in the field of German sport and that the sports associations and other institutions supported with federal funds are managed competently and with integrity. The Federal Government therefore supports sport in implementing good governance standards on its own responsibility. [...] With regard to federal funding, it is generally planned to make grants in the area of elite sport funding more dependent on compliance with central good governance standards in the future.
>
> (Deutscher Bundestag, 2023, p. 131)

Discussion

The short and superficial review of key sport policy papers suggests that at the level of explicit vision and strategy, there exists a core of commonly shared socio-cultural values among the selected EU member states. Accordingly, sport and physical activity contribute primarily to public health by inspiring life-long physical activity. The emphasis on public health is, however, hardly a European specialty, but rather reflects a general trend in global health discourses. Since the 1990s, physicians have elevated the so-called 'obesity crisis' to a major issue in the World Health Organization (WHO) after surveys indicated a global increase of obesity (James, 2008). The 'obesity crisis' has provided an irresistible exercise-is-medicine'-logic (Kirk et al., 2018, p. 72), which has first impacted physical education (Tinning, 2012; Wright, 2009). By now, this logic has been extended to the entire sport sector. Emphasizing the public health value of sport challenges existing sport models and implies organizational changes. Notwithstanding potential tensions, the policy papers continue to invoke the socio-cultural values traditionally associated with sport, that is, socialization, social cohesion, and national identification. Concerning the latter, some of the policy papers seem to be indicative of the post-national character of European societies as they seem to prioritize sport's contribution to 'nation branding' targeting audiences abroad over sport's potential to inspire patriotism. Only a minority of papers stresses the economic role of sport and its importance for national defense. Moreover, some policy papers demand sport to take a stance on political and social issues, which indicates a departure from the traditional vision of sport as an apolitical and neutral sphere.

At first glance, the emphasis on public health contributions of sport and physical activity might seem to reinforce the 'sport for all' policies. Yet, as already emphasized, the focus on the public health contributions of sport and physical activity enhances the (potential) role of alternative providers and activities. In some ways, the emphasis on public health and physical literacy is likely to revive old debates about the role of (English) sports, which have plagued the physical education profession for decades. As emphasized by Houlihan and Green (2006), there has been 'recurring value dissonance' between physical education and sports. Sport's emphasis on competition and record-seeking has been characterized as essentially elitist, in contrast to universalist and process-oriented forms of physical activity. In any case, the concept of physical literacy serves to reemphasize the public obligation to provide physical activity in a pre-school and school context and to fund public infrastructure encouraging informal participation.

Finally, a commonly shared socio-cultural value is that public authorities expect sport organizations to meet high standards in governance and service provision. As depicted, the minimum standard is that sports organizations should represent a safe, inclusive, non-discriminatory, and healthy environment. Sports organizations are further expected to adhere to principles of democracy, transparency, and accountability, and to actively mitigate the multiple forms of misconduct within sport. Some policy papers also signal that sport organizations will be confronted with expectations concerning environmental sustainability.

The emphasis on the public value and responsibility of the sport organizations illustrates that the orthodox doctrine of autonomy and self-governance of sport has been abandoned. Actual political practices as well as future visions for sport governance rather fit into what has been characterized as 'collaborative sport governance' in which public authorities and civic society organizations coordinate their efforts (Meier & García, 2021). The aim of public authorities is to improve the efficacy of the sport sector, which means that the allocation of duties and responsibilities between public sector and civic societies might be adjusted:

> We strengthen the organisational power of sporting organisations on an individual level. Sporting organisations play a key role in a strong sporting infrastructure. They need the capabilities and high-quality facilities to support sports clubs and encourage people to engage in sport and physical activities. [...] Self-sufficiency and futureproofing are key when it comes to strengthening these organisations. In order to achieve this objective, close cooperation with local authorities, local sporting companies, sports services and other relevant stakeholders is essential. How the duties and responsibilities are divided in this process is a key strategic issue, the aim being to work together on providing inspiration and support to sports clubs.
>
> (Nocnsf, 2022, p. 20: 0)

To summarize: There seems to be a consensus on key socio-cultural values in sport and physical activity among EU member states. Accordingly, sport is of instrumental value for public health, socialization and social cohesion, national pride, and nation branding. A vision shared by the selected EU member states is broad, inclusive, and life-long participation within settings characterized by good governance and high-quality service provision. Therefore, it seems fair to conclude that, at least in public policy declarations, there exists such a thing as a hegemonic European

Model of Sport. However, ideological hegemony does not necessarily translate into actual practice. The policy papers suggest that there exist at least two barriers for policy implementation:

1   In particular the policy papers from former communist countries indicate that the domestic sport infrastructure is worn-out and outdated, which implies a need for substantial public investments. Although the policy papers include commitments to dedicate public budgets to such purposes, it is difficult to assess whether the amounts will be sufficient to inspire the level of participation and physical activity desired.
2   The vision of broad and life-long physical activity implies either that sports organizations adapt their provision of physical activity or that alternative providers and forms of physical activity emerge and become more popular. When it comes to implementing the vision of life-long physical activity for all, the policy papers resort, however, to rather traditional implementation agents, that is, the public school system and the existing sport organizations, which have been able to mobilize volunteers. By implication, the ambitious policy visions might fail when the sports organizations are not willing or able to adapt their models of service provision and when there are no alternative civil society organizations with which public authorities could collaborate.

References

Aggerholm, K. & Breivik, G. (2020). Being, having and belonging: values and ways of engaging in sport. *Sport in Society*, 24(4), 1–15. https://doi.org/10.1080/17430437. 2020.1734562

Allison, L. (2001). *Amateurism in Sport*. London: Frank Cass.

Anastasiadis, S. & Spence, L. J. (2020). An Olympic-sized challenge: effect of organizational pathology on maintaining and repairing organizational legitimacy in sports governing bodies. *British Journal of Management*, 31(1), 24–41.

Braun, V. & Clarke, V. (2006). Using thematic analysis in psychology. *Qualitative Research in Psychology*, 3(2), 77–10. https://doi.org/10.1191/1478088706qp063oa

Bromley, P. & Powell, W. W. (2012). From smoke and mirrors to walking the talk: decoupling in the contemporary world. *Academy of Management Annals*, 6(1), 483–530.

Chatziefstathiou, D. (2005). *The changing nature of the ideology of Olympism in the modern Olympic era* (Doctoral dissertation, Loughborough University).

Coakley, J. (2007). Socialization and sport. In G. Ritzer (Ed.), *The Blackwell Encyclopedia of Sociology* (pp. 4576–4580). London: Blackwell Publishing.

DeSensi, J. T. (2014). Sport: An ethos based on values and servant leadership. *Journal of Intercollegiate Sport*, 7(1), 58–63. https://doi.org/10.1123/jis.2014-0097

Deutscher Bundestag. (2023). 15.Sportbericht der Bundesregierung. *Drucksache* 20/5900.

DiMaggio, P. J. & Powell, W. W. (1983). The iron cage revisited: institutional isomorphism and collective rationality in organizational fields. American Sociological Review, 48(2), 147–160.

Finnish Parlament. (2018). *Hallituksen esitys Eduskunnalle laeiksi maanpuolustuslain 1 ja 6 luvun muuttamisesta ja eräiksi siihen liittyviksi laeiksi.* https://www.eduskunta.fi/FI/vaski/JulkaisuMetatieto/Documents/VNS_6+2018.pdf

Gammelsæter, H. (2010). Institutional pluralism and governance in "commercialized" sport clubs. *European Sport Management Quarterly,* 10(5), 569–594.

Gammelsæter, H. (2021). Sport is not industry: bringing sport back to sport management. *European Sport Management Quarterly,* 21(2), 257–279.

García, B. (2009). Sport governance after the White Paper: the demise of the European model?. *International Journal of Sport Policy,* 1(3), 267–284.

Houlihan, B. & Green, M. (2006). The changing status of school sport and physical education: explaining policy change. *Sport, Education and Society,* 11(1), 73–92.

James, W. P. (2008). WHO recognition of the global obesity epidemic. *International Journal of Obesity (2005),* 32(Suppl 7), S120–S126. https://doi.org/10.1038/ijo.2008.247

Kirk, B., Cope, E., Bailey, R. & Parnell, D. (2018). What young children identify as the outcomes of their participation in sport and physical activity. *Health Behavior and Policy Review,* 5, 103–113. https://doi.org/10.14485/HBPR.5.1.11

Koenigstorfer, J. & Preuss, H. (2018). Perceived values in relation to the Olympic games: development and use of the Olympic value scale. *European Sport Management Quarterly,* 18(5), 1–26. https://doi.org/10.1080/16184742.2018.1446995

Koohsari, M. J., Mavoa, S., Villanueva, K., Sugiyama, T., Badland, H., Kaczynski, A. T., Owen, N., & Giles-Corti, B. (2015). Public open space, physical activity, urban design and public health: concepts, methods and research agenda. Health & Place, 33, 75–82. https://doi.org/10.1016/j.healthplace.2015.02.009

Kultur Ministeriet. (2016). *Idrætspolitiske sigtelinjer.* Copenhagen: Kultur Ministeriet.

Laclau, E. (1996). The death and resurrection of the theory of ideology. *Journal of Political Ideologies,* 1(3), 201–220.

McFee, G. (2004). Sport, rules and values: philosophical investigations into the nature of sport. *Journal of the Philosophy of Sport,* 32(1), 119–121. https://doi.org/10.1080/00948705.2005.9714676

Meier, H. E. & García, B. (2021). Beyond sports autonomy: A case for collaborative sport governance approaches. *International Journal of Sport Policy and Politics,* 13(3), 501–516.

Meyer, J. W. & Rowan, B. (1977). Institutionalized organizations: formal structure as myth and ceremony. *The American Journal of Sociology,* 83(2), 340–363.

Milton-Smith, J. (2002). Ethics, the Olympics and the search for global values. *Journal of Business Ethics,* 35(2), 131–142. https://doi.org/10.1023/A:1013015331517

Ministère des Sports, Comité Olympique et Sportif Luxembourgeois, Luxembourg Institute for High Performance in Sports & Sportlycée (2020). *LTAD - Lëtzebuerg lieft Sport.* Rahmenkonzept. https://sports.public.lu/dam-assets/fr/publications/DE-LTAD-Rahmenkonzept.pdf.

Nocnsf. (2022). *The world's sportiest nation.* Dutch Sport's Strategic Plan 2032. https://nocnsf.nl/media/4dpanj5w/dutch-sports-strategic-plan-2032.pdf

Parliamentary Secretary for Youth, Sport and Voluntary Organisations. (2019). *Aiming higher; An overview of the national strategy for sport and physical activity in Malta.* https://www.gov.mt/en/Government/DOI/Press%20Releases/PublishingImages/Pages/2019/May/21/pr191132/PR191132a.pdf

Republic of Bulgaria. (2011). *National strategy for development of physical education and sport in the Republic of Bulgaria 2012-2022.* Council of Ministers; Ministry of Physical Education and Sport. http://mpes.government.bg/Documents/Documents/Strategii/Strategia_2012-2022.pdf

Republic of Slovenia & Ministry of Education. (2014). National programme of sport of the Republic of Slovenia 2014-2023. https://www.google.com/url?sa=t&rct=j&q=&esrc=s&source=web&cd=&ved=2ahUKEwiIzcud6uuCAxU3S_EDHYrRBA8QFnoECBUQAQ&url=https%3A%2F%2Fwww.gov.si%2Fassets%2Fministrstva%2FMIZS%2FDokumenti%2FZakonodaja%2FEN%2FNational-Programme-of-Sport-of-the-Republic-of-Slovenia-2014-2023.docx&usg=AOvVaw19wiqTqCdCE_8-2WCgitJx&opi=89978449

Riigikogu & Government of the Republic. (2014). *Explanatory memorandum to the draft resolution of the Riigikogu "Fundamentals of Estonian Sports Policy until 2030".* file:///Users/hmeie_01/Downloads/Sport2030_Explanatory_Memorandum_ENG.pdf

Riksidrottsförbundet & SISU Idrottsutbildarna. (2023). Strategisk plan för idrottsrörelsen 2022-2025. https://www.rf.se/download/18.7e76e6bd183a68d7b7117a2/1664978260467/Strategisk%20plan%202022-25.pdf

Roberts, K. (2016). Youth leisure as the context for youth sport. In K. Green & A. Smith (Eds.), *The Routledge Handbook of Youth Sport* (pp. 18–25). Oxford: Routledge.

Rocha, C. M., Hong, H. J. & Gratao, O. A. (2023). Involvement with the Olympic and Paralympic games and the values of sport. *Journal of Policy Research in Tourism, Leisure and Events,* 15(3), 353–376. https://doi.org/10.1080/19407963.2021.1944169

Rokeach, M. (1968). A theory of organization and change within value-attitude systems. *Journal of Social Issues,* 24(1), 13–33. https://doi.org/10.1111/j.1540-4560.1968.tb01466.x

Schwartz, S. H. (1994). Are there universal aspects in the structure and contents of human values? *Journal of Social Issues, 50*(4), 19–45. https://doi.org/10.1111/j.1540-4560.1994.tb01196.x

Sport Ireland. (2023). Sport Ireland statement of strategy 2023-2027. https://www.sportireland.ie/sites/default/files/media/document/2023-09/strategy_FINAL.pdf

The Ministry of Education, Youth and Sport. (2014). Sport concept for 2016-2025. Sport 2025. https://msmt.gov.cz/file/49562_1_1/

Tinning, R. (2012). The idea of physical education: a memetic perspective. *Physical Education and Sport Pedagogy,* 17(2), 115–126. https://doi.org/10.1080/17408989.2011.582488

Wright, J. (*2009*). Biopower, biopedagogies and the obesity epidemic. In J. Wright & V. Harwood (Eds.), *Biopolitics and the 'Obesity Epidemic'* (pp. 9–22). London: Routledge.

Chapter 5

Patterns of Financing Sports in Europe

Holger Preuß and Antonia Hannawacker

Introduction

Up until the mid-1980s, Europe had an Eastern and a Western model of sport (Europäische Kommission, 1998). The European Model of Sport (EMS) as we know it today is based on a concept developed by the European Commission in the late 1990s (Jesse & Fischer, 2010; Nafziger, 2008).

Over the last century, modern sport has been strongly influenced by at least seven interacting factors. These are the individual culture of each country, the history of sport in that country, its success in international sporting events, the passion of the population for sport, the impact of the Second World War, the political systems, and finally, the values that the currently ruling politicians attribute to sport. As a result of all these seven influential factors, very different sporting structures have developed in the European countries. One notable difference is the financing of sport, which will be discussed in more detail in this chapter. To start with, a first difference can be seen by looking at how selected European National Olympic Committees (NOCs) are funded (Figure 5.1).

By using relative figures, the diversity in the financing of the European NOCs becomes visually evident. While Liechtenstein and Slovenia, for example, rely heavily on governmental funds, Türkiye and Lithuania do not receive any financial support from taxpayers. Sponsors are important for Belgium, lottery for Lithuania.

Many other areas of sport funding in Europe also show differences between countries. However, amidst these structural differences, certain common elements of sport funding in Europe emerge.

To highlight these common features in the following discussion, the European dimension of sport will be considered first, to shed light on the basis for transnational regulations in sport, and thus also in the financing of sport. It then examines some of the key structural features of EMSs that are particularly relevant to financing and which are used as a guiding framework. This is followed by an outline of the main sources used to finance sport in Europe. Next, the funding of grassroots and professional sport is discussed. Finally, the results are summarised

DOI: 10.4324/9781032665153-6

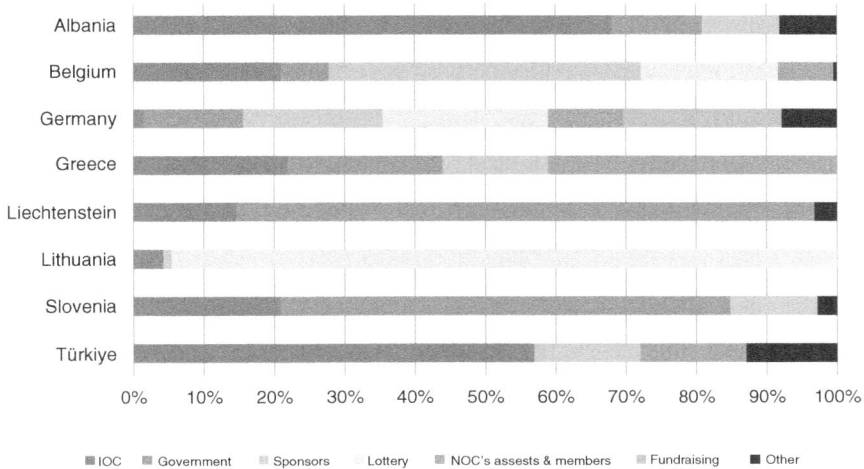

Figure 5.1 Financing structures of selected European NOCs.

Source: Preuss et al. (2022, p. 21); Reproduced with permission by the publishers Nomos Academia Verlag; data from Deutscher Olympischer Sportbund (2018).

and conclusions are drawn on the current situation and challenges of sport funding in Europe.

The European Dimension of Sport

Over the years, Europe has developed a complex system of different unions, involving increasingly diverse member countries. Each union was designed through different agreements, such as the Schengen Agreement for borderless travel, the European Free Trade Association (EFTA) for free trade, or the European Union (EU) for common overarching regulations in many areas. Overall, the EU is also involved in the regulation of sport and sport financing, which affects many European countries. However, when it comes to sport, the European members of the various European sports federations are different, e.g. in the Olympic world, the United Kingdom is one country, but in football it divides Scotland, Wales, Northern Ireland, and England. Azerbaijan is a member of UEFA, but in sport it belongs to the Olympic Council of Asia, or Israel belongs to the European sports system, although its territory is not in Europe.

For a long time, however, the European dimension was of secondary importance for sport, as today's EU is based primarily on treaties that focus on economic fields of action (Mittag, 2018). The decisive impulse to create sports policy structures at EU level was given by the Court of Justice of the EU in 1995 with the Bosman ruling. This was a decisive turning point that fundamentally changed sport and its structures. From then on, sports clubs and federations increasingly turned their attention to the EU, whose institutions also promoted activities in the field of sport (Mittag, 2018). With the publication of the White Paper on Sport in 2007, the foundations for a European policy on sport have finally been laid, but sport wasn't enshrined in primary law until the Lisbon Treaty came into force in December 2009 (Dickmann, 2018). This meant that, until then, the EU had no competence to pursue a "direct" sport policy (Parrish et al., 2010). The Lisbon Treaty and the White Paper on Sport are therefore two of the most important cornerstones for a fundamental sport policy and European cooperation in the field of sport (Katarzyna & Olivier, 2023).

The White Paper on Sport is divided into three parts. It distinguishes between the social role of sport, its economic dimension and the organisation of sport in the EU (Dickmann, 2018). The document also addresses the different roles of sport and seeks to balance several diverging interests, but also the specificities of sport and the application of EU law to it (Prets, 2009). The objectives set out in the document include the strengthening of the social role of sport, the promotion of volunteering, and the fight against doping and corruption (Katarzyna & Olivier, 2023).

With the Lisbon Treaty, the EU has begun to develop its own competence for sport and its funding potential. The overall aim of the Lisbon Treaty is to make the European states a more modern, efficient, and democratic community. In this context, the Treaty defines new areas of competence for the EU and Article 165 of the Treaty on the Functioning of the European Union (TFEU) gives the European institutions the power to actively shape policy in the field of sport for the first time (Dickmann, 2018). The main innovation of this anchoring in primary law in terms of EU financial support is the possibility of directly funding projects in the field of sport without having to justify this measure by reference to other competences in the Treaty. This means that the EU institutions can fund programmes in areas such as social inclusion, health promotion, education and training, volunteering, anti-doping, and corruption in sport (Parrish et al., 2010).

Another important document in this context is the EU Work Plan for Sport. It is a plan to promote cooperation between EU institutions, Member States and relevant stakeholders in the field of sport. Physical activity plays an important role in the current Work Plan for Sport (2021–2024), where creating sporting opportunities for all generations is one of the main priorities. Protecting the integrity and values, as well as the socio-economic and environmental dimensions of sport, are other important areas of action (Katarzyna & Olivier, 2023).

In addition to all the important areas mentioned in the documents, the economic dimension of sport remains an important consideration for the EU institutions and Member States and will be supported through both policy and dialogue.

Structural Features of the EMS Relevant for Financing

Despite the differences in the financing of sport in Europe, it is possible to identify some common patterns that result from the organisational characteristics of sport in

Europe. The following section outlines some of the main structural features of the EMS that are relevant to the financing of sport in Europe.

Pyramidal Structure

One of these key aspects of the EMS is the pyramidal structure. This leads to a close interaction between the different levels of the European sport system (Figure 5.2).

Figure 5.2 shows that the base of the pyramid is formed by local sports federations and clubs, which focus primarily on grassroots sport and youth development. It is important to note that most grassroots sport clubs in Europe are non-profit organisations. This structure has several characteristics that shape the landscape and funding of sport clubs at European level, including voluntary membership, democratic decision-making frameworks, volunteer involvement, and organisational autonomy (Nagel et al., 2023). In addition, in almost all European countries, sports clubs are important providers of sport, playing an important role in regular participation and providing a framework for regular and well-organised sporting activities (Nagel et al., 2023).

The regional sports federations are located above the local federations and clubs in the pyramid. These are responsible for coordinating local sports activities and organising regional championships, followed by the national sports federation, which organises national competitions and deals with general issues. Similarly, the European sports federations, which form the top of the pyramid, are structured and are responsible for organising competitions at the continental level (Europäische Kommission, 1998; Jesse & Fischer, 2010; Schulze, 2011). Nowadays, however, we can see that the pyramid structure is being challenged by the greed for additional financial resources, for example by sports clubs that want to create their own league (European Super League in football).

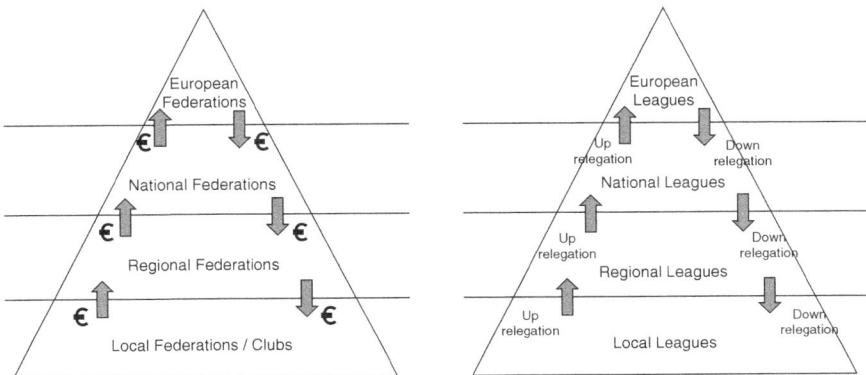

Figure 5.2 Organisation of sport federations and leagues in Europe – Pyramid model (own illustration, based on Europäische Kommission, 1998, p. 4).

It should be noted that the various continental federations, as well as the various European federations, have their own definition of their territory as outlined above. It is important to note that neither of the two models shown in Figure 5.2 includes the global federations, which would be above the continental federations in the pyramid structure. These global organisations are responsible for organising World Cups, World Tours, and World Championships (Jesse & Fischer, 2010).

The pyramid structure suggests that the different federations within the EMS are interdependent. Each federation has another federation above it, which is the coordinator of the sport on a wider level. As shown on the left side of Figure 5.2, there is a distribution of financial resources among these federations. Although higher level federations provide financial assistance and support to lower levels (e.g. sport and federation development), there is also a flow of money from lower to higher levels. It is precisely this interaction that reflects the principle of financial solidarity in European sport. This will be explained in more detail in the next chapter.

The pyramid model still applies to competitions at all levels, although there are challenges such as closed leagues. Qualification from one level to another is required for national and European championships, while the promotion and relegation system applies to different sports leagues. Every club in the pyramid has the potential to move up if they perform well, but they also run the risk of being relegated to a lower league if they don't perform well, as shown in Figure 5.2 on the right. This governance system is significantly different from the system of North American closed leagues (Andreff, 2011). The open league system has a negative effect on the finances of the clubs involved, leading to over-investment, fierce competition and, finally to so-called destructive competition, which will be discussed in more detail in Chapter 6.

Financial Solidarity

The principle of solidarity is reaffirmed in the White Paper on Sport (2007). As a fundamental aspect of sport, the EMS recognises and seeks to promote solidarity between different levels of sport. The principle of financial solidarity is designed to ensure that sport remains diverse and exciting and that revenues generated from elite sport also support the development of grassroots sport (European Commission: Directorate-General for Education, Youth, Sport and Culture, 2022).

The Solidarity Mechanism in European sport is manifested through the redistribution of financial resources from one section of sport to another and is visible in several ways. This mechanism operates in two main forms: horizontal and vertical distribution (European Commission: Directorate-General for Education, Youth, Sport and Culture, 2022). Horizontal distribution is the redistribution of funds between different sports or equal distribution between all clubs participating in the same competition. Vertical solidarity, on the other hand, focuses on the redistribution of revenues generated at the elite level, which are then redistributed down the pyramid (Figure 5.2, left). This support comes in a variety of forms, including educational programmes for officials and athletes, equipment as well as direct funding (European Commission: Directorate-General for Education, Youth, Sport and Culture, 2022). As shown in Figure 5.2 on the left, this redistribution also occurs in the opposite direction, for example when national federations receive membership fees from clubs and active athletes. However, the flow of funds from the national to the European level is not significant, as European federations mainly generate funds from sponsorships, licensing and events.

A notable example of the Solidarity Mechanism in European sport is UEFA's European football competitions. Events such as the UEFA club competitions generate revenue that is redistributed to support different levels of the sport, from European to grassroots. This financial Solidarity Mechanism helps to maintain the link between professional and amateur sport and to fund less profitable events, such as those for women and young people, which are essential for the long-term development of sport and access to it (European Commission: Directorate-General for Education, Youth, Sport and Culture, 2022).

Another example is that of sharing of broadcasting revenues. Through the Solidarity Mechanism, revenue from the sale of broadcasting rights to sporting events is not only an important source of income at the international level but also benefits member federations. It helps to fund youth development, grassroots sport, and volunteerism (Hellmund, 2017).

These examples show that solidarity in the financing of sport in Europe emphasises that financial support is not limited to individual interests or to specific types of sport, but that it has broad societal objectives to make sport accessible to all and ethically responsible. In order to ensure the continued the development of the grassroots movement and to maintain the social and educational function of sport, experts from the sports sector have stated that the Solidarity Mechanism should be strengthened and modernised (European Commission: Directorate-General for Education, Youth, Sport and Culture, 2022).

The Main Sources of Financing Sports in Europe

Sport in Europe relies on public and private sources of funding. Governments, local authorities, and gambling revenues provide public funding. Private funding, including sponsorship and personal spending on sport, is crucial to ensuring that sport remains accessible to all (Andreff, 2009). The EU also supports sport in a variety of ways, and voluntary work is another important resource in Europe, even if it is not monetary.

This section looks in more detail at each of the main sources of funding for sport in Europe mentioned above. However, the importance of the different sources of funding varies from country to country, as well as within the different sports and at the different levels at which they are practised.

Government and Local Authorities

In all the EU countries, public funding of sport by governments and local authorities is of immense importance. Grassroots sport, equal opportunities, and the access to sport for all in European countries depend on public participation. The main objective of this funding is to provide financial support to sport clubs and organisations in order to promote the participation of citizens in sport across Europe.

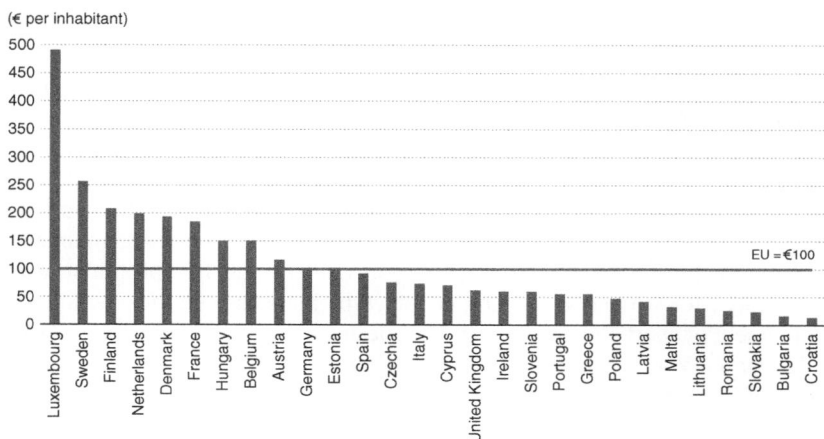

(€ per inhabitant)

EU = €100

Figure 5.3 General government expenditure on recreation and sport per capita in the EU 2017 (Eurostat dataset gov_10a_exp and nama_10_pe, 2019). Reproduced under CA A 4.0 International licence.

In 2017, public spending on leisure and sport in the 28 EU Member States amounted to €51.3 billion. Overall, public expenditure on leisure and sport in the EU has remained relatively stable as a percentage of total expenditure over the last few years (Eurostat, 2019). However, the level of government support per head varies from country to country. This is illustrated in Figure 5.3.

In 2017, public expenditure on recreation and sport per capita exceeded €200 in three EU Member States, as shown in Figure 5.3: Luxembourg (€492 per inhabitant), Sweden (€256), and Finland (€206), closely followed by the Netherlands (€199). On the other hand, Croatia (€13 per inhabitant) and Bulgaria (€16) had the lowest per capita expenditure on recreation and sport.

However, this figure should be interpreted with great caution. It only reflects the general expenditure of national governments, but it's important to note that some countries have a federal structure where significant financial contributions are also made by regional authorities. This distinction needs to be considered when assessing how resources are allocated.

Government and local authority funding is mainly for sport clubs and the development and maintenance of sports infrastructure such as sports halls and training grounds (Andreff, 2009). They also provide support through measures such as tax levies based on club income or international events, the sharing of betting and lottery revenues, the provision of office space for national federations, and direct subsidies (Andreff, 2009).

In return, governments and local authorities require sports clubs and federations and users of public sports facilities to provide open access to all interested citizens, to guarantee that no profits are made or shared, and to demand transparent accounting systems. This helps to ensure that funds are used in accordance with the club's/federation's constitution. The European Parliament also calls on countries to fight corruption and to promote ethics in sport. Therefore, the introduction of strict financial control rules for sports clubs and federations in each country is considered essential (Europäisches Parlament, 2012).

Financial support for elite athletes is another key aspect of public funding of sport by governments, as illustrated by the allocation of government funds to NOCs in Figure 5.1. These funds support elite athletes in their training and travel to global sporting events, enabling them to focus on their athletic development and represent their country effectively.

In addition to supporting sports organisations and athletes, several European countries have developed national strategies to attract major sporting events, such as the Olympic Games, to their countries. This is supported by direct and indirect subsidies for the bidding and hosting process. For example, countries such as Denmark, the United Kingdom, Germany, and Switzerland offer subsidies to support these processes.

Lottery and Gambling

Revenues generated from state-owned or state-licensed lotteries and gambling operators are an important source of income for sport in general, as the European Commission pointed out in 2011. They are also an important source of funding, particularly for grassroots sport, according to another study carried out in the same year (Hellmund, 2017). The rules governing the redistribution vary considerably from one country to another. This also applies to the sports that benefit from this source of funding.

Internationally, numerous betting companies offer a wide range of sports betting services and generate an estimated annual turnover of between 700 billion and a trillion US dollars. In Germany, annual sales are estimated to be up to 4 billion euros (Meyrahn et al., 2014). In the traditional form of betting, the customer goes to a betting shop, fills in a betting slip, and deposits the stake in cash. Today, however, betting over the internet is by far the most popular option. This is particularly important in countries without a liberalised gambling market, such as Germany and many other European countries. This has previously been a legal grey area, as it is possible for a customer to place an online bet with an online bookmaker that is not licensed in the customer's country of residence (Meyrahn et al., 2014). Many internet betting companies have their headquarter in Malta or Gibraltar. More liberal gambling laws and low taxes are the main advantages of these locations (Meyrahn et al., 2014).

Taking Germany as an example of European countries, the share of lottery funding in the budget of the German NOC (DOSB) was around 25% (Figure 5.1). In the budgets of the state sports associations, the share was up to 80% (Ashelm, 2010). This illustrates the relevance of the lottery for sports policy, as grassroots sports development is primarily the responsibility of national sports associations. The lottery is therefore the only area of sports gambling from which grassroots sport currently benefits to a greater extent.

Despite its importance in financing sport in Europe, this source of funding causes ethical debate. The European Parliament therefore calls on the Commission to take concrete measures to ensure that lotteries remain a source of funding for sport. The European Parliament also considers sports betting to be a form of commercial exploitation of competitions and calls on Member States to take measures to prevent possible match-fixing. It emphasises the recognition of the rights of organisers of their competitions to ensure that betting operators contribute to the funding of grassroots and youth sport, while safeguarding the integrity of competitions (Europäisches Parlament, 2012). Furthermore, the European Parliament stresses that the financial support of grassroots sport through lotteries and betting can only be guaranteed if the holders of the necessary national gambling licences, who pay taxes and fund other non-profit purposes in their respective countries, are legally obliged to pay levies in the "public interest" (Europäisches Parlament, 2012).

Households

Within the EMS, household sport consumption is the main source of funding, which is often overlooked. Household finance sport in various ways, such as buying tickets or sporting equipment (Andreff, 2009). It plays an important role in ensuring the diversity and accessibility of sport. This means that household funding is crucial for promoting and sustaining sport at all levels.

Households contribute to the financing of sport in three main ways. The first is health and recreational sport, characterised by, for example, the purchase of sports equipment or membership of sports clubs. The second is elite sport, which includes buying tickets and watching televised events. Finally, there is household expenditure on amateur sport, which is supported by membership of sports clubs that take part in local and national sporting competitions (Andreff, 2009).

The importance of household consumption becomes clear when considering the vast dimensions of sport at European level. To capture these, the EU has decided to develop a "Satellite Account for Sport" (SSK) at European level (Commission of the European communities, 2007). These satellite accounts show government and household consumption and their impact on the country's economy. Results are currently available for Austria, Cyprus, Poland, the United Kingdom, the Netherlands, Portugal and Germany (Ahlert & Repenning, 2023; Preuss & Alfs, 2013). Comparable indicators of sport employment, gross value added, and consumption are being discussed at international level. Table 5.1 shows, as an example, the gross value added and the consumption of private households in billions of euros and as a percentage of GDP for selected countries, once again highlighting the importance of private households in the financing of sport in Europe.

To date, the SSK has produced in-depth national studies for nine EU Member States. Cyprus and Poland have produced pilot study results, while comprehensive results have already been presented for the remaining seven EU countries (Table 5.1). Nevertheless, it is noteworthy that only Germany has included comprehensive

Table 5.1 Economic importance of sport (Ahlert & Repenning, 2023; Statistics Netherlands, 2021, Kleissner et al., 2021; Department for Culture, Media and Sports, 2018; SIRC & SPEA, 2019; SpEA, 2022; Statistics Portugal, 2016)

	Belgium	Croatia	Germany	Netherlands	Portugal	Austria	UK
Reported year	2015	2015	2019	2019	2012	2019	2016
Gross value added in billion EURO	6.6	0.9	70.2	7.6	1.7	17.2	37.3
Gross value added in % of GDP	1.8	2.4	2.2	1.1	1.1	4.8	2.1
Consumption private households in billion EURO	n.a.	n.a.	74.7	11.7	1.9	n.a.	n.a.
Consumption private households in % of total	n.a.	n.a.	4.4	3.3	1.7	n.a.	n.a.

and regularly collected data on sport-related consumer behaviour in the SSK calculations. The lack of appropriate sport-specific primary statistical data often leads to an underestimation of the economic importance of sport, including the household consumption that finances all sports clubs and organisations (Ahlert & Repenning, 2023).

Enterprises

In the early 1990s, the share of enterprises became increasingly important in professional sports financing. This marked the beginning of a fundamental change in the traditional funding model of European professional sport, which had previously relied on spectators' pockets, public subsidies, donations, and fees (Andreff, 2011). According to Andreff (2011), enterprises have been the main source of funding for professional team sports in Europe for more than 15 years.

For the funding of overall sport in Europe, enterprises are only a minor source, in contrast to North America (Andreff, 2011). However, the funding of amateur sport is increasingly dependent on enterprises. This includes sponsorship of sports clubs and donations to non-profit sports organisations (Heiden et al., 2012). Figures from Germany, for example, show that up to 19.7% of German clubs receive income from perimeter advertising (Breuer & Feiler, 2021).

European Union

Securing stable funding for grassroots sport is a challenge that the EU recognises. For this reason, the EU has taken into account developments in other areas of sport policy and promoted the exchange of best practices between organisations and Member States to address sustainable funding (Hellmund, 2017).

In general, a distinction is made between direct and indirect sport funding in Europe. Direct funding involves EU support for sport projects that provide benefits at European level and aim at improvements that can't be achieved by Member States alone or would require increased expenditure. Indirect funding involves financial support for sport projects through related action areas, contributing to specific objectives in these areas (Dickmann, 2018).

In particular, the EU aims to ensure the financing of sport in Europe through the following actions (Europäische Kommission, n.d.):

— improve the monitoring and forecasting of sport data in order to influence social and economic policy;
— identify sport's economic potential and share best practices on financing measures;
— support legislation in the areas of antitrust, merger control, and state aid under European competition law;
— determine the best options for public and private financing of sport at grassroots level; and

– create awareness of the social and economic implications of sport-related media and to safeguard intellectual property rights.

An example of an EU-funded programme that aims to support the development of sport in Europe is Erasmus+, an EU action programme in the fields of education, training, youth, and sport (Katarzyna & Olivier, 2023). Under this programme, a fixed percentage of the overall budget is allocated to sport to combat cross-border threats to the integrity of sport, to promote the principles of good governance and to strengthen support for voluntary activities. Among other things, Erasmus+ promotes collaborative communities, non-profit European sporting events, and dialogue with relevant stakeholders at the European level (Hellmund, 2015). In addition, the application of tax deductions or exemptions provided for at EU level allows sports organisations to retain a greater share of their income and thus reinvest it in the provision and accessibility of services to their members (Hellmund, 2017).

Undoubtedly, any EU regulation has the greatest impact on the financing of sport. For example, the Bosman case, which changed the liability of many sports clubs and sparked debates on international player transfers and EU competition rules for sport and related activities. Subsequently, the sports movement and the European Commission agreements have worked together to reach agreements in various areas, including rules for sports organisations, joint selling of sports media rights, and ticket sales arrangements (Hellmund, 2017).

Voluntary Work

Voluntary work is not a monetary source of funding, but it is indirectly very valuable. Sport, and especially grassroots sport, is largely run by volunteers (Hellmund, 2017). Without voluntary work, the funding of many sports clubs and organisations in Europe would not be possible as it is today.

Volunteers cover a wide range of roles in sport. While the need for volunteers directly involved in sporting activities and coaching is obvious, grassroots sport also relies on individuals who act as committee members, treasurers, legal advisers, administrators, advocates, and fundraisers. However, the role of volunteers is also changing. Volunteering is no longer associated with coaching in grassroots sport only, as it is now seen to operate at all levels. For example, volunteers are supporting the organisation of top-level sports events and activities at European and national level (European Commission: Directorate-General for Education, Youth, Sport and Culture, 2022).

Although not a direct source of funding, volunteers are provided by households and make a significant contribution by providing invaluable services that result in significant cost savings. In terms of the economic valuation of volunteering, estimates for 13 European Member States indicate that the average contribution of volunteering in sport is equivalent to 0.82% of gross domestic product (GDP) (Europäische Kommission, 2010). In line with the principles of solidarity, volunteers can therefore be seen as a symbol of the traditional European funding mechanisms for sport.

According to the 2018 Eurobarometer on Sport and Physical Activity, there are 30 million volunteers in sport across Europe (European Commission, 2018). In addition, national analysis shows that in 15 EU Member States, at least one in ten respondents say they are currently involved in volunteering in sport or intend to do so in the next two months (European Commission, 2022). The tendency is particularly strong in Ireland and Luxembourg, where almost one in five respondents (19% in both countries) express such intentions, as well as in the Netherlands with 18%. More specifically, in six EU Member States – the Netherlands (15%), Luxembourg (13%), Ireland (12%), Sweden and Slovenia (both 11%), and Denmark (10%) – at least one person in ten currently volunteers to support sports activities (European Commission, 2022). Conversely, a more modest 4% of respondents in Portugal, Greece, and Lithuania currently participate or intend to participate in a similar capacity. However, at least one in ten respondents in 21 EU Member States has volunteered for sporting activities in the past, with the highest figures in Sweden (35%), Finland (32%), and Denmark (29%) (European Commission, 2022). These numbers also fit to the finding of Scheerder et al. (2023), who examine pan-European similarities and differences in club-based sport. The results show that volunteering in sport seems to be very popular in Northern Europe, where almost one in five people say they volunteer in sport, while the number of people volunteering in sport is much lower in Southern and Eastern European countries, for example. There are also social differences according to the latest Eurobarometer on Sport and Physical Activity (European Commission, 2022): Volunteers in sport are less likely to be female, older than 55, and/or left school at the age of 15 or earlier. In addition, managers are the most likely to be currently engaged or planning to engage in the next two months and respondents who consider themselves as upper middle class are the most likely to be engaged or planning to engage (European Commission, 2022). These figures are an indication that favourable socio-cultural, political, and economic conditions are necessary for volunteering in sport to be successful (Koutrou & Kohe, 2021).

Overall, the results show that voluntary participation in sport is on the decline in all social groups (Scheerder et al., 2023). For example, according to German clubs, recruiting and retaining volunteers remained the biggest problem in 2020 (Breuer & Feiler, 2021). The fact that more than half of all respondents in all 27 EU Member States have never volunteered and do not plan to volunteer for sport activities means that a large potential financing source of funding is being missed. The proportion of not being volunteers in sport ranges from 88% in Portugal to 51% in Sweden (European Commission, 2022).

Without the support of volunteers, sport, especially at grassroots level, would face serious problems and would dramatically change the EMS. It is important that the EU raises awareness of the value of volunteering and continues to promote the informal learning and experience gained through volunteering in sport in order to counteract the decline in the number of sports volunteers. This should ensure that they continue to be involved in sports organisations (Hellmund, 2017). A good example is the Act on Sport in Slovakia, which offers people who volunteer in sport to receive tax-free compensation for the time they spend at sporting events (up to €500 per year) (European Commission: Directorate-General for Education, Youth, Sport and Culture, 2022).

Financing of Non-Professional Sport

The main source of funding for non-professional sport comes from private house-holds, followed by local authorities and corporate sports budgets (Andreff, 2011), with the latter becoming increasingly important. Regarding local authorities, there are countries where the majority of public intervention in the sports economy comes from local authorities, such as Germany or Denmark. On the other hand, there are also countries where central government sports policy plays an important role, such as Latvia or Greece (Andreff, 2011).

The income of grassroots sports clubs comes from a variety of sources, as the case of Germany illustrates. The main source of income for the clubs there is membership fees, followed by income from donations, sports subsidies from the district, city or municipality, sport events, and course fees (Breuer & Feiler, 2021).

In the EMS, athletes (consumers) pay fees to national sports federations through their sports clubs, but officially there are no fees charged by sports clubs to fund NOCs. These fees vary according to the type of sport and support the national federations in running leagues and championships. Clubs also receive services from their federations. These include insurance, legal advice, infrastructure support and, most importantly, developing young athletes to compete at the highest level. As a result, club members, clubs, and regional and national sports federations are linked to national federations through the provision of services and financial transactions. They are also linked through elections, when they elect their regional representatives, who in turn elect their national representatives. This requires adherence to the principles of good governance, such as transparency and democracy.

Financing of Professional Sport

Professional sport in Europe is financed differently from sport in general. This difference has become particularly apparent since Europe's top professional leagues began to move away from the *Spectators-Subsidies-Sponsors-Local* (SSSL) financial model, where the main sources of revenue were gate receipts, public subsidies, donations, and fees, to the MCMMG (Media, Corporate, Merchandising, Markets, Global) model in the mid-1990s (Andreff & Staudohar, 2000). This was based on the flow of money from enterprises, media, corporate involvement, trade, and markets, moving away from a local or national focus and opening up new sources of funding for professional sport (Andreff & Staudohar, 2000). This was the beginning of the dominance of private funding sources, especially in professional team sports in Europe.

The importance of private sources in the financing of sport is also evident in the results of Andreff (2009). He examines the five largest European leagues (Premier League, Lega Calcio, Liga de Futbol, Ligue 1 and German Bundesliga) and calculates their average financing structure for the years 2006–2007. Even at that time, enterprises were already the most important source of funding for professional team sports.

Fair competition and the idea of solidarity are fundamental to professional sport in Europe. However, state support can also lead to distortions of competition between clubs or sports organisations. This is the case when commercial clubs receive aid for the development of infrastructure (such as football stadiums or training facilities) or educational programmes for grassroots sport within the same clubs where the professional team competes.

Organising sport in Europe through open leagues offers the possibility of promotion and relegation and allows any club in a country to reach the top league or, if a team is not good enough, to drop down to the lower leagues. In this way, each team has the potential to qualify for prestigious tournaments such as the UEFA Champions League, the UEFA Europa League or the Conference League. Since relegation always means losses or additional financial needs, this has a significant impact on funding.

At the same time, this leads to a structural problem known in game theory as the rationality trap or prisoner's dilemma. Clubs tend to overinvest in players and coaches when facing relegation or failure to win promotion. As a result, most professional clubs are over-indebted, or at least under-indebted. In other words they are trapped in the so-called destructive competition. In some sports, clubs are even reluctant to move up a division because of the additional requirements, such as finding sponsors, larger venues to generate more revenue, or potential support from other teams within the same club.

Some European governing bodies, such as UEFA, try to prevent over-indebtedness by implementing financial sustainability rules. For example, through its club monitoring process, UEFA has established a framework to which clubs participating in UEFA's men's club competitions are committed. The system is based on clubs working together to provide a complete and true financial picture. It is based on three key pillars – solvency, stability, and cost control (UEFA, 2023).

However, leading professional sports clubs in Europe are financed in a similar way to top clubs in other parts of the world, but without government support in Europe. The EU is even trying to legislate against governments supporting clubs to maintain fair competition in European leagues. This is a fact that distinguishes them from clubs in Arab countries or China, where the clubs are heavily supported by the governments and the governments face the problem of multiple ownership.

Conclusion

In conclusion, the financing of sport in Europe is based on harmonisation and the promotion of solidarity, with the main objective of ensuring sustainable financing methods, especially for grassroots sport.

But it is a challenge – with almost 50 countries and many different sports and federations, the European landscape is very diverse and the approaches to funding are very different. Trends such as the liberalisation of TV and betting markets are affecting several countries at once, leading to Europe-wide changes in the financing of sport.

This chapter has outlined the different sources of funding that sport should use in a transparent and accountable way to strengthen sport at different levels across Europe and maximise its positive impact on European citizens. It also recalls the challenges of defining a single EMS and calls for continued efforts in this direction.

References

Ahlert, G., & Repenning, S. (2023). *Die ökonomische Bedeutung des Sports in Deutschland: Sportsatellitenkonto (SSK) 2019 und ein erster Ausblick auf das durch Covid–19 geprägte Jahr 2020.* GWS Themenreport 2023/1. Gesellschaft für Wirtschaftliche Strukturforschung. Retrieved from https://www.bisp.de/SharedDocs/Downloads/Publikationen/Publikationssuche_SSK/SSKThemenreport20231.pdf?__blob=publicationFile&v=2.

Andreff, W. (2009). Public and private sport financing in Europe: the impact of financial crisis. *Romania,* 1(4.5), 36–37.

Andreff, W. (2011). European versus American model of sports. In E. Emrich, C. Pierzdioch, & M.-P. Büch (Eds.), *Europäische Sportmodelle: Gemeinsamkeiten und Differenzen in international vergleichender Perspektive.* Hofmann.

Andreff, W., & Staudohar, P. D. (2000). The evolving European model of professional sports finance. *Journal of Sports Economics,* 1(3), 257–276. https://doi.org/10.1177/152700250000100304.

Ashelm, M. (2010). *Der große Kampf um die Wett-Millionen.* Retrieved from https://www.faz.net/s/Rub9CD731D06F17450CB39BE001000DD173/Doc~E82125BE3AF5E4BB5A7A9B54F6A95A8E9~ATpl~Ecommon~Scontent.html.

Breuer, C., & Feiler, S. (2021). *Sportvereine in Deutschland: Ergebnisse aus der 8. Welle des Sportentwicklungsberichts.* Sportentwicklungsbericht für Deutschland 2020–2022 – Teil 1. Retrieved from https://cdn.dosb.de/user_upload/Sportentwicklung/Dokumente/SEB/2022/SEB_Bundesbericht_W8_deutsch_bf.pdf.

Commission of the European Communities. (2007). *White Paper on Sports.* Retrieved from https://eur-lex.europa.eu/legal-content/EN/TXT/PDF/?uri=CELEX:52007DC0391.

Department for Culture, Media and Sports. (2018). *UK Sport Satellite Account, 2016 (Provisional).* Retrieved from https://assets.publishing.service.gov.uk/government/uploads/system/uploads/attachment_data/file/676504/Sport_Satellite_Account_2016.pdf.

Dickmann, D. (2018). Die finanzielle Dimension europäischer Sportpolitik: Das Verhältnis direkter und indirekter Sportfinanzierung in der Europäischen Union. In J. Mittag (Ed.), *Europäische Sportpolitik: Zugänge - Akteure - Problemfelder* (pp. 287–298). Nomos Verlagsgesellschaft mbH & Co. KG.

DOSB. (2018). *Leitbild.* Deutscher Olympischer Sportbund. Retrieved from https://cdn.dosb.de/user_upload/www.dosb.de/uber_uns/Mitgliederversammlung/Koblenz_2017/TOP_12_Anlage_Leitbild_MV_2017.pdf.

Europäische Kommission. (n.d.). *Sport and Economy.* Retrieved from https://sport.ec.europa.eu/policies/sport-and-economy.

Europäische Kommission. (1998). *Das Europäische Sportmodell(Diskussionspapier der GD X).* Brüssel: Generaldirektion X, Information, Kommunikation, Kultur, audiovisuelle Medien Politik im audiovisuellen Bereich, Kultur und Sport.

Europäische Kommission. (2010). *Freiwilligentätigkeit in der EU.* Retrieved from https://ec.europa.eu/citizenship/pdf/executive_summary_volunteering_de.pdf.

Europäisches Parlament. (2012). *European Dimension in Sport.* Retrieved from https://www.europarl.europa.eu/doceo/document/TA-7-2012-0025_EN.pdf.

European Commission. (2018). *Special Eurobarometer 472: Sport and Physical Activity.* European Commission. Retrieved from https://www.europarc.org/wp-content/uploads/2020/01/Special-Eurobarometer-472-Sports-and-physical-activity.pdf.

European Commission. (2022). *Special Eurobarometer 525_ Sport and Physical Activity.* European Commission. Retrieved from https://nyadagbladet.se/wp-content/uploads/2023/03/Sport_physical_activity_2022_eb525_summary_en.pdf.

European Commission: Directorate-General for Education, Youth, Sport and Culture, Sennett, J., Le Gall, A., Kelly, G., Cottrill, R., Goffredo, S., & Spyridopoulos, K. (2022). *Study on the European sport model : a report to the European Commission, Publications Office of the European Union.* https://data.europa.eu/doi/10.2766/28433.

Eurostat. (2019). *How Much Do Governments Spend on Recreation and Sport?* Retrieved from https://ec.europa.eu/eurostat/web/products-eurostat-news/-/EDN-20190923-1.

Heiden, I. a. d., Meyrahn, F. & Ahlert, G. (2012). *Bedeutung des Spitzen- und Breitensports im Bereich Werbung, Sponsoring und Medienrechte.* Forschungsbericht (Langfassung) im Auftrag des Bundesministeriums für Wirtschaft und Technologie (BMWi). Retrieved from https://sportsatellitenkonto.de/wp-content/uploads/2019/12/01_BMWi-Werbung-Sponsoring-Medienrechte-Forschungsbericht-20120117-fin.pdf.

Hellmund, F. (2015). *Sportförderung in der Europäischen Union: 2014–2020.* European Olympic Committees / EU Office. Retrieved from https://issuu.com/dosb/docs/eoc_eu-b__ro_-_sportf__rderung_in_d.

Hellmund, F. (2017). *Guide to EU Sport Policy.* European Olympic Committees & EU Office.

Jesse, B., & Fischer, C. (2010). Sportstrukturen der Länder der Europäischen Union. In W. Tokarski, & K. Petry (Hrsg.), *Handbuch Sportpolitik* (pp. 114–127). Hofmann.

Katarzyna, A. I., & Olivier, Y. A. R. (2023). *Sport | Kurzdarstellungen zur Europäischen Union.* Europäisches Parlament. Retrieved from https://www.europarl.europa.eu/factsheets/de/sheet/143/sport.

Kleissner, A., Grohall, G., Kokolakakis, T., & Papić, A. (2021). *Investments in Sport - Sport Satellite Account Croatia.* Retrieved from https://isport2020.eu/wp-content/uploads/2022/03/Intellectual-Output-No.-3-Sport-Satellite-Account-Croatia.pdf.

Koutrou, K., & Kohe, G. Z. (2021). Transnational unities, challenges and opportunities for sport volunteering: lessons from the European PlayGreen project. *Sport in Society*, 24(7), 1249–1266. https://doi.org/10.1080/17430437.2021.1925251.

Meyrahn, F., Heiden, I. a. d., Ahlert, G., & Preuß, H. (2014). *Wirtschaftsfaktor Sportwetten - Sportfaktor Lotterien: Aktuelle Daten zur Sportwirtschaft.* Berlin: Deutschland / Bundesministerium für Wirtschaft und Energie. Retrieved from https://sportsatellitenkonto.de/wp-content/uploads/2019/12/07_BISp-Wirtschaftsfaktor-Sportwetten-20141216.pdf.

Mittag, J. (2018). Europäische Sportpolitik zwischen Wachstum und Differenzierung: Entwicklungslinien, Analyseperspektiven und Erklärungsansätze. In J. Mittag (Ed.), *Europäische Sportpolitik.* Nomos.

Nafziger, J. A. (2008). A comparison of the European and North American models of sports organisation. *The International Sports Law Journal*, 3–4, 100–109.

Nagel, S., Elmose-Østerlund, K., Ibsen, B., & Scheerder, J. (2023). *Funktionen von Sportvereinen in europäischen Gesellschaften. Eine länderübergreifende vergleichende Studie.* Springer Gabler.

Parrish, R., García, B. G., Miettinen, S., & Siekmann, R. (2010). *The Lisbon Treaty and EU Sports Policy.* Belgium: EPRS: European Parliamentary Research Service. Retrieved from https://www.europarl.europa.eu/meetdocs/2009_2014/documents/cult/dv/esstudyeusportspolicy/esstudyeusportspolicyen.pdf.

Prets, C. (2009). Weißbuch Sport der Kommission – Auf dem Weg zu einer Europäischen Sportpolitik. In G. Sander, & A. Sasdi (Eds.), *Sport im Spannungsfeld von Recht, Wirtschaft und europäischen Grundfreiheiten* (pp. 171–178). Logos-Verlag.

Preuss, H., & Alfs, C. (2013). Wirtschaftliche Bedeutung des Sportkonsums in Deutschland. *Sportwissenschaft (Heidelberg)*, 43(4), 239–252. https://doi.org/10.1007/s12662-013-0311-y.

Preuss, H., Schallhorn, C., & Schütte, N. (2022). *Olympic Sport Organisations in Times of Crisis and Change*. Academia Verlag.

Scheerder, J., Helsen, K., Elmose-Østerlund, K., & Nagel, S. (2023). Untersuchung gesamteuropäischer Gemeinsamkeiten und Unterschiede im vereinsorganisierten Sport: Ein länder- und zeitübergreifender Vergleich. In S. Nagel, K. Elmose-Østerlund, B. Ibsen, & J. Scheerder (Eds.), *Funktionen von Sportvereinen in europäischen Gesellschaften. Eine länderübergreifende vergleichende Studie* (pp. 345–375). Springer Gabler.

Schulze, B. (2011). Internationale Sportentwicklung und nationale Sportstrukturen. In B. Schulze, & U. Marker (Hrsg.), *Gesellschaftlicher Wandel und Sportentwicklung* (S. 81–92). Waxmann Verlag.

SpEA. (2022). *SPORT AUSTRIA - das SPORT-DATENVADEMECUM*, Ausgabe Nr. 12. Sports EconAustria.

Sport Industry Research Centre [SIRC], & SportsEconAustria [SPEA]. (2019). *The Sport Satellite Account of Belgium – 2019 Edition*. Final Research Report, Vienna.

Statistics Netherlands. (2021). *De Nederlandse sporteconomie 2019*. The Hague.

Statistics Portugal. (2016). Sport Satellite Account.

UEFA. (2023). *Financial Sustainability*. UEFA.com. Retrieved from https://www.uefa.com/insideuefa/news/0246-0e796c23daa9-41f78afb0c7a-1000--financial-sustainability/.

Chapter 6

Sports Cultures in the European Union

An Analysis of Eurobarometer Sport and Physical Activity 2022 Data

Ramón Llopis-Goig

Introduction

Issues related to sport are of great interest and relevance to the daily lives of the general population in the European Union. In the 50 years since the Sport for All Charter was ratified in 1975, there has been an unprecedented expansion of engagement in physical activity and sport, largely due to the socio-economic development and cultural change experienced by European societies and introduction of *Sport for All* policies several decades ago.

Sport for All is an umbrella term that is typically used to refer to the need to orientate sports policies towards facilitating access to recreational, physical and sporting activities for all social groups as a means of extending the social, educational and health benefits of such activities throughout the population. However, although this approach has been adopted by most European countries, its implementation in national sports policies has taken various forms. As a result, patterns of sport participation currently vary greatly between European countries. Data from the most recent Eurobarometer on Sport and Physical Activity (European Commission, 2022) demonstrate a huge gap in sports participation rates between countries with the country with the highest weekly sports participation rate, namely, Finland (70.9%), being almost four times more engaged in sport than the country with the lowest rate, namely, Romania (19.6%). Whilst these two countries may represent opposite ends of the scale, sports participation rates between the remaining countries also exhibit great variability. The same can be said for weekly physical activity engagement rates with Eurobarometer 2022 data revealing even greater disparity between countries. Indeed, at one extreme, Portugal (16.8%) has physical activity engagement rates that are more than 70 points lower than the Netherlands (88.1%), at the other extreme. Another indicator of note, membership to sports clubs, also reveals large differences with the Netherlands (22.1%) again reporting the highest rates compared with Bulgaria (1.8%) which has the lowest rate and lags far behind. These differences are further exaggerated when focus is shifted to fitness centre membership, with Sweden and Lithuania representing the two ends of the spectrum with 34.6% and 1.9% membership rates, respectively.

DOI: 10.4324/9781032665153-7

The aforementioned disparity is not surprising since they have already been identified in previous Eurobarometer surveys on sport and physical activity (European Commission, 2004, 2010, 2014, 2018). These surveys have shown that sport participation is higher in Northern European countries compared with Southern European countries and is higher in Western European countries compared with Eastern European countries (Van Tuyckom and Scheerder, 2008, 2010). Nonetheless, aside from illustrating a fairly clear picture regarding sport participation variability across different European Union countries, findings reported by Eurobarometer surveys raise questions pertaining to the potential permeance of different sports cultures in European society, the way in which these cultures may be configured in terms of the countries in which they prevail and the characteristics inherent to them, and the most decisive factors when it comes to determining the prevailing sport culture.

More than a decade ago, Van Tuyckom sought to respond to these questions (Van Tuyckom, 2013) in a paper based on 2004 Eurobarometer on Sport and Physical Activity data (European Commission, 2004). Van Tuyckom identified the existence of six sporting clusters in the European Union with assignment to each one being based on the most prevalent sporting features within the countries examined. Groupings were denominated as follows: "non-to average fitness countries", which comprised countries such as Greece, Italy and Portugal; "active club countries", which included Denmark, the Netherlands and Austria; "average non-organised countries", which pertained to Slovenia, Malta and Cyprus; "average school countries", which were composed of Hungary, Latvia, Lithuania and Poland; "active multi-context countries", which contained Belgium, Germany, Spain, France, Ireland, Luxembourg, the UK, the Czech Republic, Estonia and Slovakia; and "very active countries", which corresponded to only Finland and Sweden.

Research presented in the present chapter aims to respond the very same questions that Van Tuyckom already sought to answer but, this time, most recent data on the subject are used, via Eurobarometer 525, for which fieldwork was carried out during May and April 2022 (European Commission, 2022). Thus, research presented in the present chapter can be considered a replica of that reported by Van Tuyckom (2013), insofar as it proposes the same objectives and is based on the same analytical approach. This being said, it is important to note that the present work differs in both a theoretical and methodological sense. On the one hand, the present contribution is theoretically grounded in the approach conceived by Inglehart and Welzel (2005), which considers the influence of interactional modernisation processes and cultural traditions that is evident within all processes of human development. On the other hand, at a methodological level, the present study extends the number of variables used to classify sports cultures and, as already mentioned, employs data gathered almost two decades after the study conducted by Van Tuyckom, which allows the analysis to be updated and the evolution that has taken place since then to be examined.

Theoretical Considerations

Despite the fact that the data on sports participation referred to in the previous section highlight the existence of large differences in sports participation patterns between EU countries, sport is often portrayed as a global and homogeneous phenomenon with hardly any significant geographical or cultural variations. This is largely due to standardisation of the rules that govern it, internationalisation of sport competitions and worldwide media coverage of major sporting events. However, the reality of sport is far removed from this simplified and homogenous vision.

As is well known, modern sport was born in the United Kingdom in the mid-19th century and, by the end of that century, it had already begun to spread throughout the rest of Europe and the world thanks to the economic and political influence of the British Empire (Mandell, 1986). However, the way in which sporting cultures were shaped in each country varied widely and was conditioned by the specific characteristics of each nation. Firstly, the timing of the introduction of modern sports and the pace at which each national sporting culture took shape depended greatly on the political situation and economic development of each country. Secondly, traditions around play and the main elements of play and popular games, which impacted the emergence of subsequent sporting characteristics, also differed between countries, with these generally being linked to local traditions and festive celebrations. It should be borne in mind that popular games constitute a core element of modern sport, insofar as the latter was derived from introduction of the type of spatial-temporal structure and criteria that was inherent to the process of industrial modernisation into traditional popular games (Van Tuyckom, 2011: 18). Thirdly, different conceptions of the body, physical culture and gymnastic traditions between countries or cultural regions also steered the course of subsequent sport.

As a result, the way in which these elements and influences were integrated and evolved has given rise to sporting cultures that are very different in nature (Heinemann, 1999: 21–22). Sporting cultures have continued to take shape throughout the 19th and 20th centuries and, today, constitute an extraordinary display of cultural diversity that cannot be ignored, even if it is often taken for granted that the processes of modernisation and globalisation undermine national differences and reduce the weight of cultural traditions. Socio-economic development has a strong influence on social change processes, as is typically espoused by modernisation theories. However, the true meaning of such development cannot be understood without referring to cultural traditions (Inglehart and Welzel, 2005). According to this standpoint, socio-economic development tends to promote cultural change that, to a certain extent, can be considered to be predictable, insofar as they point in the same direction. In this sense, technological innovation, increased productivity, labour specialisation, higher levels of education, increased income and diversification of human interactions lead to cultural changes in gender roles, attitudes towards authorities, reproductive patterns and a wide range of social and political behaviours. However, the outcome depends not only on these processes but also on the cultural trajectory historically followed by a given society (Inglehart and Welzel, 2005: 27). Indeed, one of the main limitations of classical theories of modernisation is precisely the assumption that cultural traditions and religions will gradually fade away. On the contrary, they have shown great resistance around the world. This has led authors such as Putnam (1993) and DiMaggio (1994) to assert that cultural traditions are enduring and continue to shape the cultural, economic and political bent of societies. In this sense, even if cultural patterns within all nations shift in the same direction due to them all being caught up in the same modernisation trends, attitudinal and behavioural systems will not converge because the influence of cultural traditions will not completely fade away, sustained by the resilience and durability of belief systems (Inglehart and Welzel, 2005: 26).

Transferring Inglehart and Welzels' (2005) ideas on modernisation processes and cultural change to the sporting sphere, it could be argued that socio-economic and technological development, on the one hand, increase the economic resources, opportunities, time availability and stimuli available for individuals to play sport. Consequently, this reduces some of the external constraints and obstacles that may have previously hindered sporting activity. On the other hand, socio-economic and technological development also foster a cultural context in which individuals attach greater importance to physical and emotional well-being, quality of life, physical self-care and self-expression. All of the above are directly benefits of regular engagement in physical activity and sport. These cultural changes, however, do not imply the disappearance of cultural traditions or the emergence of societies that are increasingly similar in terms of patterns of sports participation.

The study presented in the present chapter assumes that several sporting cultures prevail in the European Union and that these can be classified according to certain criteria that is related to the cultural background and traditions of each given society. A simple glance at data on sports participation in the countries of the European Union already shows that societies with higher levels of economic development achieve higher sport participation rates. The same is true for societies with lower levels of economic development. However, it is important to acknowledge that meaningful differences exist between countries. The present paper hypothesises that different sport cultures emerge in European society and that these are strongly related with the historical cultural, political and religious landscape inherent to each country. Sport culture results from the interaction between modernisation processes and traditional influences.

Method

The study presented in the present chapter is based on data from the Special Eurobarometer 525 on Sport and Physical Activity, commissioned by the European Commission (2022). A total of 26,578 residents of the 27 Member States aged 15 years and over were interviewed face to face at their homes and online. Fieldwork was carried out by the Kantar network between the 19th of April and the 16th of May 2022. As stated in technical specifications of this Special Eurobarometer

(European Commission, 2022: 91), multi-stage, random (probability) sampling was employed in all countries. Most countries secured a sample of around 1,000 interviews with only a few exceptions. Probability proportional to population size and population density sampling was used to ensure representation of each country. Sampling points were drawn systematically from pertinent administrative regional units after stratification according to individual unit and area type. This ensured that data represented the whole territory of surveyed countries according to Eurostat nuts II (or equivalent).

Statistical analyses presented in this chapter are based on 12 variables related to sports participation that corresponded to four different areas. Firstly, one variable referred to the frequency of sport engagement. Secondly, four variables pertained to the location of sporting activity (health or fitness centre, sports club, home and park/outdoors). Thirdly, six variables addressed reasons for sport engagement (improve health, improve physical appearance, counteract the effects of ageing, relax, improve fitness and control weight). Finally, one variable described health/fitness centre membership.

In terms of statistical analyses, percentages for the aforementioned variables were calculated as fractions for the 27 countries by aggregating individual data. Given that data were all reported as averages (incidence per 100 inhabitants), the unit of measurement was guaranteed and no transformation of data distribution was necessary (Diaz de Rada, 2002: 274). Percentages for each country were estimated without the application of weighting coefficients, as the focus of analysis was on national data as opposed to overall EU data.

Other variables pertaining to the location and underlying motives of sport engagement were discarded due to a lack of discriminant validity in preliminary statistical analysis. In addition, two other variables were discarded due to their high correlations with some of the other variables, namely weekly physical activity engagement (correlated with weekly sport engagement) and sports club membership (correlated with sport engagement in sports clubs). In both cases, correlations exceeded the upper threshold of 0.8 at which suppression is recommended (Lago, 2008: 90). Thus, a total of 12 variables were included in final analysis. This number can be considered adequate for type of analysis conducted here (Díaz de Rada, 2002: 276).

In order to address the research objectives, two-stage cluster analysis was carried out in accordance with the recommendations of Hair et al. (2014: 446). At the first step, the number of clusters and their initial centres was determined taking a hierarchical approach (Ward's method and square Euclidean distance). At the second step, initial outcomes were optimised to examine cluster characteristics via K-means optimisation of cluster centres. Next, bivariate analyses complemented by Chi-square tests were carried out to explore the sporting characteristics of each cluster.

Results

Preliminary first results derived from hierarchical analysis are shown in Table 6.1 and Figure 6.1, which present a proximity matrix and dendrogram, respectively.

Table 6.1 Hierarchical cluster analysis: proximity matrix (squared Euclidean distance).

	1	2	3	4	5	6	7	8	9	10	11	12	13	14	15	16	17	18	19	20	21	22	23	24	25	26	27	28
1	0.00																											
2	0.05	0.00																										
3	0.19	0.11	0.00																									
4	0.12	0.04	0.15	0.00																								
5	0.11	0.08	0.27	0.16	0.00																							
6	0.08	0.06	0.10	0.07	0.16	0.00																						
7	0.30	0.19	0.16	0.11	0.31	0.14	0.00																					
8	0.10	0.09	0.14	0.09	0.15	0.05	0.09	0.00																				
9	0.15	0.15	0.25	0.19	0.19	0.20	0.33	0.18	0.00																			
10	0.16	0.13	0.30	0.14	0.07	0.15	0.22	0.12	0.26	0.00																		
11	0.21	0.16	0.39	0.24	0.07	0.31	0.43	0.27	0.20	0.12	0.00																	
12	0.15	0.09	0.26	0.03	0.19	0.16	0.17	0.16	0.18	0.19	0.24	0.00																
13	0.39	0.26	0.21	0.19	0.45	0.19	0.18	0.28	0.38	0.45	0.61	0.26	0.00															
14	0.34	0.23	0.15	0.17	0.35	0.19	0.03	0.14	0.35	0.28	0.45	0.23	0.21	0.00														
15	0.19	0.07	0.19	0.03	0.16	0.10	0.13	0.13	0.19	0.15	0.22	0.06	0.17	0.18	0.00													
16	0.12	0.09	0.15	0.12	0.19	0.17	0.28	0.19	0.08	0.24	0.20	0.12	0.33	0.28	0.16	0.00												
17	0.14	0.10	0.27	0.06	0.13	0.08	0.13	0.06	0.21	0.10	0.25	0.08	0.20	0.07	0.19	0.22	0.00											
18	0.13	0.06	0.19	0.03	0.15	0.07	0.13	0.09	0.16	0.16	0.25	0.05	0.17	0.19	0.02	0.16	0.04	0.00										
19	0.27	0.28	0.58	0.26	0.34	0.35	0.43	0.29	0.34	0.36	0.42	0.18	0.67	0.50	0.29	0.36	0.20	0.23	0.00									
20	0.18	0.16	0.38	0.07	0.22	0.16	0.22	0.16	0.24	0.16	0.32	0.05	0.33	0.32	0.11	0.22	0.04	0.08	0.16	0.00								
21	0.29	0.30	0.64	0.23	0.40	0.33	0.44	0.30	0.39	0.37	0.50	0.17	0.61	0.57	0.27	0.42	0.17	0.20	0.07	0.10	0.00							
22	0.20	0.19	0.41	0.24	0.22	0.23	0.36	0.22	0.30	0.29	0.28	0.19	0.65	0.40	0.31	0.24	0.23	0.25	0.13	0.25	0.25	0.00						
23	0.19	0.21	0.55	0.20	0.18	0.28	0.39	0.21	0.26	0.16	0.23	0.16	0.64	0.48	0.22	0.32	0.11	0.17	0.11	0.10	0.10	0.19	0.00					
24	0.26	0.22	0.50	0.15	0.26	0.25	0.27	0.19	0.29	0.23	0.35	0.10	0.45	0.38	0.15	0.34	0.07	0.11	0.09	0.05	0.05	0.20	0.06	0.00				
25	0.19	0.14	0.24	0.07	0.31	0.14	0.26	0.23	0.28	0.26	0.41	0.10	0.24	0.35	0.12	0.15	0.16	0.12	0.35	0.11	0.27	0.38	0.32	0.25	0.00			
26	0.27	0.21	0.57	0.23	0.22	0.35	0.45	0.29	0.35	0.23	0.23	0.19	0.70	0.54	0.23	0.36	0.18	0.21	0.11	0.18	0.13	0.36	0.14	0.07	0.35	0.00		
27	0.34	0.34	0.70	0.34	0.36	0.45	0.52	0.35	0.46	0.38	0.41	0.27	0.83	0.60	0.37	0.47	0.26	0.31	0.04	0.25	0.11	0.12	0.12	0.26	0.47	0.05	0.00	
28	0.17	0.15	0.31	0.16	0.20	0.20	0.23	0.13	0.22	0.23	0.30	0.13	0.49	0.28	0.19	0.22	0.13	0.14	0.07	0.16	0.16	0.06	0.14	0.11	0.28	0.13	0.10	0.00

Source: own analysis with data from Eurobarometer 525 (European Commission, 2022).

Note: 1=France; 2=Belgium; 3=The Netherlands; 4=Germany West; 5=Italy; 6=Luxembourg; 7=Denmark; 8=Ireland; 9=Greece; 10=Spain; 11=Portugal; 12=Germany East; 13=Finland; 14=Sweden; 15=Austria; 16=Cyprus; 17=Czech Republic; 18=Estonia; 19=Hungary; 20=Latvia; 21=Lithuania; 22=Malta; 23=Poland; 24=Slovakia; 25=Slovenia; 26=Bulgaria; 27=Romania; 28=Croatia.

The proximity matrix illustrates pairwise distances between EU countries by jointly examining the 12 variables pertaining to frequency of sport engagement, location of sport engagement, reasons for engaging in sport and membership to fitness centres.

On the one hand, the proximity matrix (Table 6.1) reveals a degree of affinity between some countries. For example, outcomes for West Germany are highly similar to those coming out of East Germany, Austria, Czechia, Latvia, Slovenia and Estonia. The same is true for Luxembourg in relation to France, Belgium and Ireland, as well as for Poland in relation to Lithuania and Bulgaria, and Italy in relation to Spain and Portugal. Other countries showing similar degrees of affinity are Denmark and Sweden, and Greece and Cyprus.

On the other hand, the proximity matrix also makes it possible to identify European countries whose sporting cultures are more distant. In this sense, outcomes for Finland and Sweden are hugely disparate when compared with those produced for Hungary, Lithuania, Poland, Bulgaria and Romania. The same can be said of the Netherlands and Italy with respect to these same countries. Other disparate countries to emerge were Denmark in relation to Romania and Bulgaria, and Portugal in relation to Finland and Lithuania. This is a clear indication of the diversity of sport engagement patterns in EU member states, whilst also indicating that a huge gap exists between some of these countries.

Hierarchical cluster outcomes are presented graphically in the dendrogram shown in Figure 6.1. When interpreting the number of identifiable clusters in the dendrogram, it should be considered that small distances indicate homogeneous clusters, whilst large distances define heterogeneous clusters. It is convenient to cease the addition of new clusters before the horizontal lines start to become excessively long (Díaz de Rada, 2002: 293). According to these premises, the dendrogram derived from the 12 sport engagement variables introduced in hierarchical analysis suggests the existence of seven clusters, that is, seven sport cultures (Figure 6.1). In any case, it should be kept in mind that decisions regarding the number of identifiable clusters in a dendrogram is subject to researcher interpretation and, therefore, vulnerable to subjectivity bias. The dashed vertical line to the left of point five on the upper horizontal axis reveals the existence of seven clusters. This line could alternatively have been traced further to the right, at point five on the horizontal axis, and in that case, would have resulted in the determination of five clusters. The seven-cluster solution was chosen because this option maximises internal homogeneity of the clusters and, furthermore, because the greater differentiation afforded, in comparison to that made possible by a five-cluster solution, makes full sense from the theoretical perspective assumed in the present research.

From top to bottom, the first cluster in the dendrogram (Figure 6.1) comprises Germany, Austria, Czechia, Slovenia, Latvia and Estonia. These countries are characterised by different cultural and religious traditions. The former two correspond to the so-called conservative welfare regime (Esping-Andersen, 1990, 1999), whilst the latter four all formed part of the Communist Bloc along with Germany East.

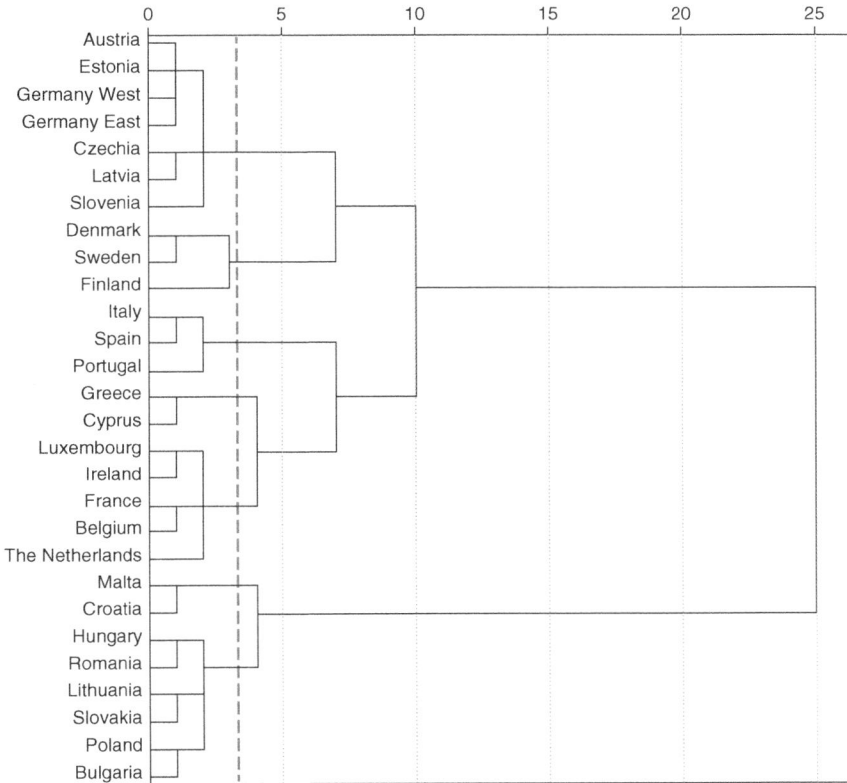

Figure 6.1 Dendrogram (hierarchical cluster analysis).
Source: Own analysis with data from Eurobarometer 525 (European Commission, 2022).

Moreover, the first four are located contiguously in the same geographical area, as are the last two. The next cluster groups three Northern European countries representing the so-called social democratic welfare regime, namely, Denmark, Sweden and Finland. The third cluster brings together three Southern European countries with Catholic traditions, namely, Italy, Spain and Portugal. The next cluster groups together Greece and Cyprus, which are also from Southern Europe but, in this case, have Orthodox traditions. Both the third and fourth clusters comprise countries from the Mediterranean welfare regime. The next cluster brings together four Western European countries with Catholic traditions, namely, Luxembourg, Belgium, France and Ireland, joined by the Netherlands. The next cluster includes Malta and Croatia and the last cluster includes six geographically contiguous former Communist countries, namely, Lithuania, Poland, Slovakia, Hungary, Romania and Bulgaria.

Following determination of the existence of seven clusters, initial cluster centres were estimated for all clusters using the 12 sports participation variables. *K*-means

Table 6.2 K-means clustering

Cluster	Country	Distance
1	06 Luxembourg	0.138
	02 Belgium	0.157
	08 Ireland	0.188
	01 France	0.211
	03 The Netherlands	0.265
2	04 Germany West	0.102
	18 Estonia	0.132
	12 Germany East	0.145
	15 Austria	0.169
	17 Czechia	0.182
	20 Latvia	0.187
	25 Slovenia	0.259
3	05 Italy	0.133
	10 Spain	0.181
	11 Portugal	0.185
4	07 Denmark	0.151
	14 Sweden	0.182
	13 Finland	0.287
5	09 Greece	0.142
	16 Cyprus	0.142
6	19 Hungary	0.180
	24 Slovakia	0.185
	27 Romania	0.192
	21 Lithuania	0.195
	23 Poland	0.201
	26 Bulgaria	0.203
7	22 Malta	0.120
	28 Croatia	0.120

Source: Own analysis with data from Eurobarometer 525 (European Commission, 2022).

optimisation was then conducted in order to obtain final cluster centres. Table 6.2 reveals the countries within each cluster, as well as the distances of the countries in each cluster from the cluster centre. The first thing to note is that the countries integrated within the seven groups resulting from *K*-means cluster analysis were exactly the same as those previously obtained through hierarchical analysis. This reinforces and adds statistical rigour to obtained results.

   K-means cluster analysis provides information on the most centred and peripheral countries within each of the seven clusters. The far-right column of Table 6.2 shows that the countries with the most centred positions within their clusters are Luxembourg (0.138) in cluster 1, West Germany (0.102) in cluster 2, Italy (0.133) in cluster 3, Denmark (0.151) in cluster 4 and Hungary (0.180) in cluster 6. In contrast, the Netherlands (0.265), Slovenia (0.259), Portugal (0.185), Finland (0.287) and Bulgaria (0.203) constitute the most peripheral countries from their respective cluster centres.

Table 6.3 Distances between final clusters centres

Cluster	1	2	3	4	5	6	7
1							
2	0.278						
3	0.363	0.390					
4	0.363	0.365	0.566				
5	0.327	0.367	0.405	0.510			
6	0.521	0.386	0.497	0.666	0.553		
7	0.421	0.413	0.458	0.586	0.457	0.304	

Source: Own analysis with data from Eurobarometer 525 (European Commission, 2022).

The distance between different cluster centres (Euclidean distance method) was also examined to verify that clusters sufficiently differed from one another. Outcomes presented in Table 6.3 show that the most distant clusters are cluster 4 (Northern European social democratic countries) and cluster 6 (former communist countries). However, large distances also emerge between the social democratic countries of Northern Europe (cluster 4) and the cluster formed by Malta and Croatia (cluster 7), on the one hand, and the Catholic countries of Southern Europe (cluster 3), on the other hand. The latter cluster is also significantly distant from cluster 5 (orthodox Southern European countries), cluster 6 (ex-communist countries) and cluster 7 (Malta and Croatia). In contrast, cluster 3 is less distant from Western European countries (cluster 1) and from Central and Northeastern European countries (cluster 2). Turning attention to cluster 5 (orthodox Southern European countries), this group is distanced from the social democratic countries of Northern Europe (cluster 4), as well as from the group of former communist countries (cluster 6). Finally, the smallest distance is found between clusters 1 and 2, although sufficient distance still emerged to be able to conclude that the two clusters are clearly separated.

Once the division into seven groups obtained through the cluster analysis has been presented, Table 6.4 shows the sporting profile of each cluster. The results have been obtained from the initial dataset of individuals, after creating a new variable to group the 27 EU countries into the seven clusters identified. To identify the existence of statistically significant differences between the clusters, the Chi-square test has been used. As revealed in Table 6.4 Chi-square test outcomes demonstrate that all variables make a significant contribution towards differentiating between the seven clusters

Countries in cluster 4 are characterised by very clearly marked sporting features. This cluster, which groups three countries usually included in the social democratic welfare model – Denmark, Sweden and Finland – reflects high scores for nine of the 12 variables under analysis. Moreover, in the case of six of these, the highest scores across all clusters were produced. Specifically, these variables pertained to playing sport on a weekly basis, engaging in sport at health or fitness centres, playing sport for the purpose of improving health, counteracting the effects of ageing

Table 6.4 Sports profiles of the clusters

	Clusters							Chi-square	
	1	2	3	4	5	6	7	Value	p
Sports activity (weekly)	48.4%	42.3%	31.4%	61.8%	25.6%	23.0%	30.6%	1772.73	<0.001
Sports activity at a health/fitness centre	12.2%	10.6%	18.2%	24.4%	21.7%	6.8%	9.6%	610.18	<0.001
Sports activity at a sports club	16.0%	9.1%	7.6%	10.8%	2.9%	4.9%	6.8%	367.07	<0.001
Sport activity at home	34.1%	50.7%	18.2%	45.6%	39.7%	59.1%	47.9%	1064.24	<0.001
Sports activity at the park/outdoors	45.4%	55.0%	51.0%	49.4%	48.3%	37.4%	21.6%	621.60	<0.001
To improve your health	55.2%	59.8%	52.5%	69.3%	61.5%	40.9%	46.2%	680.70	<0.001
To improve your physical appearance	15.8%	20.0%	27.1%	17.5%	22.8%	20.7%	25.0%	129.03	<0.001
To counteract the effects of ageing	17.0%	21.5%	13.5%	33.9%	13.5%	13.4%	16.0%	581.24	<0.001
To relax	46.7%	38.0%	37.8%	30.2%	54.2%	26.9%	34.9%	511.87	<0.001
To improve fitness	52.9%	40.9%	35.9%	53.7%	61.8%	31.8%	40.4%	669.85	<0.001
To control your weight	30.4%	25.0%	22.9%	33.7%	33.7%	19.2%	32.7%	283.31	<0.001
Health/fitness centre membership	15.9%	11.7%	11.0%	23.8%	11.3%	6.9%	13.6%	586.20	<0.001

Source: Own analysis with data from Eurobarometer 525 (European Commission, 2022).

and weight control and health/fitness centre membership. Countries in this cluster also scored highly (although not the highest) for variables pertaining to performing sports activities at home and playing sport in order to improve fitness. At the other end of the spectrum, this cluster was characterised by some of the lowest scores for playing sport in order to improve physical appearance.

Cluster 1 comprises four Western European countries with Catholic cultural backgrounds – Luxembourg, France, Belgium and Ireland – alongside the Netherlands. Countries in this cluster reported the highest scores for sport engagement at sports clubs, together with the lowest scores for sport engagement to improve physical appearance. Also of note are the above-average scores for weekly sport engagement and health/fitness centre membership and below-average scores for sport engagement at a health or fitness centre and at home. Cluster 2 stands out as being highly similar to this cluster. In fact, as already noted, clusters 1 and 2 represent the two closest clusters. Cluster 2 brings together five Central and Northeastern European countries that are geographically contiguous but have diverse cultural backgrounds and traditions, namely, Germany, Austria, Czechia, Latvia, Estonia and Slovenia. As noted above, the former two correspond to the conservative welfare regime, whilst the other four (along with part of Germany) are a part of the former Communist Bloc. This cluster is characterised by high scores for eight of the 12 variables under study. Amongst the variables with the highest scores, sport engagement at a park/outdoors stands out, alongside sport engagement both to improve health and to counteract the effects of ageing. As far as weekly sport engagement is concerned, scores are the third highest of all of the seven clusters, despite being far behind the scores reported by countries pertaining to cluster 4.

Cluster 3 groups together three countries with Catholic traditions in Southern Europe, namely, Italy, Spain and Portugal. These countries score highly in terms of playing sport at a health or fitness centre and at the park/outdoors, as well as in sport engagement to improve physical appearance. In contrast, countries in this cluster are less likely to play sport at a sports club and at home, whilst also being less likely to play sport as a means of counteracting the effects of ageing. Finally, health/fitness centre membership scores in the middle in relation to the other six clusters.

Cluster 5 groups together two more Southern European countries, namely, Greece and Cyprus. In the hypothetical case that the five-cluster solution would have been selected ahead of the seven-cluster solution, this cluster would have been merged with cluster 1. However, clear differences emerge between the countries in cluster 1 and the two countries in cluster 5, both in terms of cultural background and traditions – with countries in this latter cluster following Orthodox traditions – and in terms of patterns of sport participation. The only variables in which this cluster scores higher than the other clusters pertain to the reasons for playing sport, specifically, to relax, to control weight and to improve fitness. In contrast, this cluster registers low scores for two other variables, specifically, sport engagement activity at a sports club and health or fitness centre membership. Aside from these variables, moderate scores stand out for sport engagement at a health or fitness centre, as well as sport engagement as a means of improving health and physical appearance. On the other hand, low scores for weekly sport engagement should also be noted, as only one other cluster scored comparatively lower in this regard.

Finally, cluster 6 is composed entirely of former communist countries – Slovakia, Lithuania, Poland, Bulgaria, Romania and Hungary – while cluster 7 includes Croatia and Malta. As can be seen in Table 6.4, there are clear differences between the two clusters. Cluster 6 (former communist countries) produces the lowest scores of all clusters for seven variables, specifically, weekly sport engagement, health/fitness centre membership, sport engagement at a health or fitness centre and sport engagement for the four separate motives of health improvement, counteracting the effects of ageing, relaxation and improving fitness. On the other hand, this cluster only produced the highest scores for sport engagement at home, with scores corresponding to this cluster being amongst the lowest for all remaining variables. As far as cluster 7 is concerned, scores are mostly around average, with relatively high scores only emerging for playing sport as a means of improving physical appearance and weight control. In contrast, this last cluster is characterised by below-average scores for sport engagement at a health or fitness centre and at the park/outdoors.

Conclusions

This chapter has presented a ranking of the 27 EU member states based on most recent Eurobarometer Sport and Physical Activity data (European Commission, 2022). The study can be seen as a replication of a previous study conducted by Van Tuyckom with data from the 2004 Eurobarometer on the same topic (Van Tuyckom, 2013). The aim of this was to update this previously conducted analysis and extend it to encompass a larger number of variables in order to determine the landscape of prevailing sport culture across European society and paint a more accurate picture of the differing characteristics inherent to these various cultures. For this purpose, present research was grounded in the theoretical approach conceived by Inglehart and Welzel (2005), which considers the influence of interactional modernisation processes and cultural traditions on societal development. From this perspective, it was assumed that the nature of the evolution and transformation of sporting culture do not depend solely on the economic modernisation processes and trends towards the globalisation of social life affecting European nations, as cultural traditions continue to have a strong influence on the shaping of collective beliefs and behaviours.

Outcomes obtained through the statistical technique of hierarchical analysis reveal the existence of seven clusters, which was later fully verified by outcomes obtained through K-means cluster analysis. Profiles outlined for these seven clusters show a high degree of coherence with the theoretical starting point of the present work, insofar as all clusters reveal some link to their member countries' historical religious traditions and cultural or political trajectory, as well as to their geographical location. Thus, for example, countries comprised by cluster 6 are ex-Communist, whilst countries composing clusters 3 and 5 are located in Southern Europe and are characterised by a Mediterranean-type welfare regime with the caveat that the former cluster has an inherent Catholic tradition and the latter an Orthodox tradition. The three countries in cluster 4 are Nordic and belong to the social democratic welfare model. Four of the five countries in cluster 1 share common Catholic cultural traditions, whilst those in cluster 2 – in some ways the most heterogeneous of the seven – either correspond to the conservative welfare model or belonged to the former Communist Bloc.

This classification differs slightly from the six clusters previously described by Van Tuyckom (2013) using 2004 Eurobarometer data. With regards to Southern European countries, on that prior occasion, Greece, Italy and Portugal formed a single cluster, whist Cyprus and Malta were grouped in another cluster together with Slovenia. In contrast Spain, was included within a ten-country cluster that also included Belgium, Germany, France, Ireland, Luxembourg, the UK, Czechia and Slovakia. As for the Nordic countries, Finland and Sweden formed a single cluster together, whilst Denmark and the Netherlands joined Austria in a separate cluster. The final remaining cluster was composed of four former communist countries, namely, Hungary, Latvia, Lithuania and Poland. Changes in the composition of EU countries may have influenced the results obtained. Further, in the convening years between the 2004 and 2022 Eurobarometer, economic, cultural and sporting developments in each country are likely to have had an impact.

The cluster that emerges from the present analysis with the highest and most marked sporting patterns corresponds to Nordic countries under a social democratic welfare regime (cluster 4). These countries are characterised by the highest levels of weekly sport engagement, exhibit a strong orientation towards health, weight control and anti-ageing and, at the same time, have higher memberships to health or fitness centres. These sporting traits fit the profile of much more socio-economically developed countries. Cluster 2 shares some similarities with this aforementioned cluster, although relatively lower scores were produced for eight of the 12 sport participation variables. Aside from this, this cluster differs from cluster 4 in that its members are more likely to engage in sport at a park/outdoors and at home, but are much less likely to do so at health or fitness centres. Health-related motives for sport engagement are also seen to be important to these countries but to a lesser extent than that seen in cluster 4. Some of these patterns also appear in cluster 1. In this cluster, which comprises four countries with Catholic traditions alongside the Netherlands, weekly sport engagement is the second highest of all clusters, as is sport engagement at a sports club. However, the importance of motivational aspects related with health, weight control and counteracting the effects of ageing decreases slightly. On the other hand, sports clubs are very important in this cluster, both as a location of sporting engagement and in terms of membership rates.

Cluster 3 is made up of three countries with Catholic traditions but, in this case, this cluster comprises Southern European countries that form part of the so-called Mediterranean welfare model. Weekly sport engagement is significantly lower in this cluster compared to the previous three clusters. In terms of motivation, it should be noted that improving physical appearance emerges as a reason for physical activity to a greater extent than in all the other clusters. Further, sport is engaged in more at a park/outdoors and less at home. These trends are maintained, albeit with some nuances, in cluster 5, which is also made up of Southern European countries, although, in this case, member countries are typically Orthodox. Cluster 5 is more distant from the world of sports clubs, instead being the cluster that attributes greatest importance to relaxation and improving fitness as reasons for sport engagement. Finally, cluster 6 (ex-Communist countries) produced the lowest scores for weekly sport engagement, as well as for six other sport participation variables. This indicates a less-developed sporting culture.

The present study reveals that EU countries differ significantly in terms of their sports participation patterns, including aspects related to the frequency of sport engagement, the context in which sport is typically played, the main reasons or motives underlying sport engagement and the use of fitness or health centres as a physical space for playing sport. The differences discussed are not arbitrary and, instead, are related with the existence of a series of sporting enclaves or cultures that have been shaped by economic development and modernisation processes, as well as by the influence of political trajectories or cultural traditions inherent to each given society. As a result, the relationship Europeans hold with sport differs greatly according to their country's profile in light of the characteristics outlined for the seven clusters identified here. This means that the frequency with which sporting activities are undertaken, the location at which they take place, the reasons underlying them and the degree of membership to sporting organisations vary significantly between the seven sporting enclaves or cultures.

Conclusions reached by the present paper, however, are subject to several limitations. The first is that the work is limited to the 27 countries that currently make up the European Union. Certainly, no data are available on sport engagement at the European level beyond those provided by the Eurobarometer surveys on sport and physical activity, which are circumscribed to the member countries of the European Union. This ultimately means that a number of countries whose European affiliation is unquestionable are not considered by the present study preventing a complete analysis of sporting cultures from being performed. A second limitation pertains to the type of data used to classify sporting cultures. Data was exclusively gathered on sport engagement and, therefore, does not speak to other aspects (economic, political…) of national sports systems that are also important to be considered. Further, individual level data was obtained through interviews which is, therefore, subject to the limitations inherent to this type of approach. Finally, it should be noted that a wide range of sporting diversity may also exist within each nation, which the present study overlooks by considering each country as a unit of information. An alternative approach could have been to apply classification techniques to individual data instead of working with aggregated data at a national level. However, this would have made it more difficult to respond to some of the questions that the study sought to answer. Future research could, however, seek to take this approach when following up on the work presented in the present chapter.

References

Díaz de Rada, V. (2002). *Técnicas de análisis multivariante para investigación social y comercial*. Madrid: Rama Editorial.

DiMaggio, P. (1994). Culture and Economy. In N. J. Smelser and R. Swedberg (eds.), *The Handbook of Economic Sociology*. Princeton: Princeton University Press.

Esping-Andersen, G. (1990). *The three worlds of welfare capitalism*. London: Polity.

Esping-Andersen, G. (1999). *Social foundations of post-industrial economies*. Oxford: Oxford University Press.

European Commission (2004). *The citizens of the European Union and Sport (Special Eurobarometer 213)*. Brussels: European Commission.

European Commission (2010). *Sport and physical activity (Special Eurobarometer 334)*. Brussels: European Commission.

European Commission (2014). *Sport and physical activity (Special Eurobarometer 412)*. Brussels: European Commission.

European Commission (2018). *Sport and physical activity (Special Eurobarometer 472)*. Brussels: European Commission.

European Commission (2022). *Sport and physical activity (Special Eurobarometer 525)*. Brussels: European Commission.

Hair, J. F., Black, W. C., Babin, B. J. et al. (2014). *Multivariate data analysis*. 7th edition. Harlow: Pearson Education.

Heinemann, K. (1999). *Sport clubs in various European countries*. Schorndorf: Hofmann.

Inglehart, R. and Welzel, Ch. (2005). *Modernización, cambio cultural y democracia: la secuencia del desarrollo humano*. Madrid: Centro de Investigaciones Sociológicas.

Lago, I. (2008). *La lógica de la explicación en las ciencias sociales. Una introducción metodológica*. Madrid: Alianza Editorial.

Mandell, R. D. (1986). *Historia Cultural del Deporte*. Barcelona: Ediciones Bellaterra.

Putnam, R. D. (1993). *Making democracy work: civic traditions in modern Italy*. Princeton: Princeton University Press.

Van Tuyckom, Ch. (2011). *Sport for all: Fact or fiction? Individual and cross-national differences in sport participation from a European perspective*. Ghent, Belgium: Ghent University.

Van Tuyckom, Ch. (2013). Six sporting worlds: A cluster analysis of sports participation in the EU-25. *Quality and Quantity*, 47(1): 441–453.

Van Tuyckom, C. and Scheerder, J. (2008). Sport for all? Social stratification of recreational sport activities in the EU-27. *Kinesiologia Slovenica*, 14: 54–63.

Van Tuyckom, C. and Scheerder, J. (2010). Sport for all? Insight into stratification and compensation mechanisms of sporting activity in the EU-27. *Sport, Education and Society*, 15(4): 495–512.

Chapter 7

Redistribution and Solidarity in the European Model of Sport

Daniel Plumley and Rob Wilson

Introduction

Before we begin to explore redistribution and solidarity mechanisms present in the European Model of Sport, it is first requisite that we outline a range of broader economic principles and their relevant application to the sporting field. In doing so, we will also outline why redistribution and solidarity is an argument focused on professional team sports rather than individual pursuits and competitions. Professional team sport economics do not always function like regular economic markets. It is a unique ecosystem and often an irrational one. These pursuits are unique; and to explore and explain this uniqueness further we need to grasp some key market functions such as league structure, uncertainty of outcome and competitive balance, the economic models of professional team sports, and profit and utility maximisation. All these functions influence revenue generation for teams within league structures, and it is how that revenue is distributed that is of most interest to this chapter.

Professional team sports and economics are inextricably linked, intertwining perfectly to promote interest to different stakeholder groups within the professional team sport environment. This is not just confined to the boardrooms of individual clubs, league organisers, or sport governing bodies. It stretches far wider, to the players, the fans, and the communities that the clubs and leagues interact with in a broader societal context, becoming part of the fabric of our lives. A necessity of existence for many. Put simply, professional team sports are of interest to us, and they lend themselves to economic analysis (Plumley and Wilson, 2022).

We put this down to two main factors. First, the nature of professional team sport as opposed to sport more generally. Second, the worldwide growth (or globalisation) and commercialisation of sport. You can consider any major structural change in professional team sport and analyse it through an economic framework. The growth of the English Premier League (EPL) and the future potential for growth in the English Women's Super League (football). The shift to professionalism in rugby union. The emergence of shorter format versions in cricket. Every single example will illustrate the impact of economic principles at their core. A discussion on these principles is naturally lengthy, and beyond the scope of this

DOI: 10.4324/9781032665153-8

chapter. However, for those interested, Downward and Dawson's, *The economics of professional team sport* published in 2000, or the more recent *The economics and finance of professional team sport*, 2022, by the authors of this chapter, are a good place to start.

Professional team sports comprise of leagues and clubs who will compete on the sporting 'field' by arrangement. This arrangement will be made by those who govern the sport. For example, in English football this might be the Football Association (FA) but there are also the individual competition organisers to consider such as the EPL. In American sports, the governing body is just one organisation (e.g., the National Basketball Association (NBA) or the National Football League (NFL)). Generally, we can measure the success of each team by their standing in the league at the end of a season. Nowadays, points also mean prizes, and each position in the league table can be worth an extra couple of million pounds on the income statement. It is here that we perhaps begin to get to the crux of the issue. Principally, what matters to many of these stakeholders is the opportunity to generate revenue – which leads to an ability to buy players, build stadia, and potentially make profits. The production, distribution, and consumption of sport are what causes such money to change hands and present sporting teams with a dilemma regarding their twin objectives (Plumley and Wilson, 2022).

These two objectives cover sporting and financial performance. Teams must maintain a high level of on-field performance and simultaneously attempt to maximise off-field commercial business operations in the pursuit of revenue gains (Plumley and Wilson, 2022). The challenge in professional team sport is that the cost side of the equation (e.g., player wages) is considerably high, which makes balancing these two objectives challenging. In many cases, teams are reliant on the redistribution of league wealth to sustain the pursuit of short-term sporting success. Thus, the concept of 'earned' and 'unearned' revenue is a relevant discussion within redistribution, a concept that we unpack later in this chapter.

What is obvious is that we cannot separate the on-field/off-field juxtaposition. In practice, this means professional sport teams and leagues require a level of coopetition (defined as simultaneous cooperation and competition (Brandenburger and Nalebuff, 1996)). Opponents are competitors on the field of play, and they need each other to produce the competition and, by association, the product (a match). This reality forces teams to become joint economic partners (Plumley and Wilson, 2022) – without two competing teams you have no product (no match). Consequently, professional team sports are intrinsically different from other more mainstream businesses. In these scenarios, a firm is likely to prosper if it can eliminate competition and establish a position as a monopoly supplier (Dobson and Goddard, 2011). In sport, however, it does not pay for one team to establish such a position due to the joint nature of 'production' in sports – you can only have a match if you have two teams. Moreover, economic analysis also proves that leagues with single-team dominance do not prosper in an economic environment (see, for example, Vrooman (2009) in an American sport context and Gasparetto et al. (2023) in European football). Redistribution and solidarity payments, therefore, have a vital role to play in the ecosystem to protect the environment and, theoretically at least, attempting to maintain sporting integrity.

Models of Professional Team Sport and Profit versus Utility/'Win' Maximisation

As this book debates, the European Model of Sport can be argued as being a policy construct. Some actors agree with it, others disagree. Some will even say it does not exist. The debate is as much about how to define the model as it is about how such a model guide sport regulation in Europe. The model is often portrayed as a socio-cultural way of understanding sport, opposed to the more commercially driven American Model of Sport. It is not the point of this chapter to get drawn into a socio-cultural debate. That is a different matter. What can be determined is that the European Model of Sport is an always evolving policy construct that actors tend to use for their own benefit in policy negotiations. This notion of collective action versus vested self-interest links back to professional sport teams as joint economic partners and is something we refer to later in this chapter when we begin to put pound signs at the end of arguments.

To understand how money flows within the model, we first need to define the features of the model. A natural comparison would be to consider the European Model of Sport and the American model separately. However, this conversation also transcends sport, to a degree. Some features of the European Model of Sport are embedded within the European Commission itself – which is effectively the European Union's (EU) politically independent executive arm. It defines some key organisational structures of the European model such as the pyramidal and hierarchical structure of governance with one federation per sport that sits at the top of the pyramid and open competitions that promote the principle of sporting merit through promotion and relegation. These features are often defined in stark contrast to the American model of sport. American sports have different governance principles regarding some of these features. For example, instead of having open league structures, the predominant approach is a closed leagues system. One that lacks the critical European feature of promotion or relegation. This protects the financial value of the franchises (teams) participating in the competition. Moreover, it also cements the concept of profit maximisation for franchise owners. That is to say, they run teams to extract financial return on their investments. In American team sports, revenue (from broadcasting, ticket sales, and other merchandise) is often also shared equally amongst the franchises. Alongside the draft system, which promotes the best-performing college athletes to the worst-performing team each season, these principles protect the sporting integrity of the competitions and promote competitive balance, more than is seen in other sports in Europe.

By contrast, the European model rarely shares revenue equally and operates a transfer market where players can move freely, sometimes for agreed fees, sometimes via the end of contracts, between teams. This 'transfer' system replaces the

American 'draft system'. The final key feature of American sports is a salary cap, aimed to promote cost control. While some European sports (e.g., rugby union and rugby league) have introduced salary caps they have also retained other principles of open leagues and unequal revenue sharing. This can result in problems with salary cap adherence and wage control. Football is perhaps the best example for spiralling costs, having never deployed a salary and wage control system, these costs have initiated significant financial sustainability issues since the sport began.

The differentiated approach to the operation of the economic model mean that the unique features create a disconnect in strategy with American sports and owner motives geared towards a return on investment (profit maximisation) whereas the European model, with open leagues, revenue gaps between teams and no cost control, has fuelled a strategy of a 'winner takes all' approach based on maximising short-term sporting performance (utility maximisation). It is these factors, and the way in which they are regulated by the hierarchical structures of governance in the European model, that has led to significant financial gaps between teams and leagues, some of which is directly attributable to the distribution and solidarity payment mechanisms.

Revenue Generation and Mix

Any distribution or solidarity mechanism is dependent on money coming into the system. Revenue generation in the European Model of Sport is unique because both leagues and member teams generate their own revenue, but the league then distributes some of that revenue to its member teams. As such, we need to appreciate the revenue mix of professional sport teams and the notion of 'earned' and 'unearned' income at team level. Put simply, the revenue mix is the breakdown of different revenue components that added together make up the total revenue for the company. The word 'mix' is commonly used because analysts want to know how many different components make up the total revenues. More crucially, however, they will also be interested in the 'mix' or split of these revenues as a proportion of the total. This will allow businesses to determine where their major income streams are, where the potential for growth in revenue potentially lies and how to navigate risk through the revenue mix. Professional sport teams have a relatively simple revenue mix. Their revenue only comes from three main sources: matchday revenue, commercial revenue, and broadcasting revenue. These revenue streams have evolved considerably over the course of history as the world of sport has become more commercialised, particularly at the elite end. Two are earned by the team itself (matchday and commercial) and one is unearned (broadcasting) as that money comes into the league first before it is redistributed proportionally to teams.

By way of an example, let us consider professional football. In 2022, Tottenham Hotspur FC generated total revenues of €523 million. This comprised €125 million (24%) matchday income, €215 million (41%) commercial income and €182 million (35%) broadcast income. Leicester City FC, who competed in the same Premier League as Tottenham Hotspur FC in 2022–2023, posted total revenue of €252 million for the same season comprised €25 million (10%) match-day income, €50 million (20%) commercial income and €177 million (70%) broadcast income. The overall revenue gap between these two clubs – who compete in the same league – is significant (€271 million). However, the revenue mix is also a cause for concern, particularly as broadcast income is 'unearned' by the club and determined by the league organisers – in this case the EPL – although each member team has voting rights. Tottenham Hotspur, boosted by a new stadium completed in 2019, show a relatively balanced revenue mix. Of course, it is unlikely that any club will achieve a 33% split across the three areas, but Tottenham's is not too far away from equilibrium. Leicester City, by contrast, are reliant on unearned income for 70% of their overall revenue. This is okay while you are competing in the league that provides you with that figure, but at the end of the 2022–2023 season, Leicester City were relegated to the Championship (tier 2 of English football). Owing to the broadcasting distribution and solidarity payment mechanism present in English football (covered in more detail in the next section), the club saw c.£60 million wiped off their broadcasting revenue overnight, placing strain not only on the total revenue line, with high costs still to pay, but also the ability to generate revenue from their other two mix components in the league below. Imagine owning and running a 'normal' business where you are not in direct control of a revenue stream that accounts for 71% of your overall revenue. We would imagine you would be concerned!

As an alternative to a football club, we can also point to the English cricket system. In England, cricket is unique in its structure in that it does not have a private league organiser that sells broadcasting rights. Instead, the governing body of the sport in England (the England and Wales Cricket Board – ECB) deal with the broadcasting rights of the English national test team and then use some of that money to provide central grant funding to the domestic teams (counties). The result of this is shown in the revenue mix of Yorkshire County Cricket Club, one of the clubs in the system.

Yorkshire CCC break their income down slightly differently to the football clubs outlined above; however, we can still break this down into three main streams of matchday (ticket revenues and subscriptions), commercial (commercial income and other income) and broadcasting (effectively the ECB grant). Yorkshire CCC had total revenue of £14.1 million in 2022, comprised of £6.1 million in ticket revenue, £3.7 million in commercial revenue and £4.3 million from the ECB grant. The financial risk of unearned income here in respect of the ECB grant is the same risk with Leicester City FC and broadcasting. Additionally, in English county cricket we can see the importance of a strong English test side and hosting international test matches for the counties. Yorkshire CCC generated £4.2 million in ticket sales from England Test Matches and One-Day Internationals but only £1.5 million from their own domestic tickets sales to watch the actual county side. The number of zeros on the end of the number may differ across sports in the European model, but the balancing act of revenue mix remains complex. The precarious nature of unearned income through broadcasting also needs further analysis linked to distribution and solidarity payments in the ecosystem.

Broadcasting Rights, Distribution and Solidarity

As we saw earlier with the Leicester City example, to some, broadcasting is the most important revenue stream of them all. To outline the reasons why, we need a brief history lesson. The amount of revenue earned from television broadcasting deals for leagues and teams has grown exponentially since the early 1990s and has been primarily responsible for pushing team revenues forward. However, as we will see from some of the data in this section, it has once again benefitted only (for the most part) the teams at the very top of their respective sports and has in some way led to greater financial imbalances between leagues within certain countries – something that you will remember is supposedly not good for competition. To contextualise this further, there is an excellent quote from Morrow (2003) regarding television's relationship with football. We have amended this quote below slightly to include the word sport as we feel it holds true not just for football, but plenty of other sports in the model:

> Football's (sport's) relationship with TV is a paradox. On the one hand, television has been responsible for substantially increasing the revenues available across many different sports. At the same time, it is those very revenues, or rather the manner in which they are shared out, that has most undermined competitive league balance and has led to the emergence of financially dominant leagues and financially dominant super clubs.
>
> (Morrow, 2003)

Let us consider this quote against some of the biggest television broadcasting deals in sport. We add in the American sport for context, before focusing solely on European sports and using football as the unique case study to illustrate the breakdown of distribution and solidarity payments across a single industry. The biggest television deals in professional team sports as of 2023 are presented in Figure 7.1 below.

We can see from Figure 7.1 that the NFL is the market leader when it comes to the most lucrative television deals with the NBA and MLB the clear second and third. The Indian Premier League (IPL) cricket franchise league takes fourth spot on the list before the figure becomes dominated by European football leagues taking up five of the remaining seven spots. The EPL is the market leader in football although others have closed the gap (in domestic terms at least) in recent years.

If we focus on the domestic rights picture, the dominance of American sport becomes clear. American sports have historically been quite insular – relying on significant audiences across North America – and have not tended to generate large international television rights deals. Judging by the numbers in Figure 7.1, perhaps they don't need to, but some American sports have begun to shift their focus to

Total Domestic TV Rights ($bn)

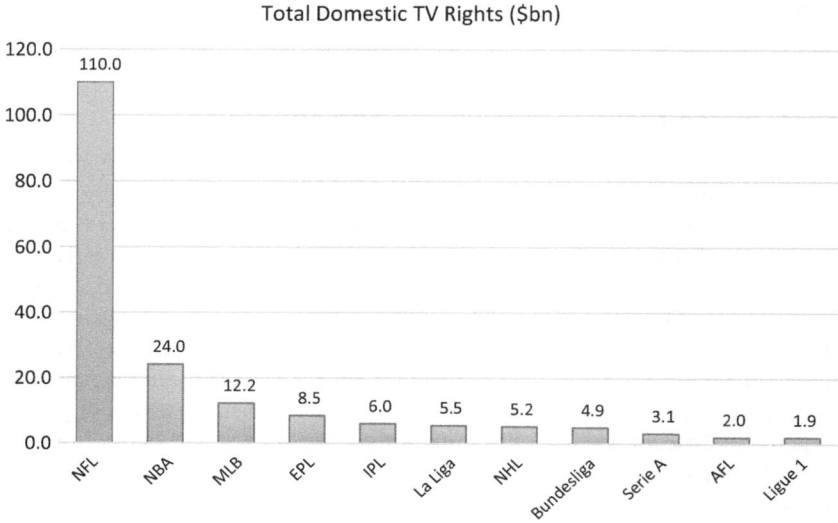

Figure 7.1 The biggest (domestic) TV deals in sport 2023.

an overseas audience to consider future growth (e.g., the NFL hosting games in England Germany, or Mexico; the NBA hosting games in Paris). American sport television deals tend to be signed on longer contracts, too. The NFL deal, for example, is eleven years long, running from 2022 to 2033 and the others follow a similar pattern. The NBA is a nine-year deal, the MLB is a seven-year deal, and the NHL is a 12-year deal. This is a good strategy as it protects the price and reduces risk for a longer period. However, signing a shorter deal, if you have a product that is attractive, could be considered more beneficial as you have the ability for more faster growth assuming you can sell for a higher price. The latter strategy has been the direction of travel for European football leagues since the early 2000s and the EPL has been at the forefront of growth. The EPL deal in Figure 7.1 is a four-year deal running from 2025 to 2029 and if we consider this contract on a per season basis it pushes clear of its nearest rivals in football and outstrips MLB in America.

However, Figure 7.1 still does not tell us the full story. If we factor in international television rights, the picture changes again. Part of the reason for this, as mentioned earlier, is that American sports tend to be American centred in terms of broadcasting. For example, all four big American sports have their deals with domestic providers. The NFL have deals with CBS, Fox, NBC and ESPN. The NBA have deals with ESPN and TNT, and the MLB have deals with Fox, TBS, ESPN. The NHL has its deal exclusively with the Canadian Network (up until 2024 at least). The difference in the European football market is the value of the overseas broadcasting market, once again dominated by the EPL. The EPL has made significant gains in the international market over the years, so much so that the total value for the 2019–2022 cycle was closer to £9.2 billion ($12.7 billion).

In the 2022–2025 cycle, the total value was estimated (because the league does not publish the specifics of overseas rights) to be closer to £10 billion, with overseas rights outstripping domestic rights for the first time ever. Once the total pot is confirmed for 2025–2029, it is likely to be more of the same. Additionally, in 2019, the 'big 6' clubs in the EPL managed to secure a vote so that the international rights are now split based partly on merit payments (they used to be split equally). More on that later.

Other leagues in European football have closed the gap in international rights value recently but still lag some way the EPL. For example, as of 2021, international rights in Serie A in Italy were only worth 21.3% of the overall total and in the Bundesliga in Germany (16.9%) and Ligue 1 in France (10.9%) they were even lower. So, if the market power for broadcasting in the European model is in football, what about other sports? How do they compare in terms of their broadcasting deals? First things first, unlike football, many of the so-called smaller sporting competitions do not publish their data, so it is not always easy to get figures, yet a small sample is provided below for context. If we look at both codes of rugby in the United Kingdom (UK), we can see the financial disparity between sports compared to football. Rugby union in the UK signed a three-year deal with BT Sport in 2021 that was worth a total of £110 million, equivalent to c.£36.6 million per season. Remember, the EPL generates around £9 million per match! The deal for rugby league was estimated to be worth £29 million per season between 2023 and 2026, but that was down from a £40 million per season deal up until 2021. In this previous deal, the Super League (and its clubs) received £30 million and the Rugby Football League (RFL) received £10 million. This was quite unique at the time. The EPL, for example, do not provide the FA with any share of its television deal. However, the same arrangement did not appear to be in place for the next deal signed so it may be that it was just a flash in the pan. In cricket in England, where we know the ECB provide central funding to the clubs, recent deals have eclipsed those found in rugby. The deal signed for English cricket in 2020 (to run until 2024) with Sky Sports and the BBC was worth £1.1 billion in total and £220 million per year. This deal guaranteed each county an extra £1.3 million and, crucially, it brought cricket back to free-to-air television for the first time in England since 2005.

Data is hard to obtain for other sports in Europe. For example, the EuroLeague basketball television deal is reported to be around €42.5 million in 2023 but there is no detail about how many years the deal relates to. Other sports in Europe such as volleyball and handball do have television deals with a range of pay-tv platforms across Europe, but the total amount is not disclosed. It is also difficult to obtain exact figures in other sports because of their complexity. For example, for a sport such as Formula 1, the deal breakdowns become infinitely more complex. This is because Formula 1 has multiple rights holders all over the world, owing to the structure of its competition (e.g., Grand Prix are hosted in different countries). This means it is a sport that does not operate in individual countries, unlike the sports we have discussed so far. However, Formula 1 is also hugely popular because of this fact. Indeed, in 2017 it was estimated that 352 m watched the sport on television.

That is one of the largest sport television audiences (in total) after the World Cup (football) and Olympic Games. In terms of the value of the broadcasting contract for Formula 1, in 2021 it was estimated that the Sky Sports deal was worth an estimated $240 million per year. Sport broadcasting makes up a huge part of the financial landscape of professional sport and has grown exponentially since the turn of the most recent millennium. It has been responsible for growing club revenues and pushing sports, teams and leagues into global marketplaces allowing them to further extend their commercial reach by engaging new fans. However, as Morrow (2003) pointed out, it is the way they are shared out, that has created issues for competitive league balance and has led to the emergence of financial gaps between leagues, dominant leagues, and financially dominant super clubs. We will again turn to football as our case study example to deconstruct this notion.

European Football Broadcasting Distribution and Solidarity

Each league within the big five in Europe (EPL, La Liga, Bundesliga, Serie A, and Ligue 1) operate their own broadcasting distributions with their own league. The EPL is perceived to be the fairest and most equitable in Europe with regards to its percentage split (note the percentages cited here are based on domestic deals only). The EPL allocates 50% of domestic broadcasting rights equally amongst all 20 teams in the league. It then allocates 25% based on performance in the current season defined as a merit payment. This is in relation to the finishing position of teams in the table. In 2022–2023, each position in the Premier League was worth around £2 million in additional broadcasting revenue. A further 25% is allocated based on the number of televised fixtures a club is allocated in the given season. This can vary depending on the club in question. Each club must be shown on television a minimum of ten times per season but there is no upper limit.

La Liga's distribution mechanism is very similar with just a couple of slight tweaks. They have moved closer to the EPL model after historically letting the big clubs dominate the market. In the early 2010s, it was commonplace for Real Madrid and Barcelona to be taking around 50% of the total pot just for themselves and La Liga's move to a fairer model of distribution was well received by the other member clubs at the time. They also now allocate 50% equally, 25% based on performance (but based on the last completed season not the current one) and 25% for viewership (but they include both stadium and TV viewership in this calculation). This still gives the bigger clubs a slight advantage as they typically have more fans and bigger stadiums, but it does appease other member clubs to a degree. Serie A (Italy) and Ligue 1 (France) also allocate 50% of broadcasting revenues equally and Serie A also follow La Liga's viewership principle of stadium and TV viewership (20%). Serie A's remaining 30% is performance based with 15% based on last season, 10% based on the last five seasons and 5% based on historical performance (this is not explicitly stated but it is rumoured that is stretches back to as far as the 1946/47 season!). Ligue 1 choose to split their remaining 50% across the last season (30%) and the last five seasons (20%). The Bundesliga (Germany) is an outlier against these other four leagues. It allocates 93% of the total broadcasting pot based on the last five seasons. This figure is also weighted so that 70% of the 93% is kept for Bundesliga clubs with a further 23% distributed to the lower leagues. The Bundesliga then gives a further 5% to its top tier clubs based on historical performance and the final 2% is based on playing time of players that have come through the club's academy system. It is the only football league, to our knowledge, that distribute broadcasting money based on academy playing time.

As we can see, the distribution mechanisms can be quite complex and different across leagues within the same sport. As such, we need to also focus our attention on not just the total value and the overall split, but the gap that such a split creates between clubs within a league and the overall amount of money distributed to each club. We noted earlier that the EPL is perceived to be the fairest distribution mechanism across European football, and this is largely due to its top to bottom distribution gap. In the EPL, based on figures for the 2022–2023 season, the broadcasting revenue gap between the top club and bottom is 1.6x. The next best on the list is Serie A in Italy (2.9x) followed by Ligue 1 in France (3.2x). La Liga and Bundesliga both have a top club to bottom club ratio of 3.8x. Such gaps can be attributed back to the distribution system including factors such as stadium viewership and historical performance, which creates a situation where the big clubs continue to stretch away from the rest and a larger revenue gap is the result. Whilst we cannot ascertain full data on the breakdown of figures for each club within each league, we can provide a worked example for the EPL (for season 2021/22) in terms of club-by-club income based on the broadcasting distribution (see Table 7.1).

Table 7.1 outlines the relative fairness in the distribution model of the EPL in relation to other leagues in Europe. The gap between the highest earning team in 2022 (title winning Manchester City) to the lowest earning team (relegated Norwich City) was £52.4 million. There is still a considerable difference, but in terms of a top to bottom ratio it is far better than the EPL's European counterparts, even when the distribution model still favours the big clubs overall. They are likely to be shown more on television and command greater facility fee payments as a result. Again, note Manchester City's 28 live television appearances in Table 7.1 versus Norwich City's 12 (the joint lowest on the list alongside Southampton and the other two relegated clubs Burnley and Watford). On the numbers relating to international rights, note the merit payment column, which used to be shared equally and is now weighted based on overall finishing position. The EPL is the fairest distribution in the big five European leagues, but it still looks after its biggest clubs internally.

Greater disparity and financial imbalance arise when we consider how (some of) this money trickles down to the leagues below (most notably the English Football League) through solidarity and parachute payments. The EPL passes on some of its broadcasting wealth to the three leagues directly below it (The English Football League Championship, English Football League 1, and English Football League 2).

Table 7.1 EPL TV payments to clubs 2021/22.

Club	Domestic rights (UK)				International rights		Central commercial	Total payment
	Live TV	Equal share	Facility fees	Merit payment	Equal share	Merit payments		
Manchester City	28	31,809,969	24,436,525	33,779,160	48,885,768	7,365,240	6,814,232	153,090,894
Liverpool	29	31,809,969	25,274,331	32,090,202	48,885,768	6,996,978	6,814,232	151,871,480
Chelsea	24	31,809,969	21,085,299	30,401,244	48,885,768	6,628,716	6,814,232	145,625,228
Tottenham Hotspur	27	31,809,969	23,598,718	28,712,286	48,885,768	6,260,454	6,814,232	146,081,427
Arsenal	29	31,809,969	25,274,331	27,023,328	48,885,768	5,892,192	6,814,232	145,699,820
Manchester United	28	31,809,969	24,436,525	25,334,370	48,885,768	5,523,930	6,814,232	142,804,794
West Ham United	23	31,809,969	20,247,493,	23,645,412	48,885,768	5,155,668	6,814,232	136,558,542
Leicester City	16	31,809,969	14,382,847	21,956,454	48,885,768	4,787,406	6,814,232	128,636,676
Brighton & Hove Albion	15	31,809,969	13,545,041	20,267,496	48,885,768	4,419,144	6,814,232	125,741,650
Wolverhampton Wanderers	16	31,809,969	14,382,847	18,578,538	48,885,768	4,050,882	6,814,232	124,522,236
Newcastle United	21	31,809,969	18,571,880	16,889,580	48,885,768	3,682,620	6,814,232	126,654,049
Crystal Palace	16	31,809,969	14,382,847	15,200,622	48,885,768	3,314,358	6,814,232	120,407,796
Brentford	16	31,809,969	14,382,847	13,511,664	48,885,768	2,946,096	6,814,232	118,350,576
Aston Villa	20	31,809,969	17,734,073	11,822,706	48,885,768	2,577,834	6,814,232	119,644,582
Southampton	12	31,809,969	11,031,621	10,133,748	48,885,768	2,209,572	6,814,232	110,884,910
Everton	22	31,809,969	19,409,686	8,444,790	48,885,768	1,841,310	6,814,232	117,205,755
Leeds United	22	31,809,969	19,409,686	6,755,832	48,885,768	1,473,048	6,814,232	115,148,535
Burnley	12	31,809,969	11,031,621	5,066,874	48,885,768	1,104,786	6,814,232	104,713,250
Watford	12	31,809,969	11,031,621	3,377,916	48,885,768	736,524	6,814,232	102,656,030
Norwich City	12	31,809,969	11,031,621	1,688,958	48,885,768	368,262	6,814,232	100,598,810
		636,199,380	354,681,180	354,681,180	977,715,360	77,335,020	136,284,640	2,536,897,044

Source: Data from premier league website (2022).

The English Football League television deal (expiring in 2024) sees the money distributed down from the EPL via solidarity payments structured as follows (data relates to per season breakdowns). The English Football League's own central revenues (media rights, sponsorships, and various levies) deliver a total of £132 million to the collective group of clubs (72 in total). An additional £130 million in solidarity payments is also passed down from the EPL. However, a further c.£200 million is also distributed in parachute payments to recently relegated clubs from the EPL and only half a dozen or so clubs share this money each year. For example, the relegated clubs (in 2022/23) of Leeds United, Leicester City, and Southampton received £47.8 million each in the season immediately following relegation (2023/24). If they fail to bounce back to the Premier League, they will all get another £39.1 million in 2024/25 and a further £17.4 million payment if they are still in the English Football League for a third season (2025/26). The addition of parachute payments plus solidarity payments means that the EPL deliver c.£350 million to the English Football League in any given season under the terms of the broadcasting deal in play up until 2024. If a club is not in receipt of parachute payments and only receives solidarity payments and EFL central revenues, then the payment per club is as follows.

Championship

On a per club basis, each Championship side receives £5.19 million in solidarity money – directly coming from the EPL's domestic and international rights – and an additional £3.92 million from central income, via the EFL. Total broadcast income of approximately £9 million.

League One

On a per club basis, each League One team receives £780,000 in solidarity payments, and an additional £950,000 in central EFL payments. Total broadcast revenue equates to £1,730,000.

League Two

On a per club basis, each League Two club receives £520,000 in solidarity from the EPL, and a further £640,000 in central payments. Total broadcast revenue equates to £1,160,000.

The figures above show a clear revenue disparity between the EPL and the English Football League, fuelled by solidarity and parachute payments. A non-parachute payment club earns c.£9 million in broadcast money per season whereas a newly relegated club competing in the same league receives £47.8 million. That means that the three relegated clubs are approximately £39 million ahead of an average Championship club before a ball is even kicked. So much for the joint nature of production and coopetition argument! The authors of this chapter conducted some research into parachute payments and competitive balance in the Championship in 2019; the findings supported this stark revenue disparity and the challenges facing non-parachute payment clubs in the Championship. Our results showed that an increase in the number of clubs with parachute payments and the overall value of these payments coincided with a reduction in competitive balance in the Championship. Furthermore, clubs with parachute payments were twice as likely to be promoted to the EPL and considerably less likely to suffer further relegation to the third tier (League 1). At the time, our paper proposed either a redistribution of parachute payments, the abolition of them completely, or a handicap points system to improve competitive balance. We updated this work directly for the English Football League in 2022 and our findings and recommendations remained the same.

A Fluid Policy Construct

Much like the European Model of Sport being viewed as a fluid policy construct, the future of English football television rights and distribution mechanisms may change in the future. At the time of writing this chapter, a new broadcasting deal in English football, to commence from the start of the 2025/26 season has recently been ratified. The full detail is not yet published but it is likely that this deal will deliver a revised distribution model, intending to provide a more equal share of broadcast revenues across the English football market. It's likely that this new approach is a direct response by the EPL to sidestep government pressure to stem the game's structural cashflow challenges, following the establishment of lobby group Fair Game, and the government white paper on the establishment of an independent regulator for football.

Despite ongoing pressure from the English Football League and government lobbyists, including the authors of this chapter, the EPL seems unwilling to scrap parachute payments – instead spreading the revenue equally (in relative proportions) across the English Football League – thus a new proposal has been tabled which may change the landscape in the future. The counterproposal (to the scrapping of parachute payments) is for the leagues to combine their net media rights and share 14.75% of that figure in solidarity payments, with a further 4.56% ring fenced for relegated clubs – to be called financial sustainability payments. This package totals c.20% of the net media rights and provides money to the Professional Footballers Association, the National League (tier below the English Football League) and football related charities.

The plan to execute this new proposal will be a two-season transition period, with the only change in formula being an immediate £88 million boost to the solidarity fund. Additionally, there will also be the inclusion of a merit-based element or 'merit rake' mirroring the EPL model where a portion of the central distribution depends on your teams finishing position. In total, the 2025–2026 fund would then stand at £733 million – £234 million more than under the current model. This drops to £466 million when excluding parachute payments, which is still £169 million higher than past values under the historical model. In terms of 'merit rakes', the model is steeper than in the EPL. Championship clubs will operate with a rake of 2:1 – meaning that the club that finishes first will have a merit payment twice as big as the team that finishes last. In League One the proposal is set at 1.5:1 and in League Two, 1.25:1. There is also a plan to make a significant change for the Championship which will see it share its money unequally within each division. The proposal suggests that the Championship's distribution model should be further enhanced by performance metrics with a 33/67 split between merit and equal shares. The proposed splits in League One and League Two are 80/20 and 90/10, respectively. We still do not quite know what the future holds, but the proposals on the table appear to suggest that the leagues are aware that financial imbalance and sporting integrity is a challenge that they need to tackle, regardless of whether or not there is also a vested interest bubbling under the surface in respect of the EPL to stave off the imposing threat of independent regulation in the game.

Parachute payments in English football tend to dominate the headlines because of the numbers involved and the arguments we have presented in the above discussion. However, it is also important to consider the amount of parachute payments distributed throughout other European leagues, circling back to our starting point of the big five leagues. Serie A in Italy, provides parachute payments for one season only, comprised of €10 million if the club is relegated after one season, €15 million if the club is relegated after two seasons (out of the last 3) and €25 million if the club is relegated after three seasons (out of the last four). La Liga also only provides parachute payments for one season which is based on 3.5% of the total broadcasting rights spent in La Liga, split according to previous broadcasting deals and seasons spent in the league. Ligue 1 provide parachute payments across two years with a fixed and variable aspect to the payments in both years. The variable amount is based on the number of seasons the club has spent in Ligue 1 in the last ten years. The Bundesliga, again, does things slightly differently. They do not provide any parachute payments at all as broadcasting revenues are already split between Bundesliga 1 and 2.

Conclusion

In this chapter, we have presented the background and development of revenue distribution models and how they can promote debate across many European professional sports. We have focused mostly on professional team sports as they operate under unique financial structures under the principles of joint production and coopetition. There are many different types of redistribution mechanisms present in the European Model of Sport, all of which have a significant impact on sporting integrity and competition.

The role of governing bodies and league organisers to control revenue distribution among its members is vital in this regard and they must prioritise collective action over vested self-interest. This is a challenge because clubs have a member vote on proposals of change in the league regulation. It is also a challenge as the broadcast market evolves in the future, particularly in relation to streaming platforms, vertical channels and different ways of packaging and selling television rights to international fans in a direct-to-consumer model. Clubs want control over these areas directly, to drive revenue diversification and remove the pressure on the unearned aspect of broadcasting through the league organisers. In our abstract for this chapter, we said we would consider the claim that redistribution is a cornerstone of the European Model of Sport. We believe this to be the case, based on the data we have provided, but we also propose that it needs to shift in the future to evolve alongside the industry and wider societal changes.

Historical structures have in some ways created a financial gap between leagues and competition, which has further disrupted the landscape regarding business sustainability and sporting competitive balance. The European Model of Sport is, and will remain, unique. A shift to a brand-new model, or a replication of the American model is, quite frankly, utopian, and in many ways the wrong argument to even propose. Instead, stakeholders must continue to review the current distribution and solidarity mechanisms, considering the financial implications and the principles of the joint nature of production in professional team sports, without which there would not be a product to sell in the first place.

References

Brandenburger, A., & Nalebuff, B. (1996). *Co-Opetition: A Revolutionary Mindset That Combines Competition and Cooperation: The Game Theory Strategy That's Changing the Game of Business*. New York, NY: Doubleday.

Dobson, S., & Goddard, J. (2011). *The Economics of Football* (2nd ed.). Cambridge, University Press.

Gasparetto, T., Mishchenko, D., & Zaitsev, E. (2023). Factors influencing competitive balance across European football top tier leagues. *Managerial and Decision Economics*, *44*(4), 2068–2078.

Morrow, S. (2003). *The People's Game: Football, Finance and Society*. London: Palgrave Macmillan.

Plumley, D., & Wilson, R. (2022). *The Economics and Finance of Professional Team Sports*. London, Routledge: Taylor & Francis.

Vrooman, J. (2009). Theory of the perfect game: Competitive balance in monopoly sports leagues. *Review of Industrial Organization*, *34*(1), 5–44.

Part II

Models of Sport in Europe

Chapter 8

The Scandinavian Sport Model

Jörg Krieger and Svein Erik Nordhagen

Introduction

The three Scandinavian countries of Denmark, Norway, and Sweden,[1] located on the Northern peninsula of Europe, have a rich sporting culture on the recreational and elite levels in both summer and winter times. Compared with other European nations, Scandinavian citizens are more frequently physically active and consequently have different perspectives on the sport system than in regions with less direct involvement in sport (Seippel, 2010; Green et al., 2019). According to the *Fifth Eurobarometer on Sport and Physical Activity* (European Union, 2022), Danes and Swedes are the European residents most likely to exercise sport or physical activity in their free time – together with individuals from neighbouring country Finland. While Norway is not represented in this study, more than half of all Norwegians over 16 years old reported in 2021 that they had exercised more than one time per week over the last 12 months (Statistics Norway, 2021).

This high engagement is also reflected in Norway's elite sport success. The 5.4 million citizen country topped the medal tables at the two latest editions of the Winter Olympic Games in 2018 and 2022, leaving sporting and economic superpowers such as the United States and Germany behind. Though Norway is not the only Scandinavian country with considerable international sporting success. Denmark is dominating men's handball, winning the past four world championships, and currently has an extraordinarily high number of world-class cyclists, including two-times Tour de France winner Jonas Vingegaard. Sweden has won 11 world titles in ice hockey and according to Andersen (2017) is amongst the top three sporting nations in the world in winter and summer sports measured against the nation's population.

The three Scandinavian countries have distinctive – though at times shared – history, culture, and traditions, as well as independent political systems and economies. Their sporting traditions have strong connections to nature, in terms of outdoor sports and outdoor activities, such recreational activities in the outdoors called "friluftsliv" (Green et al., 2019). However, there is also a high degree of influence between Denmark, Norway, and Sweden, not least due to the egalitarian characteristic of the Scandinavian welfare system. All three countries employ a

DOI: 10.4324/9781032665153-10

social democratic welfare model that grants equal social benefits to their citizens that are financed by high taxes (Esping-Andersen, 1990). They also have strong legal systems, a high degree of state bureaucracy, and a heavy reliance on public social services (Enjolras & Strømsnes, 2018). Since sport and physical activity are of public interest, the Scandinavian states provide substantial financial support to the sport sector, as with many other public culture and leisure activities. However, despite those funding streams, sport has a high degree of autonomy based on its grounding in voluntary people's movements.

For this chapter, we adopt the standpoint that it is possible to speak about a Scandinavian sport model. According to Tuastad (2019), the Scandinavian sport model consists of four building blocks: a strong volunteer tradition, a uniform organisation in each of the countries, a comparatively close connection between sport and public authorities, and egalitarianism. In the following, we will address those four blocks in outlining the Scandinavian sport model with a view on historical considerations, current organisational structures, grassroots sports, the solidarity between elite and leisure sport levels, and the role of international sporting competitions for the creation of national identities in a Scandinavian context.

Historical Considerations

Voluntary organisations constitute the backbone of democracy in Scandinavia. Despite differences in the volunteering cultures of the three countries, the overall volunteering levels in the region are very high compared with other European countries (Qvist et al., 2018). Those volunteering efforts contribute significantly to the national economies, corresponding to around 3% of the GDP in the respective countries (Stende et al., 2020). The sport sector in Scandinavia is heavily impacted and shaped by the volunteering traditions. According to Ibsen and Seippel (2010), the voluntary sport sector is larger in the Nordic countries than that in most other European countries in terms of number of associations, members, and volunteers. This direct involvement in sport of large majorities of the Scandinavian population strongly influences the way Scandinavians experience sport since they are a crucial part of the sport cultures themselves (Bairner, 2010). Since the voluntary sport sector is a key component of the Scandinavian sport model, it is important to consider the historical ties between sport and volunteering before going into more depth of the organisational systems.

In Denmark, a strong democratic and liberal movement at the end of the 19th century coincided with the development of a national gymnastics culture resulting in the establishment of the first voluntary sport organisations (Trangbæk, 2004). The voluntary clubs and federations were run by citizens in their spare times, usually without any payments. Nationalistic motives also contributed to the creation of the organisations. In both Denmark (Danish Shooting Associations) and Norway (Central Federation for the Promotion of Bodily Exercise and Weapon Use), the shooting sport movements aimed to prepare young men for military action were the rationale for the first sport organisations (Skille & Säfvenbom, 2011).

In the beginning of the 20th century, the military discourse was replaced by a health discourse (Støckel et al., 2010) and the voluntary and membership-based sport movements became increasingly popular, eventually outgrowing the gymnastics movements that were popular in Sweden and Denmark (Fahlén & Stenling, 2016). Importantly, the voluntary nature of the sports and gymnastics movements meant that they were open for individuals from all parts of society. Thus, the openness of the voluntary sport organisations has over time provided access to sport and physical activity for all citizens disregarding social markers (Peterson, 2008). This egalitarian and inclusive character of the Scandinavian sport model on the leisure sport level is still a key feature today.

Scandinavian sport was also impacted by the amateur ideology which was in essence a tool for class division and therefore in stark contrast to the openness of the voluntary sport movement. Through the domination of the Olympic Movement, to which Scandinavian individuals such as the former president of the *International Olympic Committee* (IOC) and *World Athletics*, the Swede Sigfrid Edström, contributed, amateurism became a defining ideology within Scandinavian sport organisations (Krieger, 2021). For example, all Scandinavian countries forbade sport as paid labour until the 1960s (Peterson, 2008). This limitation, however, did not affect mass participation in physical activity. Rather, it impacted the elite sport level and therewith the possibilities for individuals to make a living through sport.

Following the expansion of the welfare state in the Scandinavian countries after World War II, a division of labour emerged, with the government funding and ensuring public access to facilities while sports organisations, backed by public support, focus on the development and organisation of sporting events. By prioritising the provision of sports facilities for all as a political objective, Denmark, Norway, and Sweden now rank among the countries with the highest number of sports facilities per capita worldwide (Rafoss & Troelsen, 2010).

Sweden has had a consistent model for the organisation of sport. The *Swedish Sports Confederation* is the umbrella organisation of the Swedish sports movement since 1903, overseeing voluntarily organised sport. In Norway and Sweden, several divisions and mergers of sport organisations occurred throughout the 20th century that resulted in the current organisational forms. In Norway, the workers' sport movement that dealt with sport for all and the bourgeois sport organisation merged in 1946, maintaining their traditional responsibilities. In 1996, all Norwegian organised sport was united when the national Olympic committee was included into one umbrella organisation, the *Norwegian Olympic and Paralympic Committee and Confederation of Sports* (NIF).

The picture in Denmark is more complex and separated. Those engaged in sports without an elite focus but an orientation on health and well-being are organised by the Danish Gymnastics and Sports Associations (DGI). In contrast, the *Danish Sports Confederation* (DIF) oversees competitive sports together with *Team Denmark* (TD), the latter solely focusing on the Danish elite athletes' squads (Ibsen et al., 2013). The foundation of TD was a consequence of a decline in international sporting success for Danish athletes, also experienced by the other Scandinavian countries, in the 1970s and 1980s due to increasing global competition (Andersen, 2017). Norway responded similarly through the establishment of Olympiatoppen (OLT) as a division of NIF that solely focuses on elite athletes (Goksøyr & Hanstad, 2012). In Sweden, which until the 1990s did considerably better in international elite sports than their Scandinavian neighbours, changes took place without transforming the overall institutional structure (Andersen & Ronglan, 2012).

It is worth noting that it was predominantly men who took the leadership in Scandinavian sport. However, this is not to say that women were historically not allowed to participate in many sporting activities. Women of all classes participated in gymnastics and swimming, and in Norway did skiing and skating from the end of the 19th century (Klausen, 1996). In fact, the world's first compulsory school gymnastics classes in Denmark, introduced in 1828, were targeted at girls and boys alike. Throughout the 20th century, men limited women's access to sports they saw as their own, such as football. It was only in the 1970s and 1980s that women's participation increased significantly, and women started to demand access to decision-making processes within sport organisations (Ottesen et al., 2010). Those processes continued until today, also influenced by public equal opportunity plans particularly in Sweden and in Norway.

In sum, the history of sport in a Scandinavian context resembles the close entanglement with the voluntary sector, particularly in the organisation of leisure sport activities. However, it would be a mistake to assume that the three Scandinavian countries were operating outside the realities of the global sport system with regard to elite sport. Rather, they also had to first adhere to amateur regulations and later undertake efforts to increase their competitiveness on the international level. This led to the emergence of the current organisational structures within the Scandinavian sport model that we will discuss in the next section.

Current Organisational Structures

The democratic systems in organised sport in the Scandinavian countries resemble the political systems. The political systems in these countries can be described as a representative democracy, where elected people represent a group of people in the national assembly (legislative body), which determines the composition of the government (executive body). In the sport systems, representatives from different parts of the sport organisation constitute the general assembly, which holds the legislative power and selects the executive board. While the sport federations constitute most of the delegates at the general assembly in Sweden and Denmark, the district sport associations and the national sport federations are equally represented in Norway. The sport organisations are, like other parts of the Scandinavian civil societies and the political organisational structure (Enjolras & Strømsnes, 2018), hierarchically organised. Thus, the national sport associations have two underlying political and administrative levels: the regional level (the county councils/district sport associations), and the local level (the municipalities and the sports clubs).

The municipalities have a particularly important role to play since they are the direct reference point for local sport organisations with regard to organisational structure and financing. In Norway, for example, local sport councils within the municipal framework are created to oversee infrastructural issues (Skille & Säfvenbom, 2011). This appears to be an important characteristic of the Scandinavian organisational sport model.

Funding for sport in Scandinavia comes to a large degree from state-owned betting operators. In Denmark and Norway, this has been the case for several decades, whereas in Sweden the allocations of financial resources from the state's gambling income have increased considerably since the early 2000s (Bergsgaard & Norberg, 2010). In fact, in Sweden, a third of the funding is provided by membership fees, one-third from lotteries and sponsorships, and the final third through government funding based on tax revenues rather than gambling activities (Norberg, 2010). Swedish clubs and local sport authorities further receive direct funding from the Swedish government, including money for sporting facilities.

Despite receiving fundamental public funding for their activities, sports associations do enjoy autonomy in the spending of their budgets. This follows the generally loose and decentralised systems of political control in Scandinavia. The degree of governmental influence varies among the three countries. In Sweden, governmental control appears to be stronger since the government approves all state sport funding on an annual basis (Skille, 2011), which makes the funding of Swedish sports more vulnerable to shifts in the political landscape. In Denmark, each sport association decides independently how the government-allocated money is utilised. Similarly, in Norway, the sport organisations have a high degree of autonomy when it comes to the spending of public funding. Although the white paper forms the public guidelines for organised sport, these policies correspond significantly with the NIF's own sport strategy plans (Ibsen & Seippel, 2010). Since sport is an expression of citizen initiatives, states regard the practical development of sport predominantly to be a task of the citizens themselves via self-organisation. Thus, the Scandinavian sport model is to be considered liberal and non-interventionist.

While there are no legal regulations for sport in the Scandinavian countries and no specific sport laws, the sport organisations orientate themselves on international frameworks as well as on their own laws and regulations. However, there are a few exceptions such as Sweden's anti-doping law (Wagner & Hanstad, 2011).

The similarities between the three countries also reach into the organisation of the various sport disciplines. Sport clubs can be multi-sport clubs that oversee various sports, or single-sport clubs responsible for organising only one sport. The sport clubs are responsible for both elite and grassroot sports, for example in football (Gammelsæter, 2009). Due to their diverging interests (grassroots vs. elite level), there can be clashes of interests between top-level clubs and the grassroots sport clubs, as well as within clubs organising sports at both the elite- and grassroots levels. Even though some of the grassroots clubs may have a high number of members, the professional football section often generates the highest revenues for the club, many top-level clubs have introduced semi-autonomous sub-divisions to allow for separate financial regulations. In doing so, Danish and Swedish football clubs in the top tiers have transferred their licences to public limited companies so they can participate in national competitions. In Norway, this is not possible because of the Norwegian football association's (FA) statutes, but the clubs can transfer their marketing rights to public limited companies.

The national sport federations, such as national FAs, organise the league systems on both levels. There is an open competition in all sports, meaning that sport clubs can be promoted and relegated on a constant basis. In Sweden, a football league association had already been founded in 1928 to organise top-level football in the country. Denmark and Norway followed in the 1970s (Gammelsæter, 2009). Threat of commercialisation led to disputes over television rights in Denmark (in the mid-1990s) and in Norway (in the mid-2000s). In both cases, the national football league associations complained that the lack of revenue generation restricted the best clubs' international competitiveness (Gammelsæter, 2009). As a result, Danish and Norwegian football became highly commercialised in recent decades as they could not prevent the realities of globalisation and professionalisation to impact the sport (Carlsson et al., 2011).

The large majority of Scandinavian leagues are structured around the principles of open competitions and sporting merit and include promotion/relegation on a seasonal basis. Due to extreme weather conditions, outdoor sports such as football, hold several months of winter breaks. This can be a challenge for the clubs that are playing in European cups since potential opponents in other European leagues might still be in the regular season when they face each other. In addition, with a lack of resources for professional sport leagues, Scandinavian sport teams cannot be considered highly competitive on a continental level. The Swedish Hockey League is the only national league in Scandinavia in a team sport that can be considered of top-European level in a team sports, inspired by the dominating ice hockey models in Russia and North America (Alsarve, 2021). Swedish teams have won six of the eight editions of the Champion Hockey League, Europe's first-level ice hockey tournament introduced in 2014. In contrast, no Scandinavian football teams ever reached the Champions League semi-final stage. Even in handball, only one Danish club (Aalborg Håndbold, in 2021) has qualified for the handball Champions League's final four tournament in the past ten years. In light of the success of the Denmark's men handball team, this might be surprising, but most Danish players play in the financially more attractive European leagues in Germany, France, and Spain. In recent years, there have been increased attempts to bring back successful Danish players to the Danish league, especially by the top club based in Aalborg. The same strategy is followed by Norwegian club Kolstad Håndball.

Taken together, we concur with Skille (2011), who highlights that "historically there has been a fairly harmonic relationship between the voluntary and public sides of sport in all Scandinavian countries based on mutual dependency". We believe that the high participation rates and the bottom-up approach reflect the democratic societal cultures in the Scandinavian region and therefore sport is accepted as an integral and natural phenomenon within society.

Sport for All (Grassroots Sports)

The general participation in sport and physical activity among children, youth, and adults in the Scandinavian countries is high and higher than other European countries (Tuyckom, 2016; European Union, 2022).

The Danish National Institute of Social Research found that in 2016, 83% of children between 7 and 15 years old and 61% of adults over 16 years old in Denmark confirmed that they normally participate in sport and physical activity (Pilgaard & Rask, 2016). In Sweden, Statistics Sweden found that, in 2013, 60% of the population between 16 and 84 years, and over 70% between 16 and 24 years participated in sport and physical activity at least two times per week (Fahlén & Ferry, 2018). For Norway, the statistics show that 92% of all children under 12 years old participate in organised sports, while 75% of youth between 13 and 18 years old have been active members of sports clubs during this period (Bakken & Strandbu, 2023).

Football is the most popular sport among boys in all three countries as well as for girls in Norway and Sweden. In Denmark, the most typical sports among children include gymnastics, football, handball, badminton, and swimming in voluntary, while other activities, such as fitness and running are more popular among youth (Pilgaard, 2018). In Norway, football and handball are the two most popular sports, followed by martial arts, dance, swimming, volleyball, horse riding, athletics, basketball cross-country skiing, and tennis (Seippel & Skille, 2018). In Sweden, team sports, such as football, ice hockey, floorball, handball, and basketball are most popular, while equestrian, tennis, swimming, gymnastics, and athletics are popular individual sports (Fahlén & Ferry, 2018).

Among youth and adults in all three countries, self-organised activities, such as running, fitness, cross-country skiing, climbing, and hiking are becoming more popular. Winter sports are of natural causes most popular in Norway and Sweden, however, around 300,000 Danes go to the Alps, Norway, or Sweden to do winter sports every year (Støckel et al., 2010). Statistics from Norway shows that while the pandemic reinforced an ongoing decline in participation in organised sports, young people's interest in training did increase (Bakken & Strandbu, 2023).

The high sport participation rate among children and youth within the Scandinavian countries has several explanations. First, Scandinavian sports are considered an active and integral part of the social democratic ideology that is the basis of the Scandinavian welfare policy (Skille, 2011). According to Peterson (2008), the popularity of the sport for all movements in the Scandinavian countries further contributes to the promotion of democratic values and shaping character through sport. Since the sport movement is based on democratic values such as social life, respect, equality, and accessibility, sport promotes the same values that the welfare states foster within its society: democracy, equality, and integration.

Second, the centrality of the "sport for all" concept, a mixture with roots in popular festivity and gymnastic mass sport (Eichberg & Loland, 2010). For example, the NIFs vision «sport joy for all» implies that all people shall be given equal opportunities to participate in organised sports, regardless of features, such as gender, age, sexual orientation, as well as physical or intellectual disabilities (NIF, 2023). The NIF has recently developed a parasport strategy called *One sport – equal opportunities,* to ensure equal opportunities in sport for all, including people with disabilities (NIF, 2022).

Finally, the Scandinavian sport organisations can be understood largely as children and youth organisations. NIF's regulations for children's rights in sports are established to prevent early specialisation in one sport and reduce competitive pressure in order to maintain "participation, safety and joy of sports for every child" (NIF, 2019). In fact, all Norwegian sports clubs are obliged to appoint one person responsible for the monitoring the implementation of the children's rights regulations. While Norway's rather strict regulations for children's sport are considered unique in an international context, Sweden has some regulation and Denmark lacks such regulations (Støckel et al., 2010). Thus, among the three Scandinavian countries, the differences in the grassroots sports movements are only marginal (Book, 2022).

Solidarity Between Leisure and Sport Elite

To develop elite sport athletes at the highest international level is included in the sport for all policies. Thus, both leisure sport and elite sport are political priorities in the Scandinavian countries, which has been seen as a paradox (Støckel et al., 2010). However, the rather non-traditional talent development models stand out in an international context and has led to remarkable results in international sport, especially when considering the low population.

There is a broad awareness in Scandinavia that elite sport success, individual star athletes, or hosting sporting events does not affect an increase in children (or general public) participation in specific sports (Storm et al., 2018). A key feature of the Scandinavian sport model is that competition and specialisation amongst children and youth organised in sport clubs are not explicitly encouraged. The Scandinavian sport model does not enforce competition and specialisation on children participating in sports. Rather, there is a general understanding that motivating as many children as possible to continue practicing different forms of physical activity well into their youth is the best strategy to both reduce drop-out and produce elite athletes at the senior level. This understanding is shared by the Olympiatoppen (Olympiatoppen, 2021) and confirmed by Söderström and Garn (2022), which argue that early sport specialisation is not necessary for elite sport participation in adulthood. However, it is important to note that, although early talent development is not a core goal for the central sport organisations in Scandinavia, some federations, clubs, and coaches still drive children into specific sports from an early age, due to their disagreement or unawareness of the national policies.

Comparable to the general European model, competitive university sport is not an essential feature of the Scandinavian sport model as it is the case in North

America. University sport in Scandinavia is mainly on a recreational level, such as *Kapsejlads*, an annual regatta at Aarhus University that involves a race of an inflatable item, with over 25,000 spectators (mainly the university's students) per year. Scandinavian elite athletes are not employed by the public sector, such as the French and Russian elite athletes. Instead, both high schools and universities play an important role in the support of young elite athletes through their dual-career ambitions. Norwegian sport high schools with a sport program, both public and private, have since the 1970s integrated sport and training in the school curriculum. At the university level, the universities are obliged to support elite athletes in combining their sport careers with higher education (Ministry of Education and Research, 2005). In Sweden, for example, professional dual-career support was introduced in the early 1970s (Linnér et al., 2021). The guidelines provide student-athletes with flexible study conditions, direct cooperation with their sport federations, and access to training facilities. Team Denmark has established collaboration with a network of companies, offering their best athletes' flexible jobs (European Union, 2012).

Importantly, the rather non-traditional approach to talent development does not lead to a lack of competitiveness in the international sporting arena. Except for Norway in winter sports, the modest populated Scandinavian countries are not among the highest ranked when counting the total amount of medals in international sport. However, when counting international results per capita, the Scandinavian countries are among the highest-ranked nations at Greatest Sporting Nation's list of achievements in international sports. The last ten years (2013–2022), Norway has occupied a top three spot, Sweden has constantly been ranked in the top ten. Denmark features between ranks 4 and 25 (Greatest sporting nation, 2023). Similarly, Andersen (2017) argues that Norway is amongst the top international winter sport countries, whereas Sweden historically and Denmark currently are the best-performing Scandinavian countries in summer sports.

Even in highly globalised and less geographically restricted sports such as handball, football, tennis, and golf, all the Scandinavian countries produce world-class talents. For example, Denmark won a third successive world title in handball in 2023, becoming the first nation to achieve such a feat. This is despite the fact that the Danish handball league, though improving, is not amongst the strongest national leagues in the world, measured by its clubs' success in continental competitions. Hence, football clubs and multi-sport clubs comprise both elite football and youth and grass-root football, and the national FAs organise leagues at both professional and amateur levels, for male and female, elite and youth.

The answers to Scandinavian, and in particular Norwegian, success in international sport the last 30 years, despite low population and rather limited resources used for elite sport, has raised international attention (Farrey, 2019). Without a doubt, the philosophy and knowledge of Olympiatoppen has been essential for Norwegian success. Olympiatoppen's focus on late specialisation and versatility, in combination with integration of science and knowledge sharing between sports are important factors for international sorting success (Andersen & Ronglan, 2012).

Identity and International Competitions

As outlined above, Scandinavian countries' influence and success in global sport declined during the Cold War period due to increasing international competition. Besides a reorganisation of the elite sport systems, the countries also undertook efforts to host international sporting events at the beginning of the 1990s. Lillehammer, Norway, hosted the 1994 Winter Olympic Games, the last Olympic event held in Scandinavia to date. Sweden staged the 1992 European Football Championships, surprisingly won by neighbours Denmark, and played host to the 1994 World Athletics Championships in Gothenburg. The countries now mostly focus on international events in sports that are popular in the region. Denmark has hosted the Handball World Championships in 2019 and will co-host in 2025. Norway regularly stages world events in winter sports, and Sweden organised the World Ice Hockey Championships several times. In 2025, Denmark and Sweden will jointly host the 2025 World Ice Hockey Championships. Such collaboration between the Scandinavian countries in hosting international events provides a feasible and realistic opportunity in light of expanding costs and security at global sporting events.

This is also a consequence of the unsuccessful or withdrawn bids by Sweden and Norway for several editions of the Winter Olympic Games over the past two decades. The bid for Olympic Winter Games in Oslo in 2022 was met with strong public opposition towards extensive government funding despite the IOC publicly announcing that the city would be favourite to host the Games. Eventually, the bid was withdrawn after the Norwegian government declined granting the funding for the potential event (Mathis-Lilley, 2014). In the same application process, Sweden had put forward a bid with Stockholm as the main host city, but the Swedish ruling party did not provide its backing due to fears over high costs (Mackay, 2014). Denmark has never officially attempted to host the Olympic Games, even though in 2005 a potential bid for staging the Olympic Games in Copenhagen in 2024 was considered as part of a Danish nation branding strategy.

Even though we can speak about a Scandinavian sport model, it is important to mention that there are also intense rivalries in elite sport between the three Scandinavian countries, linked to their national identities. Those sporting enmities are most pronounced between Denmark, Sweden, and Norway and have historical roots. Norway had formed a military and political union with Denmark for more than 400 years between 1380 and 1814 but was then surrendered to Sweden after the Napoleonic wars. Until 1905, Norway remained in a union with Sweden governed by the Swedish king. During this time period, a strong sense of Norwegian national identity and opposition towards Sweden was formed (Wagner & Kristiansen, 2019). With the ambitions to become an independent country, arts, sport, and the polar explorations became an important means to express the country's separation from Sweden. This was most expressed in the sport of Nordic skiing due to the significance of the sport in a Nordic context (Goksøyr, 2005). Today, this rivalry is expressed through sport and especially winter sports, with

Norway, Sweden, and Finland, as the dominant nations in Nordic skiing disciplines (Wagner & Kristiansen, 2019).

Arguably, the biggest expression of national identity through sport in Denmark in recent years came in professional cycling that is paradoxically not organised around nations but professional sport teams. With Denmark granted the right to host the first three stages of the 2022 edition of the Tour de France, a unique opportunity was provided to showcase Danish sights and enthusiasm for cycling to a global audience. Moreover, Dane Jonas Vingegaard eventually won the 2022 (and 2023) Tour de France, further strengthening Danish national identity through cycling success, as reported in the media (Christensen, 2023).

Finally, critical thinking, which is a cornerstone of the national education policies in the Scandinavian countries, has also impacted our understanding of sport in general. As such, Scandinavian organisations and individuals have been at the forefront of reform and analysis processes within the global sport system. Sweden and Norway strongly shaped the establishment of international anti-doping regulations in the 1980s and 1990s, with Swedish medical doctor Arne Ljungqvist taking a leading role (Krieger, 2016). Similarly, Denmark is host to the Play the Game platform, an internationally recognised platform and community whose members raise awareness about critical issues in elite and grassroots sport (PlaytheGame, 2023). Taking an analytical approach, DIF regularly publishes a "Sports Political Index" that demonstrates the influence of individual countries in international sport organisations (Broberg et al., 2021). Thus, we argue that the ongoing questioning of the prevailing ideologies and power structures in global sport, is another key feature of the Scandinavian sport model.

Concluding Remarks

The Scandinavian region employs a separate societal model that is characterised by "large public sector, a universal, all-embracing welfare state, and a high degree of economic and social equality" (Enjolras & Strømsnes, 2018). In the past decades, it has proven to be a robust and stable model and has been largely unchanged for several decades. Scholarship has highlighted how sport has played a central role within the model to maintain well-being and happiness amongst the population, and "penetrated the countries from centre to periphery" (Klausen, 1996). And since the Scandinavian region is stable with comparatively little political turmoil, the Scandinavian sport model has equally lasting features as the political sector. Besides its anchoring in the volunteering sector, its democratic features, and its competitive fostering (Peterson, 2008), such longevity might be another key characteristic of the model.

Having reflected over the specific features of the Scandinavian sport model and looking for a benchmark, we conclude that the sport model is in fact very close to the visions of the founders of modern sport, such as the founder of the modern Olympic Games Pierre de Coubertin. The Scandinavian sport model is democratic, hierarchical, provides access to citizens from all social levels, is dominated by white Western ideals, and has a large basis of sporting participants to draw from to make up a small elite of top-level performers. Regarding the latter, it is close to Coubertin's Olympic pyramid (Coubertin, 2000).

Because of such similarities and with the international sport system increasingly challenged by alternative ideas and non-Western values, the Scandinavian sport model also has to constantly adapt to the global realities of sport. This can be seen in the employment of state-of-the-art organisational structures and increasing commercialism to remain competitive on the highest international level. Similarly, Scandinavian countries and cities do not want to (and in part cannot) compete for the hosting of mega-sport events with economic and political superpowers as well as autocratic regimes. Country- and city-fit is important when sport events are targeted such as the start of the 2022 Tour de France in Denmark or the Ocean Race stopover in Aarhus, Denmark, in summer 2023. Only then sport events are accepted by the public, which is crucial since both the democratic features and the volunteering culture make the Scandinavian sport model dependent on public support.

Note

1   Scholars at times refer not to the Scandinavian but the Nordic countries as a distinct region. Besides the three Scandinavian countries Denmark, Norway, and Sweden, the Nordic region includes Finland and Iceland (Jalava & Stråth, 2017). We focus here on Scandinavia since their characteristics in terms of their sport systems have more in common with each other and are to be distinguished from the models in Finland and Iceland.

References

Alsarve, D. (2021). Historicizing machoism in Swedish ice hockey. *The International Journal of the History of Sport*, 38(16), 1688–1709.

Andersen, M. (2017). *Which nation is best in Nordic elite sport: An analysis of the results of Sweden, Norway, Finland and Denmark in international elite sport - past and present.* https://idrottsforum.org/wp-content/uploads/2018/08/Which-nation-is-best-in-Nordic-elite-sport.pdf.

Andersen, S. S., & Ronglan, L. T. (2012). Same ambitions–different tracks: A comparative perspective on Nordic elite sport. *Managing Leisure*, 17(2–3), 155–169.

Bairner, A. (2010). What's Scandinavian about Scandinavian sport? *Sport in Society*, 13(4), 734–743.

Bakken, A., & Strandbu, Å. (2023). *Idrettsdeltakelse blant ungdom – før, under og etter koronapandemien NOVA Rapport 4/23.* NOVA, OsloMet.

Broberg, P., Robsøe, J., Gottlieb, P., & Hestbech, L. (2021). *The sports political power index 2019–2021.* DIF – NOC & Sport Confederation of Denmark.

Book, K. (2022). *Is grassroots sport ready for the future?* ENGSO. https://engso.eu/is-grassroots-sport-ready-for-the-future/

Carlsson, B., Norberg, J. R., & Persson, H. T. R. (2011). The governance of sport from a Scandinavian perspective. *The International Journal of Sport Policy and Politics*, 3(3), 305–309.

Christensen, M. (2023). *Du holder forhåbentlig med Vingegaard?* Feltet. https://www.feltet. dk/nyheder/du_holder_forhaabentlig_med_vingegaard/.

Coubertin, P. (2000). The philosophical foundations of modern Olympism. In N. Müller (Ed.), *Olympism: Selected Writings* (pp. 580–583). International Olympic Committee.

Eichberg, H., & Loland, S. (2010). Nordic sports–from social movements via emotional to bodily movement–and back again? *Sport in Society*, 13(4), 676–690.

Enjolras, B., & Strømsnes, K. (2018). The transformation of the Scandinavian voluntary sector. In B. Enjolras & K. Strømsnes (Eds.), *Scandinavian Civil Society and Social Transformations* (pp. 1–24). Springer.

Esping-Andersen, G. (1990). *The Three Worlds of Welfare Capitalism*. Princeton University Press.

European Union (2012). *EU guidelines on dual careers of athletes: Recommended policy actions in support of dual careers in high-performance sport*. European Union. https:// ec.europa.eu/assets/eac/sport/library/documents/dual-career-guidelines-final_en.pdf.

European Union (2022). *Eurobarometer*. European Union. https://europa.eu/eurobarometer/ surveys/detail/2668.

Fahlén, J., & Ferry, M. (2018). Sports participation in Sweden. In K. Green, T. Sigurjónsson, & E. Å. Skille (Eds.), *Sport in Scandinavia and the Nordic Countries*. Routledge.

Fahlén, J., & Stenling, C. (2016). Sport policy in Sweden. *The International Journal of Sport Policy and Politics*, 8(3), 515–531.

Farrey, T. (2019). *Does Norway have the answer to excess in youth sports?* New York Times.

Gammelsæter, H. (2009). The organization of professional football in Scandinavia. *Soccer & Society*, 10(3), 305–323.

Goksøyr, M. (2005). "Og så ein svensk-norsk landskamp! Ein bliver så patriotisk i slike stunder": Norsk-svenske idrettsforbindelser etter 1905. In Ø. Sørensen & T. Nilsson (Eds.), *Norsk-svenske relationer i 200 år* (pp. 72–86). Aschehoug.

Goksøyr, M., & Hanstad, D. V. (2012). Elite sport development in Norway - a radical transformation. In S. S. Andersen & L. T. Ronglan (Eds.), *Nordic Elite Sport: Same Ambitions - Different Tracks* (pp. 27–42). Unversitetsforlaget.

Greatest Sporting Nation (2023). *The quest for the best*. https://greatestsportingnation.com/.

Green, K., Sigurjónsson, T., & Skille, E.A. (Eds.) (2019). *Sport in Scandinavia and the Nordic Countries*. Routledge.

Ibsen, B., & Seippel, Ø. (2010). Voluntary organized sport in Denmark and Norway. *Sport in Society*, 13(4), 593–608.

Ibsen, B, Hansen, J., & Storm R. K. (2013). Elite sport development in Denmark. In B. Houlihan & K. Green (Eds.), *Routledge Handbook of Sports Development* (pp. 386–98). Routledge.

Jalava, M., & Stråth, B. (2017). Scandinavia/Norden. In D. Mishkova & B. Trencsényi (Eds.), *European Regions and Boundaries: A Conceptual History* (pp. 36–56). Berghahn.

Klausen, K. (1996). Women and sport in Scandinavia: Policy, participation and representation. *Scandinavian Political Studies*, 19(2), 111–127.

Krieger, J. (2016). *Dope Hunters: The Influence of Scientists on the Global Fight against Doping in Sport, 1967–1992*. Common Ground Research Networks.

Krieger, J. (2021). *Power and Politics in World Athletics: A Critical History*. Routledge.

Linner, L., Stambulova, N., & Ziegert, N. (2021). Maintaining dual career balance: A scenario perspective on Swedish University student-athletes' experiences and coping. *Scandinavian Journal of Sport and Exercise Psychology*, 3, 47–55.

Mackay, D. (2014). *Stockholm drops bid to host 2022 winter Olympics and Paralympics.* Insidethegames. https://www.insidethegames.biz/articles/1017899/stockholm-drops-bid-to-host-2022-winter-olympics-and-paralympics.

Mathis-Lilley, B. (2014). *The IOC demands that helped push Norway out of winter Olympic bidding are hilarious.* Slate. https://slate.com/news-and-politics/2014/10/ioc-demands-oslo-drops-bid-after-over-the-top-list-of-requirements.html.

Ministry of Education and Research (2005). *Act relating to universities and university colleges: Ministry of education and research.* Ministry of Education and Research. https://lovdata.no/dokument/NLEO/lov/2005-04-01-15.

NIF (2019). *Children's rights in sport (English version).* NIF https://flippage.impleoweb.no/dokumentpartner/8a4ab125083149639ebc3b0c0c7cd0a5/82_19_Barneidrettsbestemmelsene_EN.pdf#page=1.

NIF (2022). *En idrett – like muligheter: Parastrategi for norsk idrett 2022–2027 [One sport – equal opportunities: Parastrategy for Norwegian sport 2022–2027].*

NIF (2023). *Hvem are vi? [Who are we?].* https://www.idrettsforbundet.no/om-nif/hvem-er-vi/.

Norberg, J. R. (2010). Idrottens spelberoende: Tre tillfällen då spelmarknaden förändrat svensk idrottspolitik. *Idrott, Historia & Samhälle,* 29, 9–46.

Olympiatoppen (2021). *Talentutvikling [Talent development].* https://olympiatoppen.no/fagomrader/talentutvikling/utviklingsfilosofi/innledning/.

Ottesen, L., Skirstad, B., Pfister, G., & Habermann, U. (2010). Gender relations in Scandinavian sport organizations – a comparison of the situation and the policies in Denmark, Norway and Sweden. *Sport in Society,* 13(4), 657–675.

Peterson, T. (2008). *The professionalization of sport in the Scandinavian countries.* Idrottsforum. https://www.idrottsforum.org/articles/peterson/peterson080220.html

Pilgaard, M. (2018). Sports participation in Denmark. In K. Green, T. Sigurjónsson, & E. Å. Skille (Eds.), *Sport in Scandinavia and the Nordic Countries.* Routledge.

Pilgaard, M., & Rask, S. (2016). *Danskernes motions- og sportsvaner 2016.* Aarhus, Denmark: Idrættens analyseinstitut.

Playthegame (2023). *About.* Playthegame. https://www.playthegame.org/about/.

Qvist, H. P., Folkestad, B., Frdiberg, T., & Lundåsen, S. W. (2018). Trends in volunteering in Scandinavia. In L. Skov Henriksen, K. Strømsnes, & L. Svedberg (Eds.), *Civic Engagement in Scandinavia* (pp. 67–94). Springer.

Rafoss, K., & Troelsen, J. (2010). Sports facilities for all? The financing, distribution and use of sports facilities in Scandinavian countries. *Sport in Society,* 13(4), 643–656.

Seippel, Ø. (2010). Professionals and volunteers: On the future of a Scandinavian sport model. *Sport in Society,* 13(2), 199–211.

Seippel, Ø., & Skille, E. (2018). Sports participation in Norway. In K. Green, T. Sigurjónsson, & E. Å. Skille (Eds.), *Sport in Scandinavia and the Nordic Countries.* Routledge.

Skille, E. Å. (2011). Sport for all in Scandinavia: Sport policy and participation in Norway, Sweden and Denmark. *International Journal of Sport Policy and Politics,* 3(3), 327–339.

Skille, E. Å., & Säfvenbom, R. (2011). Sport policy in Norway. *International Journal of Sport Policy and Politics,* 3(2), 289–299.

Söderström, T., & Garn, A. C. (2022). Sport specialization in Swedish football players: Investigating a model of antecedents and outcomes. *European Journal of Sport Science,* 23(9), 1868–1876.

Statistics Norway (2021). *Idrett og friluftsliv, levekårsundersøkelsen.* Statistics Norway. https://www.ssb.no/kultur-og-fritid/idrett-og-friluftsliv/statistikk/idrett-og-friluftsliv-levekarsundersokelsen.

Stende, T., Andreasson, U., & Skjold Frøshaug, A. (2020). *Voluntary work in the Nordic region – societal cohesion in a new era*. Nordic Council of Ministers.

Støckel, J. T., Strandbu, Å., Solenes, O., Jørgensen, P., & Fransson, K. (2010). Sport for children and youth in the Scandinavian countries. *Sport in Society*, 13(4), 625–642.

Storm, R., Gjersing Nielsen, C., & Jakobsen, T. G. (2018). Can international elite sport success trickle down to mass sport participation? Evidence from Danish team handball. *European Journal of Sport Science*, 18(8), 1139–115.

Trangbæk, E. (2004). Danemark. In J. Riordan, A. Krüger, & T. Terret (Eds.), *Histoire du sport en Europe* (pp. 147–176). Aujourd'hui.

Tuastad, S. (2019). The Scandinavian sport model: Myths and realities. Norwegian football as a case study. *Soccer & Society*, 20(2), 341–359.

Van Tuyckom, C. (2016). Youth sport participation: A comparison between European member states. In K. Green (Ed.), *Routledge Handbook of Youth Sport* (pp. 61–71). Routledge.

Wagner, U., & Hanstad, D. V. (2011). Scandinavian perspectives on doping – a comparative policy analysis in relation to the international process of institutionalizing anti-doping. *International Journal of Sport Policy and Politics*, 3(3), 355–372.

Wagner, U., & Kristiansen, E. (2019). The fall of the queen of Nordic skiing: A comparative analysis of the Swedish and Norwegian media coverage of the Therese Johaug scandal. *Nordicom Review*, 40(1), 121–138.

Chapter 9

The Western and Central European Model of Sport Under Pressure

Between Societal Transformation and the Obstinacy of the Neo-Corporatist Arrangement in Germany

Mara Verena Konjer and Henk Erik Meier

Introduction

The Western and Central European sports model, which will be analysed in this chapter using Germany as an example, seems to fit into the highly idealized European sports model described in the European Commission's *White Paper on Sport* (European Commission, 2007): A pyramidal structure from the volunteer sports clubs (VSCs) at the grassroots level to the umbrella associations at the top of the pyramid, a high degree of state autonomy and a permeability in the league system with promotion and relegation of the major team sports. However, Ian Henry (2009) has already shown that the European sports model ignores the diversity of European sports models and, at best, describes a superficial antithesis to the American sports model. There are at least four different sport models to which (Western) European countries can be assigned (VOCASPORT Research Group, 2004), even if this categorization also ignores specific national dynamics and policy decisions (Henry, 2009). Germany, as well as its neighbouring countries Austria, Luxembourg, Denmark and also Italy and Sweden, therefore belong to the 'missionary configuration', which

> is characterised by the dominant presence of a voluntary sports movement with great autonomy to make decisions. The state or regional authorities delegate it much responsibility for orienting the sports policy, even though they may become gradually involved in a contractual logic with it. The social partners have little presence; legitimacy belongs more to the voluntary managers than to employees; users rarely have the chance to adopt the position of consumer, and private entrepreneurs act on the fringes of the dominant system (with a variable role).
>
> (VOCASPORT Research Group, 2004, p. 53)

In this chapter, the German sports model will be re-examined. The most recent societal and political developments (Chapter 5), which are putting pressure on the German sports model with its typical characteristics, will be taken into account.

DOI: 10.4324/9781032665153-11

First, however, the neo-corporatist autonomy arrangement, which has been characteristic for Germany will be explained (Chapter 2), before individual elements of the German sports model such as the specifics of VSCs, the professional leagues system and the particularities of federalism in Germany are discussed (Chapter 4). Finally, an outlook on the future of the German Sports Model will be presented.

The Specific Autonomy of Sport in the Federal Republic of Germany

The roots of the German sport model date back to the era of the Napoleonic wars when the German gymnastics ('Turnen') movement emerged. The Turner were a true grassroots phenomenon, which indicated the emergence of a vibrant modern civic society in Germany, which was politically fragment at the time. The Turner movement combined dedication to a specific national form of physical activity with a political and social agenda. While the Turner opposed the domination by the First French Empire, they represented not only a nationalistic but also a democratic and liberal movement (Krüger, 2020a, pp. 86–88). Accordingly, the Turner movement faced political repression under the Conservative Order. While the nationalistic leanings of the Turner movement, which prevailed after the creation of the German Empire in 1871, resulted later in a fierce opposition to the adoption of English sports, the specific organizational form characteristic for the Turner movement, that is, the democratic membership association or Verein has served as blue print for all subsequent sport organizations.

The Turner movement indicates not only the long German tradition of physical activity and sports as grassroots phenomena but also that the idea of apolitical sports never strongly resonated in Germany. After one of the original political aims of the Turner, that is, national unification was achieved, the Turner movement split into several factions in response to the class conflicts in the newly found German Empire. Later, the vibrant German sports scene in the short-lived Weimar Republic was characterized by a multitude of political, cultural, class and religious divisions (Krüger & Riordan, 1996; Krüger, 2020b, pp. 140–147). Once the National Socialists had assumed power in 1933, they subjected the sport scene to a process of Nazification ('Gleichschaltung'). The Gleichschaltung was substantially eased by willing collaboration of the rather bourgeois Vereine and their umbrella organization, while the working-class clubs and associations were banned or opted for 'voluntary' dissolution (Krüger, 2020b, pp. 165–169). The Third Reich integrated the remaining Vereine into a state sport system, which was heavily inspired by fascist Italy. The centralized sport organization of the Third Reich, the Nationalsozialistischer Reichsbund für Leibesübungen (NSRL), was subject to the NSDAP's authority (Krüger, 1986).

The historical experiences of the Weimar Republic and the Third Reich have been decisive for the specific organizational structures and political doctrines in the post-WWII German sport system. After the defeat of the Third Reich, the Western Allies were initially hesitant to readmit sports activities in occupied Germany at all since the entire sport sector seemed to have been strongly affiliated with the Nazi movement. Therefore, they insisted that any post-war sports had to be apolitical, which implied political neutrality and self-restraint on behalf of the sport organizations and the acceptance of the doctrine of autonomy of sports on behalf of public authorities. These demands fell on fertile soil as the bourgeois sport elites – who were compromised by their willing collaboration with the Nazis – were more than willing to reinvent themselves as Olympic role model. Accordingly, ideological divides within German post-war sport were significantly reduced (Krüger, 2020b, pp. 199–207). Moreover, even though sport is not mentioned in the Federal Constitution of 1949 ('Grundgesetz'), the autonomy of sport became a quasi-constitutional doctrine as lawyers interpreted the basic right on the freedom of association (Art. 9 Basic Law) as guarantee of a 'state-free' voluntary sport sector (Steiner, 1983; Vieweg, 1990).

However, sports autonomy experienced a very German interpretation according to older corporatist traditions of policy-making. At the federal level, the autonomy of sport started eroding in the wake of the 'cold war on the ash-tracks' (Balbier, 2006). The German Democratic Republic (GDR) established in the Soviet occupied zone employed elite sports to undermine the diplomatic isolation, which was enforced by the West German Hallstein Doctrine. In order to meet the challenge, both, West German sport officials and political elites, chose to re-politicize elite sports. Hence, a neo-corporatist pattern of cooperation between public authorities and sport sector emerged (Winkler & Karhausen, 1985; Meier, 1988; Heinemann, 1996; Lösche, 2002). Winkler and Karhausen (1985) were to first to provide evidence on the existence of a stable and complex neo-corporatist bargain between sports associations and public authorities. By providing funding and organizational privileges, public authorities have been able to utilize the sport organizations as agents of implementation for a number of policies. In this manner, public authorities have relieved themselves of dealing with social problems and have facilitated policy implementation by relying on the human, infrastructural and cultural resources of the sport sector (Braun, 2013, p. 147). Sport associations and federations have gotten primarily involved in these exchange relationships due to the notorious shortage of funds. However, they have also been granted privileged access to policy-making, a representative monopoly and substantial organizational autonomy (Winkler & Karhausen, 1985; Heinemann, 1996). Among others, the German Olympic Sports Confederation's (DOSB) monopoly is reflected by the fact that commercial sport providers are not entitled to receive public funding for elite sport activities (Bundestag, 2012). Moreover, in the neo-corporatist arrangement, relations were not asymmetrical or hierarchical. In contrast, the sport organizations have had a strong say in programme development and have exerted a decisive influence on implementation. Such neo-corporatist patterns of cooperation have evolved at all levels of sports policy-making in Germany's federal state structure. While the DOSB acts as sports' representative at the federal level, the state sports associations do so at the state level and the municipal sports associations at the municipal level. At all levels, elite and popular sports have been supported in a variety of ways by public authorities, whether as a voluntary provision of sports facilities by the municipalities, through tax exemptions, or through the recognition of sport as a partner of the health care system in the Prevention Act passed in 2015.

The dependence of sport organizations on direct and indirect public subsidies meant that sports associations have become increasingly responsive to political expectations, which implies that other goals, such as members' interest, have received less weight. Yet, as demonstrated by Meier and García (2019), these neo-corporatist patterns of policy development and implementation have come under increasing pressure due to their perceived inefficacy. Dissatisfaction with the declining German success in international sports since 1992 has inspired federal policy-makers to reduce the organizational autonomy of the elite sport sector by subjecting it to performance-based budgeting. Such efforts have been made repeatedly since the 1960s but mostly failed due to the opposition of multiple veto players in the complex German sport system (Meier & Reinold, 2013). Yet, in the new millennium, such reform efforts have gained increasing momentum. The federal government has aimed to disempower the DOSB and to implement a logic of deliberate delegation with regard to elite sport funding (see below). Also in other policy areas, such as the provision of children and youth welfare services, in which the DOSB has always enjoyed substantial discretion, neo-corporatist policy-making is under pressure. In contrast to the traditional provision of flat-rate subsidies for the children and youth welfare services of the DOSB, the federal government has recently pushed for more project-oriented funding, which is likely to increase political control. Moreover, the DOSB and its member VSCs face now strict regulations and scrutiny concerning preventive measures against sexual abuse (Meier & García, 2019).

Thus, in Germany, the doctrine of the autonomy of sports has inspired the emergence of neo-corporatist arrangements between public authorities and the sport organizations. Political interest in using sport as policy vehicle in combination with limited financial resources of the voluntary sport sector has given rise to close collaborations between public authorities and the DOSB where scarce resources, that is, funding, voluntary work and professional expertise are exchanged. Sports autonomy is insofar respected as public authorities and DOSB jointly develop policies in a persistent dialogue. However, the neo-corporatist consensus as well as its particular interpretation of sports autonomy has come under pressure. The neo-corporatist dialogue might be replaced by a logic of deliberate delegation.

Basic Features of the German Sports Model

Grassroots and Voluntarism

As already indicated, Germany has a long tradition of grassroots sport organizations. Moreover, the key role of the VSCs as a fundamental pillar of the German sport system was reinforced after WWII. However, although the VSCs meet the depiction of key role of grassroots organizations in the idealized European Model of Sport (EMS), the German model does not resemble a simple pyramid but rather some matrix organization. Denazification not only depoliticized but also decentralized the German sport system by combining two contradictory organizational principles: Former representatives of the worker sport movement insisted on the principle of regional organization according to which a regional umbrella confederation should represent all sports. Representatives of the bourgeois sport movement lobbied instead for the sports principle, according to which each sport should have an independent organization (Krüger, 2020b, pp. 206–207). The regional sports confederations have similar tasks to those of the DOSB at the federal level: representing the interests of the VSCs in the respective federal state, promoting the training of volunteers, supporting the financing of VSCs, the training of coaches or the construction of sports facilities, general counselling, etc., and developing new programmes (Heinemann, 2007). At the same time, the regional sports-specific federations also take on similar sport-related tasks, which regularly results in overlaps and rivalry of responsibilities.

The VSCs are characterized by voluntary membership, democratic decision-making structures, voluntary commitment and autonomy or independence from the state, a lack of profit orientation, financial autonomy and the principle of internal solidarity (Horch, 1983, 1994). In comparative perspective, the VSC model appears to be extremely successful. More than 27 million people in Germany are currently members of one of the approximately 87,000 VSCs, i.e., around one-third of the population (DOSB, 2022). Almost two-thirds of children and youngsters practice sports in the VSCs. However, membership in the VSCs shows some social bias: men and middle classes are overrepresented. The likelihood of membership increases with the level of educational attainment, i.e., people with higher formal education are more likely to become members. However, VSCs in former communist East Germany show less social bias. Recently, the proportion of female members has been increasing and the importance of education has been decreasing (for detailed analyses of membership structure, see Emrich et al., 2001; Breuer, 2011).

The VSCs are rather small-scale organizations: Half of them have fewer than 145 members. More than half of all German VSCs only organize one type of sport (Emrich et al., 2001). The key resources of the German VSCs are the members who provide fees and volunteering. In general, among all German civil society organizations, the VSCs are among the most successful when it comes to active volunteers. Yet, half of the VCS members are rather passive (Timm, 1979; Heinemann & Schubert, 1994). According to their own statements, almost half of the members are either volunteering (18.4%), have assumed honorary positions (29.8%), or are regularly helping out (Braun et al., 2021). A methodologically slightly difficult monetary estimate arrived at the conclusion that the volunteers of the German VSCs provide annually a total of about 557 million hours of unpaid work, which equals an economic value of about EUR 8.5 million (Breuer et al., 2006). Although volunteer work dominates, 40% of the VSCs employ also paid personnel

(Breuer, 2011), around 6.4% at the management level (Breuer & Feiler, 2019). According to an estimate, around 240,000 people are paid by the VSCs, which equals, however, only 36,000 full-time jobs (Breuer, 2011). Naturally, full-time employment creates an anomaly within predominantly volunteer organizations and creates substantial challenges for the professional staff (Güllich & Krüger, 2013).

The most important financial resource of the VSCs are member fees but they are also supported by tax money from the municipalities and the federal states. VSCs can receive basic funding from municipalities based on the number memberships and licensed coaches. Municipalities also fund VSCs indirectly through access to sports facilities if they do not have their own. In addition, the federal states finance other tasks of the VSCs, such as the provision of health sports (Feiler et al., 2019). The VSCs receive also indirect support from the federal government as their services are perceived to be socially and politically desirable. On the one hand, the VSCs offer 'sport for all', that is, access to instructed physical activity and sport at comparatively low cost thanks to volunteering and internal solidaric redistribution among members (Breuer & Feiler, 2021). On the other hand, besides the potential impact of services on health and well-being, the VSCs are supposed to create 'social capital' as a byproduct, i.e., social trust, tolerance and other social skills. Hence, the VSCs have been often called 'schools of democracy' since they provide manifold opportunities to participate in collective decision-making. Hence, they are supposed to contribution to the education of politically and socially competent citizens (Baur & Braun, 2003; Braun, 2011).

Governmental Organization of Sports

According to German federalism, policy responsibilities and competences are allocated across the different levels of Germany's state architecture. This applies in particular to sport policy-making for which the federal government just has 'implied powers'. Accordingly, the federal government is only responsible for providing essential support services in the area of competitive and elite sport, which is supposed to fulfil a representative mission of national importance. Hence, the primary policy-makers are – at least in theory – the federal states and the municipalities. As school authorities, the cities and municipalities have to provide the sports facilities for physical education (PE). These facilities are regularly also used by VSCs. The federal states have several responsibilities for the organization of sport: on the one hand, they are responsible for promoting and supporting popular, recreational and health sports as well as competitive sport at the state level. On the other hand, they control PE via the states' education ministries, which define binding curricular guidelines for PE. These guidelines specify both the content and scope of PE lessons in each type of school. As a rule, three hours of PE are compulsory for all pupils each week in Germany from the first schoolyear (pupils around six years old) until the tenth schoolyear (pupils around 16 years old) (DOSB & KMK, 2017).

Governmental organisations and their responsibility for sports (public sports administration)	Non-governmental organisations and their reponsibility for sports	
└─ principle of subsidiarity ─→	Non-for-profit organisations	For-profit organisations

National level

Federal Government	DOSB (Sport self-administration)		
Sports promotion within the framework of national tasks: elite sports, military sports, sports development...	Autonomous organisation, administration and promotion of sports in sports clubs and associations		
	17 associations with special tasks	66 national (sport-governing) federations / 38 Olympic and 28 non-Olympic federations	

Regional level

16 Federal States	16 regional sports confederations (one for every Federal State)	regional (sport-governing) federations (Olympic and non-Olympic)	Commercial providers	Third party providers
Sports promotion within the framework of the cultural sovereignty of the federal state: PE, University sports, grassroots sports...			gyms, sports tourism, commercial asports facilities...	Adult Education Centers, health insurance companies...

Local level

Municipalities	87.000 sports clubs and more then 27 million members	Commercial sports and recreational activities (for-profit sports)	Commercial sports and recreational activities (for-profit sports)
Support of sports clubs and sports facility construction			

Figure 9.1 The German sports model (own illustration based on Grupe & Krüger, 2007, p. 171).

Other Sports Providers

The commercial sector is playing an increasingly important role in the German sports model, as will be shown. Fitness studios, previously the most important providers in this sector, are increasingly being replaced by digital services. However, the scope of the latter is almost impossible to estimate. Figure 9.1 depicts the German sports model along its federal and hierarchical structures.

Sport Competitions

European League System – Football

Football is the most commercialized sport in Germany. Nevertheless, football has remained integrated into the open league system, which has been deemed typical for the EMS. Yet, commercialization facilitated a number of institutional changes. Even before football's rapid commercialization since the Bosman judgement, lawyers criticized that the legal form of a non-profit organization was no longer appropriate as the professional clubs were handling substantial amounts of money (Trommer, 1999). In addition, economists argued that the specific legal form created disincentives. The legal character of VSCs as non-profit organizations limits liability but demands that the Verein's entire cash flow is dedicated to its non-profit objectives, which in the case of football has implied that the cash flow has been primarily invested in players. After the Bosman judgement created a highly competitive international player market, German football clubs aimed to transform into corporate entities in order to raise capital for stadium modernization and competitive squads. In 1998, the German Football Association (Deutscher Fußballbund – DFB) had to give in to these pressures and allowed the clubs in

1998 to create a subsidiary 'football company' under private law. However, in order to prevent multiple ownership of clubs and over-commercialization, the DFB imposed the 50 + 1 rule requiring the parent *Verein* to hold the majority of voting rights in the football company. The rule limits the property rights of private investors and, therefore, maintains disincentives to overspend (Dietl & Franck, 2007). Since a couple of years, debates about an abolition of the 50 + 1 rule have intensified as some clubs aim to attract similar investments as English clubs. While the 50 +1 rule can be bypassed and does not prevent investors from assuming complete control over a club, it has in some cases also institutionalized shareholder conflicts, which allowed the parent membership association to blackmail private investors (Meier & Krüßmann, 2022). However, the 50 +1 rule has become a political fetish for rather traditional fans and has, therefore, been maintained. Concerning league structure, the professional clubs were increasingly dissatisfied with the DFB's hesitant approach to pay TV (Swieter, 2002). Thus, they pushed for the creation of an independent league organization in 2000. Since then, the Deutsche Fußball-Liga (DFL) owns and markets the commercial assets of the first and second *Bundesliga*. The DFL also got a say in all matters concerning the national team and acquired a blocking minority in the executive committee of the DFB (Meier, 2008). However, the Bundesliga is still an open league and Bundesliga clubs refused to participate in the closed Super League project (Meier et al., 2022).

Closed Leagues in Basketball Based on US Model, etc.

In contrast to football, basketball in Europe has experimented with emulating US league institutions. At the European level, the private company EuroLeague Basketball competes with the governance body FIBA Europe, which is the continental federation of the International Basketball Federation (FIBA). The EuroLeague represents a semi-closed league where most of the clubs have long-term licences or are granted wild cards. In contrast, in FIBA Europe's Basketball Champions League (BCL) clubs participate based on performances in national competitions. The German basketball league (Basketball-Bundesliga – BBL) implemented several times drastic changes in league design in order to improve financial sustainability of professional basketball. Increases in the number of BBL teams had the effect that relegation was temporarily suspended. Right now, the BBL still adheres to the European system of open leagues. Following the US model, the BBL season is split into a league stage and a playoff stage. The eight best teams of the league stage qualify for playoff matches, while the last two ranked teams are relegated to the second league.

Facing problems of financial sustainability, professional ice hockey in Germany has gone the furthest in adopting US institutions. The German Ice Hockey League (Deutsche Eishockey Liga – DEL), founded in 1994, was the first German professional league to be run by a private company and whose clubs had transformed their professional teams into corporate entities. The creation of DEL was preceded by persistent debt making and a number of insolvencies among professional teams. For the sake of brevity, it is impossible to present the entire saga of the conflicts between the DEL and the governance body, the German Ice hockey Federation (Deutscher Eishockey Bund – DEB). When DEL and DEB agreed on a cooperation agreement in 2006, relegation from the DEL was abolished, while promotion to the DEL was possible for the champion of the 2nd Bundesliga based on adherence to the economic requirements of the DEL licence. The creation of a semi-closed league did, however, not end the financial troubles in German professional ice hockey. When the new cooperation agreement between DEB and DEL of 2011 abolished also the opportunity for promotion, the second-tier ice hockey clubs walked also out of the DEB and created the DEL2. Since 2014, DEB, DEL and DEL2 have worked to reconcile, which involved attempts to reintroduce promotion and relegation. Finally, relegation was reintroduced in the 2021/22 season.

To sum up: The examples show that some minor or niche sports in Germany, which have some professional tradition and commercial potential, face substantial economic problems. As these problems relate to the fact that the system of relegation of promotion encourages overspending and debt making, these sports have explored closed league systems. However, the cases also indicate the persistence of the EMS.

Current Discussions and Developments

Sports Funding under Pressure

As already indicated, there exists a neo-corporatist bargaining system in elite sports funding, which has come under increasing pressure. The public acceptance of public funding for elite sport has been substantially declining (Breuer & Feiler, 2017). The dramatical decline of athletic success – the German team delivered a historically poor performance at the Olympic Games in Tokyo 2021 and failed to win any medals for the first time at the World Athletics Championships in Budapest 2023 – has provoked intense public discussions about the performance of German athletes and national teams.

Already before the most recent athletic disappointments, the new public management revolution encouraged a 'value for money' attitude on behalf of federal policy-makers in the new millennium. Moreover, the radical concentration of British elite sport subsidies in preparation of the London Olympics of 2012 was perceived as providing a blue print for an inevitable policy reform. Since 2016, the federal government, represented by the Federal Ministry of the Interior, started pushing for very specific organizational reforms within the sport federations and aimed to reduce the authority and discretion of the DOSB. Key aims of these reforms were the concentration of Olympic training centres as well as a reduction of squads and sports supported. Moreover, the federal government has forced the sport federations, which used to be volunteer-controlled organizations, to professionalize, to centralize decision-making and to implement systems of controlling and quality management. Finally, the government aimed to reap the competence to make decision on subsidies for elite sports from the DOSB by transferring them to an external expert committee (Thieme, 2017). The first attempts to implement these far-reaching reform efforts failed with regard to a radical concentration of public funding and side-lining of the DOSB (Meier et al., 2021). Yet, organizational structures and processes within the German sport sector have been heavily reformed. Notwithstanding changes in the composition of governing coalitions at the federal level, the federal government has kept pushing for reforms, which ultimately aim to subject the sport sector to a more hierarchical logic of delegation. The most recent legislative draft presented by the Federal Ministry of the Interior aims to establish an independent sports agency, which is supposed to decide on the allocation of public funds for elite sports. The reform would disempower the DOSB, which until now has had a decisive say on the allocation of public funds to the sports federations. Moreover, the first attempts to impose financial austerity at the federal level have resulted in the announcement of a 20% budget cut for elite sports from 2024 on (Hecker & Reinsch, 2023).

In addition, the COVID-19 pandemic, with widespread lockdowns and closures of public facilities – including schools and sports facilities in particular – has yielded serious consequences for children and young people: Studies (Dreiskämper, 2021; Mutz & Gerke, 2020; Piesch et al., 2024) confirmed a deterioration in coordinative and other movement skills and an increase in weight among youngsters in Germany. These findings prompted leading scientists and sports officials to write an open letter to the German government calling for recognition of the importance of sports and an increase in public funding for school and grassroots sports (DOSB, 2021). However, there have been recent calls for financial austerity (Tagesschau. de, 2023). It is known from countries that have already had to implement austerity policies for some time in the wake of the global financial crisis that these policies often have a negative impact on municipal sports spending, particularly on sports infrastructure (Parnell et al., 2019). The German sports infrastructure is already not in good shape.

Societal Trends and Their Influence on the Sports Model

As already indicated, the COVID-19 pandemic served to exacerbate some secular societal trends, which present a challenge to the German model of sports. During the COVID-19 pandemic, the German government enforced lockdowns with contact restrictions and school closures as well as closures of sports facilities, gyms and VSCs (Coronavirus-Pandemie: Was geschah wann?, n.d.). Sports were, thus, almost exclusively self-organized and possible within people's homes in 2020 and 2021, which had a major impact on Germans' sporting activities overall and exacerbated already existing trends. In the following, three developments will be discussed.

Membership Decline and Volunteer Crisis

Members represent the most important resource for VSCs, as their membership fees not only largely secure the funding of the VSCs, but they are also the source of the second important resource: volunteering (Braun et al., 2021). Since the COVID-19 pandemic, German VSCs have faced difficulties in attracting and retaining members (Breuer & Feiler, 2021). While representative surveys report strong waves of resignations with up to 8% loss and lower entry numbers of VSC members in the first year of the pandemic (Braun et al., 2021), DOSB statistics show relatively stable membership numbers even during the pandemic. Only for the year 2021 a decrease of more than 2% has been reported (DOSB, 2022). In addition to the perceived and actual losses of members in VSCs, popular and street running, which had been steadily gaining participants before the pandemic, must also report high losses. By 2019, more than 2 million participants were taking part in running events each year, an increasing number. During the pandemic, that number dropped to a historic low of 153,000 in 2020 and has not recovered since. In 2022, the first year without restrictions, running organizers did not exceed 1.1 million participants, less than half the pre-pandemic level (DLV, 2023).

Preliminary surveys also suggest that those who started running during the pandemic (about 12% of runners) due to lack of other offerings will not remain loyal to running over the long term (Konjer et al., in publication). Membership figures in gyms, which grew steadily to 11.7 million by 2019, also experienced a drop due to the pandemic, although these were much smaller than those in VSCs and running events. In 2022, numbers almost returned to pre-pandemic levels at 10.3 million (DSSV, 2023). During the pandemic, the number of fitness-related content and their access figures on digital platforms such as YouTube also increased significantly (Kim & Kim, 2023). However, it is hard to estimate the exact extent or supply and participation and the sustainability of these trends.

In general, VSCs in Germany also have the problem of becoming less attractive to young people. From the age of around 15 (DOSB, 2023), membership in VSCs drops sharply by more than 20%, especially among girls. As depicted above, the German model of sport relies on volunteering. Although nearly half of VSC members volunteer or engage in voluntary work, VSCs regularly find the recruitment and retention of volunteers to be their greatest challenge (e.g., Breuer, 2011; Breuer & Feiler, 2021). During the COVID-19 pandemic, an actual decline in volunteering of 3.2% was noted for the first time (Braun et al., 2021). Detailed surveys cannot find an overall decline in volunteering, but both hours worked per week and the number of volunteers holding leadership or board positions are decreasing (Simonson et al., 2021). 14.6% of VSCs feel that their existence is fundamentally threatened by this decline, and 30.1% still feel that the COVID-19 pandemic is accelerating these trends (Breuer & Feiler, 2021). Club characteristics play a complex role here: in larger VSCs and VSCs with a larger proportion of volunteers, the amount of time spent volunteering is reduced, adult members are less likely to volunteer if the club has a balanced budget, while the existence of strategic planning increases the likelihood of informal volunteering (Swierzy et al., 2018).

Emergence of Informal Sport

VSC membership rates drop significantly around the age of 15 from 60% to 40%. In general, it has been assumed that young people do less sports due to the medialization of adolescent life (i.e. Manz et al., 2014). However, studies show that sport is consistently one of the most popular and most natural leisure activities in young people's everyday lives; 70% to 80% of young people practice sport (Manz et al., 2014; MPFS, 2015; Thieme, 2015; Züchner, 2013). Informal sport is increasingly important: 70% of all young people practice sport on a self-organized basis (van Tuyckom, 2016) or in addition to compulsory club sport (Burrmann, 2005). Social background is decisive: young people with a migration background, whose proportion is growing in Germany, and girls are more likely to practice sport informally (Braumüller, 2016). Since the pandemic and the legal regulations in force at the time have forced all sports enthusiasts into informal sports formats in 2020 and 2021, and since supervised sports activities are no longer necessarily tied to clubs but are also possible online it can be assumed that informal sport will gain in importance in the future (Konjer et al., in publication).

The Role of the Health Motive

The German sports model is also facing challenges due to changing sports motives. In addition to the increased preference of young people for informal sports settings, the health aspect plays an increasingly important role among sports motives along the lifespan and is the strongest motive for doing sports among adults (Gut et al., 2021; Konjer et al., in publication). VSCs, on the other hand, traditionally serve competitive sport motives and have hardly adapted their portfolio to date despite numerous support aids from the federal states (Feiler et al., 2019). This reveals a key peculiarity of the German sports model: due to their small size, informal nature and lack of professionalization, VSCs in Germany are rarely capable of strategic planning and consistently ignore external changes (Meier et al., 2014).

Crisis of State-Organized Sport

The federal states and municipalities are responsible for both the management of PE and the provision of sports facilities. In both areas, however, major difficulties have been arising for some time, which also impacts the German sports model. PE faces persistent pressure to justify its place in German school curriculums. There have been repeated debates about the abolition of grades for PE or even PE in general (e.g., Falkenbach, 2022; Zerwosky, 2022). Moreover, under-resourcing of PE is a permanent problem. PE lessons are often cancelled or provided by non-trained staff, students and substitute teachers. This particularly applies to primary and vocational schools. The now widely implemented all-day school programme and the comprehensive requirement of inclusion also bring increased challenges (DSLV et al., 2019). Another major problem is the backlog in the refurbishment of municipal sports facilities, which the DOSB now estimates to amount to 30 billion euros. The backlog affects in particular swimming pools and school sports facilities, which are used to a large extent by VSCs, which affects, therefore, the German sports model (Friebe, 2022).

Conclusion – The Future of the European Sports Model in Germany

In many respects, the German sport model seems to be an almost perfect example of the European sport model or what the VOCASPORT Research Group has described as the 'missionary configuration' of the European sport model (VOCASPORT Research Group, 2004). The German model has been characterized by strong grassroots organizations relying on volunteers and enjoying a relatively high degree of autonomy. However, sports autonomy has been translated into neo-corporatist arrangements, which are typical for Germany. The specific German sport model faces a number of challenges.

In elite sports funding, declining athletic success, organizational inefficacy and pressures to implement budgets motivated the federal government to pursue reforms, which are ultimately likely to curtail the autonomy of sport. In popular sports, secular social changes, such as changing sporting motives and the rise of informal sports put increasing pressure on VSCs, which is reflected both in declining membership figures and (at least perceived) declines in the number of volunteers. Due to organizational inertia, VSCs are currently unable to react adequately to these developments. In addition, VSCs are dependent on their municipalities both financially and in terms of infrastructure. Assuming that Germany is entering an era of austerity policies, the German sports model faces substantial challenges in the future.

References

Balbier, U. A. (2006). Kalter Krieg auf der Aschenbahn: Der deutsch-deutsche Sport 1950–1972: Eine politische Geschichte. In *Kalter Krieg auf der Aschenbahn: Der deutsch-deutsche Sport 1950–1972*. Paderborn: Brill Schöningh.

Baur, J., & Braun, S. (Hrsg.). (2003). *Integrationsleistungen von Sportvereinen als Freiwilligenorganisation*. Aachen: Meyer & Meyer.

Braumüller, B. (2016). Hockey im Club oder Skaten im Park? Eine Sekundäranalyse der MediKuS-Studie zur Sozialisation in vereinsorganisierte und informelle Sportsettings in Abhängigkeit von sozialen, personalen und medialen Ressourcen in der Adoleszenz. *Sport und Gesellschaft, 13*(3), 215–249.

Braun, S. (2011). Sozialkapital. In T. Olk & B. Hartnuß (Hrsg.), *Handbuch Bürgerschaftliches Engagement* (pp. 53–64). Weinheim: Juventa Verlag.

Braun, S. (2013). Gesellschaftlicher Wandel als Gestaltungsoption: Eine "sportbezogene Engagementpolitik" als Zielperspektive? In S. Braun (ed.), *Der Deutsche Olympische Sportbund in der Zivilgesellschaft: Eine sozialwissenschaftliche Analyse zur sportbezogenen Engagementpolitik* (pp. 18–32). Berlin: Springer.

Braun, S., Burrmann, U., & Sielschott, S. (2021). Ressourcen der Sportvereine in Zeiten der Corona-Pandemie. *Forschungsjournal Soziale Bewegungen, 34*(4), 576–586. https://doi. org/10.1515/fjsb-2021-0057.

Breuer, C. (2011). *Sportentwicklungsbericht 2009/2010- Analyse zur Situation der Sportvereine in Deutschland.* Retrieved September 19th, 2023 from https://cdn. dosb.de/alter_Datenbestand/fm-dosb/arbeitsfelder/Breitensport/Sportentwicklung/ Sportentwicklungsbericht%202009-2010.pdf.

Breuer, C., & Feiler, S. (2017). *Sportentwicklungsbericht 2015/2016.* Retrieved October 2nd, 2023 from https://cdn.dosb.de/user_upload/www.deutsches-sportabzeichen.de/ SEB/2015/SEB15_Kurzfassung_deutsch_final_Druckversion.pdf.

Breuer, C., & Feiler, S. (2019). *Sportvereine in Deutschland: Organisationen und Personen. Sportentwicklungsbericht für Deutschland 2017/2018.* Retrieved September 29th, 2023 from https://cdn.dosb.de/user_upload/www.dosb.de/Sportentwicklung/SEB/ SEB_Bundesbericht_2019.pdf.

Breuer, C., & Feiler, S. (2021). *Sportvereine in Deutschland: Ergebnisse aus der 8. Welle des Sportentwicklungsberichts.* Retrieved September 19th, 2023 from https://www.blsa. de/images/geschaeft/2022/SEB_Bundesbericht_W8_deutsch_bf.pdf.

Breuer, C., Horch, H. D., Rittner, V., Schubert, M., Haase, A., & Hovemann, G. (2006). Sozialberichterstattung des deutschen Sports. In *BISp-Jahrbuch Forschungsförderung 2005/2006* (pp. 37–241). Bonn: Bundesinstitut für Sportwissenschaft.

Bundesministerium für Gesundheit (n.d.). *Coronavirus-Pandemie: Was geschah wann?* Retrieved September 26th, 2023 from https://www.bundesgesundheitsministerium.de/ coronavirus/chronik-coronavirus.html.

Bundesregierung (2008). *Kindergesundheit geht uns alle an. Magazin für Soziales, Familie und Bildung 7*(65). Retrieved November 2nd, 2023.

Burrmann, U. (2005). Informelle, vereinsorganisierte und kommerzielle Sportengagements der Jugendlichen im Vergleich. In U. Burrmann (ed.), *Sport im Kontext von Freizeitengagements Jugendlicher. Aus dem Brandenburgischen Längsschnitt 1998–2002* (pp. 117–129). Köln: Sport und Buch Strauß.

Deutscher Bundestag (2012). Spitzensportförderung der Bundesregierung. *Bundestags-Drucksache* 17/9827.

Dietl, H. M., & Franck, E. (2007). Governance failure and financial crisis in German football. *Journal of Sports Economics, 8*(6), 662–669.

DOSB (2021, October 21st). Offener Brief" des DOSB an die Politik. Retrieved July 16th, 2023 from https://www.dosb.de/aktuelles/news/detail/offener-brief-an-die-politik.

DOSB (2022). *Bestandserhebung 2023.* Retrieved July 16th, 2023 from https://cdn.dosb.de/ user_upload/www.dosb.de/uber_uns/Bestandserhebung/BE-Heft_2022.pdf.

DOSB, & KMK (2017). *Gemeinsame Handlungsempfehlungen der Kultusministerkonferenz und des Deutschen Olympischen Sportbundes zur Weiterentwicklung des Schulsports 2017 bis 2022.* Retrieved October 12th, 2023 from https://cdn.dosb.de/user_upload/ www.dosb.de/Sportentwicklung/Bildung/KMK-DOSB-Handlungsempfehlungen-Schulsport-2017.pdf.

Dreiskämper, D. (2021). Bewegung und körperliche Aktivität während der Corona-Pandemie: Einflussfaktoren und Auswirkungen auf Fitness, Motorik und Koordination am Beispiel einer Grundschulkohorte. https://www.uni-muenster.de/forschungaz/ project/13793.

DSLV, dvs, DOSB, & FSW (2019). *Memorandum Schulsport.* Retrieved November 13th, 2023 from https://www.sportwissenschaft.de/fileadmin/pdf/download/Memorandum_ Schulsport_2019.pdf.

DSSV (2023, March 30). *Number of gym members in Germany from 2003 to 2022 (in millions)* [Graph]. Statista. Retrieved September 26th, 2023 from https://de.statista.com/statistik/daten/studie/5966/umfrage/mitglieder-der-deutschen-fitnessclubs/.

Emrich, E., Pitsch, W., & Papathanassiou, V. (2001). *Die Sportvereine: ein Versuch auf empirischer Grundlage*. Hofmann: Schorndorf.

European Commission (2007). *White Paper on Sport* (No. COM (2007) 391 final). Brussels: European Commission. https://eur-lex.europa.eu/legal-content/EN/TXT/?uri=celex%3A52007DC0391.

Falkenbach, J. (2022, December 13). *Ändert den Sportunterricht drastisch – damit Schüler sich wieder bewegen*. https://www.noz.de/deutschland-welt/meinung/artikel/sportunterricht-abschaffen-damit-kinder-sport-wieder-moegen-43731750.

Feiler, S., Wicker, P., & Breuer, C. (2019). Public subsidies for sports clubs in Germany: Funding regulations vs. empirical evidence. *European Sport Management Quarterly, 19*(5), 562–582.

Friebe, M. (2022, August 7). *Siegel (DOSB): "Das ist nur ein Tropfen auf den heißen Stein"*. https://www.deutschlandfunk.de/sportstaetten-sanierung-102.html.

Grupe, O., & Krüger, M. (2007). *Einführung in die Sportpädagogik*. Schorndorf: Hofmann (Sport und Sportunterricht, 6).

Güllich, A., & Krüger, M. (eds.). (2013). *Sport: Das Lehrbuch für das Sportstudium*. Springer: Berlin.

Gut, V., Schmid, J., & Conzelmann, A. (2021). Ein Leben lang aktiv–sportbezogene Motive und Ziele über die Lebensspanne. *B&G Bewegungstherapie und Gesundheitssport, 37*(1), 3–8.

Hecker, A., & Reinsch, M. (2023). *Kürzungen im Sport-Budget: Stehen die deutschen Medaillenschmieden vor dem Aus?* Frankfurter Allgemeine Zeitung https://www.faz.net/aktuell/sport/sportpolitik/bundeshaushalt-budget-kuerzungen-belasten-den-spitzensport-19091879.html.

Heinemann, K. (1996). Sports Policy in Germany. In L. Chalip, A. Johnson, & L. Stachura (eds.), *National Sports Policy: An International Handbook* (pp. 161–187). Westport: Greenwood.

Heinemann, K. (2007). *Einführung in die Soziologie des Sports*, 5th edition. Schorndorf: Hofmann.

Heinemann, K., & Schubert, M. (1994). *Der Sportverein: Ergebnisse einer repräsentativen Untersuchung*. Schorndorf: Hofmann.

Henry, I. (2009). *European Models of Sport: Governance, Organisational Change and Sports Policy in the EU*. Kunitachi: Hitotsubashi University.

Horch, H. D. (1983). *Strukturbesonderheiten freiwilliger Vereinigungen-Analyse und Untersuchung einer alternativen Form menschlichen Zusammenarbeitens*. Campus: Frankfurt/M.

Horch, H. D. (1994). Does government financing have a detrimental effect on the autonomy of voluntary associations? Evidence from German sports clubs. *International Review for the Sociology of Sport, 29*(3), 269–285.

Kim, J., & Kim, Y. (2023). What is being uploaded on YouTube?: Analysis of fitness-related YouTube video titles pre- and post-Covid-19 in Korea. *Sport in Society, 26*(3), 390–408. https://doi.org/10.1080/17430437.2022.2130050.

Konjer, M., Laske, H., Kuropka, F., & Meier, H. E. (in publication). *Athletics Clubs and Runners on Different Paths? – A Post Pandemic Typology and Positioning of the German Running Scene*.

Krüger, A. (1986). The influence of the state sport of Fascist Italy on Nazi Germany. 1928–
1936. In *Sport, Culture, Society: International Historical and Sociological Perspectives. Proceedings of the VIII Commonwealth and International Conference on Sport,
Physical Education, Dance, Recreation and Health.* Conference '86 Glasgow, 18–23 July
(pp. 145–165). E. & FN Spon.

Krüger, M. (2020a). *Einführung in die Geschichte der Leibeserziehung und des Sports,*
Volume 2, 3rd rev. edition. Schorndorf: Hofmann.

Krüger, M. (2020b). *Einführung in die Geschichte der Leibeserziehung und des Sports,*
Volume 3, 3rd rev. edition. Schorndorf: Hofmann.

Krüger, A., & Riordan, J. (eds.) (1996). *The Story of Worker Sport.* Champagne, IL: Human
Kinetics.

Lösche, P. (2002). Sport und Politik(wissenschaft): Das dreidimensionale Verhältnis von
Sport und politischem System der Bundesrepublik Deutschland. *Jahrbuch für Europa-
und Nordamerika-Studien, 5,* 45–64.

Manz, K., Schlack, R., Poethko-Müller, C., Mensink, G., Finger, J., & Lampert, T.
(2014). Körperlich-sportliche Aktivität und Nutzung elektronischer Medien im Kindes-
und Jugendalter. Ergebnisse der KiGGS-Studie– Erste Folgebefragung (KiGGS
Welle 1). *Bundesgesundheitsblatt, Gesundheitsforschung, Gesundheitsschutz, 57*(7),
840–848.

Medienpädagogischer Forschungsverbund Südwest (MPFS) (2015). *JIM–Studie 2015.
Jugend, Information, (Multi-) Media. Basisuntersuchungen zum Medienumgang 12–19
Jähriger.* Stuttgart: Medienpädagogischer Forschungsverbund Südwest.

Meier, H. E. (2008). Institutional complementarities and institutional dynamics: Exploring
varieties in European football capitalism. *Socio-Economic Review, 6*(1), 99–133.

Meier, H. E., & García, B. G. (2019). *Collaborations between National Olympic
Committees and public authorities.* Retrieved November 2nd, 2023 from https://
library.olympics.com/Default/doc/SYRACUSE/353246/collaborations-between-
national-olympic-committees-and-public-authorities-henk-erik-meier-borja-
garc?_lg=en-GB

Meier, H. E., García, B., & Konjer, M. (2021). Resisting the pressures of globalisation: The
repeated failure of elite sport reforms in re-United Germany. *German Politics, 30*(4),
562–582.

Meier, H. E., García, B., Konjer, M., & Jetzke, M. (2022). The short life of the European
Super League: A case study on institutional tensions in sport industries. *Managing Sport
and Leisure, 29*(3), 1–22. https://doi.org/10.1080/23750472.2022.2058071.

Meier, H. E., & Krüßmann, D. (2022). The soft budget constraint in action: German third tier
professional football during the COVID19 pandemic. *Managing Sport and Leisure, 30*(1),
110–126. https://doi.org/10.1080/23750472.2022.2147858

Meier, H. E., & Reinold, M. (2013). Performance enhancement and politicisation of
high-performance sport: The West German 'air clyster'affair of 1976. *The International
Journal of the History of Sport, 30*(12), 1351–1373.

Meier, H., Thiel, A., & Adolph, C. (2014). Organisationales Lernen und Veränderungsbar-
rieren in Sportorganisationen. In A. Rütten, S. Nagel, & R. Kähler (eds.), *Handbuch
Sportentwicklungsplanung* (pp. 149–156). Schorndorf: Hofmann.

Meier, R. (1988). Neo-Corporatist structures in the relationship between sport and government. The case of the federal republic of Germany. *International Review for the Sociology
of Sport, 23*(1), 15–29.

Mutz, M., & Gerke, M. (2020). Sport and exercise in times of self-quarantine: How Germans changed their behaviour at the beginning of the Covid-19 pandemic. *International Review for the Sociology of Sport, 56*(3), 305–316. https://doi.org/10.1177/1012690220934335.

Parnell, D., May, A., Widdop, P., Cope, E., & Bailey, R. (2019). Management strategies of non-profit community sport facilities in an era of austerity. *European Sport Management Quarterly, 19*(3), 312–330.

Piesch, L., Stojan, R., Zinner, J., Büsch, D., Utesch, K., & Utesch, T. (2024). Effect of COVID-19 pandemic lockdowns on body mass index of primary school children from different socioeconomic backgrounds. *Sports Medicine - Open, 10*(1), 20–20. https://doi.org/10.1186/s40798-024-00687-8.

Simonson, J., Kelle, N., Kausmann, C., & Tesch-Römer, C. (eds.) (2021). *Freiwilliges Engagement in Deutschland – Der Deutsche Freiwilligensurvey 2019*. Wiesbaden: Springer VS.

Steiner, U. (1983). Staat, Sport und Verfassung. *Die Öffentliche Verwaltung, 36*(3), 173–180.

Swierzy, P., Wicker, P., & Breuer, C. (2018). The impact of organizational capacity on voluntary engagement in sports clubs: A multi-level analysis. *Sport management review, 21*(3), 307–320.

Swieter, D. (2002). *Eine ökonomische Analyse der Fußball-Bundesliga*. Berlin: Duncker & Humblot.

Tagesschau.de (2023). Auftakt der Haushaltswoche: Die fetten Jahre sind vorbei. Retrieved September 5th, 2023 from https://www.tagesschau.de/inland/innenpolitik/haushaltswoche-lindner-100.html.

Thieme, L. (2015). Kommerzieller Sport. In W. Schmidt, N. Neuber, T. Rauschenbach, H. P. Brandl-Bredenbeck, J. Süßenbach, & C. Breuer (eds.), *Dritter Deutscher Kinder- und Jugendsportbericht. Kinder- und Jugendsport im Umbruch* (pp. 162–178). Schorndorf: Hofmann.

Thieme, L. (2017). Zielsicher verteilen. *German Journal of Exercise and Sport Research, 47*(3), 264–273.

Timm, W. (1979). *Sportvereine in der Bundesrepublik Deutschland, Teil II: Organisations-, Angebots- und Finanzstruktur*. Schorndorf: Hofmann.

Trommer, H.-R. (1999). *Die Transferregelungen im Profisport im Lichte des „Bosman-Urteils" im Vergleich zu den Mechanismen im bezahlten amerikanischen Sport*. Berlin: Duncker & Humblot.

van Tuyckom, C. (2016). Youth Sport Participation: A Comparison Between European Member States. In K. Green & A. Smith (ed.), *Routledge Handbook of Youth Sport* (pp. 61–71). London & New York: Routledge.

Vieweg, K. (1990). *Normsetzung und-anwendung deutscher und internationaler Verbände: Eine rechtstatsächliche und rechtliche Untersuchung unter besonderer Berücksichtigung der Sportverbände*. Berlin: Duncker & Humblot.

VOCASPORT Research Group (2004). *Vocational Education and Training in the Field of Sport in the European Union: Situation, Trends and Outlook*. Lyon: European Observatoire of Sport and Employment. https://educamp.coni.it/images/documenti/mercatolavoro/vocasport_en.pdf.

Winkler, J., & Karhausen, R.-R. (1985). *"Verbände im Sport. Eine empirische Analyse des Deutschen Sportbundes und ausgewählter Mitgliederorganisationen"*. Schorndorf: Hofmann.

Zerwosky, L. (2022, December 16). *"Talentfächer": Thüringen will Noten für Sport, Musik und Kunst abschaffen. Richtig so?* https://www.familie.de/schulkind/schule/talentfaecher-thueringen-will-noten-fuer-sport-musik-und-kunst-abschaffen-richtig-so/.

Züchner, I. (2013). Sportliche Aktivitäten im Aufwachsen junger Menschen. In M. Grgic & I. Züchner (eds.), *Medien, Kultur und Sport. Was Kinder und Jugendliche machen und ihnen wichtig ist. Die MediKuS-Studie* (pp. 89–138). Weinheim & Basel: Beltz Juventa.

Chapter 10

Sport Governance in South-East Europe

From Socialist Self-Management to Post-Transition Politicization

Marko Begović

Introduction

When thinking about sport in the South-East Europe, the majority of research is focused on football-related topics from the perspective of historiography or post-war topics (Mills, 2018; Brentin, 2016; Wood, 2013). In reacting to the edited volume on the European Model of Sport (EMS) as a rather policy construct, due to political and developmental heterogeneity in the Eastern Europe, especially after the fall of the Berlin Wall, this chapter will be narrowed around the ex-Yugoslavia, primarily as it is the intention to grasp both geographically location and political homogeneity. Nevertheless, it is important to take this position conditionally, as early developments of sport ecosystem as part of broader socio-political realm may suggest otherwise, particularly having in mind Bunce's view on differences between Yugoslavia and Soviet lager (Bunce, 1999). That's why, it is important to inform on the early developments of sport system taking into account concept of socialist self-management, a socio-political construct of relationship that didn't bypass organized sport. The sport model that was developed with the influence from early institutional arrangements from the 19th century and as reflex of revolutionary struggle during WWII, was based on inclusive and holistic principles shaped by Marxism. The physical culture, not sport, was seen as sum up of sport-related and organized physical activities, aimed at contributing broader socio-political changes having in mind that repercussions of fratricidal wars and religions/ethnic heterogeneity. The second challenge to be resolved was understanding the physical culture will enhance workers quality of life toward industrialization of country.

The concept of physical culture was focused on amateurism and Olympism, at the first years mimicking the Soviet sport model, however, very shortly departing from the same as a part of country's orientation West to the East and East to the West (Begović, 2021). The path that was taken echoed Yugoslav foreign policy goals resulting in the establishment of Non-Alignment Movement promoting ending of colonialism, as an alternative to bipolar system. When it comes to sport, the major difference lies in attempt to democratize sport-related actors within socialist one-party system, from the central planning approach in the Soviet Union (Riordan, 1974, 1978). Yugoslavia with introduction of socialist self-management

DOI: 10.4324/9781032665153-12

system aimed at shifting the power from state to society, although carefully directed under the Communist Party of Yugoslavia (KPJ). At the time, KPJ exercised socio-political monopoly, especially through network of your-related organizations and guardian of constitutional arrangements. That said, members of the KPJ or politically exposed persons (PEPs), were engaged dominantly within governing bodies and decision-making processes within organization of physical culture, i.e. sport organizations (Begović, 2021). Considering these dynamics that after the dissolution of Yugoslavia unfolded in never-ending transition toward accepting western democracy and liberal economy, this chapter will reflect upon three interrelated phases. Firstly, an early development of Yugoslav sport model will be presented through birth of sport-related institutions and concept. As part of broader changes discussed before, the second part builds upon decentralization as pioneering attempt toward democratization and its effects on sport system. Following, the next part will discuss on the dismantling of self-management socialism led to tectonic changes that didn't bypass composition and relationship in the sport ecosystem.

The significance of this chapter is to confirm that although nominally sport in the ex-Yugoslav region as part of South-East Europe follows concept of autonomy with the pyramidal structure in place in the context of composition of sport movement (Begović, 2024). In practice, the system represents a rather flexible version of the European Sport Model, with strong political presence, either through governmentalization or politicization of sport. During the socio-political transition in the 1990s, the convergence of political and economic power stimulated reproduction of political nomenklatura (elite) that managed to takeover wider societal forums and organization, inclusive of sport-related ones (Džankić, 2018; Begović, 2021). Further, this constellation favored dominance of the PEPs within sport governing bodies, as they are successfully combining public funds through allocation from public sector and non-governmental status of sport organizations. This proved to be not a unique case. Similar pathways in utilizing sports for non-sporting objectives were undertaken in other Eastern European countries (Wojtaszyn & Melicharek, 2023). In particular, issues from politization, collectivization (collective polarizing identity building us vs. them), nationalism and (never-ending) transition from communist and socialist to post-socialist and capitalist societies represents a joint determinant (Garamvölgyi et al., 2021).

Early Development of Yugoslav Sport Model

For over five centuries this region, according to geopolitical position, didn't lose interest of great powers (Byzantine, Ottoman Empire, Austro-Hungarian Empire, Nazi Germany...), whereas redistribution of power shaped particular parts of Yugoslavia. Following the outcome of Berlin Congress in 1879, the new nation-states emerged including countries within Yugoslav geographical location (Montenegro and Serbia), leading to establishment of independent institutional settings. For sport, prior to international recognition, the Czech Sokol movement provided initial foundations as the first attempt to bridge religious and ethnical differences among South Slavs (Žutić, 1991). Based on the instructions from Czech experts, the first Sokol organization was established in today's Slovenia, Ljubljana, in 1863 as part of emancipation processes, especially focused on developing cross-border and regional cooperation upon uniting all South Slavs under the coin brotherhood and unity (Pavlin & Čustonja, 2018; Jakovčev, 1970). Subsequently, the organizations have been established through the Balkans, with the first Sokol federations in Slovenia, Croatia and Serbia (Flander, 1975, 1977). Although these organizations promoted regional cooperation and unity, there were noted first frictions on how the union should look like from institutional and organizational perspectives (Klasić, 2017). Following the developmental path of sokol, other sports received appropriate organizational structures. These processes were regulated by the competent ministry (often interior), as a public authority in charge of approving the founding act (statute) and related internal regulations. These regulations were formatted in detail, specifically paying attention on limiting the role of political influence, including provisions on democracy, transparency and accountability within sport-related activities. The establishment of the Croatian Sport Federation in 1909 served as fertile soil for umbrella organization of united South Slavs under the first Yugoslavia in 1929 (Association of Sport Federations). Although the attempt from the sport movement was to achieve greater autonomy, in practice, especially with the coup d'état dismantling parliamentary democracy and introduction of dictatorship, all organizations were subdued to the King of Yugoslavia (Graham, 1929). The Frown Prince Pavle Karađorđević was appointed to lead the Association of Sport Federations contributing to the development of patrimonial sport system; however, the opposing voices prevail as frictions between centralist and federalist remained vivid (Žutić, 1991; Klasić, 2017). Stepišnik (1967), suggested that Slovenians resisted moving the headquarter of the Association to Serbia. The political uprising led to institutional rearrangements toward centralization. Under the regime pressure and attack were specifically sport organizations managed by KPJ (Benson, 2004). Nevertheless, these organizations tried to resist, especially with support from the Red Sport International (RSI) reflecting main political doctrine – class struggle (Gounot, 2001). The centralization of power led to establishment of the Ministry for Physical Education acting and adoption of Law on Mandatory Physical Education as first *lex specialis* in the field of sport. The Ministry exercised broad jurisdictions from bypassing competencies of Association of Sport Federations as umbrella organization to creation of the curricula in accordance with the principles of Sokols (State of Archive of the SFRJ, 1932). The strategic tasks were under the Cabinet Office and General Department, while the Department for Physical Education was in charge for school sport and curricula development (State of Archive of the SFRJ, 1942). This institutional arrangement remained in power until begging of the WWII and break-up of Yugoslavia. The research on inter-war suggested that was communist sport organizations that remain active, especially within liberated territories and abroad as they were part of Peoples' Liberation Movement (Begović, 2024). During WWII, the activities of KPJ were intensified, especially from 1943, and secured international support from Allied countries. These activities included organized physical activities with the number of tournaments and friendly matches organized focusing on attracting youth and athletes (Mills, 2018). In 1942 the First Antifascist Congress of Youth marked among other topics, organized physical activity and physical education as key cohesive elements (Jašanica, 1985). The number of activities were plan, including Slet, as mass movement celebrating brotherhood and unity under the communist ideology (Mills, 2018; Erdei, 2004). Following the number of ad hoc activities organized, the first communist umbrella sport organization established with the name "Partizan", as the name of military formation of Peoples' Liberation Movement (Klasić, 2017). Consequently, organizations for physical culture within liberated territories were founded on the principles of Sokol movement and following the instructions from Partizan (Central Committee of the KPJ, 1982). Jointly with workers' movements, a conference for workers' sport was organized as a prelude for the establishment of public body responsible for physical culture, the Physical Education Committee of Yugoslavia (Kardelj, 1990).

Toward Decentralized Model of Sport

The Soviet experience and model represented a major institutional direction for establishing sport ecosystem in Socialist Yugoslavia. Especially, the KPJ under the influence of Cominform and Sportintern, applied Soviet approach in establishing organizations of physical culture and establishing centralist public sector in sport with clear political indoctrination primarily of youth population as main strategic orientation (Očak, 1985). The emphasis was on large, amateur-based events and competitions through the principles of mass sport shaped by the revolutionary movement (Saveljić, 1985). The sport events were used to commemorate revolutionary movement and to specifically emphasize connection between revolution, successful athlete and communist party. As majority of sport governing bodies were occupying by PEPs, sport organizations tried to follow the dominant direction by celebrating Yugoslavia and Partisan movement regularly. Very early, the KPJ secured monopoly with the spillover effect through a number of party commissions and other bodies for physical culture. The institutional arrangements and organizational structure were based on institutional memory of Sokol movement with omnipresence of political actor as a major socio-political driver (Begović, 2021). As the system was shaped predominantly by political preference, the reforms were often stalled and during the Second Congress just in the eve of Cominform in 1948 it was concluded on the importance of democratization of relations outside of politics, as part of preparatory processes to depart from Soviet lager. Thus, the delegate system in sport governing bodies has been introduced strongly adhering to principles of amateurism. This latter was of particular interest as dispute between professionalization and maintaining amateurism occurred at the begging of establishment of new sport ecosystem. As part of broader democratization effort, the workers' councils established as product of introduction of self-management system, were engaged in the work of organizations for physical culture (Dedijer, 1990).

Physical culture was understood as one of the major driving forces for social cohesion as post-war inequalities were great, and sport was placed as important public policy tool for community building and equally important political resource (Starc, 2010; Begović, 2021). Therefore, early development presupposed work on establishment of new institutions in sport, developing sport infrastructure and organization of mass sport-related events. The KPJ reproduce non-political umbrella sport organization as an attempt to formally lower political omnipresence. The Physical Culture Association as an umbrella organization was formed at each republic and national level. Later this organization as part of another wave of institutional reforms was reshaped as Association of Organizations of Physical Culture (SOFK) as an attempt for a more inclusive structure as it was very engaged in policy-making. Therefore, as early as in the 1950s, there were two rather theoretically and formally opposing models: (i) centralist with state as solely policy actor and the KPJ as a guardian of ideological/political consistency and (ii) self-managerial with the effort to formally decentralize organizational structure toward republics and non-state actors, e.g. SOFK (Šugman, 1998). The concept of physical culture was based on amateurism with extensive highly bureaucratic organizations connected with a range of stakeholders and shaped by the KPJ branches from national to local level (Guttmann, 2004; Begović, 2021). The development of mass sport (school and sport recreation) was a priority, but also served as foundation for high performance serving to the larger purposes, to greater unity and prosperity of Yugoslavia. The concept of self-management facilitated institutional decentralization and organizational fragmentation toward involving a broad spectrum of actors in policy-making at the public level, widening sport governing bodies and implementation of sport-related activities. The first policy changes occurred as early as in 1950s, as the fragmented governance lacked in achieving cross-republics coordination (State Archive of Montenegro, 1957). This led to the policy inconsistence and unregulated frame for organizations for physical culture. Further institutional changes from state owned to socially owned socio-political organizations facilitated even greater challenges, as number of actors multiplied with no clear delineation of competencies. The overlapping resulted that early on organizations for physical culture exercised significant level of autonomy and lack of public supervision. The establishment of Educational and Scientific Council of the Federal Assembly was an attempt to harmonize public efforts on different levels, strongly aligned on the principles of amateurism (Jašanica, 1985). Together, the new strategic plan was adopted, foreseeing needed legal changes toward transferring and broadening jurisdictions to republics bodies responsible for sport. In parallel, the opposition to amateurism has been intensified. Gradually, it was firstly in football that national federation introduced a set of regulation as an attempt to legalize practice of illegal payments to athletes. These regulations included the method of transfer of athletes, establishment of the Union of First League Clubs and Association of Football Coaches, but beyond this a number of provisions aimed at enabling medical and social coverage (Kovačić, 2018). As for the governance, the Association of Football Coaches was involved actively in decision-making bodies, contributing to the implementation of socialist self-management system with the unsuccessful attempt of maintaining strong amateur policy.

The sport in Yugoslavia was a constitutional category regulated by a number of national and republics' legislative instruments (Radunović, 1983). At the national level, following the adoption of the 1974 Constitution, the Law on Associated Labour and Law on Associations along with republics' laws in physical culture represented the regulatory essence. Prior to the adoption of new constitution, the Resolution of Physical Culture of the Federal Assembly of Yugoslavia from 1968 marked further policy orientation toward decentralization. Following, the commitment was reaffirmed within the Decision from the Central Committee of the League of Communists of Yugoslavia (SKJ) from 1974, on the political importance of further development of physical culture. These policy documents served as foundation for adoption of laws on physical culture within each republic. Besides constitutions within national and republics/provinces context and law on physical culture, the statutes of local communities, social and self-management agreements for physical culture or indirectly related (e.g. health and workers), represented main legal sources. The joint determinants reflected in decentralization as major driver for further democratization together with the aim to achieve standardized roles for different public actors. Thus, the Law on Physical Culture distinguished between natural (athletes and sport professionals) and legal persons (club, school section, association or federation), recognizing specific governmental units enabling closer exchange between public and non-public actors – self-management communities of interest (SIZ). The SIZ were government by semi-autonomous regulations, mostly as a product of agreements of various workers' council (Despotović & Baltić, 1976). The social agreements represented the foundations for organizational and administrative development within physical culture including policies on specific interest such as high-performance sport or economic status of athletes (remuneration, rewards, etc.). These regulatory changes were followed by organizational repositioning of sport-related stakeholders. Athletes were given opportunity to participate in sport governing bodies, primarily within boards of sport organizations contributing to the introduction of horizontal governance system (Begović, 2021). However, the method and the manner of nominated athlete's representative was largely unregulated, as attempt to structure sport organization based on Law on Associated Labor proved to be operationally impossible. Further, social agreements are concretized with self-management agreements, refereeing to transferring jurisdiction or competencies to specific legal entity. This legal foundation resulted in establishment of the Republic of Self-Managing Communities of Interest (RSIZ) and local self-managing communities of interest as the main public actors and the Republic Federation of organizations for physical culture (RSOFK) as the main non-governmental actor in the field of sport established with the self-management treaty. These organizations, according to their statutes, adopted a number of internal regulations for governing, organization of competition formats, financial management and dispute resolution mechanisms. Thus, hierarchically the domestic legislation recognized regulations from the International Sport Federations as an important framework for development of sport-specific rules within the doctrine of monism (Begović, 2021). Interestingly, in the work of RSOFK, the Presidency of Communist Youth (SSOJ) plays an important political role in maintaining the presence of the SKJ within organizations of physical culture. Contributing to the complex governance model, on the local level, workers' councils and organizations of associated labors are engaged within SOFKs. On the republic's level, the RSIZ was in charge of policy-making and coordinating with local SIZs.

Never-Ending Transition

The introduction of self-management was an attempt to break away from the Soviet lager as political strategic orientation and not as workers' initiative or product. This notion is important to understand the limits of this concept and consequences of dissolution of Yugoslavia on institutional setting of sport. Following political repositioning, the decentralized planned to enable more decision-making power not only to the sub-national level but also to the other non-state actors, such as works. As a part of wider regulatory and institutional changes, governance of sport organization shifted toward more horizontal and autonomous form. The illustrative example represents introduction of good governance principles as a reflex of negative phenomena being widespread in and through sport and to consolidate policy-making efforts. One of the important changes reflecting, broader political articulations, was introduction of provision to limit the term of office. This provision prescribed collegial one-year rotation within governing bodies to reduce overwhelming influence of existing stakeholders and clientelist network (Begović, 2021). Associations, such as coaching ones were particularly active in articulating voices of natural entities, including athletes and referees as indispensable actors and center of sport movement. There were two practical challenges to these efforts. First, Yugoslavia was country of different nations, a number of republics and provinces and sport movement as any other socio-political structure needed to reflect this plurality. Second, the existing nomenklatura with sport movement, opposed to any structural changes that would limit their power and influence. With these challenges, the operationalization of self-management principles in sport proved to be aggravated as decision-making processes were often stalled. That said, the efforts toward democratization through decentralization resulted in reproduction or inflation of bureaucratic and political structures as workers' councils, associated labor organization or youth organizations were directed by the SKJ representatives. Under the radar, between the 1960s and 1970s, the frictions between republics reflected limits of self-management within heterogenous society (Lampe, 2000). Following broader socio-political changes toward decentralization, the structure of sport organizations reflected self-management orientation. Practically speaking, clubs established a number of self-managing bodies including presidency, general assembly and different commissions. As local sport organizations, these bodies were supposed to coordinate activities with other socio-political organizations and institutions. In addition to this complex governance structure, members of sport organizations and particular bodies were engaged in the work of local political branches of the SKJ ensuring political dominance and continuity of self-management socialist ideology.

From the functional perspective, Yugoslavia was more confederal country, as republics exercised significant level of autonomy with limited coordination among them (Obrenović, 1994). Mills (2018) suggests that the national level didn't have proper mechanism in place to lower these frictions, especially as nationalism started to be omnipresent at sporting events (Kovačić, 2020). Especially during the late 1970s and throughout 1980s, the negative phenomena including corruption and match-fixing were widespread in which PEPs played key roles. Also, most of the clubs proved to be financially dependent on public funds, contributing to the inefficient governance structure and interplay with political organizations. PEPs continued to maintain dominance in sport governing bodies, despite poor performance and management of public funds. The funds originated mostly through self-management agreements from the public sector and various workers' organizations. The real challenge lies in reluctance to implement decentralized and depoliticized principles enacted within self-management system. Practically, athletes, coaches, referees and sport organizations should be core stakeholders, with limited presence of other stakeholders, following horizontal decision-making processes. This was solution to the growing number of problems that undermined sustainability of sport ecosystem.

However, these deficiencies reflected more serious frictions between different republics (Slovenia, Croatia and Serbia) and within Serbia (Autonomous Provinces of Kosovo and Metohija and Vojvodina), signaling political inability to tackle those challenges in a coherent manner. As an outcome of different and often opposing views within the SKJ, the dissolution of Yugoslavia started with the struggle between party branches stimulating broad polarization across republics and with all socio-political organizations including sport movement. It was the sport through a number of events that were used to facilitate nationalism and violence (Brentin, 2016; Begović et al., 2020). National sport federations from Croatia and Slovenia demanded for loose national association with limited, rather advisory roles (Kovačić, 2018). Besides nationalism, corruptive practices didn't bypass sport and similarly, federal authorities were not able to suppress this threat primarily due to ineffective institutional arrangements and lack of capacities (Jovic, 2001; Buchenau, 2021). The presence of corruption derogated principles of amateurism, while political focus shifted toward professional and elite sport, with the republics branches of the SKJ managed to maintain the grip of sport-related organizations (Begović et al., 2020). With these efforts, the reforms remained rather nominal than operational. That said, provisions that facilitated self-managerial governance model that recognized athletes and other sport professionals (e.g. coaches) as one of the major sport stakeholders within the concept of direct representation through delegate system were abandoned (Drobnjak, 1991; Begović, 2024). Operationally, limited power that athletes and other sport professions were entitled to was transfer to clubs, excluding former from participation in sport governing bodies and decision-making processes (Begović, 2022).

Within this unfavored environment, shift from socialist self-management to capitalism under the dissolution of Yugoslavia led to sharp economic decline and rise of social and economic inequality. Within emerging and reconstructed countries, sport was under pressure to ensure the continuity of organized sport, especially competition format under the new realm. The rationale behind was to confirm that new countries were capable to operate independently, and sport, due to its international success of Yugoslav teams and athletes, was particularly important (Brentin, 2014; Hrstić & Mustapić, 2015). With the repression that was practiced in all countries, the nationalistic political structures tightened the grip over the society through its influence on non-public and economic spheres. It was privatization and uneven distribution of public wealth that secured monopoly of informal groups (Uzelac, 2003). This constellation led to establishment of the state capture system with illiberal democratic practices inclusive within sport-related organizations (Kaufmann et al., 2000; Zakaria, 1997; Begović, 2024). Newly established parties from the republics' SKJ within emerged countries, maintained political monopoly beyond political sphere and keeping strong influence on sport ecosystem (Begović, 2023). Countries were quick in dismantling sport-related institutions and organizations from the self-management period, creating rather flexible institutional arrangements that will enable more control and less transparency (Begović et al., 2020). The governance re-shifted to vertical combining autocracy and clientelism with variety of formal and informal pressures in place (Begović, 2023, 2024). The process of "liberalization", resulting in loosening control primarily over public funding, while PEPs and public officials remained involved in sport governing bodies. Following Chaker's categorization, model of sport in emerging countries is mostly centralized and interventionist, strongly relying on public sector culture with bureaucratic configuration (Chaker, 2004; Begović, 2024). Sport was perceived as important asset or tool to utilize non-sportive objectives, directed to serve both as unified or polarized power with the "partocratic systems produced a country of controlled dualism where actors seemingly appear as a sort of the communicating vessels with very homogenous forces connected from its base and subjected to the same political pressure" (Begović et al., 2020, p. 1211). The reproduction of the bureaucratic elite in sport that occurred in the 1980s, remained a continued process under clientelist and informal structures, carefully crafted to maintain socio-political status quo by stretching its influence on all sport-related stakeholders (Begović, 2022). The consolidation of power was secured with transferring, often public competences within unclear or overlapping jurisdictions, as in case of financing, leaving particular entities discretionary power to decide upon allocation often without policy in place (Begović, 2020). In most of the emerging countries, the politics drives policy processes in sport, whereas dominance of political parties are prevalent in non-EU members. The level of politicization is omnipresent and the case of Bosnia and Herzegovina with fragmented, ethnically divided governance model that dominantly shaped sport ecosystem as well (Begović, 2024).

However, in the region of ex-Yugoslavia and wider Eastern Europe, the structural and organizational differences are rather formal, whereas major focus rests on high-performance and elite sport. That said, sporting excellence in these countries depends primarily on public funding, resulting in limited financial autonomy exercised by sport movement. Moreover, political support for sporting excellence with PEPs occupying major sport governing roles, significantly restricts political autonomy. The interplay between public sector and sport movement is shaped by non-sporting interest, often creating dispute between the law-on-the-books with law-in action, resulting in adapting former to serve to the informal structures (Bantekas & Begović, 2024). That said, the institutional stability is being maintained by transforming informal practices into formal regulatory regimes. Of course, it is not a new phenomenon (Mijatov, 2019); however, in the last several decades, it became pervading (Begović, 2023). Therefore, it should not be a surprise that sport for all, primarily school sport and recreation are not on the policy agenda, as political objectives steered institutional arrangements and policy development toward high-performance sport (Brentin & Zec, 2017; Begović, 2024). With this in mind, the public sector remained quite limited in operations, focusing mostly on administrative and financial tasks in supporting preferential sport-related organizations. This is in line with the Stojarová and Emerson (2013), view on the maintaining concept of state capture with recent democratic backsliding and keeping patron–client relationship as dominant (Levitsky & Way, 2015; Bieber, 2018; Garamvölgyi et al., 2021; Csaky, 2022; Begović, 2023). Consequently, these relationships with the lack of self-regulatory policy arrangements in terms of the existence or application of good governance mechanism resulted in a sort of supervised autonomy, whereas formal regulatory regimes set up architecture of sport ecosystem (Begović, 2024). As indicated earlier, the pyramidal structure nominally patronages national sport federation as major players, however, bearing in mind the importance of particular sport clubs (e.g. Crvena Zvezda or Dinamo), these clubs in practice enjoyed larger political and financial support weakening the role of NSFs.

Conclusion

Early development of sport system (Sokol movement) served as a foundation of concept of physical culture aimed to engaged broader population into organized physical activity. The focus was on mass sport, however, limited autonomy of sport movement didn't allow further or needed organizational evolution, especially as public sector directed by politics played dominant role. The paradox lies here as in fact, the attempt was to enable broader autonomy, but the decentralized concept and horizontal governance were maintained over SKJ and related political units under the control. In practice, decentralized model of governance led to functional obstruction and lack of coordination within different stakeholders within public sector. Consequently, the policy-making was often used to articulate non-sporting objectives as primary ones. With the undeveloped civil society and political omnipresence, socio-political transition just contributed to enhance politicization of sport and rise of patron–client relations (Richter & Wunsch, 2020; Begović, 2023). With slight modifications, the politicized of sport movement prevailed in majority of emerged countries, confirming continuity and stability of informal groups. The never-ending transition provided platform for the convergence of political and economic power, extending its influence beyond political arena, with PEPs maintaining reproduction of the elite and grip over sport-related bodies and organizations.

References

Begović, M. (2020). The development of sport policy in Montenegro. *International Journal of Sport Policy and Politics*, doi: 10.1080/19406940.2020.1719186

Begović, M. (2021). Athletes in socialist Yugoslavia, 1945–1992. *The International Journal of the History of Sport*, 38, 1109–1121. https://doi.org/10.1080/09523367.2021.1973442

Begović, M. (2022). Sport Governance in Times of Crisis: The Case of Montenegro and COVID-19. In Cherrington, J. & Black, J. (eds.), *Sport and Physical Activity in Catastrophic Environments*. https://doi.org/10.4324/9781003225065.

Begović, M. (2023). Corruption in sports: Lessons from Montenegro. *International Review for the Sociology of Sport*, 58(1), 126–145. https://doi.org/10.1177%2F10126902221094186

Begović, M. (2024). *Sports Policy and Politics in the Western Balkans* (1st ed.). London: Routledge. https://doi.org/10.4324/9781003246992

Begović, M., Bardocz-Bencsik, M., Dóczi, T., & Oglesby, C. A. (2020). The impact of political pressures on sport and athletes in Montenegro. *Sport in Society*, 24(7), 1200–1216. https://doi.org/10.1080/17430437.2020.1738393

Benson, L. (2004). *Yugoslavia: A Concise History*. New York: Palgrave Macmillan.

Bieber, F. (2018). Patterns of competitive authoritarianism in the Western Balkans. *East European Politics*, 34(3), 337–354.

Brentin, D. (2014). "Now You See Who Is a Friend and Who an Enemy." sport as an ethnopolitical identity tool in postsocialist Croatia. *Südosteuropa. Zeitschrift Für Politik Und Gesellschaft*, 2, 187–207.

Brentin, D. (2016). Ready for the homeland? Ritual, remembrance, and political extremism in Croatian football. *Nationalities Papers*, 44(6), 860–876.

Brentin, D., & Zec, D. (2017). From the concept of the communist 'new man' to nationalist hooliganism: Research perspectives on sport in socialist Yugoslavia. *The International Journal of the History of Sport*, 34(9), 713–728. https://doi.org/10.1080/09523367.2017.1413871

Buchenau, K. (2021). The third path into the twilight? Corruption in socialist Yugoslavia. *Tokovi istorije*, 3, 89–120.

Bunce, V. (1999). *Subversive Institutions: The Design and the Destruction of Socialism and the State*. New York: Cambridge University Press.

Central Committee of the KPJ (1982). Letter on the state and the current standings in physical education from 1952. *Fizička Kultura*, 2, 9.

Chaker, A. -N. (2004). *Good Governance in Sport–A European Survey*. Strasbourg: Council of Europe.

Csaky, Z. (2022). *Nations in transit 2022: Dropping the democratic façade*. https://freedomhouse.org/sites/default/files/2022-04/NIT_2022_final_digital.pdf

Dedijer, V. (1990). Speech during the II Congress of the Physical Education Committee of Yugoslavia 1948. In *Vukman Boričić: Historical Notes Fond of the Ministry of Physical Education, no. 71/3* (p. 49). Belgrade: State Archives of SFRJ.

Despotović, M., & Baltić, A. (1976). *Osnovi radnog prava Jugoslavije, sistem samoupravnih međusobnih*. Serbia: Savremena Administracija.

Drobnjak, D. (1991). Organizovanost fizičke kulture u Crnoj Gori [Organization of physical culture in Montenegro]. *Fizička kultura, 1*, 31–42.

Džankić, J. (2018). Capturing contested states: Structural mechanisms of power reproduction in Bosnia and Herzegovina, Macedonia and Montenegro. *Southeastern Europe, 42*(1), 83–106.

Erdei, I. (2004). "The Happy Child" as an Icon of Socialist Transformation: Yugoslavia's Pioneer Organization. In Lampe, J. & Mazower, M. (eds.), *Ideologies and National Identities: The Case of Twentieth-Century Southeast Europe*. Budapest, London: CEU Press.

Flander, M. (1975/1977). Zagreb: Jugoslovenski leksikografski zavod. In *Enciklopedija fizičke kulture 1-2 (Encyclopedia of Physical Culture 1-2)*. Zagreb: Jugoslovenski leksikografski zavod.

Garamvölgyi, B., Begović, M., & Dóczi, T. (2021). Sport diplomacy in hybrid regimes: The cases of Hungary and Montenegro. *Journal of Global Sport Management, 9*(4), 1–18. https://doi.org/10.1080/24704067.2021.2008804

Gounot, A. (2001). Sport or political organization? Structures and characteristics of the Red Sport International, 1921-1937. *Journal of Sport History, 28*(1), 23–39.

Graham, M. (1929). The "Dictatorship" in Yugoslavia. *American Political Science Review, 23*(2), 449–459. https://doi.org/10.2307/1945227

Guttmann, A. (2004). *From Ritual to Record: The Nature of Modern Sports*. New York: Columbia University Press.

Hrstić, I., & Mustapić, M. (2015). Sport and politics in Croatia-Athletes as national icons in history textbooks. *Altre Modernità: Rivista di studi letterari e culturali, 14*, 148–165.

Jakovčev, G. (1970). Sokolska organizacija u borbi za bratstvo jugoslavenskih naroda do 1918 (Sokol Organization in the Fight for the Brotherhood of the Yugoslav Peoples). In *Zagreb: Savezna komisija za historiju fizičke kulture Jugoslavije* (pp. 9–37).

Jašanica, D. (1985). Četrdeset godina Saveza za fizičku kulturu Jugoslavije [Forty years of the association for physical culture of Yugoslavia]. *Povijest sporta, 66*, 514–518.

Jovic, D. (2001). The disintegration of Yugoslavia: A critical review of explanatory approaches. *European Journal of Social Theory, 4*(1), 101–120.

Kardelj, E. (1990). *Speech during First Congress of the Physical Education Committee of Yugoslavia in 1947* Belgrade: State Archive of SFRJ.

Kaufmann, D., Hellman, J., & Geraint, J. (2000). *Seize the State, Seize the Day: State Capture. Corruption, and Influence in Transition*. Washington, DC: World Bank.

Klasić, H. (2017). How falcons became partizans. *The International Journal of the History of Sport, 34*(9), 832–847.

Kovačić, D. (2018). Politički i društveno važni problemi i teškoće jugoslavenskoga nogometa 60-ih i početkom 70-ih godina XX. stoljeća. *Časopis za suvremenu povijest, 50*(3), 535–555. https://doi.org/10.22586/csp.v50i3.81

Kovačić, D. (2020). Nogomet kao sredstvo nacionalne identifikacije Hrvata u Kraljevini SHS-u/Jugoslaviji i socijalističkoj Jugoslaviji. *Diacovensia: teološki prilozi, 28*(4), 549–565.

Lampe, J. R. (2000). *Yugoslavia as History: Twice There Was a Country* (2nd ed.). New York: Cambridge University Press.

Levitsky, S., & Way, L. (2015). The myth of democratic recession. *Journal of Democracy, 26*(1), 45–58.

Mijatov, N. S. (2019). *Sport as an Instrument of Socialism: The Yugoslav Experience* [PhD Diss.]. Faculty of Philosophy, University of Belgrade.

Mills, R. (2018). *The Politics of Football in Yugoslavia: Sport, Nationalism and the State.* London: I.B. Tauris.

Obrenović, Z. (1994). Raspad Jugoslavije u svetlu dva državotvorna projekta i "pomoć međunarodne zajednice". *Социолошки преглед, 28*(2), 167–187.

Očak, I. (1985). Gorkić i Sportintern [Gorkić and Sportintern]. *Povijest sporta, 66,* 347–348.

Pavlin, T., & Čustonja, Z. (2018). Sokol: Between making nation and state. *Kinesiology, 50*(2), 260–268.

Radunović, R. (1983). Neka iskustva iz četvorogodišnjeg rada i ostvarivanja delegatskog sistema u RSIZ (Some experiences from the 4 year work and application of delegate system in the Republic self-management communities of interest). *Fizička Kultura, 3,* 23–30.

Richter, S., & Wunsch, N. (2020). Money, power, glory: The linkages between EU conditionality and state capture in the Western Balkans. *Journal of European Public Policy, 27*(1), 41–62.

Riordan, J. (1974). Soviet sport and Soviet foreign policy. *Soviet Studies, 26*(3), 322–343. https://www.jstor.org/stable/150858

Riordan, J. (ed.). (1978). *Sport under Communism.* London: Hurst.

Saveljić, V. (1985). Fizička kultura u Crnoj Gori između potreba i mogučnosti [Physical culture in Montenegro between needs and opportunities]. *Fizička Kultura, 3,* 29–34.

Starc, G. (2010). Sportsmen of Yugoslavia, Unite - Workers' Sport between Leisure and Work. In Luther, B. & Pusˇnik, M. (eds.), *Remembering Utopia: The Culture of Everyday Life in Socialist Yugoslavia.* Washington, DC: New Academia Publishing.

State Archive of Montenegro (1957). Official Gazette People's Republic of Montenegro, no 18/57.

State Archives of SFRJ (1942). Official Gazette Kingdom of Yugoslavia, no. 2/1942.

State Archives of the SFRJ (1932). Official Gazette Kingdom of Yugoslavia, no. 76/1932.

Stepišnik, D. (1967). Razvoj sokolstva u Sloveniji [Development of the Sokol movement in Slovenia]. *Historija Fizičke Kulture, 2*(2), 11.

Stojarová, V., & Emerson, P. (2013). *Party politics in the Western Balkans* (Vol. 28). Abingdon: Routledge.

Šugman, R. (1998). *Slovenski šport v mednarodnem prostoru po letu 1991 [Slovenian Sport in the International Arena after 1991]* (pp. 1–34). Ljubljana: Fakulteta za šport.

Uzelac, S. (2003). Corruption in Transition Countries: "How to Capture a State"-The Example of Montenegro. *SEER: Journal for Labour and Social Affairs in Eastern Europe, 6*(1/2), 103–116. http://www.jstor.org/stable/43291986

Wojtaszyn, D., & Melicharek, M. (eds.). (2023). *Football in the Balkans I: Internal Views, External Perceptions.* New York: Peter Lang. https://doi.org/10.3726/b20693

Wood, S. (2013). Football after Yugoslavia: conflict, reconciliation and the regional football league debate. *Sport in Society: Cultures, Commerce, Media, Politics, 16*(8), 1077–1090. https://doi.org/10.1080/17430437.2013.801225

Zakaria, F. (1997). The rise of illiberal democracy. *Foreign Affairs, 76*(6), 22–43.

Žutić, N. (1991). *Ideologija u fizičkoj kulturi Kraljevine Jugoslavije 1929–1941. [Ideology in the Physical Culture of the Kingdom of Yugoslavia].* Beograd: Angrotrade.

Chapter 11

The UK Model of Sport
Early Pioneer and Contemporary Revisionist

Spencer Harris and Mathew Dowling

Introduction

The United Kingdom (UK) has a long and turbulent history of socio-political division intensified by unification. Over the past two millennia, there have been at least 16 distinct attempts to unify England, Scotland, Wales, Ireland or Northern Ireland into a single nation (Davies, 2000). The most recent change in the union was in 1927 when the *Royal and Parliamentary Titles Act* formally recognised the UK of Great Britain (England, Scotland and Wales) and Northern Ireland following the creation of the independent Irish Free State and the partitioning Northern Ireland (Gibbons, 2015).

While the UK's political structure could once be said to resemble an absolute monarchy, rebellion and modernity gave rise to a Democratic Parliamentary Monarchy. This political system combines a parliamentary democracy with a constitutional monarchy, underlining the sovereignty of Parliament which encompasses the two Houses (the House of Lords and the House of Commons), and the reigning monarch. While the monarch retains a central role as the UK's head of state, they have no official political or executive role in governing and their role is largely ceremonial and symbolic (Allen, 2018).

Over recent years, in response to growing calls for self-governance in Scotland, Wales and Northern Ireland, the UK Parliament has devolved powers to these home nations[1] with each nation slowly acquiring wider responsibilities and broader powers particularly in health, education, and the development of school and community sport policy (HM Government, 2020). However, there is no such delegated authority in England as decision making remains centralised within the UK Parliament.

Over the past two decades Conservative commentators have argued that the UK is experiencing a period of major decline due to EU dominance, the effects of intense immigration, and a widened multi-culturalism (Hitchen, 2008). Consequently, the UK is said to be suffering a complete identity crisis (Gilroy, in Hill, 2004), with the union collapsing before our very eyes (Nairn, 2000). More practically, the most visible threat to the continuation of the union at this time would appear to be Scottish independence, an issue that has been reignited by the UK's

DOI: 10.4324/9781032665153-13

decision to leave the European Union and inflamed by disagreements between the Scottish National Party and the UK Supreme Court (Torrance, 2022).

This chapter continues by exploring the historical development of sport in the UK, the current organisational structure of elite sport and grassroots sport across the UK, and the extent to which the UK model of sport aligns with key features of the European Model of Sport (EMS).

The Evolution of Modern Sport in the UK

Modern sport and the UK share a special relationship. British institutions, its social class structure and culture have had a considerable influence on the evolution of modern sport (Brailsford, 1992). Sport is also deeply embedded in the cultural life of British society although any "sporting patriotism" across Scotland, Wales and Northern Ireland more likely represent resistance against English dominance rather than any notion of Britishness (Holt, 1989, p. 7). The potent combination of geographical proximity and ideological distance elevates the importance of sport across the home nations, delineating each nation's identity, culture, and collective values. Where modern sport was once a cornerstone of the British Empire (de Coubertin in Holt, 1989), today it more modestly represents an integral part of the fabric of people's lives across the UK.

Modern sport in the UK emerged in the mid-19th century as a rational and orderly alternative to its traditional, often violent predecessors (Renson, 2009). This shift is reflected in the transition from disorganised traditional gatherings (e.g. mob football) to codified and regulated sports (Holt, 1989). Elias and Dunning (1986) argue that the "civilising process" and the "parlimentarization of society", which reduced class conflicts and shifted political disputes to non-violent means, led to the "sportisation" of pastimes. The first sportisation phase occurred during the 17th and 18th centuries with the early transformation of pastimes such as cricket, golf, boxing, foxhunting, greyhound coursing, and horse racing. Most significantly, these pastimes experienced a change in rules, organisation, and function heavily influenced by the higher social order (Brailsford, 1992), the emergence of a bourgeois public sphere (Habermas, 1989) and the desire for self-organisation and regulation (Elias & Dunning, 1986). For Habermas, the bourgeois public sphere represented a new civic society—a space to interact—one that would gradually replace the "public sphere in which the ruler's power was merely represented before the people, with a [bourgeois public] sphere in which state authority was publicly monitored through informed and critical discourse by the people" (1989, p. xi). For Szymanski (2008), the 17th and 18th centuries witnessed an unrelenting commitment to associativity or "the tendency for individuals to create social networks and organisations" (p. 2). It was the combination of this new civic society and these private associate activities that drove Britain's sporting revolution and laid the foundations for modern sport.

The second phase of the sportisation of pastimes occurred during the early- to mid-19th century (Elias & Dunning, 1986). This phase witnessed a considerable expansion of clubs and associations across several sports including football (all three codes—association football, rugby football union, and rugby football league), tennis, hockey, rowing, swimming, and athletics. Furthermore, the expansion of modern sport required the codification of rules to allow for fair competition and wagering. And, with a growing urban working-class showing considerable interest in sport, there was a need to reconcile how different classes might engage with sport. While space precludes a detailed sport-by-sport analysis, we generally see a sharp distinction in sport between amateurs and non-amateurs, players or professionals. In the UK, amateurism represented a classist ideology insofar as it distinguished players by class, in favour of those who were already dominant (Allison, 2001). Amateurs were those who were not paid to play, those who would likely be offended by any suggestion of payment to play and more instructively, gentlemen of means who played sports in a particular way, one that epitomised fair play—respecting rules, and committing to the spirit of the game (Holt, 1989). The establishment of the amateur hegemony, cultivated by gentleman amateurs, helped maintain their separation from and power over the working classes and provided a clear and direct response to professionalism (Allison, 2001).

Maguire (1999) expanded on Elias and Dunning's sportisation phases by adding three additional periods. During the *take-off phase* from 1870 to 1920, modern sport spread globally, international associations and competitions were formed, and rules were standardised. Britain, as a dominant imperial and economic power, significantly influenced global sporting culture during this period, particularly with the diffusion of English sports (football, rugby, cricket, tennis, boxing and athletics) throughout Europe and across the British Empire (Dunning & Sheard, 1979). Sport in the UK also experienced an intensified professionalisation during this period, allowing the upper class to maintain their amateur status and superiority (Maguire, 1999).

The fourth period represents *the struggle for hegemony,* starting in the 1920s and continuing through to the mid-20th century. During this period, the dominant British sport model influenced developments in the US, albeit with a sharper emphasis on commercialisation and achievement (Markovits & Hellerman, 2014). However, volunteerism and amateurism remained the foundation upon which local-level clubs and national sport associations were developed across the UK. And, for the UK's professional athletes, the continued professionalisation and commercialisation of sports such as football demanded a more concerted effort to build on previous efforts to unionise, to work collectively to promote their status and protect their interests (Taylor, 2014).

Finally, the mid-20th century onwards has witnessed a broad period of change and heightened uncertainty, with an increase in global competition in modern sport, with former colonies, non-western countries and women playing a more significant role in shaping western sport (Maguire, 1999). Sport in the UK over recent decades has seen major changes including increased professionalisation, commercialisation and government involvement. These developments have triggered huge governmental and lottery financial investment into sport, developed new governing structures and networks and instigated a number of new nationally coordinated programmes and initiatives (Dowling et al., 2024). These developments are discussed further in the sections that follow.

The Organisation and Structure of Sport across the UK

Given the UK's structural arrangements, sport in the UK must reconcile the need for specific home nation approaches to sport with the requirement to retain a UK-wide representation in the majority of international sport competitions. This reconciliation is achieved by establishing a two-prong approach to sport. The policies and structures for grassroots sport are led by the devolved governing structure for each home nation. The policy and structures for elite sport policy vary. For example, for the summer and winter Olympic Games and for the majority of European and world championships, the defining national unit is the UK. However, for some sports (e.g. football, cricket, rugby union) and for some multi-sport competitions (e.g. Commonwealth Games) the defining national unit is the home nation (i.e. England, Scotland, Wales, and Northern Ireland), largely a historical consequence of the varied political and social relations between associations in each home nation, across the UK, and further afield. This section will provide a brief overview of the structure of elite sport and grassroots sport across the UK, focusing attention on key stakeholders involved in policy, strategy, leadership, and implementation in each home nation.

The Structure of Elite Sport in the UK

The structure of elite sport in the UK is dominated by government and quasi-governmental agencies, National Governing Bodies of Sport (NGBs), clubs and professional sport leagues. Elite sport policy in the UK is formulated by the central government's Department of Culture, Media and Sport (DCMS) with leadership responsibility delegated to UK Sport. Exchequer (i.e. central government's budget) and National Lottery funding is then allocated by UK Sport to maximise the performance of UK athletes in the summer and winter Olympic and Paralympic Games and other major events. NGBs then work with UK Sport to develop national-level strategic plans to support talented and elite-level athletes in line with UK Sport's World Class programmes. However, the structural arrangements of NGBs across the UK are a little more complex. Over the past 150 years or so, political, cultural, social, and sporting factors have directed the slow but deliberate evolution of three different types of NGB structure: (i) sports that are governed by one single NGB with overall UK jurisdiction (for example, British Cycling, the Lawn Tennis Association, and the British Equestrian Federation); (ii) sports that are governed by one single NGB for each of the four home nations (for example, association football, rugby union, and cricket); and (iii) sports that are governed by a dual structure, with an NGB for each of the four home nations and an NGB with overarching UK jurisdiction (for example, athletics, basketball, and swimming). Importantly, only NGBs with UK-wide jurisdiction have responsibility for developing elite sport across the UK. These structural arrangements, particularly in the case of NGBs governing large team sports, exacerbate home nation tensions and hinder the formation of unified teams at multi-sport events, as has historically been the case with association football at recent summer Olympic Games.[2]

In collaboration with UK Sport, each NGB (i.e. the NGB with overall UK jurisdiction) develops the structure and focus its World Class programmes, focusing on three core elements—(i) *Podium*—programmes to support and prepare athletes with realistic medal-winning capabilities at the summer/winter Olympic Games; (ii) *Podium Potential*—programmes to support and prepare athletes with realistic medal-winning capabilities at subsequent Olympic summer/winter Games; and (iii) *Performance Foundations*—programmes to support and prepare younger athletes who demonstrate the potential to progress to *Podium Potential* in the future. These NGBs are then responsible for overseeing the implementation of their strategic plans and for ensuring that athletes in the elite-level talent pool are supported. For most NGBs, this requires collaboration with a range of partners including sport-specific training sites, specialist coaches, clubs, and higher education institutions and the decentralised UK Institute of Sport (UKIS) who provide athletes with day-to-day training and comprehensive support services including physiotherapy, physiology, biomechanics, strength and conditioning, performance analysis, nutrition, psychology, lifestyle coaching, health and wellness assistance, and general sport medicine support.

Professional sport leagues and teams are also essential components of the UK elite sports infrastructure. Association football, rugby league, and cricket, established in 1888, 1922, and 1962, respectively, have the longest history of professionalism and professional leagues in the UK. More recently, basketball (1987), rugby union (1995), ice hockey (2003), and netball (2005) have introduced league structures which may be considered professional.

The Structure of Grassroots Sport in the UK

Grassroots sport comprises both school and community sport. School sport and community sport policies are discrete and devolved areas of public policy across the UK. Policies and structural decisions for both are led by each home nation. At the national policy level, the UK-wide Department for Education (school sport) and Department for Culture, Media and Sport (community sport) set policy for England. They work with the Scottish Parliament, the Northern Ireland Assembly, and the Welsh Government, each maintaining responsibility for setting school and community sport policies in their respective home nation. Strategically, each home nation Sports Council (branded as Sport England, Sport Scotland, Sport Northern Ireland, and Sport Wales respectively) lead on and oversee the implementation of school and community sport policy and advise their respective home nation government on school and community sport matters.

At the sub-regional level, school sport policy across the UK is strategically coordinated by local education authorities, although the extent to which these authorities play any significant role in school sport varies considerably. Active Partnerships and local government represent the strategic leads for community sport policy across the UK. In England, 43 Active Partnerships have been created and funded, covering all counties and metropolitan areas across the country. The core purpose of these partnerships is to increase the number of people taking part in sport and physical activity across the partnership area. In Wales, sub-regional partnerships have been recommended albeit on a larger scale with a total of four Community Sport Active Partnership mirroring the boundaries of the four Welsh Health Authorities. In Scotland and Northern Ireland, the strategic leads for community sport policy are local government primarily due to reasons of scale and efficiency. The size and population of these home countries do not demand an additional tier of administration.

Schools lead the implementation of school sport policy across England with delivery support from a range of actors including NGBs, voluntary sport clubs, football club foundations and private sector sport coaching companies. Implementation efforts are supported with government funding as well as additional funding from the Soft Drinks Industry Levy (i.e., the sugar tax), through the PE and Sport Premium which provides at least £16,000 per school per year to spend on school sport programming. The implementation of community sport policy in England is led by a range of traditional partners including Active Partnerships, local authorities, voluntary sport clubs, and private sector providers. They have a strong focus on place-based approaches such as the local delivery pilots, 12 of which received a total of £100 million (€118m, US$ 131m) of lottery funding from Sport England. Importantly, this approach is designed to switch conventional top-down policy implementation and refocus efforts on a bottom-up approach, emphasising collaboration and working with communities rather than doing things to communities (Sport England, 2021). In Wales, school sport implementation is led by schools, working with each local authority. Importantly, for the first time in Wales, P.E. will not be a subject in its own right but will rather form part of the health and well-being area of learning. This change will likely carry significant implications for school sport policy, with the risk of a policy vacuum and a fundamentally compromised physical education experience for many young people in Wales (Bolton, 2024). Other aspects of school sport policy emphasise the after-school experience, with the Welsh government and national lottery funding investing £5 million (€5.92m, US$ 6.57m) into a three-year programme to grow participation in after-school sport activities across Wales. For community sport in Wales, NGBs are the primary implementation lead with a strong emphasis on growing mass participation through clubs, coaches and facilities with local authorities supporting NGBs with local delivery efforts. In Northern Ireland, school sport policy implementation is delegated to schools with government guidance recommending that schools provide a minimum of two hours curricular PE per week. However, research has found that these minimum requirements are not met. Only 40% of post-primary pupils receive the minimum levels of PE per week. (Connolly et al., 2020). A range of curriculum (e.g., the curriculum sports programme and daily mile) and after-school programmes (e.g., active schools and extended schools) have also been developed to provide off-the-shelf programming with national-level awareness to support schools with their implementation efforts. Community sport policy in Northern Ireland has traditionally been driven by partnerships between local authorities, NGBs and community sport clubs. The emphasis of their work has been to grow the capacity of local communities and to develop local community-based interventions to grow participation in sport. In Scotland, the Scottish government has explicit school sport policy goals stating that schools should deliver at least two hours of PE per week for all pupils in primary school and at least two 50-minute periods for all pupils in secondary school (Scottish Government, 2018). In addition, Sport Scotland support schools with implementation efforts through national programming including coordination of the Active Schools programme which works across all 32 local authorities, This network comprises over 400 managers developing opportunities for school children to engage in school and physical activity before school, during lunchtime and after school as well as developing pathways between schools and local community sport clubs. Community sport policy implementation in Scotland is dominated by local authorities and leisure trusts, with 32 community sport hubs (aligned with local authority boundaries in Scotland) providing community collectives that focus on understanding the sport and physical activity needs of each community and collaborating to provide activities and interventions that meet these needs. The Scottish Local Government and Planning Act 1982 requires that local authorities ensure that there is *adequate* provision of facilities for the inhabitants of the area for recreational, sporting, cultural, and social activities. However, Jarvie (2024) underlines the ambiguity of the term "adequate provision" and advises that local authorities remain exceptionally stretched in resource terms. Consequently, community sport has a relatively low priority status and provision is, at best, patchy.

The UK Model of Sport and the EMS: Early Pioneer or Contemporary Revisionist?

There are five core features of 19th-century British sport that are evident in the 21th-century EMS. First, it was the autonomous associative activity of individuals across Britain that triggered the creation of a network of local voluntary clubs and national associations (Syzmanski, 2006). This associativity represents the starting point in the eventual solidification of an organisational pyramid for European sport, the hierarchy of sport organisations from local-level clubs to regional bodies, and to one national, one European and one international association per sport. Second, the UK was at the forefront of the creation of cross-nation competition. For example, national football matches as seen in the plethora of friendlies between home nation teams starting with Scotland v England in 1872 and home nation rugby competition as seen the Rugby Union Home Nation Championship created in 1883 and still alive today as the Six Nations Championship. Third, the structure of British sport has been predicated on the mutual enthusiasm of volunteers and voluntary activity (Harris et al., 2009), thereby creating the early foundations of what remains today as the backbone of European sport (European Commission, 2007). Fourth, the culture of athleticism within England's public schools served to reinforce certain values such as respect, morality, and excellence and helped cultivate a wholesome commitment to fair play, "not only a commitment to respecting the written rules of the games but abiding by what was generally understood to be the spirit of the game" (Renson, 2009, p. 10). Nowadays, we see parallels in the attention given to sports social, cultural and educational function, as articulated in the European Commission working paper (European Commission, 1998), White Paper (European Commission, 2007) and the Council's resolutions pertaining to the EMS (Council of the European Union, 2021). Fifth and finally, the history of British sport demonstrates its role in forging national identity, an often-forgotten element of the EMS as first acknowledged by the European Commission in 1998. For example, in Victorian England, cricket has proved a potent symbol in demonstrating values such as respectability, morality, and the good graces of the gentleman amateur. In Wales, rugby is the ideal brand of sport to capture the enthusiasm of the bustling coal mine and metalworker industry (Holt, 1989). In Scotland, identity has historically been wrapped up in association football and in the Scots deep and bitter rivalry with England. And, for the Catholic northern Irish, the restoration of the Gaelic games has provided an ideal tool to express its cultural distinctiveness and separation from England. Today, sports relationship with British identity is more complex, challenged by "the opaque or fuzzy frontiers surrounding the very fabrication and the subsequent recasting of identity" (Cohen, 1994, p. 7), the schizoid nature of the defining unit of each home nation/British sport team (Carrington, 1999), the multiple, overlapping, and individual identities of people across the Isles (Tuck, 2005), the conflation of the terms England and Britain (Osmond, 1988) and the subsequent conflation of England identity with British (Hargreaves, 1986), and the emergence of new identities (as well as the reemergence of old identities) in a post-Brexit era (Ferdjani, 2022).

In addition to these points of alignment, we also see clear areas of revision or change between the UK sport system and the EMS. For example, while the pyramid structure and its volunteer base remain dominant features of British sport, these structures have intersected with changes including a shift from a traditional hierarchical governance to a network or polycentric governance of sport (Harris et al., 2023) and a hardened governmentalisation of sport (Houlihan & Green, 2007), that has brought about demands to modernise (Houlihan & Green, 2009) and professionalise key parts of the sport system (Harris et al., 2009). The governance of sport across the home nations and the UK today can more accurately be characterised as a network or a polycentric system rather than a hierarchy. This polycentric system is made up of multiple decision centres, with overlapping jurisdictions, guided by overarching rules and norms, and mechanisms that enable the stakeholders in the system to mutually adjust (Ostrom et al., 1961). The sustained governmentalisation of sport has added to these polycentric arrangements through the addition of government departments and a wide range of quasi-governmental agencies including home nations' Sports Councils, UK Sport, the UKIS, UK Coaching, regulatory bodies such as the NSPCC Child Protection in Sport Unit, UK Anti-Doping and sport-specific actors such as the proposed independent—but government created—football regulator. Furthermore, the modernisation of voluntary clubs, NGBs, and governmental agencies requires that these organisations update their governing structures, introduce new ways of working (e.g., commissioning, contracting), implement new public management tools and enhance their governance practices. Professionalisation is evident in the building of the professional (i.e., paid) sporting workforce across NGBs, Active Partnerships, and sports clubs but also in the attempts to cultivate a service delivery philosophy and further professionalise the work of these structures through mechanisms such as club accreditation schemes, strategies, business plans, and sport development plans (Taylor et al., 2003). When considered together, these changes in British sport demonstrate important differences in respect of its hierarchical structure, the role of the state, and the overall autonomy of sport when compared to the normative structures and features of the EMS. This is not to argue that the situation is distinctly British, rather to clarify that the reality of the current structural arrangements of British sport differ in important ways to the EMS. Other contributions to this volume address similar developments elsewhere in Europe and the world.

While there remain important differences in the structural arrangements of British sport, there is—for many sports across the country—a sustained commitment to other structural aspects of the EMS, namely the principle of sporting merit, open competition formats, together with the possibility of promotion and the risk of relegation in sports leagues. We see evidence of this across almost all professional sport leagues across the country (football, rugby union, county cricket) although there are notable exceptions of sports that have recently introduced closed or single-entity league structures with no promotion/relegation as seen with Rugby League's new licence-based Super League format and British Basketball League's franchise model. However, these recent developments represent unusual cases, developed with the aim of enhancing the professional and commercial interests of the league for a relatively small number of teams, rather than providing a pyramidical model of competition, committed to sporting meritocracy, and open to and providing for a large number of teams across the country.

The European Commission places significant importance on the grassroots approach of European sport (Garcia, 2009). For the European Commission, grassroots sport is based on voluntary work, non-profit, club-based activities, "underpinned by non-commercial support and structures", and requires strong linkages and solidarity between the top (professional) and lower (recreational) levels (European Commission, 2007, p. 117). More recently, while a weak feature of the original EMS, the European Sport Charter gives clearer and explicit attention to the role of schools at the very base of grassroots sport (Council of Europe, n.d.), including PE/sport training for teachers, community use of school sport facilities, and the development of links between schools and clubs (Council of Europe, 2022).

Across the UK, while the policy aspirations for grassroots sports do change over time and according to the political ideas of the government of the day, they tend to seesaw between sporting and social outcomes. When concerned with sporting outcomes, grassroots policy tends to emphasise increases in the number of adults playing sport and the number of young people engaged in high-quality PE and school sport. When concerned with social outcomes, policy tends to underline the power of sport to improve physical health and mental well-being as well as provide opportunities to support individual, social and community development.

As set out above, the structures governing on and implementing grassroots sport can be presented in a convenient hierarchical order from government departments, home nations' Sports Council, NGBs (at the national, regional and/or county levels) down to a variety of sub-regional and local-level partners including Active Partnerships, local authorities, community sport hubs (Scotland), schools and sports clubs of varying types (i.e. large professional football clubs, small non-profit voluntary clubs, etc.). However, while the national-to-local flow of actors involved in grassroots sport suggests hierarchical order, the structure, governance, funding, differing policy (national, regional, and local policy) and interdependent role of these actors in the grassroots system more accurately reflect network or polycentric governance arrangements. With that being said, the core funding allocated to grassroots sport flows from the central government's DCMS and the home nations' Sport Councils. Consequently, these actors lay down the policy aspirations and then allocate funding and make additional funding available (primary through the lottery sports grant programme) for NGBs, clubs, and others to develop and implement programmes aligned to national policy objectives.

These structural arrangements illustrate the ubiquitous (Foucault, 1991) and discursive, rather than purely coercive nature of power (Gaventa, 2003) as all actors in the system have the ability to comply with, avoid, or reject policy goals. Conversely, the grassroots sport policy arena exposes structural inequalities across differing actors with power unevenly distributed—or asymmetrical (Marsh et al., 2003)—largely due to different roles, resources and responsibilities of actors, and non-compliance, rejection, or manipulation of policy may affect a particular actor. While any discussion of power in grassroots sport may seem quite academic, it exposes important practical implications regarding the EMS. For example, we argue that the centre of the UK grassroots system is government and the home nations' Sport Councils, not sport. They develop and evaluate policy, and provide the lion's share of funding to support implementation efforts. While the notion of solidarity in sport, including mechanisms to redistribute revenues from professional to grassroots levels, is symbolically potent, in reality, only a small number of sports engage in such work. For example, the NGBs for football, cricket, tennis, and rugby (union and league) commit to the UK Sport & Recreation Alliance's Code for Broadcasting Rights Owners. As a result, these sports agree to make certain events available in free-to-air broadcasts as well as allocating a minimum of 30% of their pay-per-view broadcasting revenue back into development of their sport (Sport & Recreation Alliance, n.y.). Additionally, many professional football clubs across the country have developed community trusts/foundations that provide a variety of sport, education, and broader social services to their communities. However, it would be naive to suggest that this work is solely about solidarity or investing in the community as many foundations aim to promote the club, build its brand and create relationships at the local, national, and international levels. The English Premier League also allocates some of its profits to a selection of grassroots football initiatives including the Football Foundation grants scheme, the Premier League Stadium Fund, women and girls football development programmes, the Premier League Fans Fund, and a range of educational initiatives such as Premier League Primary Stars, Premier League Inspires, and Premier League Kicks (Premier League, 2023). While these examples illustrate solidarity within their respective communities, they lack the resource allocation and central coordination that is seen from government departments and home nation sports councils.

On the issue of grassroots sports, it is clear that each home nation has a state-coordinated system for driving participation in school and community sport with varied methodologies used to measure and track participation in sport, over time. In England, Sport England's *Active Lives Survey* shows that 47% of the child/young people (5–16 years) population are active (engaged in sport or physical activity for an average of 60 minutes or more per day), with 23% fairly active (engaged in sport or physical activity for an average of 30–59 minutes per week), and 30% inactive (engaged in sport or physical activity for fewer than an average of 30 minutes per day) (Sport England, 2024a). The Active Lives data also show that 63% of the adult population are active (engaged in sport or physical activity for a minimum of 150 minutes per week), with 11% fairly active (engaged in sport or physical activity for 30–149 minutes per week), and 26% inactive (less than an average of 30 minutes per week) (Sport England, 2024b). In terms of commitment to organised sport, 22% of the adult English population are members of a sports club (Sport England, 2017). In Scotland, the national health survey shows that 69% of children meet recommended physical activity levels including school-based activities (i.e. an average of 60 minutes per day) or an average of 59% excluding school-based activities (Scottish Government, 2022). For adults, 51% of the population take part in physical activity and sport at least once in the previous four weeks (Scottish Government, 2022). Annual club membership data is not collected in Scotland and the most recent data on club membership suggests that 38% of the population are sport club members (Sport Scotland, 2008). The Wellbeing in Wales 2022 statistics state that 47% of primary-aged pupils (7–11) and 48% of secondary-aged pupils (11–16) participate in sports at three times per week (Welsh Government, 2022). The National Survey for Wales shows that 60% of the adult population participate in sport and physical activity at least once during the last four weeks with 39% of the adult population participating three times or more per week. The most recent data on club membership in Wales suggests that 23% of the population are sport club members (Sport Wales, 2020). Research commissioned by Sport Ireland/Sport Northern Ireland found that 73% of primary and 71% of post-primary school children participated in community sport at least once a week (Woods et al., 2023). Additionally, primary school children in Northern Ireland spend an average of 61 minutes per week in PE, with post-primary school children spending 73 minutes per week in PE (Woods et al., 2023). The Northern Irish Household Survey found that 52% of adults participate in sport at least once a week and just over one-quarter of adults (26%) are members of a sports club (Northern Ireland Statistics & Research Agency, 2022). A final, notable concern for sport policy-makers and practitioners across the UK has been the trend away from formal, organised, sports participation towards more individualised, informal, and convenience-laden pursuits—a trend that can also be seen across much of continental Europe (Scheerder et al., 2011).

Concluding Remarks

In some respects, sport in the UK can be viewed as an early pioneer in designing and establishing some of the key structural principles presented in the EMS. For example, the pyramidal format of league competition, the creation of open competitions based on the sporting merit with a commitment to promotion and relegation, and the development of sport-specific structures based on a common model of one national association with regional, county, and local structures (clubs) were evident in the UK many decades prior to the definition of the EMS. Similarly, some of the core features of the EMS have been embedded elements of sport in the UK since the late 19th century. However, the UK sport system also reveals notable revisions away from the key features of the EMS, more likely a consequence of responding to macro- and meso-level forces than any direct or intentional response to the EMS. For example, we see changes in the governance of grassroots and elite sport from a hierarchical structure to a network or polycentric assortment of decision centres. Interestingly, within these arrangements, the state maintains a central role directing on the specific policy goals and funding for grassroots and elite sport. Similarly, we see evidence of the state intervening in matters of sport regulation, for example, the proposed creation on an "independent" football regulator. While, from a responsible governance perspective, such mechanisms may be justified, they raise questions about the extent to which sport in the UK may be viewed as having the rights and obligations of autonomy. While ministerial hands may not visibly be pulling the strings on issues that attract the IOC's attention to doubt the autonomy of British sport, the nature of their intervention adds a level of haziness to the principle of autonomy.

The hyper-commercialisation of some professional sports also presents a sustained challenge to the notion of solidarity. While football may continue to invest in grant programmes and run large foundation efforts, it is difficult to ignore the prioritisation of their brand and the work that leagues/clubs do to grow the global recognition and increase their market share. These concerns carry far greater priority for top-level professional sport—particularly Premier League and EFL Championship football—over any concern that they may have for solidarity. In response, lower league clubs perhaps retain a closer relationship, one that more accurately reflects the EMS spirit of solidarity, despite the fact that many of these clubs have limited financial capacity. Finally, commercialisation and professionalisation in some sports in the UK have driven the creation of new single-entity, closed league structures with no (or limited) opportunity for promotion and relegation. Consequently, we conclude that while the EMS may retain some symbolic value, it does not so much influence what sport is in Britain rather than reflect what it once was. While sharing many commonalities with the EMS, the UK's sport system has evolved into a distinctive hybrid, representing both an early pioneer, and a contemporary revisionist within the European sport context.

Notes

1 As of 2024, Scotland have a devolved government and directly elected Parliament; Wales have a devolved government and directly elected Parliament, and Northern Ireland have a power sharing executive and directly elected assembly.
2 It is worth noting that Team GB did manage to field a women's football team at the London 2012 and the Tokyo 2020(+1) Olympic Games. Also, in 2023, rugby reconciled these challenges, finding both the political will and the practical solutions to compete as one Team GB at the European Games and the summer Olympic Games while retaining home nation teams in the Rugby World Cup Sevens and the Commonwealth Games.

References

Allen, J. G. (2018). The Office of the Crown. *Cambridge Law Journal, 77*(2), 298–320.

Allison, L. (2001). *Amateurism in Sport: An Analysis and a Defence*. Routledge.

Bolton, N. (2024). Sport Policy in Wales. In M. Dowling, S. Harris, & C. Mackintosh (Eds.), *Sport Policy across the United Kingdom* (pp. 60–83). Routledge.

Brailsford, D. (1992). *British Sport: A Social History*. The Lutterworth Press.

Carrington, B. (1999). Too Many St. George Crosses to Bear. In M. Perryman (Ed.), *The Ingerland Factor* (pp. 71–86). Mainstream.

Cohen, R. (1994). *Frontiers of Identity: The British and Others*. Longman.

Connolly, S., Carlin, A., Johnston, A., & Woods, C., Powell, C., Belton, S., O'Brien, W., Saunders, J., Duff, C., Farmer, O., Murphy, M. (2020). Physical Activity, Sport and Physical Education in Northern Ireland School Children: A Cross-Sectional Study. *International Journal of Environmental Research and Public Health, 17*(10), 6849. https://doi.org/10.3390/ijerph17186849

Council of Europe. (2022). *European Sports Charter (Revised)*. https://edoc.coe.int/en/sport-for-all/11299-revised-european-sports-charter.html

Council of Europe. (n.d.). *Further Developing the European Sport Model*. https://rm.coe.int/further-developing-the-european-sports-model-european-sport-charter-pa/1680a1b1cf

Council of Europe Union. (2021). *Resolution of the Council and of the Representatives of the Governments of the Member States Meeting with the Council on the Key Features of the European Sport Model*. https://eur-lex.europa.eu/legal-content/EN/TXT/?uri=CELEX%3A42021Y1213%2801%29

Davies, N. (2000). *The Isles: A History*. Papermac.

Dowling, M., Harris, S., & Mackintosh, C. (2024). *Sport Policy across the United Kingdom*. Routledge.

Dunning, E., & Sheard, K. (1979). *Barbarians, Gentlemen and Players: A Sociological Study of the Development of Rugby Football.* NYU Press.

Elias, N., & Dunning, E. (1986). *The Quest for Excitement.* Blackwell.

European Commission. (1998). *The European Model of Sport: Consultation Document of DG X.* European Commission.

European Commission. (2007). *White Paper on Sport.* https://eur-lex.europa.eu/EN/legal-content/summary/white-paper-on-sport.html#:~:text=This%20white%20paper%20was%20one,of%20the%20world%20of%20sport

Ferdjani, Y. (2022). Brexit and the emergence of a new English identity. Observatoire de la Société Britannique, (28), 47–65. https://doi.org/10.4000/osb.5588

Foucault, M. (1991). *Discipline and Punish: The Birth of a Prison.* Penguin.

Garcia, B. (2009). Sport Governance after the White Paper: The Demise of the European Model? *International Journal of Sport Policy, 1*(3), 267–284.

Gaventa, J. (2003). Power after Lukes: An overview of theories of power since Lukes and their application to development. Brighton: Participation Group, *Institute of Development Studies, 8*(11), 1–18. https://www.powercube.net/wp-content/uploads/2009/11/power_after_lukes.pdf

Gibbons, I. (2015). *The British Labour Party and the Establishment of the Irish Free State, 1918–1924.* Palgrave Macmillan.

Habermas, J. (1989). *The Structural Transformation of the Public Sphere.* The MIT Press.

Hargreaves, J. (1986). *Sport, Power and Culture.* Routledge.

Harris, S., Dowling, M., & Washington, M. (2023). Political protest and Rule 50: Exploring the polycentric governance of international and Olympic sport. *International Journal of Sport Policy and Politics, 15*(3), 417–434. https://doi.org/10.1080/19406940.2023.2224345

Harris, S., Mori, K., & Collins, M. (2009). Great Expectations: The Role of Voluntary Sports Clubs as Policy Implementers. *Voluntas International Journal of Non-Profit Organisations, 20*(4), 405–423.

Hill, A. (2004, June 13). The English identity crisis: Who do you think you are? *The Guardian.* https://www.theguardian.com/uk/2004/jun/13/britishidentity.ameliahill

Hitchen, P. (2008). *Abolition of Britain: From Winston Churchill to Princess Diana.* Bloomsbury.

HM Government. (2020). *Guidance on Devolution.* https://www.gov.uk/guidance/guidance-on-devolution.

Holt, R. (1989). *Sport and the British: A Modern History.* Clarendon Press.

Houlihan, B., & Green, M. (2007). *Comparative Elite Sport Development: Systems, Structures and Public Policy.* Routledge.

Houlihan, B., & Green, M. (2009). Modernisation and Sport: The Reform of UK Sport and Sport England. *Public Administration, 83*(3), 678–698.

Jarvie, G. (2024). Sport Policy in Scotland. In M. Dowling, S. Harris, & C. Mackintosh (Eds.), *Sport Policy across the United Kingdom* (pp. 40–59). Routledge.

Maguire, J. (1999). *Global Sport: Identities, Societies, Civilizations.* Polity Press.

Markovits, A. S., & Hellerman, S. L. (2014). *Offside: Soccer and American Exceptionalism.* Princeton University Press.

Marsh, D., Richards, D., & Smith, M. (2003). Unequal Plurality: Towards an Asymmetric Power Model of British Politics. *Government and Opposition, 38*(3), 306–332.

Nairn, T. (2000). *After Britain: New Labour and the Return of Scotland.* Granta.

Northern Ireland Statistics, & Research Agency. (2022). *Experience of Sport by Adults in Northern Ireland: Findings from the Continuous Household Survey 2019/20*. https://www.communities-ni.gov.uk/system/files/publications/communities/experience-sport-by-adults-northern-ireland-201920.pdf

Osmond, J. (1988). *The Divided Kingdom*. Constable.

Ostrom, V., Tiebout, C. M., & Warren, R. (1961). The Organization of Government in Metropolitan Areas: A Theoretical Inquiry. *The American Political Science Review*, *55*(4), 831–842.

Premier League. (2023). *Premier League Annual Report 2022/23*. https://resources.premierleague.com/premierleague/document/2024/02/01/e8dee042-88c3-4d3b-8caf-294f681fcc99/PL_Annual-Report_2022-23_DIGITAL.pdf

Renson, R. (2009). Fair Play: Its Origins and Meanings in Sport and Society. *Kinesiology*, *41*(1), 5–18.

Scheerder, J., Vandermeerschen, H., Van Tuyckom, C., Hoekman, R., Breedveld, K., & Vos, S. (2011). Understanding the Game: Sport Participation in Europe: Facts, Reflections and Recommendations. *Sport, Policy, and Management, (SPM)*, *10*.

Scottish Government. (2018). *Health and Wellbeing in Schools*. https://www.gov.scot/policies/schools/wellbeing-in-schools/

Scottish Government. (2022). *Scottish Health Survey, 2019*, Volume 1. https://www.gov.scot/publications/scottish-health-survey-2019-volume-1-main-report/pages/10/

Sport England. (2017). *Active People Survey*. Sport England.

Sport England. (2021). *Uniting the Movement*. Sport England.

Sport England. (2024a). *Active Lives Survey 2022–23 (Children and Young People)*. Sport England. https://sportengland-production-files.s3.eu-west-2.amazonaws.com/s3fs-public/2023-12/Active%20Lives%20Children%20and%20Young%20People%20Survey%20-%20academic%20year%202022-23%20report.pdf?VersionId=3N7GGWZMKy88UPsGfnJVUZkaTklLwB_L

Sport England. (2024b). *Active Lives Survey 2022–23 (Adults)*. Sport England. https://sportengland-production-files.s3.eu-west-2.amazonaws.com/s3fs-public/2024-04/Active%20Lives%20Adult%20Survey%20November%202022-23%20Report.pdf?VersionId=veYJTP_2n55UdOmX3PAXH7dJr1GA24vs

Sport Scotland. (2008). *Sports Participation in Scotland 2008*. https://sportscotland.org.uk/media/mlanzyc3/sports_participation_in_scotland_2008_research_digest_july_2010.pdf

Sport Wales. (2020). *Sport and Active Lifestyles*. https://www.sport.wales/download/file/315/

Szymanski, S. (2008). A theory of the evolution of modern sport. *Journal of Sport History 35(1)*, 1–32. https://www.jstor.org/stable/26404949

Taylor, M. (2014). Trade Unionism in British Sport, 1920–1964. *Labor History*, *55*(5), 622–637.

Taylor, P., Nichols, G., Holmes, K., James, M., Gratton, C., & Garrett, R. (2003). *Sports Volunteering in England 2002*. Sport England.

Torrance, D. (2022). *Supreme Court Judgment on Scottish Independence Referendum*. House of Commons Library. https://commonslibrary.parliament.uk/supreme-court-judgment-on-scottish-independence-referendum/

Tuck, J. (2005). Rugby Union and National Identity Politics. In A. Bairner (Ed.), *Sport and the Irish: Histories, Identities, Issues*. Dublin Press.

UKIS. (2023). *Introducing the UK Sport Institute*. UKSI. https://uksportsinstitute.co.uk/who-we-are/uk-sports-institute/

Welsh Government. (2022). *Wellbeing of Wales, 2022.* https://www.gov.wales/wellbeing-wales-2022-children-and-young-peoples-wellbeing-wales-vibrant-culture-and-thriving-welsh#:~:text=Sport%20participation,-The%20latest%20school&text=There%20was%20very%20little%20difference,times%20a%20week%20in%20sports

Woods, C. B., Ng, K. W., Britton, U., McClelland, J., O'Keeffe, B., Sheikhi, A., McFlynn, P., Murphy, M. H., Goss, H., Behan, S., Philpott, C., Lester, D., Adamakis, M., Costa, J., Coppinger, T., Connolly, S., Belton, S., & O'Brien, W. (2023). *The Children's Sport Participation and Physical Activity Study* 2022. University of Limerick.

Part III

Models of Sport Around the World

Chapter 12

The American and Canadian Sport Models

Not One and the Same

Milena M. Parent and David Patterson

Introduction

In Europe and elsewhere around the world, there is a tendency to see North America as one sport system. But a deeper dive into the American and Canadian sport systems reveals significantly different approaches to each country's sport system. In fact, the Canadian sport system aligns more closely with the European Sport Model than with the American Model. Yet, there are competitive structures that straddle the American and Canadian border.

In this chapter, we compare the American and Canadian sport models between each other and with the European Sport Model. We start with a presentation of each country's sport system followed by an overview of the interrelationships between the two systems and the cross-border competition structures found within the North American professional sport leagues. Throughout, we compare these governance structures with the European Sport Model.

The American Sport System

Where a European sport system may be typically described as a pyramid, and the Canadian system as a matrix (see below), the American system defies any simple metaphor. In the case of Europe and Canada, the metaphor is anchored on a key player, be it the club or a governmental entity. There is no such anchored centre of the American system leaving us wanting for a ready metaphorical tool to explain it. In the end, it may be that the best explanation of American sport is that it is reflective of America – a dispersed network (see Figure 12.1).

The American sport system has multiple major nodes on its network with multiple other nodes connected to and through those respective areas of concentration. This section outlines some of the key nodes, some nodes that flow from those central actors, and some considerations of the relative strengths and weaknesses of the American system considering those nodal relationships.

This section will outline the following nodes for further consideration, although they are not the only important nodes in this complex, decentralised, and evolving network. Though the nodes are presented in the order of the progression of a

DOI: 10.4324/9781032665153-15

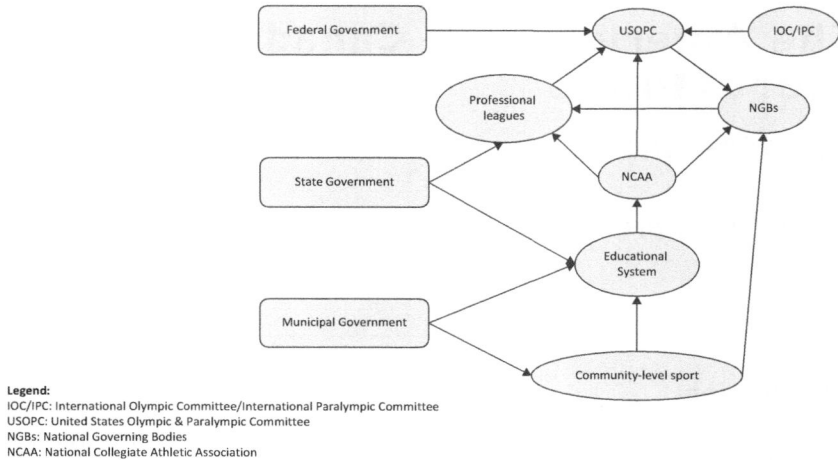

Legend:
IOC/IPC: International Olympic Committee/International Paralympic Committee
USOPC: United States Olympic & Paralympic Committee
NGBs: National Governing Bodies
NCAA: National Collegiate Athletic Association

Figure 12.1 The American Sport System in a graphic scheme.

typical athlete, from young ages through to professional sport, this is for narrative convenience and not to imply the importance of one node over the other – all nodes are dependent on each other in the network. They include:

• Community Sport
• Education Based Sport
• Olympic and Paralympic Sport
• Professional Sport

Before exploring these nodes, however, it is worth noting the role of government in American sport to juxtapose it with Canadian and European sport systems, and the impact on the autonomy of sport in the United States.

Governmental Roles in the American Sport System and the Resulting Autonomy of Sport

The role of government in America is substantial and vital to the success of the system, but that involvement takes on a very different form than it does in nearly any other nation. The role of the federal government is explicitly limited and overtly circumscribed – but remains impactful. The role of the state (regional) government is largely in support of sport through educational programming, while the municipal (city/county) level is focused on providing sport infrastructure to communities. In sum, the impacts of governmental involvement are meaningful, but as with many other elements of American sport, government interventions tend to be in a manner that is competitive rather than coordinated.

The federal government's role in sport is primarily outlined in the Ted Stevens Amateur Sport Act of 1978, which chartered the United States Olympic Committee and tasked the organisation with sending teams to the Olympic Games on behalf of the United States. Prior to the Act, the Amateur Athletic Union (AAU) was the lead body in sending teams to the Games. The changes to the Act unified the Olympic Movement under one umbrella in the USOC (United States Olympic Committee, or USOPC, United States Olympic and Paralympic Committee as of June 2019) with specific roles for the National Governing Bodies (NGBs) in each sport enumerated as well. The Act is highly prescriptive in outlining some functions of the USOC and NGBs while also being open-ended in other elements. The resulting mix is a legal structure that leaves considerable authority vested in the USOC functioning effectively as a federal amateur sport regulatory body to manage and navigate the broadly defined goals of the Act. Of note, the Act confers upon the USOC the ability to certify NGBs, meaning that the USOC can regulate and even sever relationships with NGBs from time to time.

More recently, the Empowering Olympic and Paralympic Athletes Act was passed largely in response to scandals involving youth and high-performance athletes in the sport of gymnastics (e.g., Kwiatkowski, 2021). The Act recognised some of the shortcomings of the Olympic and Paralympic system in the United States and created greater levels of transparency and accountability to remedy some of those shortcomings. Of greatest import to the system, this included the creation of the United States Center for Safe Sport (USCSS).

The USCSS (hereafter "The Center") was created to investigate allegations of abusive behaviour in sport and to act against those determined to have violated the Safe Sport Code. The centralised approach was designed to avoid any further instances of NGBs failing to pursue allegations seriously and to provide a central repository of actions taken so that offenders were not able to transfer to another sport or sport body, taking advantage of myriad enforcement mechanisms that had been in place previously. In both cases, the Center has demonstrated incremental improvement against the status quo but has inflicted substantial administrative burden on the sport system. It has also been overwhelmed at times by the volume of cases that emerged once a clear reporting mechanism was publicly available.

At the federal level, the view of sport is at times disjointed. The federal government provides real support and structure to the Olympic and Paralympic sport system, but provides no direct funding and is, in fact, legally enjoined from providing financial guarantees to the hosting of Olympic and Paralympic Games. Expectations on the structure of sport extends to only those sports and sport organisations explicitly within the Olympic and Paralympic sport system, leaving large gaps in the regulatory environment for sport.

At the state level, governmental interjections are largely filtered via the educational system. Through high school-level sports, and through sport at the postsecondary level, state funding to sport can be substantial and has created a pipeline of sport discovery and sport development in many sports, though not all. As is noted below on education, this provides a pipeline of athlete development in those sports supported by the educational system and leaves other sports (e.g., Biathlon, Bobsleigh, and Badminton) to create developmental pipelines on their own.

At the municipal (state or county in the American context) funding tends to focus on the provision of sport facilities aimed at the community level. Although there is a broader proliferation of private facilities in the United States than in many other countries (more on the private nature of community sport follows), local levels of government are often active in providing some sport facilities and facilities (e.g., walking trails) aimed at active living.

Governmental intervention in sport in the United States is substantial and makes a difference in how sport is delivered and viewed in the country. It is also meaningfully different than virtually any other nation on Earth in the form that those interventions take. That governmental role is both the product and creator of a system that emphasises the educational system as a delivery mechanism for sport. From a sport autonomy perspective, however, though there is significant government involvement at different levels of the system, sport's autonomy is maintained as governments do not normally impose government-related individuals in the running of a given sport organisation and the federal government does not fund the sport system. But the Ted Stevens Act allows Congress to remove the USOPC Board of Directors at its discretion – though it is unlikely it would ever do so.

Community Sport Provision

Community-level sport provision varies widely across sports, locations, and contexts. Though this provision results in high costs to end users and a disjointed development pathway for athletes, it also provides multiple options for participants and a resilient system able to withstand external shocks or imperatives given that there is no one "owner" of community sport in the United States.

Local governments (both municipal and county) provide facilities for many community sports but not for many others. The provision of community sport facilities sometimes includes limited programming, with community programming usually focused on introduction to sport and adult recreational sport. Local governments tend not to provide services aimed at athletes in any kind of developmental pathway.

As noted below, high schools provide considerable sport programming at the local level, and they provide facilities for those same sports in many cases. This results in many high schools having an entire suite of excellent sport facilities, but those facilities may or may not be available widely to the community, and the facilities tend not to be built in the context of a community-wide facility scope. Thus, some facilities such as tracks for athletics competitions, pools, and gyms are overbuilt in many communities, resulting in underused facilities in some areas/sports while gaps exist in others.

Educational-Based Sport

To an outside observer, the role of educational institutions in the delivery of sport is the most prominent difference between American sport and that of most other nations. The National Collegiate Athletic Association (NCAA) national championship events are massive sporting spectacles on par with major national and international professional sport events around the world. The prominence of collegiate sport in the American system is a unique and at times defining element of sport. To wit, the NCAA saw revenues of $1.14 billion USD in 2022 (Berkowitz, 2023). Although it is incredibly prominent, an examination of the sport system in the educational sphere should start in high school (grades 9 through 12), where the National Federation of High Schools (NFHS) educational-based sport often begins.

Sport at the community level is often tied to the high school system where high schools often have professional coaches, training facilities, and a public profile in their respective communities. Sport at the high school level is more open than at the collegiate or other levels, meaning a substantial portion of students can participate in sport through competition on the varsity (most competitive), junior varsity (less competitive), and sometimes freshman (aimed primarily at students in grade 9, the first year of high school). These three levels provide participation outlets and a progression pathway for students new to high school or new to a sport.

That the sport outlet at the high school level is broad (the NFHS supports 19 sports, though some state high school associations offer others) and largely inclusive leads to many opportunities to participate at the youth level, and many opportunities to discover sport and sport acumen in the educational environment. For sport development at the Olympic and Paralympic levels, it is noteworthy that, of the 19 supported sports, 18 are on the programme of the Olympic, Paralympic, or Pan American Games, ensuring that the high school system is a full element of the developmental pathway for athletes in the Olympic and Paralympic Movements. The high school sport system shares this in common with the next educational level, collegiate sport.

Those involved in sport are most likely aware of the collegiate sport system in the United States. While the NCAA is largely at the centre of this system, it is supplemented by junior college sport (mostly two-year, non-degree-granting institutions of higher learning) and by small college sport (adjudged to be "small" mostly by the number of undergraduate enrolees). Although the junior college and small college systems are important and involve many athletes, coaches and officials, the remainder of this section will focus on the composition and structure of collegiate sport contained within the NCAA.

The NCAA operates a broad sport programme on a national level, with 23 sponsored sports offered at over 1,100 member institutions with over 500,000 participating athletes. In relation to international sport, importantly, 20 of the sponsored sports are on the Olympic programme – ensuring a clear pathway for athletes through the NCAA to the Olympic and Paralympic Games. With the enormous base of sports in the NCAA system (and a parallel system of sport in the varsity club and intramural levels), the NCAA is a major provider of sport programming for thousands of athletes and a vital developmental pathway for Olympic and Paralympic athletes.

The NCAA system has become so comprehensive across multiple sports and over a large footprint of institutions that the NCAA pathway is not only important for athletes representing the United States but also for nearly the entirety of nations competing at the Olympic Games. At the 2020 Tokyo Games, athletes from the NCAA (either currently competing in the NCAA or NCAA alumni) won a total of 282 medals (NCAA, 2021): 112 were won by Team USA athletes, with another 71 won by athletes from 21 other nations. For perspective, medals won by only one athletic conference (league), the Pac12, would have placed the Pac12 fifth on the overall medals table at the Games. In terms of athlete development and podium performance, the NCAA is a driver both for American athletes and for athletes the world over.

Any discussion of NCAA sport is incomplete without a discussion of college football. Collegiate football is a behemoth on the American sport landscape with massive amounts of attendance at Games (over 100,000 fans being common at several schools), and incredible media engagement and attention. The funding flowing to and from collegiate football makes it relevant to any discussion of American sport. This drives (1) revenue to support other sports in the NCAA system; (2) athlete decision making where athletes choose football over other alternatives given its profile; and (3) brand equity of athletic departments and entire universities, with the athletic department (very often led by football) being characterised as the "front door" of the university community.

Although high-profile NCAA sports on university campuses are largely unique to the United States, club and intramural programming, common in other nations, also exists on university campuses and can be a substantial driver of sport participation and a smaller, but appreciable, driver of high-performance sport outcomes as well. In some sports (e.g., rugby), the system of student-led sport club programmes on campuses is an important vein for introduction to sport as well as development of high-performance athletes. In others (e.g., figure skating), high-performance sport outcomes are non-existent, but the club competition structure ensures continued participation by athletes beyond their high school years.

Olympic and Paralympic Sport

As is noted above, the Olympic and Paralympic sport system is headed by the USOPC. The USOPC, a creation of the United States federal government, the Olympic Charter and the Paralympic Charter, oversees the NGBs in those respective sports, as well as delivering some services directly to athletes and sport communities.

Led by a board of directors, the USOPC discharges responsibilities delegated to it by the International Olympic Committee (IOC), the International Paralympic Committee (IPC) and the federal government, all while adhering to corporate law requirements of the State of Colorado (the American state in which the USOPC is headquartered). The USOPC works through a web of regulatory imperatives and regulatory restrictions that creates a National Olympic/Paralympic Committee (NOC/NPC) unique within the Olympic and Paralympic Movements.

Apart from the requirement that the NOC certify NGBs in federal law, the UOSPC is also unique in that it delivers some services directly to sport and athletes, as opposed to entrusting that delivery to NGBs as in Canada and most European nations. The USOPC offers a suite of sport medicine and mental health services directly to athletes, provides direct financial support to athletes, and, in some cases, acts as the NGB for a sport. Finally, and significantly, the USOPC also provides health insurance coverage to many high-performance athletes and sometimes their families – a service provided by the government in nearly all other competing nations at the Olympic and Paralympic Games. As the private provision of health care is best covered by experts in that area, and at considerably greater length than this chapter can offer, it will be set aside apart from noting that this is a substantial expense for the USOPC that its colleague NOC/NPCs around the world do not need to cover nor contemplate.

The USOPC's unique role in the direct provision of NGB-like services to some sports creates a situation in which it is both the overseer of sport provision and the provider of those same services. In some sports (11 sports as of this writing), the USOPC is, in effect, the NGB for a sport or at least vis-à-vis that sport's Olympic or Paralympic high-performance programme. Delivery and oversight of delivery of these programmes are unique among most sport provision programmes around the world.

NGBs affiliated with the USOPC, as their sports are on the programme of the Olympic, Paralympic, Pan American, or Para Pan American Games, vary vastly in size, scope, and public engagement. NGBs, such as the United States Tennis Association (USTA), have hundreds of thousands of participants and substantial revenue from their marquee events (e.g., the US Open for the USTA), while others, like USA Team Handball, have very small membership bases and rely heavily on funding support from the USOPC. This variance among the NGBs creates highly variable outcomes from sport to sport, with some NGBs acting as sophisticated providers of sport to fans, media, and participants, while others struggle to provide basic services to a small group of core participants only.

In both cases, NGBs are led by volunteer boards of directors who oversee the organisation. In the larger NGBs, these boards most often provide oversight and broad direction to the organisation, while in smaller versions, the board may provide key operational support through leadership of specific functional areas like high performance, coach development, or events.

Professional Sport

With few exceptions, professional sport exists in a system that is parallel to the developmental, high performance, or community systems. Major professional leagues such as the National Football League (NFL), Major League Baseball (MLB), the National Hockey League (NHL), or the Women's National Basketball Association (WNBA) operate outside the purview or scope of their respective NGBs or the USOPC.

While this creates a system that does not explicitly dovetail with developmental levels of sport (or other professional leagues in the same sport in many cases), the professional leagues are effective at generating outcomes, athlete income, and a daily training environment. It is also common that professional leagues support the NGBs in their respective sports as sponsors/donors, helping to develop the community levels of their sports.

The American System – Disjointed and Resilient

The American system of sport delivery is perhaps the most disjointed in the world. With private providers, public sector providers, and third sector providers all working at the same time, often in the same place, the system is not readily navigable nor efficient in service provision. These clear problems are mitigated by the resilience of a system that does not rely on any one node or any one central authority in a material manner.

Without a coherent pathway, it often falls to athletes to navigate the myriad decisions that must be made to find a destination in high-performance sport or even in lifelong recreational sport engagement. Conversely, the multiple pathways and decision points often lead to more options for sport consumers and the ability to change clubs/facilities/pathways if the athlete sees the need to do so.

As with much in American life, the entrepreneurial nature of multiple actors working in an uncoordinated manner creates silos and enclaves but also creates resiliency. American identity is one of low governmental intervention in daily life, and one where competitive impulses are trusted to create positive outcomes. In these and other ways, American sport is truly an American phenomenon.

The Canadian Sport System

Canadian Sport System Structure

The Canadian sport system is a federated sport model; it is a complex multi-level, multi-sectoral system. Unlike the European Sport Model which could be characterised as pyramidal, the Canadian sport system is more of a matrix (see Figure 12.2).

The first level includes the federal government (through Sport Canada), the national multisport service organisations like Own The Podium and the Coaching Association of Canada, the national sport organisations (NSOs) or federations (terms used more than the United States-based NGB term) like Canada Soccer, and other national organisations like the Canadian Parks & Recreation Association (Government of Canada, 2022b). The Canadian sport system does not have a single technical leader organisation like Norway or Germany; instead, we find a triumvirate of Sport Canada, Own the Podium, and the Canadian Olympic and Paralympic Committees. Sport Canada funds a significant portion of NSOs' budgets through its Sport Support Program; this tool helps Sport Canada determine the level of funding for the NSO "for activities that enhance the Canadian sport system" (Government of Canada, 2022a). Own the Podium determines and recommends NSO funding levels to Sport Canada, the Canadian Olympic/Paralympic Committee, and the

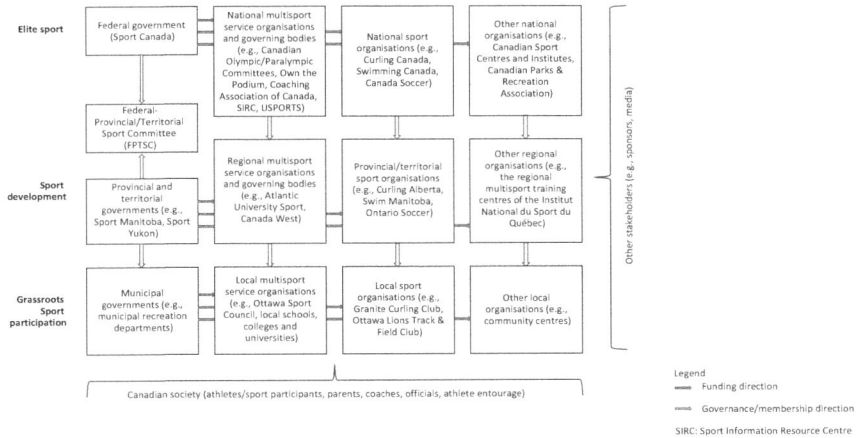

Figure 12.2 The Canadian Sport System.

Canadian Olympic Foundation "to deliver more Olympic and Paralympic medals for Canada" (Own the Podium, 2023). The Canadian Olympic and Paralympic Committees have, in recent years, taken on more funding and technical support for their affiliated NSOs, such as providing consulting assistance for specific files (e.g., branding, human resource policies, and governance). But they also receive funding from Sport Canada. Finally, all national-level non-profit organisations, be they within or outside sport, must follow the Canada Not-for-profit Corporations Act, which sets out governance guidelines such as board membership, elections, and financial reporting (Minister of Justice, 2017).

The second level includes similar organisations but at the provincial/territorial (P/T) level. In between these two levels sits the Federal-Provincial/Territorial Sport Committee (FPTSC), which oversees direction for sport in the country because sport is technically a P/T responsibility. However, the federal government and other national-level organisations are responsible for fielding the Canadian teams that represent Canada and compete internationally. Thus, we could say that the national level is responsible for elite sport, while the P/T level is responsible for the development of sport within their given jurisdiction. They also field the teams that go to the Canada Games (Canada Games Council, n.d.), Canada's premier national multisport event akin to the Olympic (Winter) Games. Some P/T governments are quite involved in the sport sector (e.g., Alberta, Ontario, Québec), establishing their own governance and funding expectations, while others – especially smaller provinces and territories – are less so.

The third level, where most of Canadian society will engage in the sport system, comprises the organisations involved in grassroots sport participation, that is, municipal departments, local sport clubs, local schools and colleges/universities, and other local organisations like community centres. Though most local clubs are non-profit in nature, some sports like soccer/football, basketball, martial arts, and figure skating, have varying numbers of for-profit clubs. In particular, soccer/football and basketball clubs recently started to follow the European model of academies, sometimes even being owned by a European entity, such as in the case of FC Barcelona having four schools in Canada (FC Barcelona, 2016).

Finally, across the whole system, we see a variety of other stakeholders involved, such as the media and sponsors.

Government Involvement and System Governance

As can be seen in Figure 12.2, the three levels of government are heavily involved in the sport system. However, a series of government decisions and policies over the past 30 years continue to influence the sport system's governance and system actors' actions and interactions.

A key issue is the separation of physical activity from sport in 1993. At the time, Prime Minister Kim Campbell put physical activity under the Health Canada portfolio and sport under the Canadian Heritage portfolio. The justification for this split stemmed from, on the one hand, sport development being a P/T responsibility and, on the other hand, the national teams that competed internationally represented Canada and therefore influenced Canadian identity, which fell within Canadian Heritage's purview. To this day, sport remains under Canadian Heritage, and efforts to engage the health/physical activity sector have been difficult and have resulted in competition for resources – especially funding – from the federal government.

In addition, the policy landscape linked to sport has become increasingly complex. Over the past 20 years, three different major policies and a multitude of topic-specific policies were developed, like on doping, women and girls, high performance, tobacco sponsorship, international sport event hosting, persons with a disability, and Aboriginal People's participation in sport (see Government of Canada, 2021; Sport Information Resource Centre (SIRC), n.d.) which influence the Canadian sport system's stakeholders. The three key policies include the Framework for Recreation in Canada from 2015, the Common Vision for increasing physical activity and reducing sedentary living in Canada from 2018, and the Canadian Sport Policy (CSP) from 2002 and 2012 (Sport Information Resource Centre (SIRC), n.d.). The CSP is relevant to understand the Canadian sport system and it illustrates how the Canadian sport system is governed, how system actors interact. Thus, we provide a brief overview of its evolution now.

The CSP 2002 was considered a policy of and for governments. It was the first time not only that Canada had a national sport policy but also that the federal level dared to include "participation" as part of national discussions. Though because the FPTSC signed off on the policy, it was still considered "owned" by the key sport portfolio holders, the P/T governments. It focused on enhanced participation, excellence, capacity, and interaction. Participation's inclusion increased the tension between participation and high-performance sport; now, Sport Canada gave itself permission to financially support participation-related initiatives instead of just elite-level sport. The CSP 2002's evaluation – in preparation for the second

CSP – noted improvements in excellence, capacity, and interaction between sport system stakeholders; however, participation rates remained a problem (Sport Information Resource Centre (SIRC), 2022).

During the ten-year CSP 2002, the Sport for Life Society (Sport for Life, 2023a) was created to spearhead quality sport and physical literacy experiences for all Canadians. It built momentum across the sport system with its long-term athlete development (LTAD) pathway (Sport for Life, 2023b). Sport Canada required all its funded NSOs to adopt and adapt the LTAD pathway for their given sport so that sport development would be not only age appropriate but also stage appropriate. Such was the strength of this movement that the Sport for Life Society became one of the most vocal organisations during the consultation process for the CSP 2012.

The CSP 2012 was a policy for the sport sector. It reflected policy development thinking at the time, that is, by using a collaborative, shared leadership approach. The CSP 2012 was developed through shared leadership between the federal and P/T governments as well as with the non-governmental sector (e.g., sport organisations, academics, and cross-country public consultations). Feedback throughout the policy's development phase asked that the policy have clear, measurable goals and that a policy implementation and monitoring (PIM) mechanism be put in place to oversee the ten-year implementation process. This mechanism became the PIM work group (for more information, see Parent & Jurbala, 2023). Though the CSP 2012 recognised the LTAD and Sport for Life's stage-based pathway, the policy writing team and approvers opted to create a dedicated taxonomy of five sport contexts within which the policy would apply: introduction to sport, recreational sport, competitive sport, high-performance sport, and sport for development. Each context had one specific goal attached to it as well as multiple objectives. In all, the 2012 policy included 30 distinct objectives. The policy also had, for the first time in Canadian history, a specific vision for the Canadian sport system, as well as values and principles.

The CSP 2012, in true Canadian fashion, was specific enough to give a general direction but vague enough to let every actor in the sport system determine how they fit and what they would do. This ambiguity meant that the CSP 2012 was perceived a successful in its summative evaluation: it "provided a common language and framework for introductory and recreational sport"; national and P/T level sport programme aligned with the CSP 2012; age-based, stage-based and physical literacy principles were incorporated into sport programming; and Canadian athletes achieved high levels of international sporting success during the life of the policy (Goss Gilroy Inc., 2021, p. 1).

Success was most notable where dedicated government funding was provided, demonstrating the strong influence of the governments on the sport system. In addition, the sport system continues to be seen as operating in a silo away from other sectors like health and education. Finally, though the national and P/T levels made progress, the local level continued to see a lack of capacity and little, if any, believed association to or even awareness of the CSP 2012.

A third CSP is currently being drafted. At the time of writing this chapter, it is meant to be a policy by Canadians for Canadians. A series of extensive cross-country consultations with various sport and non-sport stakeholders (including a survey sent to the general public), is informing the development of the new policy. This third iteration is expected to have a particular focus on the grassroots level, which has been underserved since the first CSP.

Key Systemic Characteristics and Sport Autonomy

The description of the Canadian sport system exemplifies its multi-level, multi-sectoral nature. It also highlights government involvement at all levels of the sport system. The tiered system is akin to the European Sport Model where each jurisdiction level has a set of responsibilities; however, they are not necessarily delegated from the top down given sport development jurisdiction actually lies with the P/T governments. This structure is not unique in Canada given it is a confederation; many portfolios are held by P/T governments, like health and education – though the federal government may contribute to these portfolios through various contribution agreements, the P/T governments have ultimate say in how the money is spent. As such, we see wide variations in health, education, and sport systems between provinces and territories.

Next, the above description demonstrates the dominance of non-profit sport organisations and volunteers. In particular, the Canada Not-for-profit Corporations Act (Minister of Justice, 2017) directs that non-profit organisation board members are to be volunteers elected by the membership. This aligns with the governance design archetypes Parent et al. (2023) found in their recent NSO study: thanks to national (e.g., media, sponsors, legislation) and international pressures (e.g., Olympic Movement guidelines), Canadian NSOs have professionalised their structures and activities over the past three decades but continue to be governed by a volunteer board and rely to varying degrees on volunteers. As one moves down the systemic levels, we see an increasing use of volunteers, to the point where the local level sport organisations are often run by the volunteer board without any paid staff. Likewise, major sport events like the 2010 Olympic and Paralympic Winter Games or the 2015 Pan and Parapan American Games use a high number of volunteers.

Furthermore, most sport organisations and governing bodies rely on government funding to survive. Up until the 2010 Vancouver Olympic and Paralympic Winter Games, the Quebec provincial government gave more funding to sport within its jurisdiction than the federal government did. It did so because it saw how sport could be a tool for Québec's "national" identity – Québec sees itself as a distinct nation within Canada akin to the Catalans in Spain or Scots in the United Kingdom – following the hosting of the 1976 Montreal Olympic Games. However, given Canada's lack of gold medals in 1976 and 1988 (Calgary Olympic Winter Games), the federal government increased its funding levels to ensure it would not be the only country to have hosted the Olympic Games three times and never won a gold medal on home soil. This is how Own the Podium was born.[1]

From a funding perspective, there is less of a tradition of corporate sponsorship in Canada than in the United States. This changed, somewhat, with Vancouver

2010, which saw an unprecedented interest by corporations to support Canadian efforts. The Vancouver Organizing Committee for the Olympic Games managed to obtain over 730 million CAD in domestic sponsorship (representing 38.8% of the total operating budget), which far exceeded previous support levels; in comparison, though the federal and British Columbia governments funded most of the capital budget, they only contributed 10% to the operating budget (The Vancouver Organizing Committee for the 2010 Olympic and Paralympic Winter Games, 2010). Since 2010, Canadian sport organisations and governing bodies, and especially the Canadian Olympic Committee, have continued to engage the private sector to diversify their funding options over and above government funding.

Though the federal government limits its contributions to major sport event organising committees to 50% of public funding and no more than 35% of a given budget (Sport Canada, 2008), it remains a key funder of NSOs. According to Parent et al. (2019), on average, 49% of NSOs' budgets came from public funding, followed by 31% from commercial sources (sponsorships/partnerships and event hosting), 18% from memberships, and 2% from other sources (e.g., donations).

As such, between the suite of policies and funding support the governments provide to sport organisations, it would be easy to think that sport is not autonomous. However, though sport organisations are indeed dependent on the governments to survive financially, there is little tolerance for government intervention within the sport system. On the one hand, this can be explained by the Canada Not-for-profit Corporations Act that lays out better governance guidelines (Minister of Justice, 2017), thereby eliminating the opportunity for governments to impose government-desired appointments on boards at least at the federal level – and from these authors' own personal experiences in the sport system at all three levels, there is little evidence of government intervention.

The independence of Canadian sport organisations has, however, led to unsafe sport and bad governance practices from the likes of Hockey Canada, Gymnastics Canada, and Canada Soccer (see, for example, Burke, 2022; McKeon, 2023; Sportsnet Staff, 2022) to name but three. The federal government has since intervened with a slate of parliamentary committee hearings and subpoenas. The federal government instituted an Office of the Sport Integrity Commissioner[2] to which all funded NSOs must sign on to. However, this Office is only for new complaints at the national level. Whether or not additional government oversight at the national, P/T, or local levels occurs remains to be seen.

Competition Principles in the American and Canadian Sport Systems

American and Canadian competition principles do not follow the European promotion and relegation system. Instead, like in the United States, each level can feed into the next from an athlete perspective, but not from a team or organisation perspective. Professional players can come from college/university or dedicated sport leagues, like players in the Canadian Junior Hockey League who feed into the

NHL. Canadian college and university sports, however, are not very popular, rarely filling the stands with spectators like in the NCAA sports do in the United States. USPORTS, the Canadian equivalent to the NCAA, sees athletes as students first and operates a comparatively small budget of $3.256 million CAD or $2.38 million USD (USPORTS, 2022) vs. the NCAA's $1.14 billion USD in revenues and net assets of $438 million USD (Berkowitz, 2023).

Professional sport in North America is largely the same across the United States and Canada while being distinct from models in Europe. Although the integration of the two nations in professional sport (as opposed to explicitly nationally based leagues) is unique, so too is the near complete absence of promotion and relegation models, and the arm's length relationship of those leagues with both the domestic NGBs and the international federations in those sports.

Instead of the promotion-and-relegation system, many sports have a "farm system" of affiliated teams in lower-level competition. Athletes play professionally for those teams in the hopes of being "called up" to a higher-level team in the same team system. This system is most prominent in the sport of baseball where Minor League Baseball is prominent across the continent with teams ranging from "AAA" (the level immediately below the Major Leagues) to "Low A" (a level for newly professional players to start out in the professional sport).

Another key difference in the North American model is the draft. Many professional leagues have a draft in which teams can select younger players who are finishing their amateur competition career (in the NCAA or in other structures). The draft order is determined largely by finish in the previous season, with the lower finishing teams drafting first, providing a chance for weaker teams to improve.

Finally, the relationship between the professional leagues and their corresponding NGBs/NSOs is cooperative but neither controls the other. For example, the NBA has a close working relationship with the NGB/NSO for the sport, USA Basketball, but the NBA retains control over its league play, including the playing rules, officials development, and certifications of support personnel. The parallel structures between the amateur and professional streams of the sport are distinctively North American in nature.

The Interrelationships Between the American and Canadian Sport Systems

The United States and Canada enjoy the longest undefended border in the world and enjoy an incredibly close relationship in terms of trade, diplomacy, and day-to-day culture. It is no surprise then that, while the sport systems in the two nations are different, they also overlap frequently and in substantive ways. The overlaps are most explicit in professional league settings, but they also apply throughout the respective sport systems. At the time of publishing, the United States' emerging global trade war has affected this relationship, the long-term consequences of which have yet to be determined.

Illustration of the interlocks between the American and Canadian sport systems can be ably demonstrated using the example of the sport of ice hockey. In ice hockey, the top professional league in North America is the NHL, boasting 25 teams in the United States and seven in Canada. The league is fully integrated across the border with offices in Toronto (Canada) and in New York (United States). At the same time, the nascent Professional Women's Hockey League has fully half of its six teams located in Canada. While the proportions are different, Major League Soccer (MLS), MLB, and the NBA also have teams in both countries.

The integration between the two nations extends beyond the topflight professional league. The next division of professional hockey, the American Hockey League, has teams in both the United States and Canada, as does leagues at the elite youth level (the Canadian Hockey League) and in several other developmental level leagues across the continent. Although there are elements of the sport distinct to each of nation, the sport is highly integrated and at times seamless across the border.

While the hockey system is most highly illustrative of the integration, it is common for sport in the two nations to be integrated. Given the vast size of both countries, and their shared border, it is often more practical for youth-level athletes to compete in geographically proximate competitions that may cross a border rather than travel greater distances for domestic competition.

The one exception to this cross-border integration would be American and Canadian football. Though professional soccer (football in Europe) is integrated across the nations through MLS, American and Canadian football are not. The NFL in the United States and the Canadian Football League in Canada operate independently and have slightly different rules for their sport; for instance, the field is longer in Canada.

Conclusion

Though they might appear to be similar from the outside, when examining the American and Canadian sport systems in greater depth, they are clearly different: while the United States had a disjointed system, Canada exhibits similarities with the European Sport Model. Likewise, the type and degree of government involvement and the role the national Olympic/Paralympic committees play in the system differ. Yet, the United States and Canada are highly integrated, mirroring the many other dimensions of integration (economic, social, military, etc.) between the two countries.

Notes

1 The programme was so successful Canada garnered 14 gold medals, the most for an Olympic Winter Games host until that time.
2 See https://sportintegritycommissioner.ca/.

References

Berkowitz, S. (2023, January 26). *NCAA reports loss of $59 million for 2022 fiscal year, but net assets remain over $450 million.* USA Today. https://www.usatoday.com/story/sports/college/2023/01/26/ncaa-reports-operating-losses-59-million-fiscal-year/11122997002/

Burke, A. (2022, July 29). *Crisis on ice: What you need to know about the Hockey Canada scandal.* CBC News. Retrieved 8 March from https://www.cbc.ca/news/politics/hockey-canada-sexual-assault-crisis-parliamentary-committee-1.6535248

Canada Games Council. (n.d.). *The Canada games.* Canada Games Council. Retrieved December 12 from https://www.canadagames.ca/

FC Barcelona. (2016, June 13). *A new FCB Escola in Ottawa.* FC Barcelona. Retrieved 8 March from https://barcaacademy.fcbarcelona.com/en/news/1167791/a-new-fcbescola-in-ottawa

Goss Gilroy Inc. (2021). *Evaluation of the Canadian sport policy 2012.* https://sirc.ca/wp-content/uploads/2021/09/CSP-2012-evaluation-Summary-Report-Final-Feb12-21.pdf

Government of Canada. (2021, April 1). *Sport policies, acts and regulations.* Government of Canada. Retrieved March 8 from https://www.canada.ca/en/canadian-heritage/services/sport-policies-acts-regulations.html

Government of Canada. (2022a). *National Sport Organization – Sport Support Program.* Government of Canada. Retrieved March 20 from https://www.canada.ca/en/canadian-heritage/services/funding/sport-support/national-organization.html

Government of Canada. (2022b, August 17). *Sport in Canada.* Government of Canada. Retrieved March 7 from https://www.canada.ca/en/canadian-heritage/services/sport-canada.html

Kwiatkowski, M. (2021, July 27). *Larry Nassar's abuse of gymnasts, including Simone Biles went back decades: Why it still matters in Tokyo.* USA Today. https://www.usatoday.com/story/sports/olympics/2021/07/27/usa-gymnastics-larry-nasser-abuse-scandal-looms-over-tokyo-olympics/5375279001/

McKeon, L. (2023, January 12). *The harder they fall: Inside Canada's gymnastics abuse scandal.* Maclean's. Retrieved March 8 from https://macleans.ca/longforms/gymnastics-abuse-scandal-canada/

Minister of Justice. (2017). *Canada not-for-profit corporations act.* https://laws.justice.gc.ca/eng/acts/c-7.75/

NCAA. (2021). *The road to Tokyo 2020.* NCAA. Retrieved October 13 from https://www.ncaa.org/sports/2021/7/20/the-road-to-tokyo-2020.aspx

Own the Podium. (2023). *About Own the Podium.* Own the Podium. Retrieved March 8 from https://www.ownthepodium.org/en-CA/Notre-organisation

Parent, M. M., Hoye, R., Taks, M., Thompson, A., Naraine, M. L., Lachance, E. L., & Séguin, B. (2023). National sport organization governance design archetypes for the twenty-first century. *European Sport Management Quarterly*, 23 (4), 1115–1135. https://doi.org/10.1080/16184742.2021.1963801

Parent, M. M., & Jurbala, P. R. (2023). The process of implementing a multi-level and multi-sectoral national sport policy: Cautionary lessons from the inside. *International Journal of Sport Policy and Politics*, 15(4), 1–19. https://doi.org/10.1080/19406940.2023.2228824

Parent, M. M., Taks, M., Naraine, M. L., Hoye, R., Séguin, B., & Thompson, A. (2019). *Canadian national sport organizations' governance landscape study: Survey results.* https://www2.uottawa.ca/faculty-health-sciences/sites/g/files/bhrskd346/files/2021-12/survey_results_-_canadian_national_sport_organizations_governance_landscape_study.pdf

Sport Canada. (2008, January). *Federal policy for hosting international sport events.* Government of Canada. Retrieved March 20 from https://www.canada.ca/en/canadian-heritage/services/sport-policies-acts-regulations/policy-hosting-international-sport-events.html

Sport for Life. (2023a). *About us.* Sport for Life. Retrieved March 8 from https://sportforlife.ca/about-us/

Sport for Life. (2023b). *Long-term development.* Sport for Life. Retrieved March 8 from https://sportforlife.ca/long-term-development/

Sport Information Resource Centre (SIRC). (2022). *What we heard: Findings of government consultations and a national survey to inform the Canadian Sport Policy 2023–2033.* Sport Information Resource Centre (SIRC). https://sirc.ca/wp-content/uploads/2023/01/SIRC-What-We-Heard-Report-FINAL-1.pdf

Sport Information Resource Centre (SIRC). (n.d.). *Current priorities.* Sport Information Resource Centre (SIRC). Retrieved March 7 from https://sirc.ca/canadian-sport-policies/

Sportsnet Staff. (2022, July 13). *Men's, women's national teams call for investigation into Canada Soccer's governance.* Sportsnet. Retrieved March 8 from https://www.sportsnet.ca/soccer/article/mens-womens-national-teams-call-for-investigation-into-canada-soccers-governance/

The Vancouver Organizing Committee for the 2010 Olympic and Paralympic Winter Games. (2010). *VANOC annual report: Consolidated financial statement.* The Vancouver Organizing Committee for the 2010 Olympic and Paralympic Winter Games. https://library.olympics.com/Default/doc/SYRACUSE/186598/consolidated-financial-statements-vancouver-organizing-committee-for-the-2010-olympic-and-paralympic

USPORTS. (2022). *USPORTS 2021/22 Annual report.* USPORTS. Richmond Hill, ON: Canada. Retrieved March 8 from https://usports.ca/uploads/hq/AGM/2022/Resources/USports_annualReport2122_EN_FINAL_DIGITAL_updatedFinancials.pdf.

Chapter 13

The Chinese Model of Sport
Empowered and Restrained in the New Era

Shushu Chen, Xiaoyan Xing and Qi Wang

Introduction

Sport holds a pivotal position in the socio-cultural landscape across the globe, extending its influence beyond Western nations to significantly impact the Asian-Pacific region as well. Although the concept of sport is universally recognised, its structure, governance, and societal implications vary markedly from one nation to another.

A particularly noteworthy example is China, officially the People's Republic of China (PRC). This nation merits close examination on the global stage for several reasons: (1) As of 2021, China is among the most populous countries worldwide, with a population exceeding 1.4 billion (United Nations, 2022). (2) Geographically, it ranks as the world's third or fourth largest country, covering approximately 9.6 million square kilometres in East Asia. (3) China is distinguished by its ancient civilisation, one of the earliest to develop, with a history extending over 3,000 years and notable contributions to art, science, philosophy, and technology (Fairbank & Goldman, 2006). (4) In recent decades, China has experienced rapid economic transformation, evolving from a predominantly agrarian society to an industrial superpower, now holding the position of the world's second-largest economy by nominal GDP and the largest by purchasing power parity (International Monetary Fund, 2023). Thus, one might be curious: What is the model of sport like in China? Does China view sport differently? Is the complexity in terms of running sports much more intense, given its large population, wide spread of geographic locations, and rich history? This chapter, therefore, offers an examination of the Chinese model of sport, understanding how sport is organised and governed under the broader context of socio-cultural and political dynamics, with the aim to dissect the unique attributes of the Chinese sports model.

Historical Development and the Socio-Cultural Background

The socio-cultural landscape of China, enriched by its extensive and diverse history, offers a vital context for understanding the evolution of its sports sector. Historically, the Chinese perspective on physical activity, particularly intertwined with

DOI: 10.4324/9781032665153-16

martial arts and practices like Tai Chi, emphasised not just physical fitness but also spiritual and mental equilibrium. As one of the world's oldest civilisations, China's cultural legacy has been influenced by Confucianism, Taoism, and Buddhism for over millennia. These traditional values, which highlight harmony, discipline, and collective welfare, have profoundly influenced Chinese societal norms and practices, including the perception of sports.

In contrast to Western societies, where physical prowess is often celebrated, sports in China have traditionally been regarded as secondary to academic achievement (Brownell, 1995). Even today, for example, sport is not recognised as a subject available for the normal university entrance exam. This divergence in the value placed on sports compared to academics reflects the deep-rooted influence of traditional Chinese philosophies and cultural values.

The 20th century, notably the period following the establishment of the PRC in 1949, marked a pivotal transformation. The government began to invest in sports infrastructure and athlete development, and for a short period of time, it focused on the development of mass sport to enhance public health and contribute to national defense and state-building efforts. However, this period was followed by a tumultuous phase from 1958 to 1976, coinciding with the Great Leap Forward and the Cultural Revolution, which disrupted the progress of mass sport. Subsequently, starting in 1979, there was a shift in sport policy towards prioritising elite sport, which led to a decrease in the emphasis on mass sport and a slowdown in their development.

Elite sport success—particularly success in international competitions such as the Olympic Games—as always been viewed as a vehicle for international prestige and national pride (Xu, 2008). Such successes have been methodical rather than arbitrary (Zheng et al., 2018), adhering to a centralised system led by the government, commonly referred to as the *Juguo Tizhi*, which is known for its comprehensive support for elite sport across the nation. Initiatives include systematic and intensive training programmes, the state-run sports schools, robust state support, and targeted investment in sports where China has established a competitive advantage (Zheng et al., 2018; Zheng & Chen, 2016), epitomised this approach. While this centralised control allowed for efficient resource allocation geared towards achieving specific objectives, such as Olympic success, but also posed challenges such as stifling creativity and local initiatives, and a lack of diversities in athlete development paths (Fan & Zhong, 2020). As an indication, the number of amateur sports schools, the cornerstones of China's three-tier feeder system for elite athlete development, has decreased at an alarming rate from 3,687 in 1990 to 1,552 in 2012, primarily due to recruitment issues as families, even from rural areas, were increasingly unwilling to send their children to these sport schools for a sport career as a way out (Xing, 2017).

While sport can be regarded as a significant political tool for this developing country seeking to enhance its international reputation, it is also a means of cultural inheritance and promotion, as well as a tool for stimulating the market and developing the economy.

One of the functions sports hold in China is for cultural preservation. China emphasises the accumulation and promotion of its sports culture. This cultural aspect is vividly displayed in seasonal festivals that feature traditional sports, each embedded with unique significance and cultural underpinnings. For example, the Dragon Boat Festival, which commemorates the patriotic poet Qu Yuan, is celebrated with dragon boat racing. This event transcends mere competition, serving as a reverential act honouring Qu Yuan's legacy.

Similarly, dragon and lion dancing are performed for various reasons, including praying for good weather, national prosperity, dispelling evil, and promoting peace. These activities are rich in symbolism and carry profound cultural meanings within Chinese society. These traditional sports and martial arts are not merely physical activities; they represent a rich tapestry of cultural heritage, values, and the deep interconnection between sports and society in China. This trend of promoting traditional culture through sport has been strengthened in recent years, aligning with the nation's mega-narrative to achieve the great rejuvenation of the Chinese nation (Wang, 2019; Xinhua News Agency, 2022). As a revealing anecdote, a Dragon Boat race on the day of the Dragon Boat Festival was broadcast live on prime sports channels nationwide, even at the expense of a popular NBA final (Tiyudashengyi, 2022). This exemplifies the significance and cultural importance attached to traditional Chinese sporting events where local traditions and celebrations take precedence over "other" global events.

In recent decades, China's economic transformation has greatly expanded the scope of sports development. The increased national wealth has facilitated greater investment in sports facilities, hosting international events, and participation in a broader array of sports, reflecting both an expanding economic capacity and a commitment to international engagement (Yiguan Analysis & MIGU, 2019). For example, when examining the changes in the size of the Chinese sports industry, the rapid growth is remarkable. The total size of the sports industry in China surged from 1,710 billion RMB in 2015 to 2,950 billion RMB in 2019, boasting an annual growth rate of 14.6%, consistently outpacing the overall economic growth rate (GAS, 2021). Frome then on, the earlier emphasis on allocating state resources primarily for elite sport achievements (i.e., Juguo Tizhi) has given way to a more comprehensive strategy. A contemporary approach, encompassing various dimensions of sports, has emerged, with an emphasis not only on the pursuit of excellence in elite sport but also on the promotion of widespread participation in sports and the cultivation of a thriving sports industry.

A Centralised Model for Sport Development

The origin of such a government dominated sport structure traced back to 1950s which was modelled after the former Soviet Union. At the top level, a state department for sport, commonly known as the Chinese Sport Commission, was established. The organisational and structural aspects of that traditional Chinese models of sport (especially for elite sport) have been extensively documented by numerous

Chinese scholars in other works (see, for instance, Fan & Liu, 2023). As noted by some Chinese sport historian in their work published in the 2000s, the organisation of sport in China has been highly centralised (Fan, 2008; Fan & Zhong, 2020). Since the early 2010s, however, there have been changes associated with how sport is organised. As Yang (2015) has synthesised, there are three forces driving the machinery of sport in China. Firstly, the government, which traditionally held sole responsibility for sport development, has now shifted its role to become the dominant guide in sports development affairs. The second force is the rapidly expanding group of non-governmental sports organisations, private entities that have proliferated due to the economic boom and the adoption of market economy principles following the country's economic reforms in the early 1990s. Over the past decade, there has been a significant increase in the number of sport-related companies. In fact, there are now 289,000 legal entities engaged in sports-related activities in the country, employing 5,051,000 people in 2019, a number expected to rise to 8,000,000 by 2025 (GAS, 2021). This indicates that non-governmental organisations have gradually taken the lead in implementing sports programmes and delivering sports services.

The third force comes from society itself. Improved living standards have not only increased the demand for sports but have also empowered people to self-organise for sports participation. This represents a form of social organisation that aligns with the concept of civil society, as evidenced by the numerous grassroots groups engaged in daily fitness and exercise activities, often found in parks and squares throughout the country. Consequently, society has emerged as the third force, expected to assume many of the sport development tasks, both for elite sport and mass participation, which were traditionally carried out by various administrative organisations.

Here we have a movement that seeks to equalise the influence of three forces by diminishing the government's authority and empowering social forces, which encompass commercial entities (referring to the market) and not-for-profit organisations (referring to civil society), to play active roles in sports development.

While the ideal was for the three forces to collaborate seamlessly for an efficient and equitable sport model of development, the reality was far from clear-cut with the formation of increasingly intricate relationships among the key players spanning these spheres (i.e., the government, the market, and the society). In the ensuing sections, we looked into these dynamic yet complex interplays that give shape to the contemporary model of sport in China. While there are primarily four subdomains of sport policy in China, including youth sport, sport industry, mass sport and elite sport (Xing, 2023), youth sport and sport industry can be treated either as integral parts or derivatives of elite sport and mass sport. Thus, we focus on the latter to untangle China's sport model.

Over the past few decades, two major sport reforms, both orchestrated by the state government, took place to achieve a balanced strategy, harnessing the potential of social forces, specifically the market and the societal involvement, to propel sport development. The initial reform unfolded during the 1990s in response to the transition from a centrally planned economy to a market-driven one (Xing, 2023). The second reform was merged in the backdrop of a comprehensive policy reform initiative launched in 2013. This initiative is not limited to sports alone but encompasses various sectors, including education, social affairs, health, and the environment, with the overarching goal of advancing governance reform. This reform is guided by a key concept, first introduced in the "Decision of the Central Committee of the Communist Party of China on Some Major Issues Concerning Comprehensively Deepening Reforms" during the Third Plenary Session of the 18th Central Committee of the Communist Party of China in 2013, which emphasises the modernisation of the national governance system and capacity. In the context of sport, the reform is specifically associated with an attempt to shift from a *management* of sport model to a *governance* of sport model. A well-known Chinese sport policy scholar explained the differences between these two models in the following manner:

> Today, our country's (China) sports development has entered a stage of multi-subject, multi-domain, and multi-system collaborative advancement, requiring close cooperation among multiple stakeholders such as the government, society, and the market, as well as the collective efforts of the entire society. However, we have become accustomed to a top-down, singular sports administrative system and mechanism, and the concept of governance is still relatively unfamiliar to us. Although governance and management differ by just one word, their meanings are qualitatively different. The future sports governance system will involve not only multiple subjects horizontally but also multiple levels vertically; it will encompass cooperation and collaboration, as well as constraints and conflicts; it will have the freedom of action for all parties but also adhere to the rule of law and ethical standards. This networked governance system is unprecedented in the history of China's sports development, and the capabilities required for it are lacking in the existing sports management system.
>
> (Ren, 2014, quoted in Yang's study, p. 1)

Throughout this progression, the dynamic interplay between the national governing bodies (NGBs)—the individual sport regulators—and the ministry of sport (known by different names across different periods), stood out as a prominent example of the intricate and deeply entangled interactions between governmental entities and societal forces within China's sports realm.

Under the traditional model, NGBs in China primarily operated under the nominal umbrella of the State Sports Commission, which was criticised for lacking intrinsic organisational mechanisms and structure (Song et al., 1995; Wang, 2009). In 1998, the State Sports Commission was restructured and renamed as the General Administration of Sport (GAS) with the initial aim of downsizing its department, reducing the government's control in the sports realm, and causing the NGBs to sever their direct ties with GAS.

However, this restructuring was viewed as a somewhat meaningless exercise, as the connection between state control and the autonomy of NGBs was restructured through the establishment of newly formed sport management centres (a total of 23), which functioned as quasi-governmental bodies operating at an arm's length from GAS. These centres housed 73 NGBs (Li & Zhou, 2012). For instance, the Table Tennis Sports Management Centre, which also includes the Chinese Table Tennis Association, was established in 1993 and expanded in 1997 to include badminton, resulting in a name change to the Table Tennis and Badminton Sport Management Centre.

Despite these reforms, China's sports organisations did not shake off being centrally controlled status. Leadership appointments within these management centres were still exclusively made by GAS, and their primary focus was implementing directives from GAS (Huang, 2003). The 1990s reform also saw the creation of two professional leagues: the Chinese Super League (CSL) for football and the Chinese Basketball Association (CBA) for basketball. While designed to engage the market in sports development, these leagues were closely overseen by their corresponding sport management centres—the Football Management Centre and the Basketball Management Centre—both operating under the direct purview of the GAS.

In essence, this reform resulted in little substantial change (Zhang et al., 2013) and even deviated from its initial purpose of limiting government involvement in sport. Instead, it not only increased the number of sport-related public institutions (e.g., sport management centres) directly under GAS's purview but also expanded government oversight into the domain of commercial sports (e.g., the CSL and the CBA). Thus, the 1990s reform essentially strengthened government control in sports, perpetuating the subordinate status of national sport organisations (NSOs), which were often seen as mere puppets (Huang, 2003).

The sports reform of the 2010s, therefore, began with the objective of what they termed "unhooking" (脱钩)—a process involving the separation of national sport organisations from their governmental administrative counterparts (Wang, 2020). In 2013, the GAS announced a reform pilot programme to "unhook" 18 national sport organisations from their parent administrative agencies or public institutions, making them independent social entities (Zhang & Yang, 2014). Upon closer examination of the list made public, it became evident that these NSOs did not include NGBs responsible for individual sports, particularly Olympic sports. Instead, the list comprised organisations such as the Chinese Ethnic Minority Sport Association, Chinese Sport Venue Association, and Chinese Sport Manufacturers Alliance, among others (CNR, 2015). In essence, the selection of these NSOs was carefully orchestrated to ensure that the GAS retained control over elite sport aimed at achieving Olympic medals.

In terms of Olympic sports, football took the lead. The Chinese Football Sport Management Centre was abolished in early 2017, theoretically granting the Chinese Football Association (CFA) autonomy (Xinhua News Agency, 2017). However, senior GAS officials retained leadership positions in the CFA, indicating ongoing government control. For instance, a GAS deputy minister held the positions of CPC secretary-general and vice president of the CFA from 2017 until his arrest on corruption charges in late 2023 (Titan Sports, 2023).

Following football, multiple Olympic sports detached their NGBs from corresponding sport management centres. GAS selected sports celebrities, such as retired athletes or coaches, to lead the NGBs. Shen Xue, the first Chinese figure skater to win an Olympic gold medal, became the president of the Chinese Figure Skating Association in 2021 (Zhou et al., 2021). Yao Ming, former NBA player for the Houston Rockets, became the president of the CBA in 2022 (Hu, 2022). However, unlike the football reform, the corresponding sports management centres were not abolished; instead, some of their duties were transferred to the separated NGBs. The distribution of responsibilities between management centres and NGBs varies widely across sports, ranging from full transfer of responsibilities, as in the case of the CBA, to limited involvement, such as specific tasks like national team training, coaching education, or accreditation of sports equipment.

While detaching the NSOs in name appeared straightforward, the challenge lay in establishing them as enduring and self-sustaining entities. These NGBs were fundamentally flawed, created as top-down entities despite their official recognition as social organisations with legal status. Lacking grassroots representation, they retained an administrative character and relied primarily on government funding. By the end of 2023, some NGBs, especially those overseeing Olympic sports with limited participation, reverted to their parent sport management centres due to the depletion of initial startup funds provided by the GAS.

Conversely, NGBs with a strong participation base have gained autonomy by establishing their own enterprises for sports-related marketing activities. For example, the Chinese Athletics Association (CAA) wholly owns China Athletics Sports (CAS), founded in 2019, which handles the CAA's commercialisation, including business development and operations (China Athletics, 2022). Similarly, the CBA, in addition to owning the company managing the country's professional basketball leagues, established Slam Sports in 2021 as its commercial entity responsible for managing the marketing rights of national teams and related basketball events (Slam Sports, n.d.). Thus, the sports reform of the 2010s has led to various dynamics within the Chinese sport model, involving government, market forces, and social organisations. These dynamics vary across Olympic and non-Olympic sports and those with different levels of market appeal. Nevertheless, the government maintains a strong grip on Olympic sports as it pursues international sporting supremacy (Xing, 2017).

A Market-Driven Model for Grassroots Sport Development

As early as 1995, China's "National Fitness Programme Outline (1995–2010)" laid the foundation for the active development of mass sport. However, it wasn't until the 21st century, driven by the growing demand for sports among the population and a gradual shift in the Chinese government's perspective on the role of mass sport in the country's socioeconomic development, that a more targeted approach emerged.

In 2014, China marked a significant turning point in its approach to national fitness by elevating it to the status of a national strategy. This momentous shift was articulated in a landmark policy document titled "State Council's Opinions on Accelerating the Development of the Sports Industry and Promoting Sports Consumption" (国务院关于加快发展体育产业促进体育消费的若干意见), issued by the State Council. This policy declaration represented a pivotal moment in the country's commitment to a holistic approach to the development of "sport for all."

In essence, the concept of "sport for all" or national fitness ceased to be confined solely within the realm of sports; instead, its intrinsic connection to the broader health agenda was recognised, esteemed, and pursued through collaborative efforts across various sectors. Notably, General Secretary Xi Jinping personally championed the advancement of national fitness, delivering a series of significant pronouncements on the implementation of the national fitness strategy and the expeditious construction of a sports powerhouse. The National Fitness Program has therefore been strategically planned and implemented in five-year intervals, aligning with the five-year national social and economic development plan.

The shift towards prioritising and developing mass sport over elite sport can be attributed to multiple factors. Firstly, the achievement of Olympic glory in the 2008 Olympics, where China topped the medal tally, signified the fulfilment of the political mission of prioritising elite sport. To further enhance the influence of sports, the objective of building a sports powerhouse was introduced by then-Chinese President Hu Jintao immediately after the 2008 Games. This objective was later formalised into a state policy document titled the "Outline of Building a Sports Power" in 2019 during the reign of President Xi Jinping (General Office of the State Council of the People's Republic of China, 2019). The goal of becoming a *sports powerhouse* extends China's aspirations in sports beyond Olympic medal counts, and necessitates significant growth in mass sport, the sports industry, and sports culture. Consequently, China's remarkable performance at the 2008 Beijing Olympics served as a catalyst, leading to increased investment in grassroots sports infrastructure and programmes.

Secondly, China's robust economic growth furnished additional resources for the advancement of mass sport, which had frequently been eclipsed by the prominence of elite sport. It is crucial to recognise that the emphasis on mass sport was not solely driven by a desire for broader participation but also aimed at leveraging increased sports involvement to stimulate consumption and foster potential economic growth, as pointed out by Xing (2023) in a more recent study. This perspective underscores the multifaceted nature of China's approach to mass sport, where economic considerations intersect with the broader objectives of health, fitness, and societal well-being.

Moreover, the improved social and economic conditions in China have played a significant role in driving people's enthusiasm for sports and exercise as a means of enhancing their overall well-being. The value of sport has also evolved to embrace a broader understanding of well-being that encompasses physical health (Dong et al., 2018; Chen & Wang, 2020), partly in response to contemporary health challenges such as obesity and lifestyle-related diseases. This is particularly salient among the nation's middle class as evident in the running boom since 2010s (Ronkainen et al., 2018). The outbreak of the COVID-19 pandemic further intensified people's motivation to engage in physical activities for the sake of their health. This global health crisis, which persisted for nearly three years in China, heightened awareness regarding physical well-being.

In terms of the organisation and structure of grassroots sports development, consistent with the lack of representation of Chinese NGBs, formal sports organisations at lower levels had minimal presence in people's daily sports participation. When examining the structural forms of sports organisations, data from the 2020 National Fitness Activity Status Survey provides valuable insights. It reveals that 24.7% of adults primarily engage in sports and fitness activities through informal groups formed by "friends or acquaintances," while 21.1% participate in community fitness teams (Liu et al., 2018). In stark contrast, more formal, top-down models such as "single-sport associations" (8.9%) and "social sports instructor associations" (5.5%), which are prominently featured in the government's sports development policies, appear to be less effective in reaching the wider population. This disparity suggests a gap that needs to be addressed between government-led top-down sports management models and the actual needs and preferences of those participating in mass sport.

The grassroots delivery forces primarily consist of two types of organisations. The first type comprises spontaneously organised mass sport groups, as identified by Zhang (2017). These entities are deeply rooted within local communities and are initiated by civilians. They often operate without formal regulatory recognition, relying on the social networks of their group leaders for resources (Wang, 2019). However, despite their informal nature, they share typical characteristics of civil organisations, being non-governmental and non-profit in nature. These grassroots organisations are numerous, operating on a smaller scale, and encompass a wide variety of traditional, emerging, and community-initiated fitness activities. This sets them apart from more formally established community sports organisations, such as community sports associations, community sports service centres, and neighbourhood committee cultural and sports committees. Affiliated with sub-districts, which are the most basic governmental offices responsible for overseeing all aspects of social life in communities across China, these organisations were part of the government structure. However, they often had limited human resources dedicated to planning and organising mass sport events and activities (Wang, 2004). This limitation is due to the fact that sports are just one of the many responsibilities assigned to sub-districts, typically with low priority (Xing & Chen, 2022).

The rise of community grassroots sports organisations in China is a direct result of the growing civil society, an increased capacity for self-organisation in social activities, and practical reforms in urban social sports management systems (Zhang & Cheng, 2013). Although their historical development is relatively recent, with roots in the 1980s, they represent a significant evolution within the realm of "civil organisations." In recent years, these organisations have emerged as vibrant and integral components of China's national fitness activities. However, despite their vitality and enthusiasm, community grassroots sports organisations typically fall into a smaller category of sports social organisations. Their primary focus is on organising and conducting sports activities, but they often lack the necessary qualifications to provide public sports services funded by the government. Consequently, they have limited influence in the management of community public sports affairs and are considered marginalised within the broader landscape of sports social organisations. Their historical development, although relatively recent with roots in the 1980s, represents a significant evolution within the domain of "civil organisations." In recent years, these organisations have emerged as vibrant and integral components of China's national fitness activities. However, despite their vitality and enthusiasm, community grassroots sports organisations typically fall within a smaller category of sports social organisations. Their primary focus lies in organising and conducting sports activities, but they often lack the necessary qualifications to provide public sports services funded by the government. Consequently, they have limited influence in the management of community public sports affairs and are considered marginalised within the broader sports social organisation landscape.

The second category comprises commercial sports organisations, exemplified by those offering youth sports training services and event operation companies. These organisations primarily emerged due to the absence of a grassroots, volunteer-driven sports development system in China. In contrast to the European model, which relies on numerous non-profit local sports organisations and sports clubs to deliver essential mass sport services (Henry, 2001; Houlihan & Green, 2010), China's commercial sports organisations have stepped in to fill this void. However, it's essential to note that these commercial entities are profit-oriented by nature. Youth sports training, in particular, has been identified as a lucrative market with substantial growth potential, attracting significant investment from venture capital (Wu, 2017). This burgeoning market has been fuelled by Chinese parents' strong desire to invest in nurturing their children's skills and abilities beyond the school environment. However, some of these youth training agencies, often operating under the guise of youth sports clubs, have been criticised for providing subpar services, causing widespread concern. To regulate this market, the GAS issued consecutive policy documents in 2020, including the "Opinions on Promoting and Regulating the Development of Social Sports Clubs" (GAS, 2021) and the "Code of Conduct for Extracurricular Sports Training" in 2017 (GAS, 2017). While governmental interventions are beneficial for maintaining the quality of youth sports training services, it is important to acknowledge that the commercialisation of youth sports presents a significant threat to social equality, particularly for children from economically disadvantaged backgrounds (Xing, 2023).

Event operation companies typically serve as intermediaries between various local governments and their mass sport initiatives. These local governments often possess the financial resources to fund mass sport events and activities but lack the manpower and expertise required for their successful implementation. A prime example of this dynamic can be observed in government-sponsored youth skiing and skating training programmes, as well as the organisation of mass ice-snow festivals, all aimed at fulfilling China's ambitious commitment to involve 300 million people in winter sports (Chen et al., 2022). Furthermore, the surge in the popularity of running has ignited a trend where numerous levels of Chinese local governments have taken the initiative to host their city marathons (Xing & Liu, 2023). This trend has, in turn, generated a substantial demand for event companies to orchestrate these annual running events. As an indicator of this burgeoning trend, in 2017, there were a total of 191 event companies operating running events that received certification from the CAA (Chinese Athletics Association, 2018). The strong connection between the government and these event companies is manifest in the funding structure. Government funding ranks as the primary source of revenue for these running event companies, followed by sponsorship fees and event registration fees, as observed in the Chinese running event landscape in 2019 (ChengGuangXian, 2020). This collaboration between local governments and event companies underscores the critical role played by event operators in facilitating and executing mass sport initiatives in China, ultimately contributing to the nation's sporting and recreational landscape.

Conclusion

Exactly because of the distinctive interplays between the government, market, and society, the Chinese model of sport diverges significantly from Western models, particularly the European Model of Sport, in its centralised, top-down approach to sport development. The Chinese sports model, also, intricately weaves together cultural heritage, political aspirations, and societal values, representing a dynamic and evolving component of the nation's identity and development.

As China continues to rise as a global sporting power, its sport model provides valuable insights for policy and practice. The recent shift towards a more balanced approach between elite and grassroots sports signals a promising future for the nation's physical health and well-being. For nations seeking to develop or reform their sports systems, China's experience presents an intriguing case study. It defies easy categorisation but offers lessons in the intricate balance between national objectives and individual well-being.

References

Brownell, S. (1995). *Training the Body for China: Sports in the Moral Order of the People's Republic*. University of Chicago Press.

Chen, P., Wang, D., Shen, H., Yu, L., Gao, Q., Mao, L., Jiang, F., Luo, Y., Xie, M., Zhang, Y., Feng, L., Gao, F., Wang, Y., Liu, Y., Luo, C., Nassis, G. P., Krustrup, P., Ainsworth, B. E., Harmer, P. A., & Li, F. (2020). Physical Activity and Health in Chinese Children and Adolescents: Expert Consensus Statement. *British Journal of Sports Medicine, 54*(22), 1321–1331. https://doi.org/10.1136/bjsports-2020-102261.

Chen, S., Xing, X., & Chalip, L. (2022). Planning and Implementation of Event Leveraging Strategy: China's Legacy Pledge to Motivate 300 Million People to Be Involved in Winter Sport. *Sport Management Review, 25*(5), 771–790. https://doi.org/10.1080/14413523.2021.1987737.

Chengguangxian. (2020). *2019 Nian Quanguo Paobu Saishi Guanli Congye Renyuan Diaoyan Baogao" Fabu [Release of the 2019 National Running Event Management Practitioner Research Report]*. Sina. https://sports.sina.cn/running/2021-03-09/detail-ikkntiak 6729387.d.html

China Athletics. (2022). *About Us- China Athletics*. China Athletics. https://www.chinaath. com/p/yingwenguanyuzhongtian.html.

China National Radio. (2015). *Minzhengbu: 2015 Nian 148 Jia Quanguoxing Hangyexiehui SHanghui Shidian Tuogou [Ministry of Civil Affairs: 148 National Trade Associations and Chambers of Commerce Decoupled on a Pilot Basis in 2015]*. China National Radio. https://news.cnr.cn/native/gd/20151125/t20151125_520590805.shtml.

Chinese Athletics Association, L. (2018). *Annual Report for Chinese Marathon 2017*. Marathon Gala-China 2017.

Dong, J., Ren, T., & Mangan, J. A. (2018). A Living Legacy (Part One): Japanese Imperialism and Chinese Revanchism—Modern Sport as a Modern Medium. In J. A. Mangan, P. Horton, T. Ren, & G. Ok (Eds.), *Japanese Imperialism: Politics and Sport in East Asia: Rejection, Resentment, Revanchism* (pp. 113–150). Springer. https://doi.org/10.1007/978-981-10-5104-3_5.

Fairbank, J. K., & Goldman, M. (2006). *China: A New History, Second Enlarged Edition*. Harvard University Press.

Fan, H. (2008). China. In J. Grix, B. Houlihan, & P. M. Brannagan (Eds.), *Comparative Elite Sport Development: Systems, structures and public policy* (pp. 26–52). Butterworth-Heinemann. https://books.google.co.uk/books?id=nRLO284UouYC&printsec= frontcover&redir_esc=y#v=onepage&q&f=false

Fan, H., & Liu, L. (Eds.). (2023). *Routledge Handbook of Sport in China*. Routledge. https:// doi.org/10.4324/9781003204015

Fan, H., & Zhong, Y. (2020). China and the Olympic Games. In H. Fan & Z. Lu (Eds.), *The Routledge Handbook of Sport in Asia* (1st edition). Routledge.

General Administration of Sport. (2017). *Tiyuzongju Bangongting Guanyu Yinfa 'Kewai Tiyu Peixun Xingwei Guifan' De Tongzhi*. General Office of General Administration of Sports. https://www.gov.cn/zhengce/zhengceku/2021-12/20/content_5662058.htm.

General Administration of Sport. (2021). *'Shisiwu' Tiyu Fazhan Guihua [The 14th Five-Year Plan for Sports Development of the People's Republic of China]*. The State Council of the People's Republic of China. https://www.sport.gov.cn/zfs/n4977/c23655706/part/ 23656158.pdf.

General Office of the State Council of the People's Republic of China. (2019). *Tiyu QIangguo Jianshe Gangyao [The Outline for the Construction of Sports Powers] (2019–40)*. https://www.gov.cn/gongbao/content/2019/content_5430499.htm.

Henry, I. P. (2001). *The Politics of Leisure Policy* (2nd edition). Palgrave.

Houlihan, B., & Green, M. (2010). *Routledge Handbook of Sports Development*. Routledge.

Hu, J. (2022). *Yaoming Dangxuan Xinyijie Zhongguo Lanxie Zhuxi [Yao Ming Elected as the New President of the Chinese Basketball Association]*. General Administration of Sport of China. https://www.sport.gov.cn/n20001280/n20067662/n20067613/c25022344/content. html.

Huang, Y. (2003). *Lun Zhongguo Tiyu Shetuan- Guojia Yu Shehui Guanxi Zhuanbian Xia De Tiyushetuan Gaige [On Sports Associations in China—Reform of Sports Associations under the Transformation of State-Society Relationships]* [Doctoral Dissertation]. Beijing Sport University.

International Monetary Fund. (2023). *World Economic Outlook database*. https://www.imf. org/en/Publications/WEO/weo-database/2023/October/download-entire-database.

Jinming Zheng, Shushu Chen, Tien-Chin Tan, & Barrie Houlihan. (2018). *Sport Policy in China*. Routledge. https://doi.org/10.4324/9781315168234.

Li, Q., & Zhou, Y. (2012). Quanguoxing Danxiang Yundong Xiehui Xianzhuang Yu Fazhan Duice Yanjiu [Research on the Current Situation and Development Countermeasures of National Individual Sports Associations in China]. *Journal of Beijing Sport University, 35*(12), 29–34. https://doi.org/10.19582/j.cnki.11-3785/g8.2012.12.007.

Liu, H., Guan, B., Wang, W., & Song, N. (2018). Guojia Tiyu Zhili De Jiceng Luoji: Sheqv Tiyu De Kunjing Yu Chaoyue [Basic Logic of National Sports Governance: Predicament and Transcendence of Community of Sports Governance]. *Journal of Sports and Science, 39*(2), 77–83. https://doi.org/10.13598/j.issn1004-4590.2018.02.013.

Ren, H. (2014). Yi Qunzhong Tiyu Cujin Shehui Jianshe [Propel Social Construction by Mass Sport]. *Journal of Beijing Sport University, 37*(9), 1–9. https://doi.org/10.19582/j.cnki. 11-3785/g8.2014.09.001.

Ronkainen, N. J., Shuman, A., Ding, T., You, S., & Xu, L. (2018). "Running Fever": Understanding runner identities in Shanghai through turning point narratives. *Leisure Studies, 37*(2), 211–222. https://doi.org/10.1080/02614367.2017.1324513.

Slam Sports. (n.d.). *Gongsi Jianjie- Shenlan Tiyu [Company Profile Slam Sports]*. Slam Sports. Retrieved 17 December 2023, from https://www.slamsports.cn/introduction.html.

Song, S., Zhang, L., Lei, J., Yao, B., & Zhang, R. (1995). Cong Bijiao Zhong Kan Woguo Danxiang Yundong Xiehui Guanlitizhi Cunzai De Wenti [Problems in the Management System of China's Single-sports Associations from a Comparative Perspective]. *Sports Culture Guide, 2*(5), 19–21. https://www.cnki.net/KCMS/detail/detail.aspx?dbcode=CJF D&dbname=CJFD9495&filename=TYWS502.005&uniplatform=OVERSEA&v=gNSY CG8yOJK03cPKSUIrfvGI-mz2p65fl1RKOzwZB8h03iq7vxDuyWSuY0K0wITu

Titan Sports. (2023). *Duzhaocai De Zuxie 6 Nian: Guli Guihua, Beichuan yu Nvlaoban Guanxi Feiqian [Du Zhaocai's 6 Years in the Football Association: Encouraging Naturalisation, Rumoured to Have a Close Relationship with a Female Boss]*. Titan Sports. https://www.titan24.com/publish/app/data/2023/10/08/493521/os_news.html.

Tiyudashengyi. (2022). *Youyici Rang NBA Zhibo Ranglu, Longzhou Zhexiang Xiaozhongyundong Jiasu Ruao [Another NBA Broadcast Gives Way as Dragon Boat, a Niche Sport, Accelerates into the Olympics]*. NetEase News. https://www.163.com/dy/article/ H93AU26N0529818P.html.

United Nations, Department of Economic and Social Affairs, Population Division. (2022). *World Population Prospects*.

Wang, Z. K. (2004). *Shehui Zhuanxin Yu Zhongguo chengshi Sheqv Tiyu Fazhan [Social Transformation and the Development of Community Sport in China]*. Beijing Sport University.

Wang, L. (2009). Quanguoxing Tiyu Danxiang Xiehui Gaige De Huigu Yu Sikao [Review and Reflections on the Reform of National Sports Associations]. *Research of Administration of NPOs, 2*, 32–36.

Wang, L. (2019). Research on the Operation Mechanism of Community Sports Organization Based on Case Study. *Journal of Capital University of Physical Education and Sports, 31*(1), 28–32. https://doi.org/10.14036/j.cnki.cn11-4513.2019.01.007.

Wang, Z. (2019). Minzu Chuantong TIyu Wenhuazixin Heyi Chengwei Keneng?- Jiyu Wenhua Zixin Shengcheng Lilun Jichu Yu Shijian Luoji Fenxi [Why Is Self-confidence of National Traditional Sports Culture Possible?——Logic Analysis Based on the Theory of Cultural Confidence]. *Journal of Sports and Science*, *40*(237), 28–38. https://doi. org/10.13598/j.issn1004-4590.2019.01.019.

Wang, Y. (2020). *Houtuogou Shidai Quanguoxing Danxiangtiyuxiehui Zhili Chuangxin Yanjiu [Study on the Governance Innovation of National Individual Sports Associations in the Post-Decoupling Era]* [Doctoral Dissertation]. Beijing Sport University.

Wu, B. (2017). *"Xinghuo Zhinan" Quanguo Qingshaonian Tiyu Peixun Jigou Pingxuan [Selection of National Youth Sports Training Organisations by Spark Guide]*. NetEase News. https://www.163.com/sports/article/CPPNM1T300058TS4.html.

Xing, X. (2017). China. In E. Kristiansen, M. Milena, & B. Houlihan (Eds.), *Elite Youth Sport Policy and Management: A Comparative Study Analysis* (pp. 185–208). Routledge.

Xing, X. (2023). Mass Sport and Its Role in Economic Development. In F. Hong, & L. Li (Eds.), *Routledge Handbook of Sport in China* (pp. 143–151). Routledge.

Xing, X., & Chen, S. (2022). One World, One Dream: Beijing 2008. In S. Harris, & M. Dowling (Eds.), *Sport Participation and Olympic Legacies: A Comparative Study* (pp. 79–104). Routledge.

Xing, X., & Liu, Y. (2023). Case Study 4.2 Running Events in China and Their Impact. In K. Alexandris, V. Girginov, & J. Scheerder (Eds.), *Running Events: Policy, Marketing and Impacts* (pp. 123–131). Routledge.

Xinhua News Agency. (2017). *Guojiatiyuzongju Zuguanzhongxin Zhuxiao [Write-off of the Football Management Centre of the General Administration of Sport]*. Chinese Government Website. https://www.gov.cn/xinwen/2017-01/06/content_5157448.htm.

Xinhua News Agency. (2022). *Wei Zhonghua Tiancai Wei Shidai- Tiyu Wenhua Jifa Zhongguo Liliang [Adding Colour to China Singing for the Times—Sports Culture Inspires the Power of China]*. Guangming Net. https://m.gmw.cn/baijia/2022-12/26/36255998. html.

Xu, G. (2008). *Olympic Dreams: China and Sports, 1895–2008* (1st edition). Harvard University Press.

Yang, H. (2015). Zhongguo Tiyu Zhili Tixi He Zhili Nengli Xiandaihua De Gainisn [Modernization Conception System of China Sports Governance System and Governance Ability]. *Journal of Beijing Sport University*, *38*(8), 1–6. https://www.cnki. net/KCMS/detail/detail.aspx?dbcode=CJFD&dbname=CJFDLAST2015&filena me=BJTD201508001&uniplatform=OVERSEA&v=LK65fy8bSb4WnrH2geLQ E1K_h3byKVJDxgoiaPQtDZrHk61PN1elArKqcDbx7fnJ.

Yiguan Analysis, & MIGU. (2019). *White Paper on Sports Development in China 2019* [Online]. https://www.analysys.cn/article/detail/20019479.

Zhang, H., & Cheng, P. (2013). Shequ Caogen Tiyu Zuzhi De Hanyi 、 Shengcheng Yu Gongneng Dingwei [The Definition, Formation and Functional Orientation of Community Grassroots'Sports Association]. *Journal of Beijing Sport University*, *36*(6), 12–16. https://doi.org/10.19582/j.cnki.11-3785/g8.2013.06.003.

Zhang, Y., Peng, D., & Liu, M. (2013). Woguo Quanguoxing Danxiang Yundong Xiehui Gaige De Lishi Huigu Yu Sikao [The Research on the Policy Reform on Chinese National Sport Association]. *Journal of Sports and Science*, *34*(5), 27–30.

Zhang, F., & Yang, L. (2014). Yang Shu'an: 18 Ge Quan'guoxing Danxiang Yundong Xiehui Ni Chedi Tuogou [Yang Shu'an: 18 National Single-sports Associations to Be Completely Delinked]. *Xinhua News Agency*. http://sports.people.com.cn/n/2014/0308/ c128547-24572808.html.

Zhang, W. (2017). Woguo Tiyu Shehui Zuzhi Zhili Jiegou Fenxi [An analysis of sports social organization governance structures in China]. *Physical Education Journal., 24*(04). https://doi.org/10.16237/j.cnki.cn44-1404/g8.2017.04.004

Zheng, J., & Chen, S. (2016). Exploring China's Success at the Olympic Games: A Competitive Advantage Approach. *European Sport Management Quarterly, 16*(2), 148–171. https://doi.org/10.1080/16184742.2016.1140797.

Zhou, H., Li, M., Zou, S., Kui, X., Zhang, J., & Zheng, X. (2021). *Zhongguo Huayanghuabingxiehui Zhuxi Shenxue: Jianchi Jiushi Zuihao De Reai [Shen Xue, President of China Figure Skating Association: Persistence Is the Best Love].* People's Daily Online. https://baijiahao.baidu.com/s?id=1716755266933752108&wfr=spider&for=pc.

Chapter 14

Model of Sport in the Arab World

A European Approach?

Sarah Muhanna Al-Naimi and Mahfoud Amara

Introduction: Debate on the European Sport Model and Colonial Legacy

Post-colonial theory offers a framework through which we can examine the enduring impacts of colonialism on the sports model in the Arab World. It delves into
how colonial legacies have molded present structures and practices, providing a
critical analysis of the power dynamics at play (Said, 1978). In the context of the
Arab World, European colonization established power dynamics characterized by
a binary and non-asymmetrical relationship between the colonizer and the colonized territories. Originally, colonization, as a concept, was used by Europeans
to describe the migration of segments of their population, such as scholars and
Christian missionaries, to non-European regions. Beyond elevating their living
standards in these new non-European areas, this endeavor also aimed at exerting
intellectual and cultural control (Carrington & Césaire, 2015). Thus, colonization
became entrenched in a hegemonic relationship, contrasting the non-European
destinations as an antithesis to the European colonizer. The latter was depicted as
possessing superior characteristics, such as greater civility, power, and intellectual-
ity. Carrington and Césaire (2015) define colonization as a system of domination
employed by a colonizing nation to manipulate another. The colonizer imposed
passivity by assuming complete control over the affairs of the colonized nations.
Bilgin (2004) notes that by 1914, only 15% of the globe remained unaffected by
European colonialization. However, the aftermath of World War I (1914–1918)
weakened the global influence of European colonization due to population losses
suffered by the Allies, particularly colonial powers like France and Britain. The
decline of colonial powers paved the way for the rise of anti-colonial movements
in colonized countries (Sondhaus, 2020). Although colonialism diminished after
World War II, the connections between Europe and its former colonies in Africa,
Asia, and the Middle East still reflect influences from a colonial intellectual framework. European colonization significantly contributed to the diffusion of modern
sports across the globe. The process of colonization led to the spread of European sports like rugby, cricket, netball, hockey, and organized mountaineering to
regions such as Africa in the late 1800s and early 1900s. Colonized peoples were

DOI: 10.4324/9781032665153-17

encouraged to play sports by the government, church, schools, and army as a means of discipline and civilization.

Post-colonialism is a theoretical perspective that scrutinizes the power dynamics of colonization through various mediums, including art and sport. Furthermore, it analyzes the colonial impact across political, sociological, economic, and intellectual domains (Carrington and Césaire, 2015). It is important to distinguish between post-colonialism (with a hyphen) and post-colonialism (without a hyphen). Vijay Mishra and Hodge (1991) differentiate between these terms, referring to post-colonialism as positional colonialism, representing resistance by independent states against the historical phase following the end of colonial rule. They describe post-colonialism as complicit post-colonialism, which examines certain ingrained aspects of colonialism that may persist even after formal decolonization. Sport serves as a dual platform for representation: a tool for control by colonizers and a form of resistance by colonized populations. Although Edward Said, Gayatri Spivak, and Homi Bhabha did not explicitly analyze sport in their post-colonial works, they addressed aspects of representational dynamics in sport for both the colonizer and the colonized. Edward Said's Orientalism describes a Western system of dominating non-Western areas, founded on an intellectual dichotomy between the colonial West (The Occident) and non-Western territories (The Orient). Said argues that Orientalism not only penetrated the geographical spaces of the Orient but also the intangible ones, dominating them culturally, artistically, historically, and identifiably (Burney, 2012). Gayatri Spivak's concept of the Subaltern highlights the representational inequality between colonizers and colonized peoples (Clevenger, 2017). By underscoring the plight of marginalized colonized communities, particularly women, Spivak suggests the importance of diverse voices in producing knowledge in sports history. Embracing multiple analytical perspectives allows for a reimagined understanding of sports that transcends Eurocentrism (Clevenger, 2017). Post-colonial African nations used sports as a platform to consolidate national and pan-African identities after gaining independence. Sport provided a means for these nations to assert their power in the international community and resist colonial hegemony and racist regimes on the continent. Despite some divisiveness, sport also played a role in integrating communities and asserting independence from colonial influences (Gems, 2006)

European Sport and the Formation of Arab Nation States

The colonial era marked a significant period in the introduction of modern sports to the Arab World. European colonizers viewed sports as a means of control and "civilization." According to post-colonial theory, this represented a form of cultural imperialism aimed at imposing European norms and values on colonized societies (Said, 1978). Sports such as football, cricket, and rugby were introduced through colonial institutions such as schools, military bases, and social clubs. These sports were not just recreational pursuits but were infused with the colonial agenda of discipline and hierarchy (Bairner, 2015).

Two examples from the Arab World illustrate how sport can function as a tool of colonial resistance, as seen in the case of football in pre-independence Algeria, and how it can embody a post-colonial notion of hybridity, as exemplified by Qatar's hosting of the 2022 FIFA World Cup. Before gaining independence, Algeria utilized sport, especially football, to foster unity among its diverse ethnic and social groups, challenging the colonial narrative of superiority and legitimacy. Despite its colonial origins, Algeria leveraged the universality of football to assert its distinct identity. According to Amara (2012), during Algeria's pre-independence era, sports, particularly football, served as a means of resistance against French colonial rule. Football provided a promising avenue for bringing together various Algerian social groups and countering the cultural dominance imposed by the colonizer through the pursuit of "high-quality sporting performances" (Amara, 2012, p. 32).

On the contrary, traces of Bhabha's notion of hybridity manifest in both sport and small and medium enterprises (SMEs) hosted by formerly colonized nations. SMEs, exemplified by the FIFA World Cup 2022 hosted by Qatar, a former British protectorate from 1916 to 1971 (Rolim, 2019), can serve as arenas for hybrid identity akin to Bhabha's concept of the Third Space. Griffin (2019) elucidates Bhabha's notion of the Third Space as a realm characterized by the contradictions between colonizer and colonized, engendering a landscape where cultural differences are accentuated while simultaneously nurturing elements of hybridity. This space encapsulates various filters for hybrid identity, delineated between colonized/colonizer, East/West, and conceivably, the Qatari populace (comprising Bedouin and Hadar) vis-à-vis other global identities. The Western world often resorts to a blanket stereotype when depicting the Gulf Cooperation Council (GCC) populace and, more specifically, the diverse groups within Qatar. This stereotype portrays them as a homogeneous Bedouin entity, traversing the desert on camels and in perpetual motion from one locale to another. Consequently, Western perspectives are colored by these stereotypical depictions, casting the populations of GCC countries in a negative light and implying a perceived backwardness and lack of civilization by Western standards.

The institutionalization of sports in the Arab World closely mirrored the European model. Sports clubs, leagues, and federations were established, often with direct support or oversight from colonial authorities. These institutions served as channels for European sports culture, governance models, and competition formats. They also became arenas where colonial power dynamics were perpetuated, often favoring European forms of cultural capital (Bourdieu, 1986). The legacy of this colonial introduction of sports persists to this day. Many sports institutions founded during the colonial era remain influential players in the sports landscape of the Arab World. According to post-colonial theory, these institutions can be viewed as "hybrid" forms, blending elements of both European and local cultures (Bhabha, 1994). However, the power dynamics established during the colonial period often endure, with European sports models and standards continuing to wield significant influence.

For instance, the effectiveness, viability, and reliability of institutions such as FIFA and the IOC, which were formed by western European standards and inherited some colonial legacies in terms of power relations, are under scrutiny. Parvis (2022) discusses two factors contributing to this scrutiny. Firstly, the West acts as the ultimate autonomous power, functioning as the "moral police" of the Third World, including the Middle East and North Africa. Consequently, the tired dichotomy between the West and the Orient persists. For the Gulf region to gain acceptance from the West on moral issues such as labor rights, the GCC must promptly fulfill Western mandates. However, the West sometimes overlooks the fact that sustainable change requires a careful and thorough transformation process. The second factor relates to the debates on human rights during the World Cup. Addressing complex issues like human rights requires comprehensive and sustained efforts. The World Cup tournament, which is held for one month can be a catalyst for change while preserving the internal dynamic of a society such as Qatar, which is undergoing rapid change. A country where the majority of the population is non-Qatari. That being said, Qatar has made significant reforms, particularly in addressing labor human rights, with the establishment of a minimum wage being a notable example, this change was lauded by the US Embassy as "the first of its kind in the region" (Reiche, 2021).

As further discussed in the subsequent section the close geographical proximity of the Arab World to Europe has facilitated various sports exchanges, including friendly matches, training camps, and even joint hosting of sporting events. These interactions have played a pivotal role in the adoption of European models within the sports systems of the Arab World. Globalization theory aids in understanding how these exchanges are integral components of broader global flows that influence local practices (Robertson, 1992). Furthermore, this geographical closeness has enabled regional partnerships in sports development, often receiving funding or support from European organizations. These partnerships can be analyzed through the lens of cultural capital theory, as they frequently involve the transfer of skills, knowledge, and expertise (Bourdieu, 1986).

European Model of Sport as a Product of Globalization Trends

Globalization theory serves as another critical framework, allowing us to understand how global forces, including economic relations and cultural exchanges, influence local structures and practices in the Arab World's sports model (Robertson, 1992). Globalization, as a phenomenon, refers to the interdependence of states. In other words, it denotes the "process fueled by, and resulting in, increasing cross-border flows of goods, services, money, people, information, and culture" (Held et al., 1999, p. 16, cited in Gems, & Pfister, 2014, p. 51). This diffusion occurs due to a transnational process involving diverse channels, such as the exchange of commodities, data, ideologies, and culture, including sport. The multifaceted nature of globalization is highlighted by its multidimensional character, encompassing economic, cultural, and institutional dimensions. The interconnectedness of a global economy, shared culture, and international organizations significantly shape the modern world and the interactions between nations and societies (Malcolm, 2008).

Arjun Appadurai, a notable theorist on globalization, highlighted that globalization can be classified into different levels or "scapes." The complexity of the modern world cannot be interpreted anymore in terms of traditional hierarchical analysis that divides elements into central and peripheral ones (Appadurai, 1990). The suffix "-scape" indicates the fluid, irregular shapes of these levels (Appadurai, 1990, p. 297). According to Arjun (1990), these scapes include:

* ethnoscapes: movement of people;
* technoscapes: movement of technologies;
* Finance-scapes: movement of capital;
* Media-scapes: movement of technologically mediated information, especially in the form of images or narratives; and
* Ideoscapes: movement of ideologies, including chains of ideas, terms, and images.

Globalization has aided in shifting the Major Sports hosting centers from the global north to the global South (Dubinsky, 2023). When South Africa had the privilege of hosting the FIFA World Cup in 2010, it marked a momentous occasion as it was the first time the tournament was held on the African continent. This presented an unprecedented opportunity. The shift in the choice of location for the FIFA World Cup was highly significant. South Africa successfully secured the bid to host this event back in 2006. The decision to entrust this major sporting event to a developing country like South Africa carried important implications. It indicated a shift away from the traditional Western-centric approach, signifying a redistribution of power and a move toward diversifying the pool of developing nations as hosts. These nations had previously been marginalized in the realm of international relations (IR) (Dowse, 2018).

A state's desire to utilize globalization in sports in upgrading its international stage determines the global identity of such a state (Houlihan, 2008). For example, the GCC countries utilized sport's global appeal to disseminate an appealing global image to the foreign public. Not only did these countries participate in sport international events, but they also presented themselves as equal partners to Western countries in hosting SMEs. Small GCC countries, such as Bahrain, UAE, and Qatar, emerged as potential sports hubs by hosting popular sports competitions, starting from the Formula 1 races hosted by Bahrain in 2004 and the UAE in 2009, and the FIFA World Cup 2022 in Qatar recently (Amara & Al-Naimi, 2023). The same strategy has been adopted by Saudi Arabia in positioning the country in the global sports arena and market. The same strategy that was established by economically developed countries in Europe, in the US, and then in Asia. The rise of these GCC countries can be interpreted politically and economically in the platform of global sports. Edgar (2020) explains that economic diversification and enhancement of the soft power of these GCC countries represent the motivations behind their investments in sport. However, their sport ventures have been questioned. Globalization facilitated by the technological advances in media and communication led to the dissemination of negative images about these non-European countries. The GCC countries' penetration into the sport realm has been criticized for demonstrating a façade for their sportwashing attempts. Sportwashing refers to using sport to beautify their image from human rights exploitations (Chadwick, 2023). To reduce the strategy of the GCC countries to mere sportwashing and other political ideological agendas is to ignore other commercial and financial motives, to diversify the national economy and source of investment nationally and internationally. Furthermore, to integrate sport in the urban and tourism development of these countries, to develop elite sport, and the promotion of physical activity in countries where the level of non-communicable diseases due to lack of physical activity in the highest in the world due to rapid sedentarization. Furthermore, globalization has led to structural shifts in traditional sport in the GCC countries. Heritage sports, on top of which camel racing has been impacted by global institutionalization. The location of the GCC countries as a center point linking the West and the Middle East (Amara, 2012) played a role in not only reviving a heritage tradition (camel racing) but also presenting the GCC countries' interpretation of their version of modernity. That is, modernity that balances Western modern sports values and organization with Arab and Islamic authenticity (Amara, 2009).

Debates on Good Governance in Sport

In addition, globalization has led to challenging conventional social structures in the GCC region by opening the door to the participation of GCC females in the sports arena. Besides accentuating their traditional sporting heritage, the GCC countries aim to make their citizens globally equal to their peers worldwide through their modernization quest. Empowering GCC women to participate in sports, which are traditionally male-dominated, represents an example of the global values that the GCC countries are attempting to embrace and foster. Sports serve as an invisible motor that helps foster and accept the Western visualization of a globalized world (Gems and Pfister, 2014). External influences, primarily from international bodies like the International Olympic Committee (IOC), are pressuring GCC nations to include women in their sports teams and decision-making positions in national sport governing bodies, particularly when participating in significant events like the Olympics (Lysa, 2019).

Prior to the 2012 London Olympics and after Qatar's win of the bid to host the World Cup 2022 in 2010, one of the first state-led attempts at empowering females in sports in Qatar was by forming the Qatari Female Football team in 2011 (Knez et al., 2014). However, this team did not continue due to societal disagreement and sensitivity in the community. The single official global mention of the Qatari female football team emerged in 2013 when it was ranked no. 112 in the FIFA female football global ranking (Lysa, 2020). Female athletes in Qatar and the GCC are at the center of societal resistance due to the invisibly inherited patriarchal traditions and the liberal values infused by the modernization processes of the GCC region (AlKhalifa & Farello, 2021). Hosting the World Cup 2022 in Qatar has opened the door to creating change and normalizing the participation of females in football. One of the tools is through organizing school female football competitions across the School Olympic Program. The School Olympic Program aims to discover school talents from both sexes in private and public schools in Qatar in partnership with the Qatar Olympic Committee and the Ministry of Education and Higher Education, Aspire Academy, and Qatar Foundation (Olympic. qa, 2023). This year's program included the participation of female students in several sports, including football for the first time, besides handball, volleyball, and basketball. Qatar Foundation's Vice-Chairperson, CEO, and a female triathlon royal, Sheikh Hind Bint Hamad Al-Thani, attended the closing ceremony. It is noteworthy to mention that Sheikh Hind was elected in 2022 as a member of the IOC's Olympism 365 Commission, Olympic Education Commission, and Olympic Programme Commission (QNA, 2012). The venues and facilities of the Education City offer the chance for females ranging from children (4–12 years), teenagers (12–16 years) and women (16–55 years) to learn football indoor (futsal) to preserve their privacy and the traditions of Qatari society by offering different age-based classes inside.

Arab Investments in European Football

European sports content often overshadows local sports in the Arab World, influencing not just viewership but also sponsorship and advertising revenues (Rowe, 2004). This can be understood as a form of cultural imperialism, where European sports become the dominant form of cultural capital in the Arab World's sports landscape. The rights to broadcast European leagues are hot commodities in the Arab World, often leading to bidding wars among local broadcasters. This economic aspect can be analyzed through globalization theory, which helps us understand how global economic forces shape local practices and preferences. From an economic perspective, GCC countries, exemplified by Qatar, aimed to position the country in the global sport-media landscape, through investing in sports broadcasting of SMEs and football leagues in Europe and globally (Atlantic Council, 2022). The internationalization of the BeIN Sports Network represents a vehicle to achieve economic sustainability for future generations (Amara & Ishac, 2021), as indicated in Qatar National Vision 2003, which represents a developmental national framework to prepare Qatar for a post-oil era. Another motivation is the maximization of Qatar's international image and amplifying its national branding efforts through visibility in sports media, as explained by Le May (2022). Sport media is a highly lucrative field, with the international value of global sport-media rights reaching $55.07bn in 2022 (Sportbusiness, 2022). Established in 2013, BeIN Sports Network became the region's dominant sports media network, holding more than 50% of the MENA sports media market through exclusive coverage of elite-tier sporting events, including the 2022 FIFA World Cup, and expansion regionally and internationally (Le May, 2022). However, the regional and international success of BeIN was negatively challenged during the Gulf Crisis 2017–2021. In 2017, Saudi Arabia, the UAE, Bahrain, and Egypt imposed a blockade on Qatar, leading to the emergence of a sport-media network, BeOut, by the blockading countries. The piracy outcomes of BeOut on BeIN resulted in financial losses and staff downsizing at BeIN, with losses reaching approximately $1 billion in 2019 and a halving of staff numbers at the Doha headquarters (Le May, 2022). BeINsport played a pivotal role in the diffusion of European top leagues and the marketization of European clubs, players and coaches in the region. European clubs increasing the fan base in the Middle East and North Africa. Saudi Arabia and the record signing of European players and coaches in 2023–2024 season to join the Saudi Professional league. Transforming the league to one of the most lucrative in the region and internationally.

The ownership of clubs like Manchester City by the UAE and Paris Saint-Germain by Qatar has shifted the center of gravity in European football, making Arab investors key stakeholders (Wilson, 2012). This influx of Arab investment can be analyzed through globalization theory, which explores how global economic relations shape local realities. Arab companies are increasingly significant sponsors of European sports events and teams, further intertwining the economic relations between the two regions. The concept of cultural capital provides a lens through which we can understand how these sponsorships serve as a form of cultural validation, enhancing the status and prestige of Arab companies globally (Bourdieu, 1986).

The economic benefits of Arab investment in European sports are multifaceted, ranging from direct financial returns to softer benefits like increased global visibility and prestige. These can be analyzed through a combination of globalization and cultural capital theories. Investments from the GCC region have attracted international media attention, with various GCC sovereign wealth funds, individuals, companies, and enterprises expanding their investments into the sports industry beyond their geographic region. These investments are seen as crucial components of GCC economies' strategies to transition from controlled liberalism to market-oriented economies, integrating into the global economic system (Amara, 2008). Furthermore, investments in prominent European football teams would further link GCC countries to European commercial networks and aid in shifting these countries toward economically diversified futures (Thani & Heenan, 2017). The rise of football's neoliberal economy and advancements in media technologies and transnational marketing strategies have empowered the GCC region to enter the global sports market by investing in sports media channels and sponsoring elite football clubs (Thani & Heenan, 2017). Since 2008, top European football clubs have faced financial difficulties due to the global financial crisis, prompting select elite European football clubs to seek investments from GCC SWFs and corporations to enhance their global appeal and reduce mounting debts.

Conclusion

In summary, the European Model of Sport stands as a testament to the enduring power of sport as a means of cultural expression, social integration, and international collaboration. This chapter has elucidated the model's foundational principles, governance structures, and the delicate balance it strikes between commercial interests and the preservation of sporting integrity and community values. As the world of sports continues to evolve, the European Model offers valuable lessons in sustainability, inclusivity, and the promotion of fair play. The challenges of globalization, technological advancement, and changing societal norms present opportunities for the model's adaptation and innovation. Moving forward, it will be imperative for stakeholders within the European sports ecosystem to embrace these changes, ensuring the model remains relevant and continues to contribute positively to the global sports dialogue. By doing so, the European Model of Sport can continue to inspire and influence the governance of sport worldwide, fostering a future where sport remains a powerful force for good in society.

It could be argued that the influx of Arab investment is a manifestation of broader global economic trends, redefining power dynamics and creating mutual dependency between the Arab World and Europe in the realm of sports. This raises several questions about the governance system of European sport, particularly regarding the link between these investments and state funds, the potential imbalance created between clubs in European leagues that are receiving significant investment, and other clubs with a lower budget. Some of the fear of this investment coming from Arabs may also be a product of an orientalist vision about the other, portraying the rich Arab as taking over our football (Garcia & Amara, 2013). One should also consider the positive impact of this investment on the market value of teams such as Paris Saint-Germain and the French Professional League. Investments from Qatar, the UAE, and more recently from Saudi Arabia are maintaining the influx of star players to European leagues, as well as offering these players in their 30s opportunities to continue their professional careers in local leagues in the region with a more developed business and financial capacities.

References

Alkhalifa, H. K., & Farello, A. (2021). The soft power of Arab women's football: Changing perceptions and building legitimacy through social media. *International Journal of Sport Policy and Politics*, 13(2), 241–257.

Amara, M. (2008). The Muslim world in the global sporting arena. *The Brown Journal of World Affairs*, 14(2), 67–75.

Amara, M. (2009). The Middle East and North Africa. In *Routledge Companion to Sports History* (pp. 514–525). Routledge.

Amara, M. (2012). Football sub-culture and youth politics in Algeria. *Mediterranean Politics*, 17(1), 41–58.

Amara, M., & Al-Naimi, S. (2023). Geopolitics of sports in the MENA region. In W. Chadwick, D. Widdop, & D. L. J. Goldman (Eds.), *The Geopolitical Economy of Sport: Power, Politics, Money, and the State* (pp. 127–133). Routledge.

Amara, M., & Ishac, W. (2021). Sport and development in Qatar: International and regional dynamics of sport mega-events. In *Sport and Development in Emerging Nations* (pp. 141–153). Routledge.

Appadurai, A. (1990). Disjuncture and difference in the global cultural economy. *Theory, Culture & Society*, 7(2–3), 295–310.

Atlantic Council. (2022). Many European soccer teams are owned by Gulf states. But why? [Online]. https://www.atlanticcouncil.org/blogs/menasource/many-european-soccer-teams-are-owned-by-gulf-states-but-why/

Bairner, A. (2015). *Sport, Nationalism, and Globalization: European and North American Perspectives*. State University of New York Press.

Bhabha, H. K. (1994). *The Location of Culture*. Routledge.

Bilgin, P. (2004). Is the 'Orientalist' past the future of Middle East studies? *Third World Quarterly*, 25(2), 423–433.

Bourdieu, P. (1986). The forms of capital. In J. G. Richardson (Ed.), *Handbook of Theory and Research for the Sociology of Education* (pp. 241–258). Greenwood Press.

Burney, S. (2012). Chapter one: Orientalism: The making of the other. *Counterpoints*, 417, 23–39.

Carrington, B., & Césaire, A. (2015). Post/colonial theory and sport. In R. Giulianotti (Ed.), *Routledge Handbook of the Sociology of Sport* (pp. 105–116). Routledge.

Chadwick, S. (2023). Formula 1 in the Gulf region: The fast and the furious. In H. E. Næss & S. Chadwick (Eds.), *The Future of Motorsports: Business, Politics and Society* (pp. 13–23). Taylor & Francis.

Clevenger, S. (2017). Sport history, modernity and the logic of coloniality: A case for decoloniality. *Rethinking History*, 21(4), 586–605.

Dowse, S. (2018). Mega sports events as political tools: A case study of South Africa's hosting of the 2010 FIFA Football World Cup. In S. Rofe (Ed.), *Sport and Diplomacy* (pp. 70–86). Manchester University Press.

Dubinsky, Y. (2023). *Nation Branding and Sports Diplomacy: Country Image Games in Times of Change*. Springer Nature.

Edgar, A. (2020). Contemporary art and contemporary sport in the Arabian Peninsula. *Sport, Ethics and Philosophy*, 14(3), 339–354.

Garcia, B., & Amara, M. (2013). Media perceptions of Arab investment in European football clubs: The case of Málaga and Paris Saint-Germain. *Sport&EU Review*, 5(1), 5–20.

Gems, G. R. (2006). Sport, colonialism, and United States imperialism. *Journal of Sport History*, 33(1), 3–25.

Gems, G. R., & Pfister, G. (2014). Sport and globalization: Power games and a new world order. *Movement & Sport Sciences-Science & Motricité*, 86, 51–60.

Griffin, T. (2019). National identity, social legacy and Qatar 2022: The cultural ramifications of FIFA's first Arab World Cup. *Soccer & Society*, 20(7–8), 1000–1013.

Held, D., McGrew, A., Goldblatt, D., & Perraton, J. (1999). *Global Transformations: Politics, Economics and Culture*. Stanford University Press, cited in Gems, G. R., & Pfister, G. (2014). *Understanding American Sports*. Routledge.

Houlihan, B. (2008). Sport and globalisation. In B. Houlihan & D. Malcolm (Eds.), *Sport and Society: A Student Introduction* (pp. 553–537). SAGE Publications.

Knez, K., Benn, T., & Alkhaldi, S. (2014). World Cup football as a catalyst for change: Exploring the lives of women in Qatar's first national football team – A case study. *The International Journal of the History of Sport*, 31(14), 1755–1773.

Le May, C. (2022). Qatar's BeIN sports and football broadcasting in the Middle East: International influence and regional Rancor. In A. Al-Arian (Ed.), *Football in the Middle East: State, Society, and the Beautiful Game* (pp. 303–322). Oxford University Press.

Lysa, C. (2019). Qatari female footballers: Negotiating gendered expectations. In D. Reiche & T. Sorek (Eds.), *Sport, Politics and Society in the Middle East* (pp. 73–92). Oxford University Press.

Lysa, C. (2020). FIFA World Cup 2022: Increased opportunities for Qatar's women footballers? [Online]. Retrieved on 22nd October 2023, https://cirs.qatar.georgetown.edu/fifa-world-cup-2022-increased-opportunities-qatars-women-footballers/

Malcolm, D. (2008). *The SAGE Dictionary of Sports Studies*. SAGE Publications.

Mishra, V., & Hodge, B. (1991). What is post(-)colonialism? *Textual Practice*, 5(3), 399–414.

Olympic.qa. (2023). Schools Olympic Program new season to begin on September 25. [Online]. Available at https://www.olympic.qa/media-center/schools-olympic-program-new-season-begin-september-25

Parvis, Z. (2022). The World Cup and the Utopian promise of upholding human rights. [Online]. Available at https://cirs.qatar.georgetown.edu/the-world-cup-and-the-utopian-promise-of-upholding-human-rights/

QNA. (2022). Sheikh Joaan, Sheikha Hind appointed to IOC commissions. [Online]. Retrieved on 22nd October 2023, https://www.qna.org.qa/en/News-Area/News/2022-10/02/0054-sheikh-joaan,-sheikha-hind-appointed-to-ioc-commissions

Rowe, D. (2004). *Sport, Culture and the Media: The Unruly Trinity* (2nd ed.). Open University Press.

Reiche, D. (2021). Why the FIFA World Cup 2022 in Qatar should not be boycotted. [Online]. https://cirs.qatar.georgetown.edu/why-the-fifa-world-cup-2022-in-qatar-should-be-not-boycotted/

Rolim, L. H. (2019). Qatar in the Olympic system: The emergence of the Al-Thani nation representatives and diplomatic recognition (1971–1981). *Diagoras: International Academic Journal on Olympic Studies, 3*, 132–152.

Robertson, R. (1992). *Globalization: Social Theory and Global Culture*. Sage Publications.

Said, E. W. (1978). *Orientalism*. Pantheon Books.

Sondhaus, L. (2020). *World War One*. Cambridge University Press.

Sportbusiness. (2022). Jeff Zucker named CEO of sports media investment firm RedBird IMI. [Online]. Available at https://www.sportbusiness.com/news/jeff-zucker-named-ceo-of-sports-media-investment-firm-redbird-imi/. Retrieved on 24th March 2025.

Thani, S., and Heenan, T. (2017). The ball may be round but football is becoming increasingly Arabic: Oil money and the rise of the new football order. *Soccer & Society*, 18(7), 1012–1026. https://doi.org/10.1080/14660970.2015.1133416

Wilson, J. (2012). The outsourcing of football: Gulf ownership in European football. *Soccer & Society*, 13(2), 409–419.

Chapter 15

Exploring Colombia's National Sports System through the European Model of Sport

Decentralisation, Solidarity, and Sport

Mauricio Hernández Londoño
and Néstor Ordóñez Saavedra

Introduction

In Colombia, sport is recognised as a distinct human activity marked by a playful mindset and a competitive drive for validation or challenge, demonstrated through both physical and mental exercises (LEY 181 DE 1995, 1995). This definition was established in the National Sports Act of 1995, which also created the institutional framework known as *Sistema Nacional de Deporte* (National Sports System—NSS). The right to the practice of sport is recognised in the country's legal framework through the sports act, but it does not have the legal status of a constitutional fundamental right (Constitutional Court of Colombia, n.d.). In Colombia, rights are classified within the Constitution into three main categories: Fundamental, Economic, Social, and Cultural Rights (ESCR), and collective rights. The first category, such as the right to life, liberty, and dignity, has immediate protection and is enforceable through mechanisms like the *Tutela*.[1] In contrast, ESCR, which includes the right to sports, are generally recognised but not enforceable in the same immediate manner as fundamental rights. However, ESCR can sometimes acquire constitutional protection when they are linked to fundamental rights, under a legal doctrine known as *conexidad* (connection or nexus) (Constitutional Court of Colombia, n.d.).

Therefore, the right to sport in Colombia, falling under the ESCR category, is an important tool for personal and social development. Although it is a governmental priority, it does not have the same constitutional enforceability as fundamental rights such as health or education. This means that while the state has a duty to promote and facilitate access to sports, the practice of sport as a right cannot always be claimed through judicial means with the same imminence as other fundamental rights. Instead, its enforceability depends on state resources and progressive realisation (Constitutional Court of Colombia, n.d.).

The NSS: Institutional Design

Established in 1995, the NSS plays a crucial role in guaranteeing Colombian citizens' access to sports, including leisure activities, physical education, and recreation.

DOI: 10.4324/9781032665153-18

The 1995 Colombian National Sports Act declares the practice of sport as a right, which makes it mandatory for the State to promote it nationwide (Ley 181 de 1995, 1995).

This law establishes a framework for promoting sport, recreation, leisure activities, extracurricular education, and physical education. Notably, sports are divided into eight distinct subcategories: Formative, community, university, associative, competitive, high performance, amateur, and professional.

Additionally, the International Charter of Physical Education, Physical Activity, and Sport, initially adopted by UNESCO in 1978 served as a key framework for promoting the universal right to physical education, physical activity, and sport. Over time, it became clear that societal changes required a revision, which led to its update in 2015, keeping those categories (physical education, physical activity, and sport) (UNESCO, 2015).

One limitation of the Colombian 1995 National Sports Act (Law 181) was the creation of a sport system with categories that did not align with UNESCO's Charter. As a result, many individuals outside the federated and institutionalised sport structures felt excluded from the national sport system, leading to confusion and tensions—issues that Coldeportes (the National Institute of Sport) largely overlooked.

Hence, the sector's evolution has led to an overlap between recreational sport, federated sport, and physical activity/education, often diluting recreation's distinct role in the development of a sporting culture in the country due to the focus on institutionalised/federated sport. It has been recently suggested that recreational sport should be treated as a cross-dimension connected to education and physical activity rather than a standalone component of sport, in order to align Colombian Law with UNESCO´s Charter (Ordoñez-Saavedra, 2023).

Evolution and Alignment with the European Model

Sport development in Colombia can be divided into three clearly defined stages: before 1968, from 1968 to 1995, and from 1995 to the present (Morales Fontanilla, 2020). This chapter focuses on the events from 1995 to the present, considering the extent to which sport in Colombia might resemble any elements of the EMS. Since its beginning, the government has privileged the groups dedicated to delivering sports because the NSS provided an institutional design to recognise sports organisations (i.e. clubs, governing bodies) over other types of voluntary or community associations. Non-governmental sport organisations, such as the National Olympic Committee, National Paralympic Committee, National Federations, Regional Leagues, and local clubs were strengthened by the 1995 sports act because they were recognised as strategic partners of the government in the NSS.

The National Sports Act states that public and private actors are 'harmonically articulated' to grant public access to sports, from grassroots to elite, including other manifestations of physical activity, recreation, and physical education.

In summary, the development of sport in Colombia, institutionalised through the NSS as recognised in the 1995 National Sports Act, highlights how federated sports organisations, such as national federations and local clubs, were given prominence. This created a structured and regulated environment very much similar to the pyramidal governance structures defined in the EMS. Although the Colombian NSS' legal framework does not make any explicit references to the EMS, it incorporates key elements of the model such as solidarity mechanisms, national coordination, and the principle of a single federation per sport. This indicates that, despite its unique cultural and legislative context, the Colombian approach mirrors the EMS in important ways, particularly in its focus on institutionalisation and the hierarchical organisation of sports.

Decentralised Governance: Tensions Between Financial Constraints and Institutional Sustainability

Colombia is a social state governed by the rule of law, organised as a unitary republic with a decentralised administrative structure that grants autonomy to its sub-national territories. The country's administrative division consists of 32 departments (i.e. regions), 1,102 municipalities, and special districts, such as Bogotá, D.C. (Constitución Política de la República de Colombia 1991, 1991).

The public sector has three levels of governance (national, regional, and local), each with autonomy and a budget to deliver their policies within their jurisdiction. This has implications for the governance of sport because it makes it very difficult to create a sports system that articulates harmonically at the national, regional, and local levels. Indeed, the administrative and multi-level complexity of the Colombian state underpins the complex and fragmented structures of the Colombian sport system.

Although Law 181 of 1995 established the creation of sport authorities/departments at the local level within municipal governments, by the year 2000 more than 50% of these entities had disappeared due to insufficient resources to sustain them. To address this problem, the Fiscal Adjustment Law (Ley 617 de 2000, 2000) was enacted to impose limits on municipal and departmental spending, particularly in public administration. The aim was to reduce fiscal deficits and enhance the financial stability of local governments, ensuring proper resource allocation for essential services, including sports and recreational programmes. This law introduced fiscal corrections to help municipalities better manage their budgets and prevent the collapse of local sports authorities due to financial mismanagement (Ley 617 de 2000).

Pyramidal Governance: A Dual Structure

The NSS has a dual structure that incorporates governmental and non-governmental (i.e. private) actors. On the governmental side, the Ministry of Sport (formerly known as Coldeportes—*Instituto Colombiano del Deporte*), holds the highest position in the sports hierarchy. Under the Ministry's structure, but not subordinate to it as they have large levels of independence, there are institutions known as 'regional secretaries' or 'institutes of sports and recreation', which cover each one of Colombia's 32 regions. At a local level, there are local bodies or municipal institutes for sport known as IMDERs.[2] It is discretional for local governments to decide the best administrative structure to deliver sports and recreation services at the local level. Therefore, in many cases for budgetary reasons, sports, tourism, culture, and education are joined together under one single department in the municipality (Ley 617 de 2000, 2000). Although coordination from top to bottom amongst public authorities across the different geographical level is expected, the reality is that political, cultural, and institutional differences make harmonic articulation unrealistic. Colombia's governmental sport system is, therefore, an excellent example of a multi-level and fragmented governing structure.

On the private/non-governmental side, we find the Olympic and Paralympic Committees at the top at the national level. They are followed by National Sport Federations, one per sport. The same model appears at a regional level, with one regional governing body (known in Colombia as *liga*—'league') for each sport.[3] At a local level, many clubs are expected to be created to promote sports. This institutional design relies on the idea that the best way to encourage sport participation is to have as many clubs as possible at the bottom and stretch the pyramid at regional and national levels with only one league by sport and region, and one national federation by sport, respectively.

Since the passage of Law 181 in 1995, sport clubs in Colombia can only dedicate themselves to a single sport. That is to say; the legislation does not recognise multi-sport clubs. This restriction resulted in financial unsustainability for many clubs, forcing them to depend on local government funding. Something that is not extremely different to what happens in Europe, as Chapters 5 and 7 in this volume explain. It is not only clubs, as most actors in the Colombian sport's institutional framework rely on the state to provide financial support for their training, operational, and competition needs (Ordoñez-Saavedra, 2023). A trend that, again, is not very dissimilar to what is found in European countries and elsewhere in the world, as pointed out in several contributions elsewhere in this volume.

From Coldeportes to the Ministry of Sport: Power Concentration and Source Dependency

Following the establishment of the NSS in 1995, Coldeportes underwent significant changes in governance and structure. Initially, it operated under the Ministry of National Education, as dictated by Decree 1228 of 1995 (Decreto 1228 de 1995, 1995). However, in 2003 Decree 1746 placed Coldeportes under the Ministry of Culture, reflecting a broader cultural approach to sports and physical activity (Decreto 1746 de 2003, 2003). Yet, Coldeportes (the country's highest sport authority in the governmental side) remained as a sub-ministerial level department.

This changed in 2011 with a significant decision. Coldeportes was elevated to the status of the Administrative Department of Sports, Recreation, Physical Activity, and the Use of Free Time through Decree 4183 (Decreto 4183 de 2011, 2011), granting it greater autonomy and a more prominent governmental role. It was not a cabinet-level ministerial body, but this decision enhanced the profile and operative autonomy of

Coldeportes. This evolution culminated in 2019 with the creation of the Ministry of Sport, established by Law 1967 (Ley 1967 de 2019, 2019), ensuring a dedicated and autonomous governance structure for sports in Colombia. For some academics, the creation of the Ministry of Sport was a cosmetic adjustment or a naming change because its functions and operations remained business as usual (Hernández, 2021; Ordoñez-Saavedra, 2023, 2024; Ramos Acosta et al., 2022). The Ministry of Sport was charged with responsibility in six main areas: Policy formulation, coordination of the NSS, inter-ministerial coordination, promotion of sports, infrastructure development, and ensuring compliance with regulations (Ley 1967 de 2019, 2019).

The Ministry for Sport has not had an easy time since its creation in 2019, though. Colombian President Gustavo Petro made a statement on sport policy in 2022 in which he urged his newly appointed Minister for Sport to prioritise investment in education over infrastructure projects. He criticised the focus on constructing sports facilities, arguing that such investments often lead to corruption and should not be the primary concern in sports policy. President Petro emphasised his government's commitment to 'more education, less cement', reflecting a shift towards educational initiatives rather than sport infrastructure. This statement, which indicates a willingness to change the focus of the government's sports policy, needs some context to be better understood. President Petro's statement followed the resignation of the previous minister for sport (on 15th February 2022) shortly after Barranquilla was stripped of its status as host of the XX Pan American Games 2027 due to missed payments totalling US$ 8 million. Critics blamed the minister for that failure, further fuelling Petro's criticism of the way in which the Ministry of Sport had acted. The president questioned in that statement the value of raising Coldeportes to a ministerial level, suggesting that it had been 'a waste of time'; he also highlighted the problematic emphasis on infrastructure over education in the current sports policy (Romero, 2024).

The governmental side of the sport system moves on to the regional level. Here we find regional bodies known as Departmental Sports Entities. Their functions are linked to coordination, development, promotion, and technical and administrative assistance to the municipalities and other organisations of the NSS in the territory of their jurisdiction. A certain level of coordination and cooperation between them and other municipal entities is expected to promote and disseminate physical activity, sports, and recreation. As pointed out above, it is important to remind that these regional sport authorities have political, administrative, and economic autonomy from the Ministry of Sport.

Finally, the IMDERs, or local sports institutes, are part of the public sector and sit at the base of the pyramid. Like those above them, their functions involve cooperating and coordinating policies and plans related to sports and recreation. Additionally, they are expected to propose local plans for sport and recreation, allocate funding within their jurisdiction, encourage participation, and align with other policies and programmes. Developing venues for sports and recreation is another key responsibility for these entities.

To sum up, the transformation of Coldeportes into the Ministry of Sport was intended to enhance the coordination, promotion, and development of sports across Colombia by centralising authority and expanding responsibilities. However, the complexity of implementing these policies in a context characterised by significant political, cultural, and institutional diversity poses substantial challenges. The Ministry of Sport was set up to perform a vertical coordinating role of various actors, from national to local levels. This top-down coordination is crucial for the effective functioning of the NSS. Still, it is complicated by the very heterogeneous priorities, resources, and capacities across different regions, municipalities, and sport organisations across the country. Effective policy implementation in sport often requires clear governance structures and strong horizontal and vertical coordination among multiple stakeholders (Houlihan, 2012), a particularly pronounced challenge in decentralised political systems like Colombia's.

The adoption of such a sport governance model in Colombia's context, with its diverse and decentralised landscape, underscores the difficulties of replicating traditional European governance structures in countries with distinct political and cultural dynamics. The Ministry's broad mandate, ranging from policy formulation to infrastructure development and inter-ministerial coordination, risks being undermined by these systemic coordination issues, suggesting that simply creating a new ministry does not automatically resolve the complexities inherent in governing sports at a national level.

The Sport Non-Governmental Side: Exercising Democracy from Top to Bottom

The structure of private sports organisations at the national, regional, and local levels is determined by their statutes, as long as they are based on the principles of democratisation and participation. Starting from the top, we first find three main actors: the National Olympic Committee, National Federations (Olympic and Paralympic), and the National Paralympic Committee.

The Colombian National Olympic Committee is a private organisation with national and international operations. The IOC recognised it in 1936, and it is known as the *Comité Olímpico Colombiano* (COC in its Spanish acronym).

The National Sports Law grants the COC a coordinating role for federated sports (this category encompasses competitive, high-performance, and amateur sports) and binds it to develop social and public-interest programmes. From a managerial perspective, this acknowledgment generated tensions between the Ministry of Sport and the COC because of overlapping functions and responsibilities operating with public funding.

The National Sports Law (Ley 181 de 1995, 1995) assigns seven functions to the COC: developing programmes approved by the Ministry of Sport, coordinating a national sports competition calendar, monitoring federations' compliance with international obligations, managing the organisation and funding of competitions, tracking athletes' progress and well-being, establishing agreements with public or private entities, and preparing training plans with the National Sports Federations.

The National Paralympic Committee is the top non-governmental body of paralympic sport in Colombia. The Colombian Paralympic Committee (CPC) and Paralympic system were initially organisationally structured around types of disabilities (physical, sensory, or mental disabilities). Subsequently, with Law 1946 (Ley 1946 de 2019, 2018), the Colombian Paralympic system was restructured, aligning it with international standards to mimic the organisational structures and divisions of the International Paralympic Committee. Therefore, in Colombia, sports for persons with disabilities can be organised either by sport or by type of disability, in coordination with the respective International Federations for Sport and International Sports Organisations for people with disabilities.

Public policy on paralympic sport in Colombia has been criticised for its narrow focus on high-performance para-sports, neglecting inclusive sport policies for all people with disabilities. Once driven by community and participation, these spaces are now influenced by political and economic interests, leading to division and dissatisfaction, with concerns about the fairness and inclusivity of the current sports sector.

Following down from the Olympic and Paralympic committees at the national level, the non-governmental sport structure finds two types of organisations at the regional level: sports leagues and associations. Both are defined as private organisations constituted by a minimum number of clubs to promote the sport; they can affiliate with the national federations. There are three substantial differences between leagues and associations: First, the leagues are created to encourage a single sport and its modalities, while the associations are constituted to promote several sports. Second, a sports association cannot be recognised in the departments when the government already recognises a league. Third, the creation of a league is promoted by clubs (private initiative), while the constitution of an association is endorsed by the government (public initiative). There may not be more than one league for each sport within each region. This was settled by the Constitutional Court in judgement 802-00 (*Competencia para regular estructura de entidades encargadas de fomentar, patrocinar y dirigir la actividad deportiva*, 2000).

At the base of the pyramid are sports clubs, divided into sports clubs, promoters, and professional clubs. Overall, they are private, voluntary, and not-for-profit organisations. They are constituted by individual members, primarily athletes, to promote and sponsor the practice of a sport, as well as promote public and social interest programmes in the municipality.

Other organisations, such as social clubs, universities, high schools, community organisations, and private or public companies that develop organised sports activities, may act as sports clubs for each sport and participate in elections for leagues or associations at the regional level.

Similarly to sports associations, promotional clubs promote the practice of several sports and recreation, but they are promoted by the public entity of sport when the discipline does not have enough athletes to create their own sports club.

The institutionalisation of the NSS and the creation of the Ministry of Sport has both positive and negative aspects. On the positive side, the institutionalisation of sport under the NSS has fostered a structured environment, aligning Colombia with international standards, with many elements similar to the EMS. This has strengthened key organisations such as national federations and regional leagues, ensuring better coordination and support for high-performance sports. However, this system has also generated tensions, particularly regarding the overemphasis on high-performance sport at the expense of recreation, physical activity, and inclusive sports. Critics argue that the Ministry of Sport, while a formal advancement, has not sufficiently addressed the needs of broader sectors of society, such as people with disabilities or smaller municipalities, which receive significantly lower funding levels. These tensions between centralisation, resource distribution, and inclusivity highlight the challenges of achieving equitable sports governance in a decentralised political structure like Colombia's, where cultural, political, and institutional differences complicate policy implementation at multiple levels.

The development of the NSS shares several structural similarities with the EMS, particularly in its hierarchical organisation and reliance on a centralised framework to regulate and promote sport. Both models emphasise the coordination between public and private actors, the promotion of a pyramid-like structure with grassroots clubs at the base, and national federations as key intermediaries for elite sports. In Colombia, the Ministry of Sport and organisations like the Colombian Olympic and Paralympic Committees mirror the EMS's focus on solidarity and a single federation per sport. However, while the EMS operates within a well-established tradition of solidarity and subsidiarity across European nations, Colombia faces challenges in decentralisation and equity, especially in resource distribution and inclusivity. The Colombian NSS privileges high-performance sports, much like the EMS, but struggles to replicate the same level of grassroots support and community involvement that is central to the European model. These differences underscore the complexities of adapting European sports governance principles in a context characterised by significant political and economic disparities.

The Struggle for Independence: State Intervention and the Autonomy of Colombian Sports Entities

This section delves into the ongoing debate regarding the autonomy of sport organisations in Colombia, particularly in relation to state intervention and governance. While entities such as the National Olympic and Paralympic Committees are designed to function independently, their autonomy is often questioned due to their dependence on public funding and the influence of regulatory frameworks imposed by the government (Ley 181 de 1995, 1995; Ley 1946 de 2019, 2018). This section explores the delicate balance between preserving sports organisations' independence and ensuring their accountability, transparency, and compliance with national and international regulations.

If the system's governance is understood from bottom to top, it is expected that many clubs elect their representatives democratically at a regional level. Then, these members lead the League's interests to the national federations and the Olympic Committee, respectively. All are under the oversight of public entities at all levels, preserving the principles of democratic participation.

Academics have raised some criticism because they claim that the NSS privileged the structure of sports organisations over leisure or recreation associations because it provided special recognition for them (Mesa Callejas et al., 2010) Even when elite sport is not defined in the Sports Law, almost all the attention has been given to the structures of federated sport, which is internationally known as elite sport.

The NSS has faced significant criticism for its slowness, passivity, and limited operational capacity (Hernandez, 2018). While it appears well-structured on paper, it often fails to function effectively in practice. Over two decades of diagnoses and evaluations have highlighted the complexities in managing the system. A detailed assessment conducted by the National Ten-Year Plan (2009–2019) identified several key issues. These include disarticulation between the actors, subsystems, and subsectors within the NSS, as well as the neglect of recreation, community, and physical activity organisations (Coldeportes, 2013).

Additionally, the NSS suffers from a lack of clarity regarding the roles and relationships between its various actors, and it exhibits a low capacity for planning and engaging both public and private stakeholders. The system struggles to demonstrate its impact on national development goals, has weak fundraising capabilities, especially for new or less popular sports, and remains heavily dependent on public funding. This dependency, combined with the poor sustainability of public policies and insufficient resource management planning, further hampers the NSS's effectiveness.

An excessive culture of centralisation has exacerbated these challenges. The system's focus on centralised control has limited its ability to adapt to regional and local needs, ultimately hindering the overall development of sports in Colombia. In a recent article about the uncertainty within the sports ecosystem, Ordoñez Saavedra (2024) analyses how the broader climate of uncertainty in Colombia—stemming from political, economic, and policy instability—affects the sport ecosystem. It is argued that these uncertainties hinder effective governance, planning, and funding within sports organisations, leading to challenges in the long-term development of athletes and the overall functionality of the NSS.

The national sports law grants autonomy to sports organisations. The autonomy of sports organisations at national, regional, and local levels is acknowledged. This implies that their governance structures depend on their own statutes and governing bodies, even when they run social and public-interest programmes with public funding.

The autonomy and independence of sports organisations in Colombia have attracted great interest, mainly due to problems linked to football's governance. Three specific scandals in that sport triggered wider discussions about the autonomy of sport organisations in the country and the need for further or stronger intervention by the state. The first was the participation of the former president of the Colombian Football Federation (FCF), Luis Bedoya, in the so-called FIFA Gate. Bedoya was banned for life by the FIFA Ethics Committee for racketeering and wire fraud (Gill, 2017). The second was the proven cartel for touting tickets for the qualifying matches to Russia's World Cup (Pavitt, 2020). The third was the allegations of abuse of former players against the head coach of the women's national team in 2019 (Pinochet, 2019).

The last scandal prompted the intervention of the Constitutional Court following multiple complaints by female players in judicial actions accusing Colombian football authorities of unequal treatment (including issues related to contracts, salaries, and overall working conditions). The Constitutional Court delivered a landmark ruling in 2020 whereby it found that FCF had violated the labour and constitutional rights of women footballers by perpetuating discriminatory practices rooted in machismo (Dejusticia, 2021). The Court mandated that the FCF implement measures to address these inequalities, including providing equal pay, fair contracts, and improved working conditions for female players. Furthermore, the ruling sought to dismantle deep-seated cultural biases in Colombian football, emphasising that the sport must be inclusive and respectful of the rights of all athletes, regardless of gender. The Constitutional Court's decision marked a significant legal step in addressing gender inequality in sport in Colombia, holding the FCF accountable for its discriminatory practices and pushing for structural changes to ensure the protection of women's rights within football. Despite the Supreme Court of Justice's extensive recommendations to the FCF, no structural changes happened within the system.

Recent research on autonomy in Colombian sports organisations revealed a systemic problem in the country's elite sports sector. On the one hand, non-governmental stakeholders such as federations, leagues or clubs seem to lack of capabilities for a correct management of their organisations; on the other hand, inadequate oversight from the Ministry of Sport, formerly Coldeportes: 'Most sports managers lack the time or expertise to effectively run their organisations, and Coldeportes lacks the administrative capacity to fulfil its role as the lead regulatory agency for sport in Colombia' (Villareal, 2017).

The autonomy of sports organisations remains a contentious issue both internationally and in Colombia. While autonomy allows these organisations to self-regulate, ensuring flexibility and independence from direct state control, it also raises significant concerns about accountability, transparency, and governance. The scandals involving the FCF highlighted the risks associated with unchecked autonomy, leading to judicial interventions like the Constitutional Court's ruling. Despite calls for reform and greater oversight, the principle of self-regulation persists, often shielding sports organisations from substantial changes. This ongoing tension between maintaining independence and ensuring compliance with national and international norms is at the heart of governance debates in Colombia, reflecting broader global discussions on the balance between autonomy and accountability in sport.

Good Governance: Need or Fashion?

Colombian debates about the level of autonomy that the sport model needs to concede to sport non-governmental organisations are often linked to questions of sport organisations' good governance. In that respect, this is a very similar debate to that found around the European Model of Sport. Indeed, good governance in sport is essential for ensuring ethical, transparent, and accountable management of sports organisations (PTG, 2019), and that is no different in Colombia. Recent political and academic debates in Colombia have highlighted the need to promote international standards of good governance in the country, involving clear decision-making processes, democratic structures, and inclusive stakeholder participation, fostering trust and integrity in the system (Hoye & Cuskelly, 2007).

As part of this rising debate in Colombia on sport governance, recent research assessed and compared the knowledge and perceptions of elite athletes and federations' in Colombia about the International Olympic Committee's (IOC) Basic Universal Principles (BUP) of good governance in sport (IOC, 2016). The conclusions revealed statistically significant differences in perceptions of BUP's implementation (Hernandez, 2018). Athletes generally held negative views of governance in the country, except in the areas of athlete participation and autonomy. Executives had positive perceptions across all principles. The study highlighted the limitations of the top-down approach to governance used in Colombia (and advocated by the traditional structures of the EMS). The study also indicated that different stakeholders had very different perceptions of the quality of sport governance in Colombia.

This, one would note, is not dissimilar to what is also found in Europe in relation to the European Model of Sport. As Richard Parrish argues elsewhere in this volume, the Court of Justice of the European Union (CJEU) has had to adjudicate in several sport-related cases that were brought up to the Court by dissatisfied stakeholders. The intervention of the Colombian Constitutional Court explained above could be understood very similarly to those of the CJEU. The negative perception of Colombian athletes of sport governance can also be clearly related to the motives that encouraged stakeholders in Europe to seek protection from the European court, as explained by Richard Parrish in his contribution.

Therefore, we can see that many of the governance-related features and debates that are prominent in the European Model of Sport, can also be found in Colombia, probably because the organisational structures of the NSS are similar.

Having established the raising importance of sport governance to understand the development and current state of the Colombian sport system, we want to finish this section with a short look at a recent governance audit of some Colombian sport federations.

Measuring the Unmeasurable: The National Sports Governance Observer (NSGO)

The NSGO project aimed to promote and enhance good governance within national sports organisations by providing a systematic framework for assessing their governance practices (Geeraert & Anagnostopoulos, 2018). Launched by Play the Game, the NSGO evaluated sports organisations across multiple countries, using a set of principles to measure transparency, democracy, internal accountability and control, and societal responsibility.

In 2019, Colombia participated as one of the countries in the NSGO. The evaluation showed that Colombia's National Olympic Committee and seven national federations (athletics, football, handball, swimming, tennis, cycling, and fencing) scored 45% (out of 100%, with 65% seen as acceptable) in terms of good governance, which was categorised as a 'moderate' score according to the NSGO's benchmark tool. That same year, the Ministry of Sport, along with the COC and the national federations, signed a declaration adhering to the principles of good governance under the *Agreement for Governance and Transparency in Elite Sport* (Ministerio del Deporte, 2019). Interestingly, the principles in this agreement mirrored those outlined by the IOC in 2008, yet no concrete evidence has been found of their implementation, raising questions about the practical impact of these commitments on sports governance in Colombia.

The NSGO audit of Colombian sport governance raised questions about sport federations' legitimacy in the system (Ramos Acosta et al., 2022). Key issues included a lack of transparency, insufficient accountability, and concentration of power in leadership positions, which undermine the democratic functioning and legitimacy of these organisations (Ramos Acosta et al., 2022). The audit results highlighted the need for greater stakeholder engagement, including athletes and local communities, to improve governance practices (Ramos Acosta et al., 2022), something that is perhaps unsurprising given the interventions of the Colombian Constitutional Court and other scandals that have been mentioned above. Ultimately, reforms are needed to enhance transparency, increase accountability, and promote more democratic decision-making in Colombian sport organisations. Better governance is essential to strengthening the legitimacy and effectiveness of sports federations within Colombia's NSS. This chapter turns now to examine a fundamental component of any sport model: Funding of the Colombian sport system.

Sport Financing: Where Is the Money Coming From?

Sport financing in Colombia can be divided into two key periods: before 1993 and after 1993. In both cases the two main funding sources were the public and private sectors, creating a mixed model of financing with a predominant reliance on public resources. The private sector has typically concentrated its investments on sports with mass appeal or entertainment value, such as men's football and cycling. Before 1993, sports funding primarily came from public resources, including taxes on cigarettes, public entertainment, and national, regional, and municipal budget allocations. However, after the 1993 reforms, particularly with the introduction of Law 181 of 1995, additional public financing mechanisms were introduced, such as allocations from the national budget distributed to regions based on population size. Despite these changes, private investment has continued to focus on commercially lucrative sports, while other sports have remained heavily reliant on state support.

After 1993, an annual national budget for sports was established. This allocation corresponds to a percentage of the national general budget, distributed equitably among departments, municipalities, and Bogotá C.D., primarily based on population size. Other sources have included mobile phone taxes, the 'pro-sport' tax, scholarships, tax-related projects, public–private partnerships, private sector donations, contributions from the IOC, and support from International Sports Federations.

Consolidating a single figure for sport investment and expenditure in Colombia is a complex task due to the decentralised nature of the funding and the varied sources of financial support across levels of government and private contributions. However, for the year 2024, the Colombian government allocated approximately US$ 325 million to the Ministry of Sport (Ministerio del Deporte, 2023). Additionally, the Bogotá D.C. Recreation and Sports Institute (IDRD) was allocated around US$ 75 million to support sports programmes in the capital. Despite these substantial investments at the national and metropolitan levels, there remains a significant disparity in funding across the country. Approximately 70% of Colombian municipalities receive an average of just US$ 50,000 annually for their sports development needs (DNP, 2024). This uneven distribution of resources highlights the ongoing challenge of promoting equitable access to sports infrastructure and opportunities throughout the country, particularly in rural and less economically developed regions.

Sports betting corporations have increased their sponsorship activities globally over the past two decades (Salamanca, 2023). In Colombia, sports betting is regulated by *Coljuegos*, which has overseen gambling activities since 2012. This makes the country the first in Latin America to implement comprehensive rules for physical and online casinos, sports betting, and other formats (Salamanca, 2023).

The market has evolved significantly over the past few years, with sports betting companies becoming prominent sponsors, particularly since the legalisation of online gambling in 2016 (Salamanca, 2023). Large online sports betting corporations sponsor both individual teams and the professional football league itself (Moreno, 2024).

Although online gambling heavily sponsors football, revenue does not directly support the sport or any solidarity mechanisms within. Instead, these funds are directed to the national healthcare system, per Law 643 of 2001 which regulates gambling in Colombia. This law promotes responsible gambling while ensuring that the industry contributes to societal welfare, reinforcing the healthcare system rather than directly benefiting football. This model exemplifies the broader social responsibility embedded in Colombia's gambling framework (Congreso de Colombia, 2001).

On the other hand, according to the 2024 report on the financial information of Colombian football clubs (Saavedra, 2024), the state-owned body responsible for overseeing professional football clubs reported that as of December 31st, 2023, there are 35 professional football teams in Colombia, 34 of which are incorporated as joint-stock companies. Of the 19 First Division (top tier of Colombian football) teams that submitted their financial information, the consolidated revenue figures for 2023 were as follows: US$ 49 million from ticket sales and season passes (31.5%); US$ 36 million from television rights (22.7%); US$ 37 million from advertising and sponsorship (23.2%); US\$ 18 million from participation in national and international events (11.4%); US\$ 19 million from the sale of sports merchandise (8%); and US\$ 5 million from transfers made by the FCF, DIMAYOR, and CONMEBOL (3.2%). Notably, five of the 35 football clubs are undergoing business rescue proceedings.

Thus, as can be seen in this quick overview, sport funding structures in Colombia are not very dissimilar to what can be found in some European models of sport, as pointed out by Holger Preuss and Antonia Hannawacker in this book. The involvement of the private sector is focused on top elite professional sport, whereas the development of the system, and specially amateur grassroots sport relies heavily on public state funding. A particular feature of Colombia, perhaps, is the major imbalances in public investment between different parts of the country, with Bogota and the largest and richest regions far ahead of other areas that, however, are in dire need of investment to facilitate local population access to sport.

Having looked at the financing structures of the Colombian model of sport, we cannot finish this chapter without discussing what is, perhaps, one of the particularities of the Colombian sport system that sets it apart from other countries in the Latin American context: The hosting and organisation of relatively large national and international sport events.

Colombia as a Regional Sports Power: Sports Megaevents and Olympic Medals

The history of hosting sports events in Colombia highlights the country's growing role in organising significant international sporting competitions. Since the late 20th century, Colombia has hosted major events such as the Pan American Games in Cali in 1971, the Central American and Caribbean Games in 1978, and the South American Games in 2010, showcasing its evolving capacity to manage large-scale events. In 2011, Colombia took centre stage by hosting the FIFA U-20 World Cup, followed by notable events like the World Games in Cali in 2013, the Pan American Games of Speed Skating in 2018, and the Tour Colombia cycling race in 2019. Although Colombia was selected to cohost the 2021 Copa América, political unrest led to its withdrawal (AP, 2021). These events have not only boosted the country's infrastructure and economy but also strengthened its international reputation as a prime destination for global sporting events (Hernández & Ramírez, 2014).

The organisation of sport events is a particular feature of the Colombian sports model that sets it apart from other countries in the Latin American context and, perhaps to some extent, also to some countries in Europe. It is important to note that hosting of events is not relevant per se, but because of the impact these events have had on the development of the sports system in Colombia. On the one hand, hosting of events was perceived as important by the state to project the country's international image during a period of economic and social instability due to the internal struggles with violence. On the other hand, those events have served to consolidate the role of the National Olympic Committee and National sport federations in the system, as they are key actors in bringing those events to Colombia. Moreover, the hosting of sport events has been used also by regional and municipal authorities to spearhead projects of infrastructure development. Thus, we find a dynamic whereby different stakeholders see different advantages and interests in the organisation of those large-scale sport events, shaping the development of the sports system in the country.

Similarly, some of those events have also had negative consequences. Mostly due to poor administration or management. A recent scandal unfolded in 2024, when Panam Sports revoked Barranquilla's hosting rights for the 2027 Pan American Games due to the Colombian government's failure to meet a US$ 8 million payment deadline by 31st December 2023. Although Barranquilla had been awarded the hosting rights in 2021, the government did not fulfil the required payments in 2022 and 2023, and the city lost its rights as a host for the 2027 games. Due to space constraints, we can only highlight the significance of event hosting within the Colombian sports model, which distinguishes it from other regional models. However, it is evident that this area warrants further investigation.

Finally, the analysis of the Colombian sports model will not be complete without a mention to the efforts made by both governmental and non-governmental actors to improve results in the international sporting arena, normally measured by the number of Olympic medals achieved. As we pointed earlier in this chapter, there is a clear imbalance in the Colombian sport system between the focus on elite and grassroots sport, with the former being clearly privileged due to institutional, policy, and budgetary reasons. Thus, it is relevant to reflect on whether that focus on elite sport might be delivering results or not.

Table 15.1 can offer valuable insights into the country's sport development and international competitiveness.

Colombia's Olympic journey has seen moments of individual brilliance and milestones that mark institutional shifts in its sports policy. Athletes like Ximena Restrepo, who won a bronze medal in the 400 metres at Barcelona in 1992, and Hellmut Bellingrodt, a silver medallist in shooting at Munich in 1972, stand out as rare cases of success from a time when Colombia lacked a coherent high-performance sports strategy and institutional design. The country's first gold medal,

Table 15.1 Olympic medals won by Colombia in the last five Summer Olympic Games

Olympic Games	Gold	Silver	Bronze
Beijing 2008	0	2	1
London 2012	1	3	5
Rio 2016	3	2	3
Tokyo 2020	0	4	1
Paris 2024	0	3	1
Total	4	14	11

Source: Own elaboration with data from Ministerio del Deporte (2023).

won by María Isabel Urrutia in weightlifting, at Sydney 2000, directly resulted from an institutional decision to concentrate resources on sports where Colombia had competitive potential.

Compared to neighbouring countries such as Ecuador, Peru, Panama, and Venezuela, Colombia's Olympic performance is more robust and consistent. For instance, Ecuador and Panama have only achieved isolated successes, such as gold medals in athletics and boxing, respectively, while Peru's medal count remains modest across all Games. However, Colombia's achievements remain limited compared to regional powerhouses like Brazil, Cuba, or Argentina. Brazil's dominance, highlighted by seven gold medals in Tokyo 2020, reflects its robust investment in diverse sports disciplines. Similarly, Cuba, with its long-standing focus on boxing and athletics, consistently outperforms Colombia despite fewer resources. Argentina, with a strong tradition in team sports and individual events, also showcases a more balanced Olympic track record. These comparisons underline Colombia's relative progress within its immediate region but reveal the gaps that must be bridged to compete with the broader Latin American leaders on the world stage.

Conclusion

In conclusion, the development of National Sport System in Colombia reflects a complex interplay of public and private interests, where sports governance has evolved through multiple phases since 1995. On the positive side, the system has provided a structured framework that aligns with elements of the EMS, emphasising the hierarchical organisation of federations, the principle of a single federation per sport, and a collaborative approach between public and private entities. This institutional design allowed Colombia to strengthen elite sports, as seen in the discrete success of its athletes on the international stage and the organisation of sports events.

However, several challenges persist within the NSS. In some regions, the overemphasis on elite sports reflects an imbalance in resource distribution. This has led to social inequalities, particularly in less economically developed areas and among marginalised groups, including people with disabilities. Furthermore, the decentralisation of governance, though intended to grant autonomy to local sports entities, has often led to inconsistencies in policy implementation and financial instability at the local level.

The EMS-inspired model has successfully centralised decision-making for elite sports while supporting solidarity mechanisms. Nevertheless, the NSS's limited alignment with the broader social goals of inclusivity and grassroots development points to a need for reforms. Addressing these issues will require a better balance between elite sports goals and broader societal inclusion in sports, echoing the solidarity principles central to the European model but not fully realised in Colombia.

Notes

 1 Tutela in Colombia is a legal mechanism that allows individuals to request immediate protection of their fundamental constitutional rights when they believe those rights are

being violated or threatened. Established by Article 86 of the Colombian Constitution, it provides a swift and straightforward process for individuals to seek judicial protection, with rulings typically issued within ten days. The Tutela can be filed against public authorities or private entities if their actions infringe upon fundamental rights such as life, health, or dignity.

2 *Institutos Municipales de Deporte y Recreación.* Municipal Institutes of Sports and Recreation in Spanish.

3 These organisations, known as *ligas* (which translates as 'leagues' in English), are regional sport federations. This chapter will use the term league in English to refer to them, and needs not to be confused with sport league tournaments (e.g. the Premier League).

References

AP. (2021, May 20). Colombia removed as co-host of next month's Copa America. https://www.Foxsports.Com/Articles/Soccer/Colombia-Removed-as-Cohost-of-next-Months-Copa-America

Coldeportes. (2013). Plan Decenal del Deporte 2009–2019- Coldeportes. https://www.mindeporte.gov.co//recursos_user///documentos/planeacion/planes/PLAN%20DECENAL%20COLDEPORTES.pdf

Competencia Para Regular Estructura de Entidades Encargadas de Fomentar, Patrocinar y Dirigir La Actividad Deportiva (2000). https://www.corteconstitucional.gov.co/relatoria/2000/C-802-00.htm

Congreso de Colombia. (2001, January 16). Ley 643 de 2001. *Función Pública.*

Constitución Política de la República de Colombia 1991, Función Pública (1991). https://www.funcionpublica.gov.co/eva/gestornormativo/norma.php?i=4125

Constitutional Court of Colombia. (n.d.). Constitutional court of Colombia. *Corte Constitucional.* Retrieved September 9, 2024, from https://www.corteconstitucional.gov.co/english/

Decreto 1228 de 1995, Función Pública (1995). https://www.funcionpublica.gov.co/eva/gestornormativo/norma.php?i=1485

Decreto 1746 de 2003, Función Pública (2003). https://www.funcionpublica.gov.co/eva/gestornormativo/norma.php?i=65492

Decreto 4183 de 2011, Función Pública (2011). https://www.funcionpublica.gov.co/eva/gestornormativo/norma.php?i=44639

Dejusticia. (2021, June 16). ¡Golazo al machismo! Corte Constitucional protege los derechos de las mujeres futbolistas. *Dejusticia.* https://www.dejusticia.org/golazo-al-machismo-corte-constitucional-protege-los-derechos-de-las-mujeres-futbolistas/

DNP. (2024). Distribución de los recursos del Sistema General de Participaciones (SGP). https://www.dnp.gov.co/LaEntidad_/subdireccion-general-inversiones-seguimiento-evaluacion/direccion-programacion-inversiones-publicas/Paginas/sistema-general-de-participaciones.aspx

Geeraert, A., & Anagnostopoulos, C. (2018). *National Sports Governance Observer.* Play the Game.

Gill, S. (2017, November 27). *Colombia Reports.* Colombia's Former Soccer Chief Admits to Taking Bribes in FIFA Corruption Scandal. https://colombiareports.com/amp/colombias-former-soccer-chief-admits-taking-bribes-fifa-corruption-scandal/

Hernandez, M. (2018). *Basic Universal Principles of Good Governance in the Olympic and Sports Movement: Perceptions of Athletes and Executives in the Elite Sport in Colombia.* Seoul National University. https://doi.org/10.13140/RG.2.2.25183.51362

Hernández, M. (2021, October 24). Políticas Públicas: Cinco tropiezos monumentales. https://www.hernandezmauricio.com/skininthegame/cinco-tropiezos-monumentales-en-politicas-publicas

Hernández, M., & Ramírez, C. G. (2014). Factores críticos de éxito en la gestión de los grandes eventos deportivos en Medellín. *VIREF*, *3*(4), 30–76. https://revistas.udea.edu.co/index.php/viref/article/view/338573

Houlihan, B. (2012). Sport policy convergence: A framework for analysis. *European Sport Management Quarterly*, *12*(2), 111–135. https://doi.org/10.1080/16184742.2012.669390

Hoye, R., & Cuskelly, G. (2007). *Sport Governance*. Elsevier.

IOC. (2016). Consolidated minimum requirements for the implementation of the basic principles of good governance for nocs. https://stillmed.olympic.org/media/Document%20Library/OlympicOrg/IOC/What-We-Do/Leading-the-Olympic-Movement/PGG-Implementation-and-Self-Evaluation-Tools-23-12-2016.pdf

Ley 181 de 1995, Función Pública (1995). https://www.funcionpublica.gov.co/eva/gestornormativo/norma.php?i=3424

Ley 617 de 2000, Función Pública (2000). https://www.funcionpublica.gov.co/eva/gestornormativo/norma.php?i=3771

Ley 1946 de 2019, Función Pública (2018). https://www.funcionpublica.gov.co/eva/gestornormativo/norma.php?i=90141

Ley 1967 de 2019, Función Pública (2019). https://www.funcionpublica.gov.co/eva/gestornormativo/norma.php?i=97210#18

Mesa Callejas, R. Javier, Arboleda Sierra, Rodrigo, Gaviria Garcia, N. Albeiro, & Guzman Finol, Karelys (2010). *Estado de desarrollo de las organizaciones deportivas en Colombia*. Universidad de Antioquia.

Ministerio del Deporte. (2019, March 28). *Coldeportes y el COC firmaron el Pacto por la Gobernanza y Transparencia en el Deporte Asociado Colombiano - Mindeporte*. https://www.mindeporte.gov.co/sala-prensa/noticias-mindeporte/coldeportes-coc-firmaron-pacto-gobernanza-transparencia-deporte-asociado-colombiano

Ministerio del Deporte. (2023). *Solicitud de información*.

Morales Fontanilla, M. (2020). Sport policy in Colombia. *International Journal of Sport Policy and Politics*, *12*(4), 717–729. https://doi.org/10.1080/19406940.2020.1839531

Moreno, C. (2024, January 12). Conozca cómo se mueve el mercado de patrocinadores dentro del fútbol profesional. *Diario La República*.

Ordoñez-Saavedra, N. (2023). El pasado, presente y futuro de la reforma del sector de la educación física, actividad física y deporte en Colombia. *Revista Digital: Actividad Física y Deporte*, *9*(2), 1–3. https://doi.org/10.31910/rdafd.v9.n2.2023.2472

Ordoñez-Saavedra, N. (2024). El ambiente de incertidumbre también impacta el ecosistema deportivo colombiano. *Revista digital: Actividad Física y Deporte*, *10*(2), 1–3. https://doi.org/10.31910/rdafd.v10.n2.2024.2692

Pavitt, M. (2020, July 11). *Colombian Football Federation fined over World Cup ticket scam*. Inside the Games. https://www.insidethegames.biz/articles/1096205/colombia-football-ticket-scam-sanctions

Pinochet, J. (2019, March 1). El escándalo que sacude el fútbol femenino en Colombia: abuso sexual, maltrato y desigualdad. *BBC*. https://www.bbc.com/mundo/deportes-47402553

PTG. (2019, October 14). Good governance-the new sport mantra. *PlaytheGame*. https://www.playthegame.org/news/comments/2019/088_good-governance-the-new-sport-mantra/

Ramos Acosta, J., Arias Castaño, A. M., Gómez Solano, J. H., Ordoñez Saavedra, N., & Carrillo Barbosa, R. L. (2022). Gobernanza y legitimidad en las federaciones deportivas colombianas

(Governance and legitimacy in Colombian sports federations). *Retos, 45*, 851–859. https://doi.org/10.47197/retos.v45i0.89338

Romero, P. (2024, March 5). Presidente Petro criticó duro al Ministerio de Deporte: "Es una pérdida de tiempo." *El Tiempo.* https://www.eltiempo.com/deportes/otros-deportes/gustavo-petro-critico-el-ministerio-de-deporte-y-lo-califica-como-perdida-de-tiempo-861570

Saavedra, F. (2024, August 13). Los ingresos de Millonarios superaron a los de Atlético Nacional, según informe de la Superintendencia de Sociedades. *Infobae.*

Salamanca, G. S. (2023, July 10). ¿Cuáles son las normas que hay en Colombia para las apuestas deportivas? *El Tiempo.*

UNESCO. (2015). *Carta Internacional de la Educación física, la actividad física y el deporte.*

Villareal, L. M. (2017). *Exploring a sustainable autonomy of sport organizations: A study of relationship between government and elite sport organizations in Colombia* [Seoul National University]. https://s-space.snu.ac.kr/handle/10371/137784?mode=full

Chapter 16

The African Sport Model

Between Pan-Africanism and European/Olympic Hegemony

*Pascal Camara, Louis Moustakas
and Maximilian Seltmann*

Introduction

Organised sport on the African continent is heavily influenced by the legacy of the colonial era. Historical research illustrates how the colonial powers used sport as a strategic tool to dominate local cultures in different African countries and regions in an attempt to advance their imperialistic endeavours (cf. Mählmann, 1988; Melo et al., 2018). While different colonial powers promoted different forms of physical activity (e.g., German gymnastics in East Africa, cf. Ndee, 2010, or British sport in Kenya, cf. Mählmann, 1988), the colonial era dispersed European sporting practices across the African continent, thereby largely replacing local indigenous practices and traditional games (Keim & De Coning, 2014). To date, the legacy of the colonial era is still the source for sports-political conflicts in several African countries (see, e.g., Nauright & Amara, 2018).

In its recent analysis of sport models around the globe, the Association of Summer Olympic International Federations (ASOIF, n.d.), establishes the "solidarity model of organised sport" as the dominant model the Olympic Movement promoted internationally. The key features of this proposed model are largely reflected in the European Model of Sport (EMS), as discussed throughout this volume. Consequently, the characteristics of the model, like the pyramidal structure of sport with a strong role played by private sport governing bodies (SGBs), are promoted by the Olympic Movement on a global scale, including on the African continent. Alternative models with differing characteristics identified in the study include the "North American Model" and the "Eastern Model" which are seen as a threat to the solidarity model (ASOIF, n.d., p. 25f.). A distinct African Sport Model, according to this study, cannot be identified.

Against the backdrop of the enduring legacy of European colonialism in the governance and organisation of sport in Africa, the aim of this chapter is to trace the development of a Pan-African Model of Sport. The study focuses on trans- and supranational developments aimed at utilising sport as a tool to promote Pan-Africanist values centered around unity of all Africans and the elimination of colonial influence. In a historical analysis, the activities and policies of transnational public and private actors in the area of sport are illustrated to show that the

DOI: 10.4324/9781032665153-19

conflict between (neo-)colonial concepts to the organisation of sport and a distinct African approach to sport policy transcend national boundaries. The study builds on existing literature as well as on primary data in the form of archive material of the respective actors. Moving forward, we first trace the general historical evolution of sport policy and structures at the continental level and then conclude by contrasting the current state of African sport with the values and assumptions inherent to the dominant European model.

SCSA, the Architect of a Distinct African Sport Model

To date, the African sport model is not a defined policy construct and is not anchored in any policy documents. Notwithstanding, past and present political developments on the African continent allow us to trace a distinct model for the governance of sport. Of key importance to such conceptualisation are the activities of the Supreme Council for Sport in Africa (SCSA) and its successor entities. Originally founded in 1966, and today known as the African Union Sports Council (AUSC), the SCSA was envisaged as an intergovernmental body responsible for promoting and developing sports in Africa.

The African sport model envisaged by the SCSA was based on two important pillars. On the one hand, the SCSA intended to position itself and Africa in the world of sport as an evolving and influential figure. On the continent, the SCSA intended to rely on the African Games as a platform to promote unity and interaction among African youth. Contrary to the concept of the Games of the New Emerging Forces (GANEFO), which posed a direct challenge to the Olympic Movement (GANEFO, 1963), the African Games were intended to exploit the power of sport to enhance a prospective African sport model. Though the African Games started before the formation of the SCSA, the latter provided the framework for the former and sport development in Africa as an overarching transnational organisation.

Following its formation in Bamako in 1966, a year after the first African Games in Brazzaville, the SCSA did not have the initial supranational status and authority over sport organisations in member states, though it had gained appeal throughout the continent due to its stance against apartheid in sport (Camara, 2023a,b). The SCSA was formed and constituted by a large and diverse pool of "civil society" stakeholders which included members of sports federations, International Olympic Committee (IOC) members in Africa, representatives of National Olympic Committees (NOCs), national sports authorities and central government ministries and department representatives responsible for sport. It was not until 1977 when it was formally integrated into the structures of the then Organisation of African Unity (OAU) and now African Union (AU) as a specialised agency in matters of sport (SCSA, 1977). The OAU, which was established in 1963 with 32 signatory, was a union of African Heads of State which sought to promote unity and solidarity among independent African nations. In addition, the OAU intended to ensure the continent's socio-economic potential is harnessed through cooperation while also actively supporting the liberation of African states still under colonial control

(OAU, 1963). The OAU elevated the SCSA to the status of a formal supranational sport organisation within the Pan-African project, and the SCSA was to coordinate and harmonise sport in order to consolidate African unity (Camara, 2023a). Though it gave up some of its powers to the OAU, the SCSA's task was to fulfil a limitation of the OAU at the time, that is, interference in internal matters of member states. In the context of the Pan-African movement on the continent, SCSA was positioned as a negotiator and tasked to cooperate with national liberation movements in the African countries where they existed and recognised by the OAU like Angola (SCSA, 1977). In the memorandum of understanding, the OAU would in turn fill the financial gap left by the IOC and fund the SCSA as well as encourage member states to pay their annual subscription fees to the SCSA (SCSA, 1977). This agreement propelled the SCSA to become a powerful supranational state agency with the powers to represent and take decisions on behalf of the OAU and African states. On the other hand, the memorandum of understanding relegated the SCSA to the second fiddle on the continent. In addition, it provided an opportunity to formally integrate sport into the structures of Pan-Africanism and advancing the course of Africa in and outside the continent. With this agreement, the African Games became the exclusive property of the OAU and no more the SCSA as was the first edition of the games. The SCSA clearly delineated the roles and responsibilities of African sports confederations and their interaction with organisations outside the continent. The envisaged Pan-African model was intended to be explicit in the structures and interactions of all African sports organisations (SCSA, 1975). To this effect, it was necessary to have and exercise absolute control and supervision over sport on the continent. Among the elements that legitimised the African sports model was that membership to the SCSA was subjected to the independence status of the respective country. Participation of all independent African countries and the promotion of African unity was of utmost importance.

The Conference of Ministers

Other than the structures that were initially created by the SCSA following its foundation, the OAU added an intermediary structure and organ in its relations with the SCSA, the Conference of Ministers of Sport. Another organ was the Council of Ministers which consisted of foreign ministers designated by the member states and was responsible for preparing matters of concern for discussion at the SCSA General Assembly as well as coordinate the implementation of the decisions of the Assemble in the member states (Makinda & Okumu, 2007). The Council of Ministers was a technical organ of the OAU that was composed of ministers of foreign affairs of all member states. This organ exercised its influence over the SCSA in its decision to boycott the Montreal 1976 Olympic Games, a year before formalising relations with the OAU (Ganga, 1977). To cater for the specialised supervisory needs of the SCSA, the OAU would form the Conference of Ministers of Youth and Sport which directly scrutinised and supervised the SCSA. One such instance was during its 10th session in 1983 where the Nigerian delegate lamented certain illegalities and constitutional irregularities within the SCSA. He cited the reservation of positions of the Secretary-General, Treasurer, Financial Secretary, and Auditor to only French-speaking countries as well as the reporting the SCSA meeting proceedings in only one language, French (SCSA, 1983). Following the institutional transformation of the OAU into the AU, the functions of other organs in the former were adjusted. The Conference of Ministers of Youth and Sports would in 2006 be renamed as African Union Conference of Ministers of Sports. One of the consequences of the institutional changes was the integration of a larger pool of stakeholders and social movements in the structures of the AU. While the OAU was considered a union of Head of States, the AU came to be considered as a broader union of African people encompassing a parliament, an assembly of heads of state, a conference of ministers, as well as a professional, bureaucratic staff (Hushagen Langerud, 2016). These changes had a direct impact on the structure of sport on the continent and the SCSA. The Conference of Ministers also saw the need for reforms in the SCSA which it claimed remained in the old format of the OAU (AU, 2012). Though the proposed reforms by the conference of ministers were not well received by the SCSA Executive Committee, they proposed to set a time frame for the dissolution of the organisation during its 42nd Session of the SCSA Executive Committee in Maputo (Mozambique) during the tenth edition of the Games in 2011 (SCSA, 2012). In 2012, the SCSA Executive Committee decided that the decision taken by the African Union Conference of Ministers of Sports to dissolve the SCSA does not respect the decisions of the AU Head of States and Governments which called for more support from member countries and therefore recommends that the decision be rescind (SCSA, 2012). However, in July 2013, the African Union Conference of Ministers of Youth and Sport finally dissolved the SCSA and formed the AUSC as a specialised technical office for sport matters in the continent (AU, 2012). The AUSC is now directly under the Sport Division in the Department of Social Affairs of the African Union Commission and the Specialized Committee on Youth and Sports (AU, 2012, 2013). It is important to highlight that the power dynamics between the organisations had significantly changed. The AUSC has incorporated a broader mandate than the SCSA which now includes to "Promote and defend sport development and development through sport (sports-for-development)" among others. The Executive Committee of the AUSC is now more closely linked to the agenda of the AU than the independent SCSA. The African Union Conference of Ministers of Youth and Sports still reserves the power to recommend for the dissolution of the AUSC.

SCSA and the Functions of Its Regional Zones

One of the structures that were created by the SCSA during its formation was the so-called regional zones. These structures had dual responsibilities. On the one hand, they were to act as the strategic representatives of the SCSA in the identified regions and facilitate the engagement of member countries to stimulate continent-wide interest and participation in SCSA activities. On the other hand, the zonal structures were to trickle down the knowledge and expertise to stakeholders in the member countries that would otherwise not benefit from SCSA's Africa-wide initiatives.

During the identification of the zones in 1965, the ideological differences that marred the formation of the OAU three years earlier with the disagreements between Casablanca, Monrovia, and Brazzaville Groups also translated to the sport structure. Discussions ensued regarding dividing the continent into zones, though the basic idea of a regional, or zonal, structural representation had already been agreed. Tunisia, Morocco, Algeria, and the Egypt suggested that Africa should be divided into vertical zones because they believed that the formula would prevent the continent from being divided into black, white; French-speaking, English-speaking and Arab-speaking Africa. On the other hand, Mali, Madagascar, Kenya, Nigeria, Gabon, the Democratic Republic of Congo, and Ethiopia suggested that for economic reasons, the zones be drawn up according to geographical proximities. A third alternative ensued from Ethiopia and the Democratic Republic of Congo who proposed the adoption of the zonification employed by the Confederation of African Football which is not quite identical to the one used for the First African Games. The Secretary-General then proposed that the assembly should keep with the alternative that considered the geographical proximity due to the "restricted financial means" at the disposal of the organisation (SCSA, 1966). Compared to the discussions on the OAU groups, there were evident sport-specific deviations by some countries. Tunisia, for example, was not part of the Casablanca Group of the OAU in 1961 while Mali and Ghana who formed part of the Casablanca group shifted in the sport context. In addition, considerations of Ethiopia and Democratic Republic of Congo seem to be of purely sport context (Camara, 2023a). The disruption by the IOC on the African sports model did not reflect on the zonal structures because they were unique to the context. However, the disruptions also trickled down to the national level. To this effect, many African countries still have the existence of an NOC and a government agency responsible for sport which often function in a parallel way within the same system.

ANOCA and the Disruption of the Pan-African Model of Sport

The then Coordinator of Olympic Solidarity Giulio Onesti expressed concern over the coordination of the funds in Africa as the three Africans nominated to be part of the Olympic Solidarity programme had already partitioned the continent and threatened African unity as envisaged by the IOC (Onesti, 1974). By 1978, NOCs had been established in 20 African countries. Lord Killanin, then President of the IOC, would change his approach and task the SCSA to complete the formation of the 13 remaining NOCs in the continent. The IOC in return would release US$ 30,000 for the said mission. This would eventually lead to the consolidation of the Association of National Olympic Committees in 1979 and establishment of the Association of National Olympic Committees for Africa (ANOCA) in 1981

(Ganga & Ordia, 1978). The formation of ANOCA by the IOC, which was supported by the SCSA in 1981, saw the emergence of a parallel and rival organisation to the desired model and authority of the SCSA on the continent. This produced a direct disruption to the African sport model and reduced the influence of the SCSA as most Olympic sport organisations were now directly answerable to ANOCA. The Executive Committee of the SCSA would acknowledge the disruption produced by the IOC and try to remedy this by adjustments in the 1977 constitution as most of the African IOC members in the SCSA were also in support of this move by the IOC (IOC, 1977, 1980a). Up until the 1980 Moscow Olympic Games, the IOC and the Olympic Movement did not have a firm grip of the NOCs on the African continent. Individual member countries and the SCSA still had counter influence on NOCs. A case in point was the issue of an African-led boycott of the Moscow 1980 Olympic Games. Following a statement from the President of the Republic Kenya, Daniel Arap Moi, the Kenyan Olympic Association informed the IOC of its decision to decline the Soviet invitation "in the light of the statement made by the President [...]" (IOC, 1980b, p. 54). Other countries like the Gambia also boycotted the games due to national political positions on the Russian invasion of Afghanistan (Sey, 1980).

Complementing the formation of ANOCA, the Association of African Sports Confederations (AASC) would also be formed in 1983 as an additional element to consolidate the disruption of the structure. As an umbrella organisation of continental sport federations, the AASC assumed a large part of the responsibilities previously occupied by the SCSA on the African sports landscape. Among its responsibilities included representing African sports confederations before international organisations and cooperating with African states to implement sport policies (AASC, 2024). Ultimately, these developments in African sport would eventually affect the main platform for the celebration of the African sport model, the African Games. Over time, the Games have shifted from an event organised under the auspices of African-initiated organisations to being staged by organisations associated with the dominant model of sport. Indeed, today ANOCA and AASC, assume a significant role in the realisation of the games as key partners. Though the games are still technically the property of the AU, since 2016, its organisation is embedded in a tripartite relationship between the AUSC, ANOCA, and AASC (Pavitt, 2018), a relationship which has more hindered the exploitation of the potential of the games than enhanced it. For instance, in some countries such as Botswana, this multi-party relationship has bred conflict over whether Olympic or governmental sport structures are responsible for the preparation of their own national delegations.

Sketching an African Sports Model?

Looking at the historical review above, our analysis highlights that any potential African Model of Sport aligns quite clearly with some of the main features of the EMS, namely in terms of the promotion of national or, in this case, regional identity as well as the existence of international competitions as a centrepiece of the sporting calendar. Reflecting on the first point, as this text has tried to make explicit above, the birth of many of the region's sporting structures, including especially the SCSA, was done with explicitly anti-Colonial and Pan-Africanist ideals in mind. Likewise, the African Games provided a regular, quadrennial platform for different independent African countries to compete against each other and solidify their national identities. In fact, this aspect of African sports has expanded in recent years, with the addition of events like the African Youth Games or the African Beach Games to the sporting calendar (ANOCA, 2023).

However, beyond promoting vague ideas of national or regional identity, such as the promotion of so-called "European values" within the EMS, the nascent African sports movement of the 60s, 70s, and 80s aligned with more clearly defined ideals such as Pan-Africanism, liberation, and anti-colonialism. These values were further enforced and promoted through the hosting of regional sport events and direct protest, most notably by way of the mass boycott of the Montreal Olympic Games by African NOCs. Thus, though structurally there may be overlaps between the dominant, or European, model and the African model, the identity and associated values promoted differ notably.

The analysis furthermore reveals that, historically, public organisations assumed a central role in promoting sports on the African continent. Yet, as documented above, the initially Pan-Africanist ideals of the SCSA were not left unscathed by the broader forces of the dominant sports model. The development of NOCs across the continent, combined with the formation of entities such as ANOCA and the AASC provided in many ways a direct contrast or even challenge to the SCSA. Though ANOCA or the AASC may discursively position themselves as supportive of African unity and identity, these organisations mainly focused on integration into the global sporting infrastructure and largely moved away from any explicit focus on ideas of anti-colonialism or liberation. Indeed, the formation of ANOCA and the development of funding mechanisms for NOCs, including Olympic Solidarity, could be understood as a direct reaction to African states boycotting the 1976 Montreal Olympic Games. Be that as it may, the formation of differing continental entities ultimately bred a two-headed structure at the national level of many countries, whereby governmental sport organisations or ministries aligned with the SCSA, and NOCs aligned with the dominant sport model. In turn, this fed into often divided or even conflictual national sport structures, including in countries such as Botswana (García et al., 2023), the Gambia (Camara, 2023b), and others (Keim & De Coning, 2014).

The Pan-African analysis above highlights many of the overlaps or divergences between any potential African Model of Sport and the features of the so-called dominant model. However, some questions remain open, and it is not possible for this chapter, in its current scope, to provide a comprehensive or generalisable answer. In particular, two relevant areas of comparison with the EMS could be worth of further exploration. First, this chapter and other existing academic work do not provide a continental or regional overview of the organisational structure of competitive sport. Though numerous football leagues operate as open competitions featuring promotion and relegation (e.g. Botswana, Nigeria, South Africa), it is not clear if this model is widely adopted by other sports, especially if those sports do not necessarily enjoy the wide public or commercial support of football. Second, and relatedly, there has been, to our knowledge, no comprehensive analysis of the role of sports clubs and the organisational structure of grassroots sport (cf. Breuer et al., 2015). Though anecdotal evidence and some limited academic work suggest that private firms may play a significant role in the financing and organisation of sport (e.g. Torres Solís & Moroka, 2011) and that, as with Europe, volunteers play a key role in sports delivery (e.g. Camara & Seltmann, 2018; Maralack & Jurgens, 2018; Moustakas, 2018), there is still a need for future work to truly map out how these elements are structured within the African context. In short, if there is to be any clearly defined African Model of Sport, and if the Pan-Africanist ideals that initially propelled the African Sports movement are to be further promoted, then there is significant work to be done to not only understand African sports history but also clearly define the status of African sport today.

References

AASC. (2024). *Missions.* https://www.ucsa-aasc.org/about-us/missions

ANOCA. (2023). *2nd African Beach Games, We Are Ready!* https://africaolympic.com/en/2nd-african-beach-games-we-are-ready/.

ASOIF. (n.d.). *The Solidarity Model of Organised Sport in Europe and Beyond: A Stable Platform for Collaboration.* https://www.asoif.com/sites/default/files/download/the_solidarity_model_of_organised_sport_in_europe_and_beyond.pdf.

AU. (2012). *Decision on the Fourth Session of the African Union Conference of Ministers of Sport Including the New Sport Architecture for African Sport – Doc, EX.CL/697(XX), Decisions, Executive Council Twentieth Ordinary Session 23 - 27 January 2012 Addis Ababa, Ethiopia, EX.CL/Dec.668-695(XX) Original: English/French.* https://au.int/en/decisions.

AU. (2013). *Fifth Session of the African Union Conference of Ministers of Sport 22-26 July 2013, Abidjan Ivory Coast, CAMS5/MIN/Rpt(V).* https://au.int/en/newsevents/20130722/5th-session-au-commission-conference-ministers-sport-cams5-abidjan-cote-d-ivoire

Breuer, C., Hoekman, R., Nagel, S., & van der Werff, H. (2015). *Sport Clubs in Europe: A Cross-National Perspective.* Springer Cham.

Camara, P. M. (2023a). A Divided House: The Foundation and Evolution of the Supreme Council for Sport in Africa, 1965–2013. *Sport in History, 43*(4), 490–510. https://doi.org/10.1080/17460263.2022.2157868

Camara, P. M. (2023b). Sport Policy in the Gambia: Power Imbalances between the Government and the NOC. *International Journal of Sport Policy and Politics, 15*(3), 549–561. https://doi.org/10.1080/19406940.2023.2219268.

Camara, P. M., & Seltmann, M. (2018). The Gambia. In K. Hallmann & S. Fairley (Eds.), *Sports Volunteers around the Globe* (Vol. 15, pp. 93–102). Springer International Publishing. https://doi.org/10.1007/978-3-030-02354-6_9.

GANEFO. (1963). *Documents of the Ganefo Preparatory Committee.* Library repository of the German Sport University Cologne.

Ganga, J. C. (1977). *Letter to Honourable Commissioner for Sports and Physical Culture of Ethiopia (January 10, 1977), File SD5 Correspondence 1976–1977: Box E-RE02-CSSA.001*. SCSA Collection, IOC Historical Archive.

Ganga, J. C., & Ordia, A. (1978). *Letter to Killanin, L. (October 2, 1978): File SD6 Correspondence 1978, Box E-RE02-CSSA.001*. SCSA Collection, IOC Historical Archive.

García, B., Meier, H. E., & Moustakas, L. (2023). Racing to Win: Competition and Co-operation Between the National Olympic Committee and Public Authorities in the Development of the Botswana Sport System. *Journal of Southern African Studies, 49*(4), 637–659. https://doi.org/10.1080/03057070.2023.2289806.

Hushagen Langerud, M. (2016). *From the Organisation of African Unity to the African Union: From a Policy of Non-interference to a Policy of Non-indifference?* Master's thesis. Department of Archaeology, Conservation and History, University of Oslo.

IOC. (1977). *Study of the Minutes of the SCSA Meeting in Rabat, November 1977: File 7e Assemblé Général du Conseil Supereur du Sport en Afrique, Rabat (Maroc) les 21-13 Novembre 1977. Box E-RE02-CSSA.0013*. SCSA Collection, IOC Historical Archive.

IOC. (1980a). *File SD1 Rapport su la réunion au CIO, Janvier 1980: Box E-RE02CSSA.0013*. SCSA Collection, IOC Historical Archive.

IOC. (1980b). *Press Release from the Kenyan Olympic Association Concerning Participation in the Games of the XXIIND Olympiad in Moscow (February 4, 1980), Minutes of the Meeting of the Executive Board in Lausanne 21-23 April, 1980, Annex 11*. IOC Historical Archive.

Keim, M., & Coning, C. de (Eds.). (2014). *Sport and Development Policy in Africa: Results of a Collaborative Study of Selected Country Cases* (Second edition). Sun Press.

Mählmann, P. (1988). Sport as a Weapon of Colonialism in Kenya: A Review of the Literature. *Transafrican Journal of History, 17,* 152–171.

Makinda, S. M., & Okumu, F. W. (2007). *The African Union*. Routledge. https://doi.org/10.4324/9780203940112.

Maralack, D., & Jurgens, D. (2018). South Africa. In K. Hallmann & S. Fairley (Eds.), *Sports Volunteers around the Globe* (Vol. 15, pp. 213–224). Springer International Publishing. https://doi.org/10.1007/978-3-030-02354-6_19.

Melo, V., Bittencourt, M., & Nascimento, A. (2018). Sport and Colonialism in Lusophone Africa—An Introduction. *The International Journal of the History of Sport, 35*(4), 293–295. https://doi.org/10.1080/09523367.2018.1538029

Moustakas, L. (2018). Botswana. In K. Hallmann & S. Fairley (Eds.), *Sports Volunteers around the Globe* (Vol. 15, pp. 33–42). Springer International Publishing. https://doi.org/10.1007/978-3-030-02354-6_4.

Naughright, J., & Amara, M. (eds.) (2018). *Sport in the African World.* London: Routledge.

Ndee, H. S. (2010). Prologue: Sport, Culture and Society in Tanzania from an African Perspective. *The International Journal of the History of Sport, 27*(5), 733–758. https://doi.org/10.1080/09523361003625808.

OAU (1963). Resolutions Adopted by the First Conference of Independent African Heads of State and Government Held in Addis Ababa, Ethiopia, from 22 To 25 May 1963. African Union Common Repository. https://au.int/sites/default/files/decisions/32247-1963_cias_plen_2-3_cias_res_1-2_e.pdf

Onesti, G. (1974). *Letter to Ganga, J.C. (June 8, 1974): File SD4 Correspondence 19721974, Box E-RE02-CSSA.001*. SCSA Collection, IOC Historical Archive.

Pavitt, M. (2018). *ANOCA Formalise Agreement to Take Control of African Games.* https://www.insidethegames.biz/articles/1061781/anoca-formalise-agreement-to-take-control-of-african-games.

SCSA. (1966). *Minutes and Appendices of Constitutive General Assembly 12-14 December, 1966 in Bamako. File SD2 Assemblé Genérale Constitutive 12-14 Decémbre 1966 á Bamako, proces verbal (Angláis): Box E.RE02-CSSA/10.* SCSA Collection, IOC Historical Archive.

SCSA. (1975). *Resolution of the Representation of Member States in pan-African Sports Bodies. Resolutions on General Assembly of the SCSA 1-3rd May 1975, Kinshasa.* SCSA Archive.

SCSA. (1977). *Draft Cooperation Agreement Between the OAU and the SCSA, p.2-5. 7th General Assembly Rabat, 21-13 November 1977. File "7e Assemblée générale du Conseil Supérieur du Sport en Afrique, Rabat (Maroc) les 21-13 Novembre 1977": Box E-RE02CSSA.0013.* SCSA Collection, IOC Historical Archive.

SCSA. (1983). *Remarks Made at the (10th Session) Ministerial Commission of SCSA 1st December 1983 Oaugadougou [sic], Upper Volta.: File SD5 Correspondence 1983–1988. Box E-RE02-CSSA.002.* SCSA Collection, IOC Historical Archive.

SCSA. (2012). *SCSA Executive Committee Report on the Dissolution of the SCSA, the 43rd Ordinary Session of the Executive Committee 14-15 March Asmara, Eritrea, 2012.* SCSA Archive.

Sey, O. (1980). *Letter to Killanin, L. (April 22, 1980) "Re: Participation in the Games of the XXIInd Olympiad in Moscow", Minutes of the Meeting of the Executive Board in Lausanne 21-23 April, 1980, ANNEX 18.* IOC Historical Archive.

Torres Solís, J. R., & Moroka, K. (2011). Innovative Corporate Social Responsibility in Botswana: The Debswana Mining Company Study Case. *Contaduría Y Administración* (223).

Chapter 17

Conclusion

The European Model of Sport, a Mythical Reality

Borja García and Vanja Smokvina

The European Model of Sport (EMS) has been ever present in the development of European Union sport policy and law since the 1995 CJEU's judgement in the Bosman case prompted EU institutions and sport organisations to reflect on the application of European policies and law to sport. Defined in simple, but precise, terms by the European Commission in 1998, and later apparently dismissed by the Commission's very own *White Paper on Sport* in 2007, the EMS has survived in the policy agenda until 2025, though; and it is unlikely to go away.

Most debates about the EMS have focused on two features: Its pyramidal governance structure (including the – legal or illegal – monopoly of sport governing bodies), and the importance of sporting merit in open competitions. Other EMS elements have featured less in political, academic, and legal debates, such as the grassroots approach and the sociopolitical relevance of sport for European identities.

This book has explored understandings of European sport at length, providing a comprehensive platform to discuss the extent to which one can recognise something distinctively European in a 'European Model of Sport'. As we explained in the introduction, our objective was to go beyond a discussion on whether a/the/several model(s) of sport can be identified in Europe. In doing so, we wanted the book contributions to critically analyse different dimensions in which Europeans might 'think about', 'participate in', or even 'feel about' sport. In short, we wanted to take the 'European Model of Sport' for an academic walk and see how much we could stretch its conceptual legs to increase our understanding of the relationship between Europe, the world, and sport. We have now reached the home straight of this endeavour after reading the different chapters, and we feel it is fair to say that there is a particular way in which Europeans understand sport. Yes, there is a diversity of understandings in the EMS that needs to be acknowledged and properly managed by those in charge of designing public policies and regulation, but it is equally true that there are values, identities, and structures attached to sport that can be considered of public interest and deserve protection.

Our contributors have identified three broad areas shaping the way European citizens and institutions 'think about' sport: The importance of sociocultural values attached to sport, the integration of physical activity, amateur and professional

DOI: 10.4324/9781032665153-20

sport to fully understand the dynamics of sport in Europe, and the increasing focus on good governance as a driving paradigm of European sport regulation.

A Values-Driven Model of Sport

The contributions in the book suggest there are important normative sociopolitical values underpinning the EMS. Or, at least, underpinning the way sport is socially constructed in Europe. Henk Erik Meier and Merle Wiehl (in Chapter 4) identify a core of commonly shared sociocultural values among EU member states linked to sport. They argue that sport is perceived as playing a role in socialisation, social cohesion, national pride, and nation branding, amongst other values. And this is paramount, in turn, to understand the repeated calls for financial redistribution in sport analysed by Daniel Plumley and Rob Wilson in Chapter 7. Financial redistribution is, furthermore, accepted as a legitimate objective by the CJEU's 2023 rulings, as explained by Richard Parrish in Chapter 3.

There is, in sum, an overarching feeling in the contributions to the book that, as Hallgeir Gammelsaeter (2021) put it, sport 'is not [only] an industry'. The regional chapters confirm this analysis, highlighting that many of these values can also be found at national level, albeit to different degrees. Hence, Jörg Krieger and Svein Erik Nordhagen confirm how values such as participation and volunteering underpin the models of sport in Scandinavia, whereas Spencer Harris and Mat Dowling describe a UK model of sport that is far more focused on results, professionalisation, and modernisation.

This diversity is excellently analysed by Ramón Llopis-Goig in Chapter 6. In his work, he identifies seven sport cultures in the EU using data from the Eurobarometer. One could take this chapter as suggesting that there is too much diversity in the way Europeans engage with and participate in sport. That would be a 'half-empty glass' way of looking at the EMS. A more positive and 'half-full glass' way of looking at this is realising that Llopis-Goig also explains that those differences are rooted in economic development, political context, and inherent cultural traditions. That is to say, the link between sport and social values/traditions is strong in Europe. Moreover, the fact that Ramón Llopis-Goig has constructed a statistically significant cluster analysis of sporting cultures in Europe based on grassroots sport practices vindicates the paramount importance of this dimension (grassroots/amateur sport) in the EMS. This is a strong argument in favour of considering how values are shaping the way Europeans understand sport.

Yet, we also must acknowledge that the contributions in the book identify how these values are facing increasing challenges, mostly from the commercial development of sport. The market-driven orientation of sport in the UK discussed by Harris and Dowling can also be seen in Germany and other central European countries to a certain extent, as argued by Mara Verena Konjer and Henk Erik Meier in Chapter 9. They explain how secular social changes, such as declining membership or the rise of informal sports put increasing pressure on volunteering and amateur sport clubs. These challenges are excellently seen in Dan Plumley and

Rob Wilson's analysis of redistribution. In their contribution, Plumley and Wilson argue that, based on their data, redistribution is indeed a cornerstone of the EMS. But they also clearly warn that current redistribution mechanisms need to evolve alongside sport and wider societal changes.

These tensions between commercialisation and a more sociocultural approach to sport spill over the borders of Europe. They are excellently seen in the case of Canada, presented in Chapter 12, where Milena Parent and David Patterson highlight how the Canadian system aligns more closely with the European Sport Model's grassroots and amateur ethos, yet there are commercial and professional sport structures that straddle the US and Canadian border. Similarly, in Colombia, the attention to commercial sport might be hindering a wider development of physical activity and community sport, as argued in Chapter 15 by Mauricio Hernández Londoño and Néstor Ordóñez Saavedra.

We have, therefore, a model of sport in Europe that cherishes values associated with participation, grassroots, culture, volunteering, and redistribution. In other words, a socially constructed vision that considers sport to be 'more than an industry' (Gammelsæter, 2021). This, at the same time, cohabits with increasing commercialisation and globalisation of sport. The development of an increasingly lucrative sports market (which is primarily funded by household sport consumption, as pointed out by Holger Preuß and Antonia Hannawacker in Chapter 5) plays directly into the market-oriented and liberalising pulsion of the European Union and its common market. Indeed, EU institutions acknowledge the relevance of sport for economic development (European Commission, 2007), and there is a well stablished economic dimension in EU sport policy priorities (see e.g. Council of the European Union, 2020).

There is, therefore, a natural interest embedded in the EU's very own DNA to allow the economic and commercial dimension of sport in the single market. However, this puts EU regulators in the difficult position of adjudicating between the sociocultural values of sport as 'more than an industry' and the intrinsic economic and commercial nature of the single European market, as Richard Parrish argues in Chapter 3. Whilst EU institutions, and particularly the CJEU, have often been attacked as insensitive to the specific nature of sport (e.g. Blatter, 2007), Richard Parrish in his chapter identifies a comprehensive list of sport 'legitimate objectives' recognised by the CJEU in its 2023 and 2024 judgements. They range from the training of young athletes, to preserving the openness and fairness of competitions, or even financial redistribution (for more on this see also Weatherill, 2004). It is not very difficult to see the connection of these 'legitimate objectives' recognised by the CJEU to the values of the EMS.

The CJEU does not mention a single time the words 'European Model of Sport' across the judgements, but their presence can strongly be felt (García, 2023), like dementors circling around Hogwarts. Even for the Court of Justice of the European Union, with its zealous protective role of the single market, sport seems to be not only an industry. Even for the CJEU judges there are values that seem to set apart European sport. They just do not like to call it the EMS.

The EMS Starts at the Base

A second dimension to the way sport is understood in Europe flows almost naturally from the ongoing discussion on the values underpinning the EMS. Several contributions in the book have identified the significance of physical activity and amateur sport to understand sport in Europe. This is paramount to explain the way in which sport is currently regulated, financed, practiced and used as a tool for public policies in the EU. Indeed, Ramón Llopis-Goig, in Chapter 6, identified European sporting cultures based on grassroots sport practices. Not only that, Henk Erik Meier and Merle Wiehl in chapter 4 pointed how grassroots sport is normatively driving public sport policy in Europe. The way in which that base of the EMS is structured differs across the continent, though. For example, Ramón Llopis-Goig has identified clear differences between clusters in the north of the continent (encompassing western, central and Eastern Europe: Luxembourg, France, Belgium, Ireland, Netherlands, Germany, Austria, Czechia, Latvia, Estonia, and Slovenia), and along the Mediterranean in southern Europe (Italy, Spain and Portugal, Greece and Cyprus) in terms of the role of voluntary sport clubs.

Similarly, a collective reading of the 'regional' chapters in Part II of the book illustrates the different ways in which governments approach grassroots sport and its organisational structures. From the high politicisation in Eastern Europe and the former Yugoslavia highlighted by Marko Begovic (Chapter 10), to the profound civic and social capital ethos of sports clubs in Scandinavia, passing through the commercially minded professionalisation that has been instilled in the UK since the Tony Blair's government.

But despite different approaches, we argue that the EMS cannot and should not be understood without having regard to the importance of grassroots sport; and the chapters in this book clearly demonstrate this point. This dimension of the EMS has often been neglected, although it was widely used in political discourses to argue in favour of a protectionist regulation of professional/commercial sport. There is a need to research even more the grassroots approach of the EMS.

First, we need to explore deeper the European Model of Grassroots Sport to understand the intricate motivations that lead different Europeans to be (or not be) active. And to further the contribution to social and personal well-being generated in and through sport. Second, it is necessary to explore and critically discuss the links between the bottom and the top of sport. This has been traditionally described as a pyramid, but there are those who disagree with that metaphor. Others, of course, do their outmost to demonstrate there are no links at all; something that is difficult to sustain reading the contributions in this book, though. Third (and linked to the previous point), there is a need to review current redistribution mechanisms in the EMS as Dan Plumley and Rob Wilson argue in their chapter. There is a need to assess the extent to which current redistribution mechanisms are effective; it is also necessary to adapt redistribution to the changing context and conditions of European sport, as Plumley and Wilson argue.

Redistribution is perhaps one of the stickiest points in relation to the EMS' grassroots approach given the challenges posed by commercialisation. One only needs to look at the proposal of the so-called European football superleague, or the struggles in England to agree on a financial solidarity package between the Premier League and the English Football League to understand the resistance towards redistribution of some actors that prioritise financial profit over sport development. At the same time, Richard Parrish in Chapter 3 also reminds that the CJEU demands objective demonstration that effective redistribution is done in a transparent and non-discriminatory manner by sport governing bodies. The CJEU is adamant, as Parrish points out, that redistribution (whilst recognised as a legitimate objective and, therefore, part of the EMS although the judges prefer not to employ those words) is not used just as a smokescreen to perpetuate ineffective governance practices.

Good Governance and (Supervised) Autonomy in the EMS

The third broad dimension that we have identified in the book contributions is the paramount importance of good governance in the EMS. It could be considered as one of the values underpinning the EMS explored earlier in this chapter. This is, for example, the argument that Member States put forward in their 2021 Council resolution (Council of the European Union, 2021). However, given the relevance that good governance has reached as a key foundation in the development of a European sport model (clearly demonstrated throughout the chapters in the book), we feel it deserves to be singled out.

The initial European Commission definition of the EMS in 1998 – and later the Helsinki Report on Sport (European Commission, 1999) – explored governance structures in European sport; but it did not make references to good governance principles. The Commission, back then, analysed the systemic governance (Henry & Lee, 2004) of European sport, but it did not discuss good governance. This is probably understandable given the context, because sport good governance has only risen in relevance since the IOC corruption scandal in the selection of Salt-Lake City as host for the 2002 Olympic Winter Games (Wenn et al., 2011).

The authors in our book have delved deep into this new 'good governance turn' of the EMS, discussing the definition of governance principles to maintain the autonomy of sport governing bodies within the EMS. Richard Parrish (in Chapter 3), Henk Erik Meier and Merle Wiehl (in Chapter 4), and Rob Wilson and Daniel Plumley (in Chapter 7) identified respectively legal, regulatory, and financial dimensions of good governance shaping public authorities' requirements for sport organisations within the EMS. The regional chapters in Part II reinforce the importance of good governance in public sport policy, best seen in the efforts of the British government to enhance professionalism and governance practices in sport organisations discussed by Spencer Harris and Mat Dowling in Chapter 11. A trend that is not just European, but global, as can be seen in the case of Colombia in Chapter 15.

The EMS' good governance turn is interpreted as a normative collection of minimum standards that sport (non-governmental) organisations should comply with.

They include a safe, inclusive, non-discriminatory, and healthy environment for sport practice. They are further expected to adhere to principles of democracy, transparency, and accountability, and to actively mitigate the multiple forms of misconduct within sport.

The European Commission in 1998 made scarce mention of governance standards whilst pointing out the (monopolistic) role of sport governing bodies in the EMS' systemic governance structures. This changed rapidly, though. Good governance issues featured heavily in CJEU rulings, Commission decisions in competition policy cases (García et al., 2017), and it was fully embraced in the White Paper on Sport (Weatherill, 2009). Good governance is one of the priorities since the first EU work plan for sport and continues to be there (e.g. Council of the European Union, 2020). Some of the first policy deliverables under the newly adopted Article 165 TFEU were, actually, on good governance in sport (Council of the European Union, 2016; European Union Expert Group in Good Governance, 2013).

The good governance dimension of the EMS relates almost entirely to the role of sport non-governmental organisations within the model. As Richard Parrish argues in Chapter 3, the CJEU has acknowledged the legitimate role of sport governing bodies to regulate their respective sport and to pursue legitimate objectives for the proper and healthy development of sport (see also on this García, 2023). Governing bodies, however, must act in strict observance of good governance standards such as transparency, democracy, non-discrimination, proportionality, and efficiency. The CJEU has given legal weight to the governance requirements in the EMS, something that other institutions such as the Commission, Council or Parliament have been unable to do given that Article 165 TFEU only concedes a supporting competence on sport to the EU. The problem with the Court defining those standards for the EMS is that it will only do it, naturally, on a case-by-case basis; and that, some would argue – although others would disagree – the Court might be unable to fully comprehend the complexities of sport and the EMS (see on this debate Weatherill, 2024). A number of prestigious academics have recently suggested that it is now the time for the EU to directly regulate sport and sport governance in order to protect the values of European sport, including the definition of good governance (Weiler et al., 2021).

Thus, the 'good governance turn' of the EMS is directly linked to the role of sport federations in the model and the extent to which they should be granted a level of autonomy to regulate their sport. Henk Erik Meier and Merle Wiehl argue in Chapter 4 that the concept of sport's full autonomy and self-regulation, whilst valued, has been abandoned. They point out that actual political practices, as well as future visions for sport governance, fit much better into what has been characterised as 'collaborative sport governance' whereby public authorities and sport governing bodies coordinate their efforts (Meier & García, 2021). This is reinforced by Richard Parrish's analysis of the CJEU 2023 and 2024 sport-related judgements. The Court, he argues, has set clear demands for the governing bodies to comply with, but at the same time, the Court has recognised (and protected) their legitimate role as sport regulators. Similarly, the 'regional' chapters in Part II suggest an important role of the state in sport policy and governance across the continent that, albeit to different degrees, range from a more hands-off approach in Scandinavia to a managerial touch in the UK and the explicit hands-on approach in the former Yugoslavia and Eastern Europe. Finally, the intricate collaborative nature of the EMS that brings together public and sport actors is also seen in the importance of state public funding in European sport, as highlighted in Chapter 5.

Good governance, therefore, delineates an EMS characterised by co-operation of public authorities and sport non-governmental organisations. The EMS is anchored on this co-operation that is developing into different types of collaborative governance. Whereas early defenders of the EMS might have highlighted sport autonomy as a basic structural feature of the model, this 'good governance turn' has changed that. The EMS and EU institutions, as discussed in various chapters, recognise the legitimate role of governing bodies as regulators within the model. However, their autonomy must be earned. Autonomy in the EMS is now contingent upon the adherence to and implementation of good governance standards. Autonomy in the EMS is under control. Using the words of Ken Foster (2000), autonomy in the EMS is 'supervised autonomy' under the spotlight of good governance.

Is It European, or It Is Global?

Part III of the book explored models of sport across the world. Our objective was not to conduct a comprehensive or highly detailed comparison. Rather, we aimed to provide an overview of global models of sport to consider the extent to which they exhibit similarities with the EMS. The combination of these five chapters paints an interesting picture to start dialogues and debates that, surely, will deserve further research in the future as several authors in that section already point out in their contributions.

The central theme of Part III is that the debates, divisions, and regulatory dilemmas surrounding models of sport beyond Europe are comparable to those observed in the EMS, although the solutions may differ. Accordingly, the chapters address topics such as the role of grassroots and amateur sport, the values underpinning sport development, the commercialisation of sport, and the roles of the state and non-governmental sport organisations.

The chapters suggest that the two models that diverge most from the EMS are two polar opposites: The US model with its strong focus on sport business commercialisation, closed leagues and almost negligible public intervention, on the one hand; and the Chinese model of sport with a strong top-down and authoritarian structure driven by government policy based on Confucianism and physical activity ethos, on the other hand. The Chinese sport system is especially interesting in that it distorts greatly the autonomy of sport, with sport organisations directed to implement governmental policy. Yet, some could argue that is not extremely different to what happens in some European states (see Chapters 10 and 11), where governmental intervention is perhaps more subtle or indirect (see the use of funding in the UK, for example), but it still steers sport organisations' strategies. The Chinese sports model also weaves together cultural heritage, political aspirations, and societal values, representing a component of the nation's identity and development.

Other models of sport have more similarities with the EMS, although each one does also present particularities stemming from their local sociopolitical and cultural heritage. One area that is mentioned in several chapters, especially those on the Arab World and the African model of sport, is the legacy of European colonialism. Sarah Muhanna Al-Naimi and Mahfoud Amara explain in Chapter 14 that the geographic proximity of the Arab World to Europe, including the North African region in particular, has significantly contributed to the strong European influence in the regulation and organisation of the national sports system and market, including, for example, the domain of sport TV broadcasting. On the other hand, Pascal Camara, Louis Moustakas, and Maximilian Seltmann argue in Chapter 16 that African models of sport need to be understood as a reaction to the colonial ideals and their development was anchored on values of pan-Africanism. Therefore, though structurally there may be overlaps between the European model and the African model, the identity and associated values promoted differ notably.

Chapters in Part III provide insights on how the EMS with its associated values and structures is perceived beyond Europe. It is extremely interesting that Sarah Muhanna Al-Naimi and Mahfoud Amara praise the EMS' delicate balance between commercial interests and the preservation of sporting integrity and community values. They go on to argue that 'as the world of sports continues to evolve, the European Model offers valuable lessons in sustainability, inclusivity, and the promotion of fair play'. Similarly, Mauricio Hernández and Nestor Ordóñez underline the positive contribution of what we have labelled the EMS 'good governance turn'. In their chapter, they make use of these good governance principles to assess some of the Colombian sport model structures and recommend further and deeper embedding of the 'good governance turn' in the Colombian sport model.

But there are also notable clashes and misfits between the EMS and other global models. Chapter 14 explains how the growing influence of Arab sport investment in the European sport market is questioning the structures of European sport. It is argued that the influx of money from the Gulf region is affecting (and defining) the relationships between Europe and the Arab World in sport. The authors critically discuss that Arab investment raises several questions about the governance system of European sport, particularly regarding the link between those investments and state funds.

Similarly, Chapter 16 on the African model of sport explains how the initial pan-Africanist development of sport systems in the continent clashed with Global North structures. Whereas governmental organisations assumed initially a central role in promoting sport on the African continent in the post-colonial era, the development of National Olympic Committees across the continent, combined with the formation of entities such as the Association of National Olympic Committees for Africa provided a direct contrast or even challenge. These organisations mainly focused on integration into the global sport system and largely moved away from any explicit focus on ideas of anti-colonialism or liberation.

Indeed, whereas our contributors identify EMS legacies in their respective parts of the world, these chapters also confirm that governance transplants (García & Meier, 2022) originating in the Global North (such as EMS' values and structures) are likely to encounter policy and institutional misfits in Global South countries as they negotiate local sociocultural, economic and political structures (García et al., 2023; García & Meier, 2022).

Finally, we can see that sport models around the world are facing similar challenges to the EMS, especially in the balance between sport development and commercialisation. The case of Colombia is illustrative, with governmental and public opinion attention mostly dedicated to professional sport and hosting sport events, which neglects sport development in poorer areas of the country and amongst marginalised populations.

Thus, chapters in this final Part III provide a wide (albeit not systematic) overview of the variety of sport models across the world, and how they negotiate similar dilemmas to those faced by the EMS. Although further research is needed, one important lesson is that the constant attention to the American Model of Sport (including the European Commission from the very first moment – that is to say, the 1998 document) might be preventing European sport from learning valuable lessons that can be found elsewhere in the world.

Conclusion: Myth or Reality?

When we started this project, we wanted the book to go beyond a mere debate to ascertain whether the EMS exists or not. Social sciences are rarely at their best in dichotomic scenarios. We are firm believers that social sciences produce extremely valuable scientific knowledge of the reality around us; and that they have the capacity to delve into concepts through thorough examination and critical discussion deeper than some natural sciences might be able to do. Thus, with this book, we wanted to learn deeper and richer lessons about European sport, its development, regulation, and protection for future generations. We also sought to open new avenues for further research to motivate both seasoned and upcoming academics to contribute to this research agenda.

We feel we have achieved our objective. And the book presents the most rigorous, comprehensive, and interdisciplinary academic interrogation of the EMS. However, it is perhaps unavoidable human nature to contribute to a debate that, at the end of the day, has dominated much of EU sport policy academia for three decades. As academics, we want our collective work to be impactful and to inform solutions for relevant real-world challenges. We are tremendously fortunate, because we now find ourselves in a privileged position as editors of an excellent collection of first-class authors. Having read all their contributions, we feel that it is probably true that one cannot identify *A European Model of Sport* given the heterogeneity of European sport, as the White Paper in Sport (European Commission, 2007) aptly put it. Indeed, Jaime Andreu in Chapter 2 revealed that it was never the European Commission's intention to homogenise European sport to a single model.

However, it is also extremely clear to us that there is a very particular way in which Europe and Europeans relate to sport that shapes our sporting culture. It might seem surprising and counterintuitive, but it is the way that Europeans *feel about sport* what makes the EMS different and identifiable. It is the shared values attached to sport what make the EMS. These values are the protection of amateur/grassroots sport, the fairness of open competition, training of young athletes, the connections between amateur and professional sport, which has a duty of redistribution towards wider society. Those values are underpinned by a conviction that sport plays an important role in socialisation, social cohesion, and local and national pride, resulting in a strong link between sport and social values/traditions in Europe.

The values we have observed in the EMS are further supported with a recent 'governance turn', which demands transparency, democracy, accountability, proportionality, and non-discrimination, in the organisation of the EMS to protect and support its foundational values. Those standards are to be applied not only by the international sport governing bodies but also at national and local level. The 'governance turn' is paramount to understand the EMS in the 21st century, because it has fundamental implications for European sport's systemic governance that challenge the suitability of the traditional organisational structures and the autonomy of sport. In institutional/organisational terms, we can identify a trend that supports collaborative governance between public authorities and sport non-governmental organisations that reduces the level of autonomy of sport governing bodies, which need to act responsibly under 'supervised autonomy' in the EMS.

Yet, theory and practice are not always aligned. As Henk Erik Meier and Merle Wiehl argue in Chapter 4, ideological hegemony does not necessarily translate in actual practice. More so when that hegemony is contested. The contributions in the book have identified trends that actively challenge the values underpinning the EMS. There are even those that negate the EMS because they perceive it to be too normative (García, 2009). Indeed, another conclusion of this project is that one of the EMS' most defining features is the unstable equilibrium between grassroots sport and the commercialisation of sport. Although the EMS' ability to maintain such an equilibrium is praised by some beyond Europe (see e.g. Chapter 14), others might argue that the single market's very own legal and institutional nature is at the base of the EMS instability; unless EU institutions take the political courage to challenge the *status quo* (Weiler et al., 2021).

Despite the comprehensive coverage of the book, there are areas that remain unexplored. We feel the book has been successful in moving academic research on the EMS beyond the existing focus on policy and legal issues. The book has also identified different variations of the EMS that can be found across the continent. But more research is clearly needed. First, a more systematic content analysis of EU institutions documents, including those that are traditionally left behind such as the European Parliament and the Economic and Social Committee, could uncover nuances on the different definitions of the EMS. Second, it would be interesting to research the role of the Council of Europe in defining values behind the EMS, and the extent to which the Council of Europe's European Sports Charter overlaps with meanings behind the EMS. Article 165 TFEU makes explicit mention of the Council of Europe and calls EU institutions to collaborate with it in defining EU sport policy. Thus, it is an active stakeholder whose research could add significant value. Third, we would suggest that research to understand European citizen's individual feelings and views on sport is necessary. Most of the work in this book stems from an institutional perspective. However, recent analysis of the football superleague's failed launch argues that the project failed due to popular opposition underpinned by social understandings of fair competition and opposition to closed leagues (Meier et al., 2022). This suggests that, as we have concluded in this book, there are indeed shared meanings attached to sport by Europeans. Something that is also argued by recent research on Europeanisation through football (Biel et al., 2024; Niemann et al., 2024). A deeper and more comprehensive exploration of those values and meanings can shed significant light on the EMS.

As we reach the finish line of this collective endeavour, can we answer our very own question: is the EMS a myth or a reality? We feel that the book provides a reliable and robust contribution, although perhaps not all the answers. We have identified meaningful shared values and understandings attached to sport in Europe. In this respect, the EMS is certainly not a myth. There is a very particular way to understand sport across the continent. This also translates in organisational regulatory structures that, whilst challenged and in need of adaptation, are also acknowledged. The EMS is characterised by collaborative governance between public and private organisations that adopts, however, different shapes and forms. At the same time, the undeniable economic contribution of sport as an industry questions some of the assumptions of the EMS. Thus, it seems naïve (and perhaps disingenuous) to pretend that the EMS is set in stone. It is not only evolving but also adapting to societal norms and values. In the end, the EMS is certainly not an illusion. It is not a myth. But it is not a simple reality either. As most things in life, the EMS is complex and complicated. It is, perhaps, a mythical reality.

References

Biel, J., Reinke, V., Finger, T., & Niemann, A. (2024). No longer sidelined? Football fandom, belonging, and the boundaries of Europe. *Journal of Contemporary European Studies*, *32*(4), 1343–1365. https://doi.org/10.1080/14782804.2024.2358364

Blatter, J. (2007). Sport must retain its autonomy. *FIFA.Com*. https://www.fifa.com/aboutfifa/federation/president/news/newsid=109957.html (Accessed 5 August 2007).

Council of the European Union. (2016). *Conclusions of the council and of the representatives of the governments of the member states, meeting within the council, on enhancing integrity, transparency and good governance in major sport events*. OJ C, C/212, 14.06.2016, p. 14. https://eur-lex.europa.eu/legal-content/EN/TXT/?uri=CELEX:52016XG0614(03)

Council of the European Union. (2020, December 4). *Resolution of the council and of the representatives of the governments of the member states meeting within the council on the European Union work plan for sport (1 January 2021–30 June 2024)* (2020/C 419/01). Art. 2020/C 419/01. https://eur-lex.europa.eu/legal-content/EN/TXT/?uri=CELEX%3A42020Y1204%2801%29

Council of the European Union. (2021, November 30). Sport: Council resolution stresses key features of values-based sport model. *Press Release.* https://www.consilium.europa.eu/en/press/press-releases/2021/11/30/sport-council-resolution-stresses-key-features-of-values-based-sport-model/

European Commission. (1999). The Helsinki report on sport. In *Report from the European Commission to the European Council with a View to Safeguarding Current Sports Structures and Maintaining the Social Function of Sport Within the Community Framework* (Issue COM (1999) 644 final).

European Commission. (2007). *White Paper on Sport* (Issue COM (2007) 391 final). https://ec.europa.eu/assets/eac/sport/library/documents/whitepaper-full_en.pdf

European Union Expert Group in Good Governance. (2013). *Deliverable 2: Principles of good governance in sport.* European Council. https://ec.europa.eu/assets/eac/sport/library/policy_documents/xg-gg-201307-dlvrbl2-sept2013.pdf

Foster, K. (2000). Can sport be regulated by Europe? An analysis of alternative models. In A. Caiger & S. Gardiner (Eds.), *Professional Sport in the European Union: Regulation and Re-regulation* (pp. 43–64). TMC Asser Press.

Gammelsæter, H. (2021). Sport is not industry: Bringing sport back to sport management. *European Sport Management Quarterly, 21*(2), 257–279. https://doi.org/10.1080/16184742.2020.1741013

García, B. (2009). Sport governance after the White Paper: The demise of the European model? *International Journal of Sport Policy and Politics, 1*(3), 267–284. https://doi.org/https://doi.org/10.1080/19406940903265541

García, B. (2023). Down with the politics, up with the law! Reinforcing EU law's supervision of sport autonomy in Europe. *The International Sports Law Journal, 23*(4), 416–421. https://doi.org/10.1007/s40318-024-00264-x

García, B., & Meier, H. E. (2022). The "autonomy" of developing countries in the Olympic Movement: Assessing the fate of sports governance transplants in the Global South. *Frontiers in Sports and Active Living, 4*, 972717. https://www.frontiersin.org/articles/10.3389/fspor.2022.972717

García, B., Meier, H. E., & Moustakas, L. (2023). Racing to win: Competition and cooperation between the National Olympic Committee and public authorities in the development of the Botswana sport system. *Journal of Southern African Studies, 49*(4), 637–659. https://doi.org/10.1080/03057070.2023.2289806

García, B., Vermeersch, A., & Weatherill, S. (2017). A new horizon in European sports law: The application of the EU state aid rules meets the specific nature of sport. *European Competition Journal, 13*(1), 1–34. https://doi.org/10.1080/17441056.2017.1311146

Henry, I., & Lee, P. C. (2004). Governance and ethics in sport. In S. Chadwick & J. Beech (Eds.), *The Business of Sport Management* (pp. 25–41). Pearson Education.

Meier, H. E., & García, B. (2021). Beyond sports autonomy: A case for collaborative sport governance approaches. *International Journal of Sport Policy and Politics, 13*(3), 501–516. https://doi.org/10.1080/19406940.2021.1905035

Meier, H. E., García, B., Konjer, M., & Jetzke, M. (2022). The short life of the European Super League: A case study on institutional tensions in sport industries. *Managing Sport and Leisure, 29*(3), 1–22. https://doi.org/10.1080/23750472.2022.2058071

Niemann, A., Brand, A., & Weber, R. (2024). *Football Fandom and Identity in the 21st Century: Europe on Their Minds.* Palgrave McMillan. https://doi.org/https://doi.org/10.1007/978-3-031-40631-7

Weatherill, S. (2004). Sport as culture in EC Law. In R. Craufurd Smith (Ed.), *Culture and European Union Law* (pp. 113–152). Oxford University Press.

Weatherill, S. (2009). The White Paper on Sport as an exercise in 'better regulation'. In S. Gardiner, R. Parrish, & R. Siekmann (Eds.), *EU, Sport, Law and Policy: Regulation, Re-regulation and Representation* (pp. 101–114). TMC Asser Press.

Weatherill, S. (2024). Protecting the conditional autonomy of governing bodies in sport from review 'From a competition standpoint'. *European Competition and Regulatory Law Review*, *8*(2), 67–82. https://doi.org/10.21552/core/2024/2/5

Weiler, J., Poiares Maduro, M., Mavroidis, P., & Weatherill, S. (2021, November 12). Only the EU can save football from itself. *Euronews*. https://www.euronews.com/2021/11/12/only-the-eu-can-save-football-from-itself-view

Wenn, S. R., Barney, R., & Martyn, S. G. (2011). *Tarnished Rings: The International Olympic Committee and the Salt Lake City Bid Scandal*. Syracuse University Press.

Index